SP

CLASSES

SPLINTERED CLASSES

Politics and the Lower Middle Classes in Interwar Europe

Edited by
RUDY KOSHAR

HM *HOLMES & MEIER* New York London

Published in the United States of America 1990 by
Holmes & Meier Publishers, Inc.
30 Irving Place   New York, NY 10003

BOOK DESIGN BY DALE COTTON

The paper used in this publication meets the requirements
of the American National Standard for Permanence of Paper
for Printed Library Materials, Z39.48-1984.

Library of Congress Cataloging-in-Publication Data

Splintered classes : politics and the lower middle classes in interwar
  Europe / edited by Rudy Koshar.
     p.   cm.
  Includes bibliographical references and index.
  ISBN 0-8419-1124-X (cloth, alk. paper). — ISBN 0-8419-1243-2 (pbk., alk. paper)
     1. Middle classes—Europe—History—20th century. 2. Europe—
  Politics and government—1918–1945. I. Koshar, Rudy.
  HT690.E73S65   1990
  305.5'5'094—dc20   90-4867
                                                                    CIP

MANUFACTURED IN THE UNITED STATES OF AMERICA

Contents

Preface

This book discusses the politics of the urban lower middle classes in Europe between 1918 and 1939. It deals with an array of groups—small artisans and shopkeepers; minor public officials, low-level administrators in the private sphere, and salespeople; and professionals such as nurses, school-teachers, actors, and even modestly paid lawyers and professors. Its writing was prompted by the need to address an imbalance, now slowly changing, in interwar political history that either concentrated on big labor and capital or, when it did discuss the lower middle classes, relegated them to a secondary role at best, and one of fearful resentment or reaction at worst. At its most extreme, this history reduced the lower middle classes to marginal "little men" who could easily become little Hitlers. There is much to recommend such arguments, but there is even more evidence for interpretations that stress variability rather than uniform reaction, unpredictability rather than a natural proclivity for authoritarian politics. It is around such evidence that this volume builds its central theme, namely that the lower middle classes, whether they reasserted notionally threatened group interests or made new demands in public life, were not simply objects of state and elite manipulation but also active, often autonomous agents of political change.

A useful rethinking of petit-bourgeois politics in the nineteenth century is already under way; as the introduction will suggest, we have numerous points of entry in both history writing and political sociology for a similar rethinking of the interwar decades. Yet there are limits to this recent research. The interwar era was more than a simple extension of prewar trends; most historiography of the interwar decades has failed to move beyond older habits of treating the lower middle classes as subsidiary agents; and political sociology's interest in the middle strata has concentrated mainly on contemporary events. We hope to refine, extend, and criticize this literature, and place the petite bourgeoisie center stage in the drama of European history between the world wars.

This book originated in a panel on the European lower middle classes at the American Historical Association annual conference in New York City in December 1985. Organized by Steven Zdatny, who gave a paper on French artisans that has been revised and extended for this volume, the panel also featured my paper on German associational life and Tom Jeffery's study of British white-collar activism, both likewise revised for this volume. After several publishers expressed interest in broadening the panel into an anthology of current research on the subject, I took responsibility for soliciting more contributions, which were selected according to five criteria that are discussed in the introduction, and for steering the final product into port.

Several people provided assistance by suggesting contributors and offering bibliographic advice. They include Edward Berenson, James Cronin, Geoffrey Crossick, Donald Bell, Gøsta Esping-Andersen, Daniel Levine, Michael R. Marrus, Arno Mayer, John Merriman, Leslie Page Moch, Philip Nord, Carl Strikwerda, Charles Tilly, and Steven Zdatny. I want to acknowledge our editors Barbara Lyons and Sheila Friedling, whose interest and patience are appreciated. Two anonymous readers for Holmes & Meier contributed substantially to making the last revisions of the study. My thanks also to Brenda Rena Johnson and Martha Rothermel, who retyped parts of the manuscript.

RUDY KOSHAR
Claremont, California

SPLINTERED CLASSES

On the Politics of the
Splintered Classes:
An Introductory Essay

RUDY KOSHAR

The past is always modern. Whether we form our views from historiographical debates or more directly from "the leading tensions of the contemporary
political situation"[1]—the two realms are difficult to separate completely—
present-day concerns permeate the narrative we construct of previous eras.
This point, obvious but therefore often forgotten, is particularly relevant
when we turn to the subject of the present volume, the European lower
middle classes between the world wars. Many contemporaries of interwar
Europe were convinced that the lower middle classes experienced the era
uniformly as one of wrenching social conflict, bitter economic despair,
and escalating political irrationality. The imagery surrounding these groups
came from many different and often mutually antagonistic sources, from
perspicacious observers such as the iconoclastic socialist George Orwell,
who spoke one-sidedly in 1937 of a "wretched shivering army of clerks
and shopwalkers" in England, to rabble-rousers such as the French fascist
Pierre de Taittinger, who said of small merchants in 1926 that "their work
and their money are being stolen from them" through excessive taxation.[2]
   Scholars traded in a similar currency. Writing in 1935, the U.S. economist
David Saposs argued that the "economically unstable middle-class and
worker elements" harbored a "compensatory belligerence" that was expressed in "chauvinism, jingoism, provincialism, fraternalism, hero wor-
ship, faddism, and styles."[3] The psychological dimensions of this assumed
belligerence were explored by the exiled German psychoanalyst Erich
Fromm, who in 1941 portrayed the independent artisans, small retailers,
and other members of the traditional lower middle class as the shock troops
of an age of authoritarianism and fascism. Fromm maintained that the
lower middle classes were sick: "for great parts of the lower middle class

in Germany and other European countries, the sado-masochistic character is typical, and . . . it is this kind of character structure to which Nazi ideology has its strongest appeal."[4] Fromm stated in his earlier research on manual laborers and white-collar employees that the Left could have some attraction for "the petite bourgeoisie, and above all the younger generation," but that National Socialism had a greater impact on them.[5] If one looked for real or potential gravediggers of democracy—and thoughtful people had to in that violent age—then it seemed easy to identify who held the shovels.

But language has begun to shift. Once written of in terms of vulnerability and reaction, the lower middle classes are now associated by some scholars with durability, persistence, and even political innovation. The images of economic despair and political authoritarianism have not disappeared, as they should not, but other images compete for legitimacy. The reasons for this change can only be suggested. "Economic history's reluctant disenchantment with growth" has sparked a new interest in small-scale production and urban services and a renewed appreciation of the contribution of master artisans and shopkeepers to nineteenth-century working-class formation.[6] Reappraisals of the social composition of European fascism, discussed in more detail below, have shifted emphasis away from seeing this dangerous politics as a solely "middle-class" movement. Recent social theory on commercial and technical employees has convinced numerous scholars that "the conclusion that lower white-collar employees constitute an inherently reactionary class is a form of sociological reasoning that deserves to be relegated to the dustbin of history."[7] Deeper changes in the political culture of Western states have played an equally important role. In the United States, journalists detect signs of a new, post-Reagan "middle-class Populism," distinguished from "right-wing selfishness or left-wing altruism" and heartily endorsed by the lower middle classes. Environmentalists and Eurocommunists stress cross-class coalitions in which middle strata play a key role, while scholars urge the Left to overcome its uneasiness about living "without an historical agent"—without the assurance that the working class is the harbinger of democratic socialism and the middle class the patron of reaction.[8] For conservative thinkers (but also for a few radical ones) meanwhile, self-employed retailers or master craftsmen, supposedly rooted in a moral economy of family business and individualism, appear to be almost exotic time-travelers in an age of large-scale organization, bureaucracy, and high technology. The "ma-and-pa store," or what Germans refer to as the "Aunt Emma shop," appears to some people to be an island of autonomy in a sea of dependence.

There is good reason to rethink the political history of the interwar lower middle classes given such changes in attitude and the comparatively scant scholarly attention paid to these groups in fields other than German historiography for the period. To push this rethinking forward is the goal of this volume. Our aim is not to promote a uniform political outlook or historiographical approach, but to present a substantial range of recent research that deals with how the lower middle classes defined (or failed to define) themselves politically, and how they identified, pursued, and defended certain common interests. We ask the following questions: Which political options were available to the lower middle classes of various European countries after World War I? Which options were chosen, and why? How were the lower middle classes organized politically, and did their organizations facilitate or hinder political mobilization and identity? What were the central themes and symbols of associational leaders and politicians who said they represented the lower middle classes? Were these themes and symbols derived from the language of other collective actors—especially from the upper and upper middle classes—or were they generated "autonomously" or shaped by the interests and traditions of specific lower-middle-class groups? More broadly, what was the relative importance for petit-bourgeois politics of changing rhetorics by elites and national states, long-term economic and social change, short-term material hardships, and shared ideologies?

Definitive answers for such questions are impossible on the basis of current scholarship, and thus prudence is in order. The same applies for sociographic and definitional issues. Arno Mayer remarked in 1975 that the term *lower middle class* "can be assigned no fixed meaning for all times and places."[9] This is an accurate statement today just as it was more than a decade ago, and the widely debated "boundary problem," the issue of how we define the middle classes or middle strata, will necessarily occupy a small part of these introductory remarks.[10] It is impossible to argue that there was a single "lower middle class" or a coherent "lower-middle-class" politics in interwar Europe or at any other time, partly because only a minority of these or other classes were politically active, partly because the groups that were active had different social profiles and political affiliations. Yet scholars have also argued that in times of heightened conflict, the lower middle classes, or key occupational groups in the lower middle classes, achieve an unstable political solidarity that bridges very distinct ideas about family, consumption, work habits, political affiliation, urban space, and historical time. The subjects of this volume were indeed politically splintered and resistant to cut-and-dried categorization; but they were also capable of collective action whose rhetorical conventions and expectations gave brief meaning to a deeply fissured political world.

Allowing for individual differences of approach and emphasis, all the essays in this volume address such questions and caveats. Cumulatively, they go beyond this, questioning the full validity of a traditional literature that thought of the formulation of lower-middle-class interests as a secondary phenomenon of elite and state manipulation, and finding their central theme in the argument that a dynamic, relatively autonomous, and often unpredictable process of asserting or reasserting group claims was inscribed in petit-bourgeois politics.

All nine chapters were written specifically for this book. The contributions by Jeffery and Livezeanu stem from projects on key petit-bourgeois groups between the wars whereas the others originate in research that engages in one form or another with the general subject. The shape of such undertakings is inevitably determined by the balance of current research, but the nine contributions represent much more than a random selection. Indeed, the articles were solicited and edited according to five criteria that seemed especially useful. First, I wanted a good representation of both major and "minor" countries, and the volume provides that by including essays on England, France, Germany, Italy, Belgium, Denmark, and Romania. Second, I hoped to have essays on both the "old" and "new" lower middle classes, terms that will be specified more thoroughly below. We have two essays that deal solely with the former groups, three dealing with the latter, and four that discuss both. Third, I wanted to include countries that experienced different levels of political conflict in the interwar era. Thus we have essays on Germany, Italy, and Romania, where nationalist disaffection and social conflict opened the way to political crisis and dictatorship; on France and Belgium, which experienced much conflict but held to preexisting parliamentary arrangements before the start of World War II; and Denmark and England, where the disruption of prior party loyalties and class conflict were low or sporadic by comparison to other countries. Fourth, I wanted to have a mix of essays that ranged from closely detailed local studies to more synthetic arguments. Three of the following articles deal with the national scene, two discuss the grass roots, and four move between national and local conditions. Finally, I wanted to ensure that the contributions reflected a substantial variety of petit-bourgeois politics. Four of the articles—those by Zdatny, Christiansen and Lammers, Berezin, and myself—try to address this variety, whereas Livezeanu and Haupt and Niermann focus on right-wing activity, and Jeffery and Pennybacker discuss left-wing politics. Given the emphasis of past literature on petit-bourgeois proclivities for right-wing politics, the latter two essays on England are crucial contributions to the volume insofar that they pinpoint a white-collar radicalism that fits uneasily with many previous models. The volume cannot claim to be comprehensive; that would be impossible on the basis of current research, which is surprisingly thin for the interwar lower middle classes once one leaves German territory. Yet I think we have achieved a rather substantial coverage that meets the criteria laid out above, presents a good sampling of current thinking on the subject, and points to issues involving not simply these groups but the whole political history of the era.

I will return briefly to the development of thinking about the political history of the lower middle classes, suggest which recent scholarship has been of greatest relevance for this volume, and then embed the contributions in a discussion that I offer consciously as a possible point of departure for further debate.

The foregoing contrast of past and present perspectives should not leave the impression that there was little justification for the dark appraisals of the 1920s and 1930s. World War I caused an unprecedented loss of life; it accelerated preexisting social changes; it exacerbated old political conflicts and created new ones; it placed big burdens on European states and economies; and it convinced many Europeans that they lived in a dangerous world of mass unrest. Given such uneasiness, the popular culture of the 1920s became not just a sign of new markets but a ritual of foreboding. The Depression had by 1932 thrown 13.7 million people out of work in the United States, 5.6 million in Germany, and 2.8 million in Britain. Most of the unemployed were manual laborers, but many were "nonmanual" workers such as commercial or technical employees. Some self-employed artisans, small shopkeepers, and tavern owners faced bankruptcies, while most small enterprises faced serious declines in business. Deflationary policies in some countries resulted in public-sector cutbacks that hurt officials, clerical employees, and schoolteachers. Already disappointed by narrowing professional chances in the 1920s, many university-educated men and women in West Europe, but especially in Central and East Europe, added to the growing ranks of an intellectual stratum whose economic existence put it barely above, if not sometimes below, the employed working classes. These tensions, varying in scope and intensity, seemed to slide all too easily into support for an antidemocratic politics, whether in the violent form of German and Italian fascism, the disgruntled nationalism of Romanian or Hungarian students, or a less sensational disillusionment with the parliamentary system in England, France, Denmark, Belgium, and elsewhere. The links between economic crisis, the political rancor of the lower middle classes, and antidemocratic sentiments seemed close and indisputable. The rhetoric of lower-middle-class despair spoke of harsh material and political conditions.

Although the Italian theorist Luigi Salvatorelli, responding to the rise of the fascist dictator Mussolini in the early 1920s, was among the first explicitly to link the lower middle classes to fascism,[11] it was in Germany that this theoretical tradition resonated most deeply and widely. No country after World War I seemed to offer a more powerful example of the effects of economic hardship, political upheaval, and lower-middle-class reaction. The efforts of Social Democrats, leftist liberals, and Catholics to establish a democratic republic in 1918 were thwarted by the disorganization of the Left, the antidemocratic resistance of German elites and the largest part of the middle classes, the breakdown of state authority, and the bitter effects of the Depression. Contemporary observers argued convincingly that in the context of such political drama it was mainly the lower middle classes that supported Adolf Hitler's National Socialist party, although already in 1930 Carl Mierendorff realized Nazism's appeal to a minority of young manual laborers outside the socialist movement and trade unions.[12] No country had a longer or more developed intellectual tradition of writing on the politics of the lower middle classes. Since the last two decades of the nineteenth century, Marxist and non-Marxist scholars had debated the economic and political fate of craftsmen, shop owners, clerks, and minor officials. German leftist intellectuals had strong hopes that white-collar workers would support democratic socialism immediately after World War I, but soon such hopes gave way to the idea that economic "panic" made these groups susceptible to political demagogy. Other influences shaped this analytical tradition, including the orthodox Communism of the Third International and the Marxism of Antonio Gramsci (who, as Mabel Berezin notes in her contribution to this book, referred to the lower middle classes as "monkey people"), Daniel Guerin, Leon Trotsky, and Clara Zetkin.[13] But Germany often remained the point of reference—partly for reasons already mentioned, partly because it shaped the history of interwar Europe more than any other country after 1933. Germany thus cast its considerable shadow over contemporary opinion about the wavering democratic or outright authoritarian sympathies of the lower middle classes.

Germany continued to influence intellectual discourse on the lower middle classes after 1945. The prevalent views of lower-middle-class authoritarianism were fueled in part by the dominance of North American social science in Western thought, to which the migration of predominantly German-Jewish and Austrian-Jewish intellectuals to the United States contributed mightily.[14] Seymour Martin Lipset's *Political Man,* which used German National Socialism as the ideal type of radical fascist movements, was most influential in bringing the argument of petit-bourgeois authoritarianism to a wide audience. There are several good discussions of the work of Lipset, Talcott Parsons, and William Kornhauser, all variously influenced by the German example, and it would hardly be useful to recapitulate them.[15] What needs to be emphasized is that the tradition of identifying the lower middle classes as actual or potential threats to parliamentary democracy survived the specific conditions in which it took shape. Scholars working in this tradition raised one significant feature of the interwar political experience to the status of a general law, creating a "restraining myth" that persisted in spite of disagreements over the economic, political, cultural, and psychological causes of the alleged lower-middle-class threat to freedom.[16]

Significantly, the extension of Italian, and especially German, "models" to other countries was based on thin empirical foundations. For, once we go beyond the interwar and postwar scrutiny of Nazism and Fascism, we find that the politics of the lower middle classes in interwar Europe remains one of the least researched fields in twentieth-century history writing.[17] Two recent developments, alluded to earlier, suggest a change. The first is a reinvestigation of the social basis of fascist movements, the second a growing interest in lower-middle-class groups in the nineteenth and early twentieth centuries.

As for the first development, the last twenty-five years have produced a wealth of material on the origins, evolution, social composition, and rule of fascist movements in interwar Europe.[18] In one sense, the sheer amount of research has had a dampening effect on synthetic thinking of the kind that characterized the first decade after World War II, when sweeping generalizations could be made in good conscience and relatively data-poor conditions.[19] Unsurprisingly, debates on German fascism were in the forefront of this research.[20] Thus Canadian sociologist Richard Hamilton's study of the Nazi electorate of July 1932, which combined empiricism and theory, was bound to have a wide effect. Hamilton analyzed electoral returns from a handful of big German cities. He argued that only a large minority of the urban lower middle classes voted for the National Socialist German Workers' party (NSDAP), while upper- and upper-middle-class voters in Berlin, Hamburg, Cologne and other big cities were far more sympathetic to Hitler than had previously been thought.[21] The implication went well beyond the social roots of Nazism, for Hamilton attacked a long-established tradition of pinpointing petit-bourgeois authoritarianism.

Reviews of Hamilton's work were mixed, but there was little doubt of its impact. In a balanced discussion of recent literature, historian James Sheehan responded to Hamilton's critique of previous arguments of disproportionate lower-middle-class susceptibility to fascism by saying, "one can't help but wonder how so many could have believed something for so long on the basis of so little."[22] Yet Hamilton's powerful challenge was hardly a call in the wilderness. Several years before the publication of Hamilton's book, the work of Juan Linz, among others, implied (if it did not directly assert) the untenability of "lower-middle-class" theories of European fascism. And soon after Hamilton's work appeared, Thomas Childers' more comprehensive *The Nazi Voter* demonstrated convincingly that the Nazi electorate had by 1930 "begun to transcend its lower-middle-class origins" without abandoning its all-important social anchor of self-employed artisans and retailers. Although Michael Kater insisted that the lower middle class was the "prototypical exponent" of National Socialism, he also demonstrated upper-class overrepresentation and significant participation by a working-class minority in the Hitler movement.[23] Notwithstanding Hamil-

ton's iconoclastic aims, the general thrust of this research was not to abandon the idea of lower-middle-class attraction to Nazism, but to relativize
it and to identify more precisely than before exactly which lower-middle-
class groups supported Hitler and which did not. At the same time, the
new research cautioned that lower-middle-class attraction to Hitler's party
occurred as part of wider Nazi mobilization of working-class, middle-class,
and elite groups. The debate also intersected with an important rethinking
of pre–World War I German history that stressed the self-organization of
non-elite groups, including the lower middle classes.[24] The implication for
this discussion was that if non-elite classes were less susceptible to the
manipulative political strategies of agrarians, industrialists, and the state
in Germany prior to World War I than had been assumed, then what was
the scope and nature of collective responses to Hitler's propaganda both
inside and outside the Nazi movement?

Defenders of older arguments have hardly conceded, as Kater's argument
suggests. In 1981 Amos Perlmutter wrote that Hitler was "modern tyranny's most illustrious petit bourgeois," a statement that coupled the
lower middle classes and all forms of twentieth-century dictatorship. Klaus
Tenfelde used Lipset's notion that German fascism was a form of "extremism of the center" (which emphasizes *lower*-middle-class susceptibility
to Nazism more strongly than it stresses the Nazification of the middle
strata generally) in his otherwise compelling case study of the Bavarian
town of Penzberg. Arguing that historians have overlooked the social-
psychological dimensions of Hitler's alleged attractiveness for the "ordinary
man," Kettenacker wrote that Hitler was the "mouthpiece of the German
lower middle class" and "the most outspoken representative of his generation as well as of his social class"—suggesting that Hitler was not only
representative of the lower middle class but that the lower middle class
was representative of the war generation. Not many scholars would second
Leppert-Fögen's claim that fascism was a "revival of petit-bourgeois *(klein-
bürgerlichen)* revolt" dating back to the French Revolution and Jacobin-
ism.[25] Yet many scholars, perhaps the majority, would insist on a unique
identification between most parts of the lower middle classes and fascism.
Even those who do not may still use Germany as the negative model of
petit-bourgeois authoritarianism. This statement applies to several participants in this volume.

For all the disagreements of current debates, the relevance of recent research for the following essays is unambiguous. If European or German
fascism must be thought of in terms of cross-class coalitions in which the
petite bourgeoisie played a significant but variable role in specific political
contexts, then what of the wider linking of the lower middle classes and
political reaction in interwar Europe? Scholarship has barely scratched the
surface of this problem, as some of the contributors to this book suggest.

The question points directly to a second current of research, more recent than the first, that deals mainly with the lower middle classes in the century before the Great War. Here the emphasis has often been on social and economic behavior rather than political action, although politics still clearly matters in this research, as demonstrated in Crossick and Haupt's outstanding collection of essays on master artisans and shopkeepers in Germany, Britain, France, Belgium, and Austria.[26]The significance of this and related work for our purposes is twofold. First, there is a strong emphasis on political contingency. Nord's work suggests that Parisian shopkeepers' turn from Left to Right at the turn of the century depended very much on the impact of the political moment rather than an assumed structural propensity of the lower middle classes for right-wing extremism.[27] His methodology and conclusions are therefore compatible with a part of recent political sociology, which also stresses "concrete analysis of political trends and strategies."[28]

The second significant feature is an emphasis on multiple political meanings. Crossick and Haupt note that, although one can detect a rightward tendency in the pre-1914 "old" lower middle classes, mainly self-employed craftsmen and shop owners, this appears to have meant very different things in different national milieux. Do flat and rather one-dimensional characterizations of "the Right" capture the plurality of interests and choices of the lower middle classes when they gravitated to orthodox liberalism in England; to the economic liberalism of Liberal and Catholic parties in Belgium; to the nationalism and conservatism of Raymond Poincaré, elected president of the Third Republic in 1913, in France; or to the antisocialism and contentious nationalism of Germany?[29] The state of research on the nineteenth century allows this question to be posed, but certainly not answered definitively. Research for the interwar period has rarely posed the question of multiple political meanings at all.

Both developments—a rethinking of lower-middle-class involvement in European fascism and a dual emphasis on political contingency and multiple political meanings—find an echo in the following essays in ways that the remainder of this introduction will spell out in general terms. But the contributors address other, more specific points raised by the literature, and the remaining pages will also suggest what these points are.

The "variable geometry"[30] of the lower middle classes has bedeviled scholars, creating much debate over who should be included in the category and who should be left out. In some recent scholarship on fascism, the issue of categorization dominated the literature. Here and in other places, it was "as if the assignment of persons into classes were sufficient to determine the nature and outcome of political struggle."[31] This volume avoids such preoccupations; but it also recognizes the need for categorization.

Building on previous practice, our focus is on the non-farm lower middle classes, which include small-scale, self-employed artisans and retailers; sales and clerical personnel, minor administrators and government officials, and modestly paid professionals such as nurses and schoolteachers or even certain doctors, professors, and lawyers; and some groups of university students. One problem in suggesting these categories is of course that terms such as "small," "minor," or "modestly paid" are open to considerable ambiguity, which cannot be resolved without detailed study of each group across communities and national boundaries. It is possible to include still other groups, including supervisory workers such as shop foremen[32] and small pensioners, but this book does not have material on them. Were we to abandon the non-farm distinction, we might also include small farmers in the category.

It has been commonplace since the late nineteenth century to distinguish between two groups: an "old" lower middle class, or traditional petite bourgeoisie, which usually encompasses trades and activities (such as artisanal production) that predate industrial capitalism; and a "new" lower middle class, or middle strata, or new petite bourgeoisie,[33] consisting of groups whose growth and prominence originate in modern statemaking, bureaucratization, the growth of large-scale manufacturing, the rise of a "mass culture" industry, and other processes connected to the industrial capitalism of the last 150 years. Many scholars argue that the long decline of the old lower middle classes is offset by the growth of new groups whose economic center of gravity is not small-scale production or traditional commerce, but new information technologies and urban services. The distinction is somewhat arbitrary, given that parts of the traditional petite bourgeoisie have arisen or benefited from industrial capitalism. Nonetheless, the trusty division into "old" and "new" middle strata captures an important reality, and we use it in this volume.

Having listed these groups, we have not necessarily defined a "class" or "classes." For this we need to make three other points. First, drawing on Marxist tradition, it is essential to note that the groups mentioned above, like all social groups, occupy "empty slots" in the socioeconomic structure "that exist as a result of the division of labor and that have meaning independent of the attitudes or behavior of the individuals who occupy them."[34] The empty slots occupied by all middle strata have in common a distance from both manual labor and capital, but this does not imply a necessary form of political activity (a point taken up momentarily). Second, the groups discussed here have less access to market resources such as education, real estate, and consumer goods than the upper strata of the middle classes do, but more access to these things than manual laborers and the poor. In terms of the Weberian notion of class, which emphasizes, not what people do in the production process, but what they have and can get from the market,[35] these groups belong to the "lower" middle classes. They form an aggregation whose size and well-being varies in each country according to the level and character of industrialization, urbanization, and political conflict, and whose boundaries cannot be drawn neatly in relation to either the middle and upper-middle classes or the working classes.

Third, classes are dynamic, unstable, and contingent. They are linguistic and political creations, collective ways of imagining social boundaries based ultimately on the production process, and giving voice to the solidarity that arises from recognizing such boundaries in the pursuit of power.[36] None of the essays confronts this problem head-on; that was not our task. But all the essays, and some more than others, assume that the lower middle classes find solidarity mainly in collective political action. In this they extend and refine previous research,[37] making it possible to conceptualize not a single lower middle class, but certainly lower middle *classes* whose shared rhetoric marks them off from industrial workers, the owners of capital, and the middle class.

Of course numerous obstacles stood (and stand) in the way of the formation of the lower middle classes. Scholars find very real differences in relations to capitalist economies, social life, and political outlook between independent artisans and shopkeepers. Others have commented on the significant contrasts in pay, status, political behavior, and relations to big capital between high- and low-level white-collar workers; and still others comment on significant national differences in determining the status of white-collar and blue-collar jobs. The forces pulling the petite bourgeoisie toward identity with the working class, other than those pinpointed in crude proletarianization theses, have also been noted. For instance, technical or administrative personnel may have superiority over the working class in the workplace, but they enter more equal social relations in neighborhoods where work roles jostle with identities based on home ownership or consumption patterns that manual laborers share. Family ties have been shown to play a role also, as when white-collar workers from working-class backgrounds continue to identify with the laboring class rather than with the new middle classes.[38]

Yet such issues can receive undue emphasis. Some artisans and retailers inhabited similar social worlds based on family labor or on limited exploitation of non-family members. The social boundaries between white-collar workers and the independent lower middle classes could often be very fluid, as when the sons or daughters of artisans and shopkeepers found jobs as clerks or salespeople, a practice increasingly common as the nineteenth century selectively diminished the opportunities of small enterprise in specific branches of activity. Intermarriage could also make the lines between self-employed and dependent groups increasingly indistinct.[39] If they acquired small property, employees and independents might also have gained increasingly similar perceptions of time and space, a point briefly taken up in my article but in need of more research.[40] My research and other literature also suggest that dependent and independent groups gained a sense of common purpose in local voluntary associations, especially those in smaller or less industrialized communities where class differences and the development of pressure groups based on specific sectional interests were not yet as pronounced as they were in big urban centers.[41] Later we will turn to some of the more explicitly political ways in which the lower middle classes achieved a feeling of having common goals.

The unevenness of short-term material hardships in interwar Europe further complicates the issue of class formation. The aim of this book was not to offer a detailed discussion of economic differences, but all the contributors share a sensitivity for the variable economic conditions—by country, region, economic branch, town, and occupation—that confronted the lower middle classes. The point has been made for the nineteenth century, but it deserves mention for the interwar era, for which the postwar recovery and the Depression appear all too often in popular accounts as brackets for an age of uniform economic despair. We know that the Depression of 1929 had a checkered impact, creating severe strains in Germany, Austria, the Netherlands, and Poland, but having a relatively mild effect in the Scandinavian countries or in already depressed Romania and Yugoslavia. Other countries—Belgium, France, Britain—took their places between these extremes in terms of unemployment, declines in industrial production, and cuts in per capita income.[42] Yet even in countries such as Germany, as Haupt and Niermann and I note in this volume, the effects of the Depression could vary tremendously. None of the contributors doubts that Orwell's shivering clerks were a reality, or that the wish of millions of Europeans "to live a normal life" was shattered by economic circumstances.[43] But there is a sense that, at least at the present state of research, one must remain cautious about the scope and effect of economic hardship.

References to social structures and uneven economic circumstances reaffirm the centrality of politics in the formation of the lower middle classes. Remarking on the persistent political power and volatility of small enterprise in France in the post–World War II era, Suzanne Berger argued that "differences that the simple play of economic forces might have distributed over a continuum are by political decision clustered into distinct and discontinuous segments."[44] She was referring to legislation by the French state that legitimized and perpetuated small business. If we are to understand the relation between this kind of "political decision" and the lower middle classes, two perspectives must be discussed, one dealing with state agencies and elites, the other with the leaders and organizations of the lower middle classes themselves. This dual perspective needs to be stressed if we want to avoid a distorted view of the lower middle classes as completely malleable subjects of elite and state policies.

State and elite interest in the lower middle classes in the modern period arose before 1848, but it became especially strong after that revolutionary year, when bourgeois groups and governments worked to detach the lower middle classes from a popular politics that had challenged existing power structures so mightily. Varying greatly according to time and place, elite concern with maintaining a politically useful—which often meant quiescent—petite bourgeoisie persisted throughout the following century, although the working classes aroused greater attention because they grew more dynamically, were seemingly more dangerous, and were thus more needful of special care and discrimination.[45] Of central importance in understanding elite and official strategies in the interwar years was a reshaping of the state and public life that had begun in the 1880s and 1890s. It featured growing state action in the provision of welfare and education, and in the redistribution and management of economic resources. Before the Great War, government activity in these areas was modest by present-day standards, but state involvement in economic and social life increased in 1914–1918, when national states rationed food supplies, allocated raw materials, supervised transport and shipping, and managed their economies more completely than ever before. Partially dismantled after 1918, state regulation would be revived and extended in the interwar period, and especially in World War II, then maintained in far larger degree after 1945 than after 1918. Simultaneously, growing public involvement in political life after the 1880s brought about the increasing self-organization of the working and middle classes, although once again there were significant variations within and between countries. Throughout such changes, populations looked for new forms of state authority—liberal, socialist, communist, and fascist—that admitted more groups into the political process, whether as passive audiences or as contentious agents of change. The type of mobilization of these audiences and agents was linked in turn not only to the level of group solidarity but also to the power of the state against which collective action was directed.[46]

World War I accelerated social and economic trends, created new political conditions in which prewar developments had unexpected effects, and touched off unprecedented social conflict. One crucial outcome of this combination of accelerated change and conflict was "corporatism," which refers to elite responses to the struggle over organizing state authority in interwar Europe. From the point of view of European ruling classes outside the newly formed Soviet Union, corporatism meant "dealing with unions (or creating pseudo-unions as in [fascist] Italy), giving state agencies control over the market, [and] building interest group spokesmen into the structure of the state."[47] Corporatism was an approach to interest representation in which major economic groups cooperated with the state to guarantee political stability and economic productivity, often through bureaucratic rather than parliamentary channels. The amount of state involvement varied considerably, from comparatively restrained intervention in the liberal democracies to more active and brutal intrusions in authoritarian systems. Wolfe argues that in the liberal democracies corporatism was abandoned in the decades between the Depression and the 1950s in favor of a "franchise state" in which economic groups wielded public power and limited state interventions. Some states, such as Nazi Germany, claimed they were corporatist but actually rejected this mode of political organization.[48] Despite these complexities, there can be little doubt that interwar politics featured growing interaction between diffuse state agencies, whether heavily interventionist or not, and "private" groups. Accompanied by violence, experimentation, and much uncertainty, increasingly routine exchanges between national states and social organizations presupposed highly structured economic interest groups that could transmit their claims to the state and that could in turn control and channel the actions of their memberships. Sociopolitical arrangements thus created environments in which many different kinds of previously created or newly formed pressure groups could—and had to—flourish.

Historians have focused on the two major actors in the recasting of interwar politics, big labor and capital, a point taken up critically in Strikwerda's discussion of Belgium in this volume. A corollary has been that some historians have thought of groups such as white-collar workers as "unorganized" or "unorganizable," a perspective related in this case to the fact that service sectors had large proportions of female laborers who were allegedly less militant than their male counterparts. On the other hand, some historians have thought of artisans and shopkeepers as reluctant to adapt to the new age of mass organization, a perspective often reinforced by the evidence of political alienation so prevalent in these groups between the wars.[49] There is of course substantial reason to emphasize contrasting levels of organization and responses to state formation and mass politics in these populations. Yet unambiguous evidence for an unorganized or "maladapted" petite bourgeoisie will not be found in the following pages. Instead, the essays suggest that the interwar decades were crucial in terms of increasing the scope of organization and political involvement of the lower middle classes. Political alienation stemmed less from disgruntlement over the lack of organization for economic and political interests (although this was present) than from a deep engagement in the conflicts of interwar politics.

Yet political engagement depended very much on the coalitions that were formed, the unfolding of conflict in each polity, and the "coloration" of specific political regimes.[50] Here Germany should be not a yardstick but the example of what could happen to parts of the lower middle classes when a state moves very rapidly across a continuum from weakened parliamentary democracy to authoritarian politics. German National Socialism was successful in mobilizing a significant minority of the lower middle classes. But this occurred in a context of disillusionment with democracy and deep mobilization against the Weimar state. The state had failed all around: it was attacked by Right and Left, and, by the early 1930s, never passionately defended by its supporters, many of whom shared a feeling with the opponents of parliamentarism that something had to change.[51] The lower middle classes who gravitated to Nazism interpreted the increasingly nationalist, antidemocratic, antisocialist, and anti-Semitic language of the polity in their own terms, as the articles on Bremen retailers and German associational life suggest. Of the countries covered in this book, only Italy and Romania, for reasons much different than those of Germany, gave lower-middle-class students, professionals, and officials a comparably powerful language of nationalist disaffection and substantial opportunities to attack an already-weak state. Where by contrast preexisting parties remained influential; where parliamentary democracy was more deeply rooted if not unanimously cherished; where leftist mobilization did not represent as substantial a threat to the middle classes as it did in Germany and Italy; where fascist influences were muted; where economic hardships were less sudden and severe; and where states used legislation to address, symbolically or substantively, economic grievances of lower-middle-class groups—there the language of disaffection employed by traders, artisans, officials, professionals, and clerks remained within established political channels.

But what were the specific party political options? One can identify four trajectories, none of which can be discussed in full detail in the following pages, but which the essays and much of the existing literature consider in one way or another. The first and most widely chosen trajectory was to vote for or join political parties of the established Center or Right. Subject to numerous variations of timing and scope, this pattern obtained in France, Belgium, Denmark, Britain, and elsewhere for most of the interwar years. It encompassed many different organizations with unique traditions and constituencies—one need only think of the contrasts between the orthodox liberalism of the Conservative party in Britain and the small-town and rural Republicanism of the Radical party in France[52]—and reflected the wide national variations in lower-middle-class politics. More importantly, this pattern suggests that the lower middle classes were anything but the threats to parliamentarism that literature based on the German experience identified. Whether they were seen as subordinates in the maintenance of *laissez-faire* capitalism, as in Britain, or as an independent collective force, as in Belgium or France, the lower middle classes could indeed appear as forces of conservatism, resistance to change, and preservation of social order, given this pattern of political action. One would want to caution against a one-dimensional perspective on this adherence to preexisting ideologies and organizations, however, as the earlier discussion of multiple political meanings suggested.

Such considerations also apply to the other trajectories, the second of which refers to a subject well known for the nineteenth century but perhaps underemphasized for the interwar years; namely, the involvement of lower-middle-class groups, both dependent and self-employed, in the European Left, especially the socialist movement. One can refer to various examples in the literature: artisans in the Social Democratic party in Finland; white-collar employees in socialist unions in post–World War I Germany; and various middle strata in the interwar Socialist party in provincial France.[53] This volume also presents evidence of such involvement, including specific information on white-collar supporters of the British Labour and Communist parties and somewhat more general discussion of petit-bourgeois socialists in Italy and Denmark.

The third and fourth trajectories were taken by fewer groups than the first and second. The third, more interesting for its complete lack of success than for its resonance in European politics, has to do with attempts to establish, outside existing party structures, independent political parties representing "the" middle class, or parts of it. The participants in this tradition of failure included groups that our contributors touch on—the Economic party in Germany, the Trades and Industry party in Denmark, the Middle Classes Union in Britain, the National Union of the Middle Classes in Belgium—but also groups treated in other analyses, such as the short-lived white-collar party (Angestelltenpartei) in Switzerland in 1919–20.[54]

The fourth trajectory, finally, was followed by a variegated assemblage of fascist, fascist-like, and radical nationalist parties. Electoral support and membership numbers for these groups varied widely, from nearly forty percent of the total vote in July 1932 and nearly 850,000 members for the Nazi party before Hitler's gaining of the Chancellorship in 1933, to much smaller totals for groups in other countries. The foregoing discussion makes it unnecessary to belabor my criticism of the argument of a typically lower-middle-class authoritarianism, just as it makes it unnecessary to stress that there was petit-bourgeois support of such movements. But it is useful to reinforce the argument of multiple political meanings. For, even when we have evidence of substantial if varying lower-middle-class support for Nazism, for Italian fascism, for the Romanian Iron Guard, for Belgian Rexism, or for the British Union of Fascists, we cannot avoid the different motivations underlying such support and the different uses to which it was put. Fascism and radical nationalism could serve in Germany as a defense of local interests against the corporatist management of class conflict, in Italy as a "conservative reshuffling of the middle and upper classes," or in Romania and Hungary as a reaction to expanding occupational and political possibilities and dashed nationalist expectations.[55] Unlike the three previous trajectories, this trajectory appeared only when a profound shock to the state and public life had occurred. Just as fascism and radical nationalism were volatile reactions to such shocks, so petit-bourgeois involvement in these movements was provisional, fluid, and based on sometimes-contradictory calculations of interest and threat.

The social heterogeneity of the lower middle classes is undoubtedly one of the central reasons for this splintering across the political landscape, and there are numerous examples of the interaction between mutually antagonistic social claims and political fragmentation in the following pages. But I would like to refer to another factor, which has only recently received systematic attention in scholarly literature, and for which this volume provides evidence; namely, the expectations and images of the petite bourgeoisie formed by state agencies, ruling classes, and the press. It seems that the very positing of a uniform image of the lower middle classes by elite groups produced its own fragmented counter-images and changing political loyalties, a function of that petit-bourgeois "volatility" so effectively discussed by Blackbourn for pre–World War I Germany.[56]

This resistance to being put into preconceived linguistic and political slots was expressed in many different ways. The British National Government, formed in August of 1931 and made up of representatives from the Labour, Liberal, and Conservative parties, thought of the lower middle classes not as an active buffer, but, in Jeffery's words, a "political reserve army," quiescent and without aspirations for public commitment. Whereas there was much to recommend this assumption, Jeffery and Pennybacker demonstrate that a small but vocal minority of left-wing blackcoated (or white-collar) workers had an alternative and activist image of their role in the national community that would have profound effects in World War II and the postwar world. Fascists praised the peasants or small artisans, thinking of them as the basis of an invented racial purity, whether of the "people's community" of the "Third Reich" or the proposed Carpatho-Danubian Great Fatherland of a Hungarian master race.[57] Yet even where such visions found direct expression in a political regime, as in Hitler's Germany, the lower middle classes met such expectations with a mixture of feverish support, defense of traditional practices, selfish consumerism, criticism, and retreat into private life.[58] This failure to completely toe the expected line prompted Hitler to devise his own reading of the old argument of the lower middle classes' predicted demise. Artisans, small traders, and employees would not disappear into the proletariat due to the dynamics of capitalism, as so many orthodox Marxists had argued; they would instead disappear altogether, as they deserved to in Hitler's eyes, in a racial war finished off by Allied bombs and Soviet armies. Elites could of course learn from and adjust to the inadequacies of their expectations, as Strikwerda and Christiansen and Lammers show for Belgium and Denmark, where the lower middle classes became key contributors to political stabilization. But the evidence suggests more in the way of significant disparities between elite assumptions of petit-bourgeois uniformity and the more variegated reality of lower-middle-class political action and reaction.

Socioeconomic heterogeneity, multiple political meanings and trajectories, unreasonable assumptions of petit-bourgeois conformity to elite models—these shape the picture of the splintered classes. Yet it is possible to overlook certain shared characteristics, such as the already-mentioned tendency of an indeterminate majority of the European lower middle classes to support parties of the Center and Right. Another common feature is petit-bourgeois localism, a problem taken up in my essay, in Haupt and Niermann's piece, and in less direct fashion in several other essays. Here historians of the interwar era can begin with rich evidence from research on the nineteenth century.[59] Localism could take the form of insularity, disengagement from national concerns, and political apathy. There is a good, concrete account of the distance of the lower middle classes from the national polity in Robert Roberts' discussion of the early-twentieth-century political life of the working-class slum Salford, where Roberts' parents were modest shopkeepers.[60] The political involvement of the community was distantly symbolized in two buildings: Hyndmann Hall, home of the Social Democratic Federation, which Henry H. Hyndmann had founded in 1884; and the Conservative Club. The former "remained for us mysteriously aloof and through the years had, in fact, about as much impact on the neighborhood as the near-by gasworks," recalled Roberts, whereas the latter "was notable usually for a union jack in the window and a brewer's dray at the door" and "except for a few days at election times, didn't appear to meddle with politics at all." For all the unique qualities of the author of *The Classic Slum,* Roberts' situation was typical insofar as the urban lower middle classes usually found themselves dispersed in neighborhoods of mixed class makeup.[61] It was typical in a different sense also, because it, like so many autobiographical accounts of youth, emphasized too much the distance of the family from public involvement.[62] Nonetheless, Roberts' remarks capture something of real concern for understanding petit-bourgeois localism.

If localism seemed to separate the neighborhood or street from national life, Roberts' recollections provide evidence that it could also nurture an intense concern with questions of power and social justice. When the Salford constituency elected its first Labour party representative to the national parliament in 1924, the year in which a minority Labour government took power for the first time in British history, Roberts said, "simple socialists like my mother wept for joy and we, the young, felt ourselves the heralds of a new age."[63] Here "localism" meant actively viewing a contentious world through the prism of shop, neighborhood, district, or region rather than succumbing to apathy or solipsism. This kind of localism could connect directly with the political frustrations of the lower middle classes discussed throughout the essays, for, as Castells has argued, "when people find themselves unable to control the world, they simply shrink the world to the size of their community."[64] This remark applies in some degree to many groups—to the French artisans of Zdatny's discussion, the Bremen shopkeepers of Haupt and Niermann's article, the joiners of my essay, or the activist white-collar workers of Pennybacker's detailed research on the London County Council. And it suggests that petit-bourgeois localism was not exclusively backward-looking because it could be connected to the preservation of local systems of communication and meaning threatened by unbridled industrial and technological change. Localism could be used as a form of future-oriented "camping-out . . . in the windy interstices of a generally hostile society."[65] In this sense, interwar petit-bourgeois localism, whether of the Left or Right, prefigures certain preservationist and grass-roots impulses in current politics.

Another widely shared feature is frustration with the lower middle classes' political power in relation to the state and other groups. The hateful criticisms of the German parliamentary system within artisans', retailers', or white-collar employees' groups are certainly well known. Here criticisms were aimed at corporatist arrangements that reduced political life to bargaining between highly organized pressure groups and that left key parts of the lower middle classes permanently disadvantaged. Nazism promised to destroy this system, only to replace it with its own chaotic machinery of intraparty and interest-group bargaining that benefited parts of the petite bourgeoisie and hurt others. The political frustrations of lower-middle-class intellectuals in Italy, Romania, or Hungary also made fascist and radical nationalist ideas acceptable there. But as our essays suggest, frustrations with the competition and compromises of mass politics were also evident in more stable polities: Christiansen and Lammers demonstrate that Danish artisans and retailers criticized the "party clichés" of political elites, and Strikwerda records Belgian petit-bourgeois attacks on a "rule of parties" (particratie) shaped by Catholics, Liberals, Socialists, Christian Democrats, conservatives, and Flemish and French speakers. One need only recall Hoffman's classic essay on France between the wars to see that such resentments could thrive in the countries that seemed firmly wedded to the rules of the parliamentary game.[66]

These political resentments often found expression in a hyperbolic language, surely an extension and "democratization" of the demagogic style that began to pervade European politics before World War I.[67] The present volume contains several examples, of which the Danish *Trades and Industry Daily* remark that the "road to a socialist state goes over the dead body of the middle class" is just one. An age that witnessed the rhetoric of a Hitler or a Mussolini could not help but be home to violent political language. Beyond this environmental issue, however, some scholars have suggested psychopathological reasons for the petite bourgeoisie's language. Others have seen the reflection of deep economic despair in such linguistic volatility. Without indiscriminately lumping the following essays together, the contributors to this volume generally find political explanations to be more convincing. Following Berger's analysis of French small-business groups after World War II, one could argue that the lower middle classes were more sensitive to political conflict than big labor or capital because they had less economic power to manage the effects of political change.[68] They thus responded to political strife more often and more heatedly than other groups. Yet the language of resentment, tied perhaps to collective memories of powerlessness and crisis, seemed to have gained an autonomy that persisted even when the conditions that gave rise to it had been changed. If the following essays do not provide decisive proof for this argument, they justify pursuing it in future research.

Nationalism is certainly part of this language of resentment, and understandably the lower middle classes have been thought of as especially quick to pound the nationalist drum. The preceding suggests that, for large parts of the lower middle classes, the referents of national loyalty were local.[69] They comprised not primarily the far-off symbols of national power and industriousness such as the Eiffel Tower,[70] although such structures were prominent in nationalist thought at the local level, but mainly monuments, buildings, institutions, and landscapes that were literally closer to home. If nationalism had its strong local dimensions, it was also a way for many (but not all) petit-bourgeois local notables to enter a wider nationwide web of institutions and practices shaped by the middle class, that "quintessential patriotic class" that used national loyalty to overcome its social fragmentation, "recognize itself collectively," and admit limited numbers of working-class and lower-middle-class individuals to its ranks.[71]

Yet these brief remarks are merely background for a point that comes through more clearly in the following pages, namely that, for the interwar lower middle classes, beneath the heated expressions of nationalism were strong currents of collective disillusionment. This is most obvious in Livezeanu's discussion of Romanian state officials and officials-to-be, who were crucial elements in the creation of a national community out of disparate territories, ethnic groups, and political identities. But these individuals felt thwarted in their national mission, and their political irascibility, hatred for the ruling elite, and antipathies against the Jewish bourgeoisie were outcomes of this sense of disillusionment. One finds parallels in the disgruntlement of Hungarian officialdom in the same period.[72] For such individuals, placed precariously between a weak national state and the impoverished mass of the population, nationalism became a source of tense frustration. Despite many dissimilarities of context and outcome, the examples from Italy, France, Belgium, Denmark, and Germany suggest that in these countries, also, the lower middle classes felt a deep sense of frustration about their role in building the cultural and political nation. Their loud proclamations that they represented the mean, that they were, in the case of French small enterprise, "the average honest Frenchman with common sense and a normal education," had something to do with a sense of thwarted national centrality.[73] The articles by Pennybacker and Jeffery are useful in this connection because they show that a feeling of thwarted centrality could lead to political activism of a kind that is rarely associated with the interwar lower middle classes.

Given its emphasis of cross-class identities and its powerful identification with the Right, nationalism could quickly issue into a renunciation of languages of class. This took several forms, one being the well-known opposition of artisans, traders, employees, and officials to the idea of a bipolar society in which most middle strata would eventually find themselves in the working classes. The efforts of white-collar employees in some countries to have social legislation that distinguished them from blue-collar groups, the clamoring for tax legislation favorable to small enterprise, the heated criticisms of the materialism and instrumental attitude toward labor of the working classes (an instrumentalism that allegedly reduced a job to just a job rather than a way of life)—all pointed in this direction. Another form of the renunciation of class was an emphasis on individualism or personal autonomy, difficult and ambiguous terms that nonetheless evoked important images for both the dependent and the self-employed lower middle classes. "Pull yourself together, don't just be a workhorse" said a Swiss employee to his colleagues in 1919.[74] This was a sense of individualism, an injunction to educate oneself, round out one's personality, and move beyond the concerns of the workplace in forming one's identity. This notion connected easily with the employed lower middle classes' openness to mass leisure—the cinema, bicycling, paperback books, the popular press, weekend outings.[75] Pennybacker and Jeffery refer to this phenomenon, uncovering an individualism that was compatible with traditions of collective political action on the British Left and thus not inevitably tied to the denial of class. Yet for the majority of white-collar workers, such marketplace individualism placed the employee above the worker and denied the workplace the centrality it had in the working-class movement. On the other hand, individualism had its progressive side, since it placed new pressure on hitherto authoritarian forms of management in both business and government by being linked to demands for fairer treatment, better pay, and the rewarding of merit.[76]

Some artisans and shopkeepers were also drawn to the "weekend," the symbol and temporal location of so many new forms of mass leisure. Yet these essays and other literature remind us that older themes also nurtured a sense of personal autonomy for these groups. Bechhofer and Elliott's work on the post–World War II petite bourgeoisie point to the persistence of a moral economy in these groups that was based on a peculiar mix of small capital, skill, family labor, and limited use of non-family workers.[77] Here the workplace or shop was central rather than subsidiary. The moral economy privileged individualism, autonomy, and thrift; it was deeply anti-pathetic to "materialism," whether this was perceived in the form of big capital or militant trade unionism; it was connected to deeply conservative attitudes toward sexuality and religion, issues that this volume must necessarily leave aside. One finds clear echoes of the moral economy in Zdatny's discussion of the social thought of French artisans, who in this respect perhaps were the "French version of the cowboy," and in Christiansen's and Lammers' remarks on Danish artisans and retailers. Moreover, as Strikwerda shows, the popularity of small retailing in Belgium was itself an indication of how widespread such ideas were. It would be mistaken to see this moral economy as uniformly retrogressive. Zdatny and others have pointed to a willingness, sometimes halting but nonetheless present, to adopt new machines in artisanal work or use modern business methods in small enterprises; and small shopowners and others benefited from the evolution of mass leisure in still incompletely understood ways. It would be similarly mistaken to see the moral economy as having little impact outside the traditional petite bourgeoisie. Individuals in the new middle strata also embraced a part of these values, such as that numbing penuriousness compellingly described in A. J. Cronin's novel of the orphaned grandson of a minor public official in Scotland before the Great War.[78]

These are some of the major issues this volume addresses. Contained in these pages is additional discussion, undeveloped in comparison with the above-mentioned themes but nonetheless important, on an array of subjects: the uneven resonance of anti-Semitism; the role of women in the political activity of the lower middle classes; the centrality of the family in the economic and social life of the traditional petite bourgeoisie; electoral behavior, an especially thorny problem given the dispersed residential patterns of the groups in question; and the involvement of shopkeepers, artisans, or minor government employees in specific political events or highly visible movements, a perspective that until recently dominated scholarship on the lower middle classes but that still requires continued study and rethinking. We could continue the list, just as we could build a long roster of items that this book necessarily leaves out.

But there is a wider implication of these essays that subsumes specific issues. Study of the lower middle classes between the world wars is significant, not only because scholarship has concentrated on labor and capital, but because the lower middle classes had a far greater impact on the course of European history than was previously thought. We are dealing with important collective political actors whose influence spread beyond the interwar era. Indeed, this volume suggests how one-sided older arguments were that portrayed the lower middle classes as retrograde groups struggling against change and doomed to fail once the unsettled conditions of the interwar period were swept away. To be sure, this backward-looking element was present in much of the political behavior discussed in this book. Yet even in the clearly antidemocratic currents of petit-bourgeois politics, or in the political ideas directed mainly to the tensions of the interwar years, there were forward-looking qualities that, for better or worse, would influence European history after World War II. One need only think of the French Poujadists, mobilizers of disgruntled shopkeepers in the 1950s whose outlook reminded Roland Barthes of the poisoned language of the 1930s; or of the heritage of "radical antiliberal slogans" of shop owners and artisans that gained expression in the recession of 1966–1967 in the Federal Republic of Germany.[79]

But there were mainly constructive, if at times ambiguous, long-term influences, which we find in a British blackcoated activism of the 1930s that contributed to the ambitious social programs of the first majority Labour government in 1945–1951[80]; in lower-middle-class participation in the first "golden age" (Christiansen and Lammers) of class compromise in Denmark that would extend beyond the Nazi occupation into the postwar era; in the endeavors of the Belgian lower middle classes to help in the making of a corporatist state; in the 1930s neo-Catholicism of clerical and technical employees in France, a movement with significant implications for post-1945 politics in that country;[81] and more generally in the growing efforts of groups such as storeowners and government employees throughout the twentieth century to build the kinds of nationally organized pressure groups that increasingly dominated repertoires of collective action in modern European politics.[82] This list, too, could continue.

Given the centrality of Germany in the interwar literature, it is useful to start with two pieces on that country. The first is a more general essay that deals not with classes *per se* but with voluntary associations as tracers of petit-bourgeois politics. The second, by Haupt and Niermann, is a case study of retailers in the North German city of Bremen. It parallels the first essay insofar as it concentrates on the Weimar Republic, stresses the centrality of local politics, and highlights the importance of voluntary groups. Both pieces call for a substantial rethinking of key parts of previous history writing on the German lower middle classes. The second pair of articles, on the relatively unmapped subject of blackcoated activism in interwar Britain, also combines a more general piece and a case study. It features Jeffery's probing discussion of the British new lower middle classes and the political nation in the 1930s and Pennybacker's richly detailed look at London County Council employees. The next three articles deal in varying depth with specific groups within the lower middle classes. Zdatny's engagingly written contribution focuses on French artisans, Berezin's essay discusses the so-called (and still largely unexamined) humanistic lower middle classes of Italy, and Livezeanu's research deals with the little-known subject of the lower-middle-class intelligentsia in Romania. What follows are two articles that discuss both the old and the new middle classes and that deal with Western countries often overlooked by Anglophones writing on interwar politics. These are Christiansen's and Lammers' article on Denmark and Strikwerda's comprehensive analysis of Belgium.

Notes

1. For the reference to a modern past and the quote, see Patrick Wright, *On Living in an Old Country: The National Past in Contemporary Britain* (London, 1985), 2. My thanks to Geoff Eley for informing me of this source.

2. George Orwell, *The Road to Wigan Pier*, reprint ed. (New York, 1967), 187; *Jeunesses Patriotes* party program, 1926, cited in Robert Soucy, *French Fascism: The First Wave, 1924–1933* (New Haven and London, 1986), 74.

3. David J. Saposs, "The Role of the Middle Class in Social Development. Fascism, Populism, Communism, Socialism," in *Economic Essays in Honor of Wesley Clair Mitchell* (New York, 1935), 415.

4. Erich Fromm, *Escape from Freedom*, reprint ed. (New York, 1964), 163–64.

5. Erich Fromm, *The Working Class in Weimar Germany*, trans. Barbara Weinberger (Cambridge, Mass., 1984), 226 for the quote, 227 for the remark on National Socialism.

6. Geoffrey Crossick and Heinz-Gerhard Haupt, "Shopkeepers, Master Artisans and the Historian: The Petite Bourgeoisie in Comparative Focus," in *Shopkeepers and Master Artisans in Nineteenth-Century Europe*, ed. Crossick and Haupt (London and New York, 1984), 3–4.

7. Val Burris, "The Discovery of the New Middle Class," *Theory and Society* 15, 3 (1986): 345.

8. For the point on populism, see Harry C. Boyte, "Populism Is Back, Redefined, and Redefining the Mainstream," *Los Angeles Times*, 13 Oct. 1987; on the working class and the Left, see Zygmunt Baumann, "The Left as the Counter-Culture of Modernity," *Telos* 70 (Winter 1986–87): 93.

9. Arno Mayer, "The Lower Middle Class as Historical Problem," *Journal of Modern History* 47, 3 (Sept. 1975): 411.

10. Nicholas Abercrombie and John Urry, *Capital, Labour and the Middle Classes*

(London, 1983), 47–48; for a concise discussion of definition problems, see also Jürgen Kocka, *White Collar Workers in America, 1890–1940: A Social-Political History in International Perspective*, trans. Maura Keeley (London and Beverly Hills, 1980), 1–33, *passim*. The issue of whether one can use the term *classes* in reference to the groups discussed in this volume is itself a matter of debate: see Frank Bechhofer and Brian Elliott, "Petty Property: the Survival of a Moral Economy," in *The Petite Bourgeoisie: Comparative Studies of the Uneasy Stratum*, ed. Bechhofer and Elliott (New York, 1981), 183. My position is that the term may be used only with the kinds of qualifications developed throughout this introduction.

11. Burris, "Discovery of the New Middle Class," 334. See Mabel Berezin's discussion of Salvatorelli in her article in this book.

12. Ibid., 324–43, which contains numerous references; Carl Mierendorff, "Gesicht und Charakter der Nationalsozialistischen Bewegung," *Die Gesellschaft* 7, 6 (June 1930): 497.

13. Burris, "Discovery of the New Middle Class," 324–43; Heinrich August Winkler, *Mittelstand, Demokratie, und Nationalsozialismus: Die politische Entwicklung von Handwerk und Kleinhandel in der Weimarer Republik* (Cologne, 1972), 35–39.

14. For a recent discussion of the emigration, see Irving Louis Horowitz, "Between the Charybdis of Capitalism and the Scylla of Communism: The Emigration of German Social Scientists, 1933–1945," *Social Science History* 11, 2 (Summer 1987): 113–38.

15. Seymour Martin Lipset, *Political Man: The Social Bases of Politics* (New York, 1959). For three of many critiques see Burris, "Discovery of the New Middle Class," 338–39; Richard F. Hamilton, *Restraining Myths: Critical Studies of U.S. Social Structure and Politics* (New York, 1975), 33–146, *passim*; idem, *Who Voted for Hitler?* (Princeton, 1982), 13–16, 19–32.

16. Hamilton, *Restraining Myths*, 126–39.

17. Geoffrey Crossick has noted that research on nineteenth-century artisans and shopkeepers is also sketchy in that it has focused on specific issues and events rather than broader trends. See "The Petite Bourgeoisie in Nineteenth-Century Europe: Problems and Research," in *Arbeiter und Arbeiterbewegung im Vergleich: Berichte zur internationalen historischen Forschung*, ed. Klaus Tenfelde (Munich, 1986), 227–77.

18. To cite only English-language books: Francis L. Carsten, *The Rise of Fascism* (London, 1967); Renzo de Felice, *Fascism: An Informal Introduction to Its Theory and Practice* (New Brunswick, N.J., 1976); Walter Laqueur, ed., *Fascism—A Reader's Guide: Analyses, Interpretations, Bibliography* (Berkeley and Los Angeles, 1976); Stein Ugelvik Larsen, Bernt Hagtvet, Jan Petter Myklebust, eds., *Who Were the Fascists. Social Roots of European Fascism* (Bergen, 1980); Barrington Moore, Jr., *Social Origins of Dictatorship and Democracy: Peasant and Lord in the Making of the Modern World* (Boston, 1966); George Mosse, ed., *International Fascism* (London and Beverly Hills, 1979); Detlef Mühlberger, ed., *The Social Basis of European Fascist Movements* (Beckenham, U.K., 1987), which was unavailable to me at the writing of this introduction; Ernst Nolte, *Three Faces of Fascism* (London, 1965); Stanley Payne, *Fascism: Comparison and Definition* (Madison, 1980); Nicos Poulantzas, *Fascism and Dictatorship* (London, 1974); Philip Rees, *Fascism and Pre-Fascism in Europe, 1890–1945* (Sussex, 1984); Hans Rogger and Eugen Weber, eds., *The European Right: A Historical Profile* (Berkeley and Los Angeles, 1966); Peter F. Sugar, ed., *Native Fascism in the Successor States, 1918–1945* (Santa Barbara, 1971); Eugen Weber, *Varieties of Fascism* (New York, 1964); John Weiss, *The Fascist Tradition* (New York, 1967); S. J. Woolf, ed., *The Nature of Fascism* (London, 1968); idem, ed., *Fascism in Europe*, 2nd ed. (London and New York, 1981).

In terms of analysis of the social bases of fascism, there are far more historical studies of Germany than of Italy. William Brustein's work on Italian Fascist party membership is of real significance in this context, as suggested by Mabel Berezin in note 17, p. 144.

19. See Geoff Eley, "What Produces Fascism: Preindustrial Traditions or a Crisis of a Capitalist State," *Politics and Society* 12, 1 (1983): 53–82.

20. Already somewhat outdated but still valuable as a systematic introduction: Pierre Ayçoberry, *The Nazi Question: An Essay on the Interpretations of National Socialism (1922–1975)*, trans. Robert Hurley (New York, 1981).

21. Hamilton, *Who Voted for Hitler?*

22. James Sheehan, "National Socialism and German Society," *Theory and Society* 13, 6 (Nov. 1984): 853. But see also the criticisms in Thomas Childers, "Who, Indeed, Did Vote for Hitler?" *Central European History* 17, 1 (March 1984): 45–53; Rudy Koshar, "Political Gangsters and Nazism: Some Comments on Richard Hamilton's Theory of Fascism," *Comparative Studies in Society and History* 28, 4 (Oct. 1986): 785–93.

23. See Juan Linz, "Some Notes Toward a Comparative Study of Fascism in Sociological Historical Perspective," in *Fascism—A Reader's Guide*, ed. Laqueur, 3–121; and Peter H. Merkl, "Comparing Fascist Movements," in *Who Were the Fascists*, 765–67, 773–80; Thomas Childers, *The Nazi Voter: The Social Foundations of Fascism in Germany, 1919–1933* (Chapel Hill and London, 1983), 178; Michael Kater, *The Nazi Party: A Social Profile of Members and Leaders, 1919–1945* (Oxford, 1983), 126.

24. David Blackbourn and Geoff Eley, *The Peculiarities of German History: Bourgeois Society and Politics in Nineteenth-Century Germany* (Oxford, New York, 1984).

25. Amos Perlmutter, *Modern Authoritarianism: A Comparative Institutional Analysis* (New Haven and London, 1981), 84; Klaus Tenfelde, *Proletarische Provinz: Radikalisierung und Widerstand in Penzberg/Oberbayern, 1900–1945* (Munich and Vienna, 1982), 200; Lothar Kettenacker, "Hitler's Impact on the Lower Middle Class," in *Nazi Propaganda: The Power and the Limitations*, ed. David Welch (London, 1983), 11, 14; Annette Leppert-Fögen, *Die deklassierte Klasse: Studien zur Geschichte und Ideologie des Kleinbürgertums* (Frankfurt/Main, 1974), 268–69.

26. See note 6. The Crossick-Haupt reader is a product of a larger international effort consisting of a series of round tables and publications since 1978 on the petite bourgeoisie. For an example of this activity, see David Blackbourn's report on the 1984 round table in Paris-Nanterre in "Economic Crisis and the Petite Bourgeoisie in Europe During the Nineteenth and Twentieth Centuries," *Social History* 10, 1 (Jan. 1985): 95–104.

27. Philip Nord, *Parish Shopkeepers and the Politics of Resentment* (Princeton, 1986), 486–96.

28. Burris, "Discovery of the New Middle Class," 345.

29. Crossick and Haupt, "Shopkeepers, Master Artisans and the Historian," 5–6, 15–17.

30. The term is used by George Ross, "Destroyed by the Dialectic: Politics, the Decline of Marxism, and the New Middle Strata in France," *Theory and Society* 16 (1987): 7.

31. Burris, "Discovery of the New Middle Class," 345.

32. Joseph Melling, "'Non-Commissioned Officers': British Employers and Their Supervisory Workers, 1880–1920," *Social History* 5, 2 (May 1980): 192.

33. Nicos Poulantzas, *Classes in Contemporary Capitalism* (London, 1975); and commentary on Poulantzas' general perspective by Erik Olin Wright, "Class Boundaries in Advanced Capitalist Societies," *New Left Review* 98 (1976): 3–41. Here and elsewhere, Wright stressed the "contradictory class locations" of new middle strata, but he has since altered this argument in *Classes* (London, 1985). For a recent discussion

of Wright's perspective, see Uwe Becker, "Class Theory and the Social Sciences: Erik Olin Wright on Classes," *Politics and Society* 17, 1 (March 1989): 67–88.

34. Gøsta Esping-Andersen, *Politics Against Markets: The Social Democratic Road to Power* (Princeton, 1985), 27.

35. This distinction is made by Göran Therborn, *What Does the Ruling Class Do When It Rules? State Apparatuses and State Power Under Feudalism, Capitalism and Socialism*, 2nd ed. (London, 1980), 140–41.

36. For an excellent discussion of the relation of language and politics, see Raymond Williams, *Marxism and Literature* (Oxford, 1977), 21–44. Recent work on the discursive features of class includes most notably Gareth Stedman Jones, *Languages of Class: Studies in English Working Class History* (Cambridge, 1984); for two responses to Jones' work, see: James Cronin, "Language, Politics and the Critique of Social History," *Journal of Social History* 20, 1 (Fall 1986): 177–83; Robert Gray, "The Deconstructing of the English Working Class," *Social History* 11, 3 (Oct. 1986): 363–73. In addition, see Lynn Hunt, "Introduction: History, Culture, and Text," *The New Cultural History*, ed. idem (Berkeley and Los Angeles, 1989), 5–6.

37. Suzanne Berger, "Regime and Interest Representation: The French Traditional Middle Classes," in *Organizing Interests in Western Europe: Pluralism, Corporatism, and the Transformation of Politics*, ed. Berger (Cambridge, 1981), 83–88; Esping-Andersen, *Politics Against Markets*, 26–30; Mayer, "Lower Middle Class as Historical Problem."

38. David Blackbourn, "The *Mittelstand* in German Society and Politics, 1871–1914," *Social History* 4 (Jan. 1977): 409–33; Crossick and Haupt, "Shopkeepers, Master Artisans and the Historian," 10–14, 18–23; Burris, "Discovery of the New Middle Class," 343–45; Jürgen Kocka, "Class Formation, Interest Articulation, and Public Policy: The Origins of the German White-Collar Class in the Late Nineteenth and Early Twentieth Century," in *Organizing Interests*, 63–82; Robert Zussman, "The Middle Levels: Engineers and the 'Working Middle Class'," *Politics and Society* 13, 3 (1984): 217–37; Hamilton, *Restraining Myths*, 104–13. Michael Mann refers to such familial, local, and other relations as "nonclass horizontal organizations." See his *The Sources of Social Power*, vol. 1, *A History of Power from the Beginning to A.D. 1760* (Cambridge, 1986), 216.

39. Bechhofer and Elliott, "Petty Property," 182–83; Crossick and Haupt, "Shopkeepers, Master Artisans and the Historian," 20–21.

40. Christian Lalive d'Épinay, "Time, Space and Socio-Cultural Identity: The Ethos of the Proletariat, Small Owners and Peasantry in an Aged Population," *International Social Science Journal* 107 (1986): 97–100.

41. Rudy Koshar, *Social Life, Local Politics, and Nazism: Marburg, 1880–1935* (Chapel Hill and London, 1986).

42. David S. Landes, *The Unbound Prometheus: Technological Change and Industrial Development in Western Europe from 1750 to the Present* (Cambridge, 1969), 391.

43. R. Stollmann, *Ästhetisierung der Politik: Literaturstudien zum subjektiven Faschismus* (Stuttgart, 1978), 43, 146, as quoted in Christoph Schmidt, "Zu den Motiven 'alter Kämpfer' in der NSDAP," in *Die Reihen fast geschlossen: Beiträge zur Geschichte des Alltags unterm Nationalsozialismus*, ed. Detlev Peukert and Jürgen Reulecke (Wuppertal, 1981), 37.

44. Berger, "Regime and Interest Representation," 86.

45. For elites and the lower middle classes, see Crossick and Haupt, "Shopkeepers, Master Artisans and the Historian," 16; on the issue of the relation between workers and the middle classes and elites before World War I, see Jürgen Kocka, ed., *Arbeiter*

und Bürger im 19. Jahrhundert: Varianten ihres Verhältnisses im europäischen Vergleich (Munich, 1986).

46. Peter Flora, "Solution or Source of Crises? The Welfare State in Historical Perspective," in *The Emergence of the Welfare State in Britain and Germany, 1850–1950,* ed. Wolfgang Mommsen (London, 1981), 343–89; Keith Thomas, "The United Kingdom," 82–83, and Raymond Grew, "The Crises and Their Sequences," 22–24, in *Crises of Political Development in Europe and the United States,* ed. Raymond Grew (Princeton, 1978); Peter N. Stearns, *European Society in Upheaval: Social History Since 1750,* 2nd ed. (New York, 1975), 200–211. For a discussion of state-making, changing popular organization, and political contention over four centuries, see Charles Tilly, *The Contentious French* (Cambridge, Mass., 1986). On the relationship of state power and character of mobilization, see Pierre Birnbaum, *States and Collective Action: The European Experience* (Cambridge, 1988).

47. Charles Maier, *Recasting Bourgeois Europe: Stabilization in France, Germany, and Italy in the Decade after World War I* (Princeton, 1975), 594.

48. Alan Wolfe, *The Limits of Legitimacy: Political Contradictions of Contemporary Capitalism* (New York, 1977), 108–45. For further considerations on the Nazi state, see Michael Geyer, "The State in National Socialist Germany," *Statemaking and Social Movements: Essays in History and Theory,* ed. Charles Bright and Susan Harding (Ann Arbor, Mich., 1984). The broader question of the complexities of the term *intervention* with regard to state activity is taken up in Charles Maier, "The State and Economic Organization in the Twentieth Century," in *Experiencing the Twentieth Century,* ed. Nobutoshi Hagihara et al. (Tokyo, 1985).

49. The idea that white-collar workers were badly organized or resistant to unionization is criticized for France in Michel Crozier, *The World of the Office Worker,* trans. David Landau (Chicago, 1971), 41–65, 148. For two more recent statements on the subject, both concentrating on women workers, see Ursula D. Nienhaus, "Weibliche Angestellte in den U.S.A., Frankreich und Grossbritanien 1850 bis 1930—Arbeitsmarkt, Arbeitsplatzsituation, soziale Lage, Organisation: Ein Literaturbericht," *Internationale wissenschaftliche Korrespondenz zur Geschichte der deutschen Arbeiterbewegung* 21, 3 (1985): 330–54; Gary Cross and Peter Shergold, "'We Think We Are of the Oppressed': Gender, White-Collar Work, and the Grievances of Late Nineteenth-Century Women," *Labor History* 28, 1 (Winter 1987): 23–53. A vivid example of the thesis of maladapted organizational life with reference to the German middle classes can be found in Hermann Lebovics, *Social Conservatism and the Middle Classes in Germany, 1914–1933* (Princeton, 1969), 36–37. See also the references to the literature in my contribution to this volume.

50. Esping-Andersen, *Politics Against Markets,* 30, uses the term *coloration* in reference to new middle strata.

51. Detlev J. K. Peukert, *Inside Nazi Germany: Conformity, Opposition, and Racism in Everyday Life,* trans. Richard Deveson (New Haven and London, 1987), 41–42.

52. Geoffrey Crossick. "The Petite Bourgeoisie in Nineteenth-Century Britain: The Urban and Liberal Case," in *Shopkeepers and Master Artisans,* 75, which refers to the interwar period; Nord, *Paris Shopkeepers,* 5, for the pre-1914 Radical party, and Soucy, *French Fascism,* 74–77, for the 1920s.

53. David Kirby, "'The Workers' Cause': Rank-and-File Attitudes and Opinions in the Finnish Social Democratic Party, 1905–1918," *Past and Present* 111 (May 1986): 130–64; Jürgen Kocka, "Soziale Entwicklung und politische Orientierung der Angestellten im Ersten Weltkrieg und in der Weimarer Republik (1914–1933)," in *Die Angestellten in der deutschen Geschichte, 1850–1980* (Göttingen, 1981), 142–48; Tony Judt, *Marx-*

ism and the French Left: Studies in Labour and Politics in France, 1830–1981 (Oxford, 1986), 129–44.

54. Mario König, Hannes Siegrist, Rudolf Vetterli, *Warten und Aufrücken: Die Angestellten in der Schweiz* (Zürich, 1985), 191, 463.

55. Rudy Koshar, "From *Stammtisch* to Party: Nazi Joiners and the Contradictions of Grass Roots Fascism in Weimar Germany," *Journal of Modern History* 59 (March 1987): 1–24; Alice A. Kelikian, *Town and Country Under Fascism: The Transformation of Brescia, 1915–1926* (Oxford, 1986), 205; Andrew C. Janos, *The Politics of Backwardness in Hungary, 1825–1945* (Princeton, 1982), 247–312; and for Romania, see the literature cited in Livezeanu's contribution to this volume.

56. David Blackbourn, "Between Resignation and Volatility: The German Petite Bourgeoisie in the Nineteenth Century," in *Shopkeepers and Master Artisans*, ed. Crossick and Haupt, 35–61.

57. On Hungary: Janos, *Politics of Backwardness*, 277.

58. Ian Kershaw, *Popular Opinion and Political Dissent in the Third Reich, 1933–1945* (New York, 1983); Peukert, *Inside Nazi Germany*, 86–100.

59. Crossick, "The Petite Bourgeoisie in Nineteenth-Century Europe," 260–61.

60. Robert Roberts, *The Classic Slum: Salford Life in the First Quarter of the Century*, reprint ed. (Harmondsworth, 1983), 16–17, for the ensuing quotes.

61. Hamilton, *Restraining Myths*, 25.

62. Crossick and Haupt, "Shopkeepers, Master Artisans and the Historian," 20; more generally on the problem of memory and autobiography, see Popular Memory Group, "Popular Memory: Theory, Politics, Method," in *Making Histories: Studies in History-Writing and Politics*, ed. Richard Johnson et al. (Minneapolis, 1982), 205–52.

63. Roberts, *Classic Slum*, 221.

64. Manuel Castells, *The City and the Grassroots: A Cross-Cultural Theory of Urban Social Movements* (Berkeley and Los Angeles, 1983), 331.

65. Wright, *On Living in an Old Country*, 207. More generally on the problem: Jürgen Habermas, "New Social Movements," *Telos* 49 (Fall 1981): 33–37.

66. Michael Geyer, "Nation, Klasse und Macht: Zur Organisation von Herrschaft in der Weimarer Republik," *Archiv für Sozialgeschichte* 26 (1986): 47–48; David D. Roberts, *The Syndicalist Tradition and Italian Fascism* (Chapel Hill, 1979); Eugen Weber, "Romania," in *The European Right*, ed. Rogger and Weber, 514–15; Janos, *Politics of Backwardness*, 247–312; Stanley Hoffman, "Paradoxes of the French Political Community," in *In Search of France: The Economy, Society, and Political System in the Twentieth Century*, ed. Hoffmann et al., reprint ed. (New York, 1965), 21–32.

67. David Blackbourn, "The Politics of Demagogy in Imperial Germany," *Past and Present* 113 (Nov. 1986): 152–84.

68. Berger, "Regime and Interest Representation," 87.

69. For a recent, stimulating discussion of nationalism, see Benedict Anderson, *Imagined Communities: Reflections on the Origin and Spread of Nationalism* (London, 1983); for the local basis of nationalist loyalty, see the remarks in Crossick, "The Petite Bourgeoisie in Nineteenth-Century Europe," 260–61.

70. See Miriam R. Levin, *Republican Art and Ideology in Late Nineteenth-Century France* (Ann Arbor, Mich., 1986), 41–45.

71. Eric Hobsbawm, "Mass-Producing Traditions: Europe, 1870–1914," in *The Invention of Tradition*, ed. Eric Hobsbawm and Terence Ranger (Cambridge, 1983), 302.

72. Janos, *Politics of Backwardness*, 247–312.

73. *Guide des carrières: Les Carrières du commerce* (Paris, 1927), as cited in Joseph Jones, "Vichy France and Postwar Economic Modernization: The Case of the Shopkeepers," *French Historical Studies* 12, 4 (Fall 1982): 544. There is a long literary tradition

of criticizing the lower middle class precisely because it seems to represent "the average."
See Urs Jaeggi, "Zwischen den Mühlsteinen: Der Kleinbürger oder die Angst vor der
Geschichte," *Kursbuch* 45 (Sept. 1976): esp. 151–52.

74. König et al., *Warten und Aufrücken*, 192.

75. Stearns, *European Society in Upheaval*, 230. For Germany, see Sandra Coyner,
"Class Consciousness and Consumption: The New Middle Class During the Weimar
Republic," *Journal of Social History* 10, 3 (1977): 310–31; Reinhard Spree, "Angestellte
als Modernisierungsagenten: Indikatoren und Thesen zum reproduktiven Verhalten von
Angestellten im späten 19. und frühen 20. Jahrhundert," in *Angestellte im europäischen
Vergleich: Die Herausbildung angestellten Mittelschichten seit dem späten 19. Jahrhundert*, ed. Jürgen Kocka (Göttingen, 1981); and Kocka's criticism of Coyner and Spree
in "Soziale Entwicklung und politische Orientierung," 166–67. For an argument stressing National Socialist policies that broke down the special status of new middle strata
in culture, work, and organization, see Michael Prinz, "Der Unerwünschte Stand: Lage
und Status der Angestellten im 'Dritten Reich'," *Historische Zeitschrift* 242, 2 (1986):
348–49. See also idem, *Vom neuen Mittelstand zum Volksgenossen: Die Entwicklung
des sozialen Status der Angestellten von der Weimarer Republik bis zum Ende der NS-Zeit*
(Munich, 1986).

76. König et al., *Warten und Aufrücken*, 99, 102, 192.

77. Bechhofer and Elliott, "Petty Property."

78. A. J. Cronin, *The Green Years* (Boston, 1945).

79. Roland Barthes, "Einige Worte von Herrn Poujade," *Bourgeois und Volk zugleich?
Zur Geschichte des Kleinbürgertums im 19. und 20. Jahrhundert*, ed. Heinz-Gerhard
Haupt (Frankfurt/Main, New York, 1978), 182–84; Winkler, *Mittelstand, Demokratie,
Nationalsozialismus*, 189.

80. Beside Jeffery's remarks, see James Cronin, *Labor and Society in Britain, 1918–
1979* (New York, 1984), 126–32.

81. On neo-Catholicism, see Jesse R. Pitts, "Continuity and Change in Bourgeois
France," in *In Search of France*, ed. Hoffmann et al., 280-81.

82. Tilly, *Contentious French*, 388.

2

Cult of Associations? The Lower Middle Classes in Weimar Germany

RUDY KOSHAR

A leitmotif of German historiography of the interwar period is that voluntary groups in which substantial parts of the lower middle classes *(Kleinbürgertum)* participated were incubators of National Socialism. It would be difficult to find a more direct expression of this notion than in Lothar Kettenacker's portrayal of the Nazi "national community" as a "stylization, based on military models, of a lower-middle-class *(kleinbürgerlich)* associational life that was now compulsory for everyone."[1] Embedded in this statement are two assumptions. The first is that the German lower middle classes were especially devoted to voluntary organizations and compulsive about getting others to join in a moralistic community of repression. This is the idea that there was a cult of associations among the German lower middle classes. The second assumption is that compulsive joining was linked to a *typically* lower-middle-class political outlook characterized by narrowness, militarism, reaction, and a general unwillingness to confront the realities of political power in a modern national state—traits that allegedly made these groups susceptible to fascism in the political crisis of the Weimar Republic (1918–1933). This essay critically discusses both assumptions, arguing that the wider social-political character of the cult of associations in the lower middle classes has been misunderstood. We begin with a brief look at the social history of petit-bourgeois involvement in German associational life, continue with a discussion of the political role of voluntary groups, and conclude with some remarks on the relation of associations and the Nazi movement.

The lower middle classes defy precise social description. Hamilton's endeavors in studying urban electoral districts in 1932 convinced him that it was "virtually impossible to isolate lower-middle-class populations in a way that allows acquisition of compelling evidence establishing their voting behavior."[2] Moreover, the lower middle classes made up an uncommonly disparate social configuration of groups with many different and often mutually opposed interests. Efforts to see the lower middle classes as a homogeneous whole stem from a number of sources: from conservative commentators' idealization of the "little man" as a survivor in the age of mass society; from orthodox Marxism's simplistic prediction that the lower middle classes would eventually fall into the proletariat; and, more seriously, from the allegorical quality of history writing itself, which "overplots" our construction of the past through a process of rigorous selection of data that suppresses nuance.[3]

Thus, one can make only general statements about the composition and size of the non-farm lower middle classes, which for the present discussion include self-employed artisans and retailers, professionals such as schoolteachers and nurses, clerks, middle- and low-level administrators, and minor officials. Having noted in the Introduction the limitations of establishing precisely the proportion of the lower middle classes in the population, we may rely on Hamilton's estimate that about twenty-five percent of the non-farm labor force in Germany during the Republic belonged to these groups.[4] This may be compared to the working classes, who made up sixty percent of the non-farm laboring population; the upper middle classes, who accounted for fourteen percent; and the upper classes, who made up one percent. Of course, this is a static measurement that masks considerable change and flux within the lower middle classes. Between 1882 and 1925, for instance, the absolute number of white-collar workers (*Angestellten*) and civil servants (*Beamte*) increased fivefold, while the absolute number of manual laborers did not quite double.[5]

It is impossible to deny the existence in Germany of a complex world of ostensibly narrow voluntary associations (*Vereine, Verbände*) inhabited in part by the lower middle classes. All voluntary groups have interests, but we must distinguish groups whose main activity is face-to-face contact and sociability from those that defend or pursue collective political and economic interests in the polity. The former type, undoubtedly more numerous and more attuned to grass-roots social life than the latter, included a panorama of veterans' associations, cultural groups, and numerous social clubs. The names of the associations reflected the extraordinary range of local activities: Dance Club Red-White (Gießen), Gardening Club "Flora" (Tübingen), Historic Preservation Society "Düsseldorfer Jonges" (Düsseldorf). If one focuses on particular types of associations, the same rich picture of local social ties emerges. In 1933 in the Prussian Rhine province, for instance, there were more than 2,000 sharpshooting clubs, some of them claiming fifteenth-century origins.[6] As for groups with direct economic and political aims, which also pursued sociability and developed elaborate internal rituals, it is well known that the lower middle classes were no strangers to these organizations. In the mid-1920s, 70.9 percent of all self-employed artisans were trade guild members; in 1931, 36.5 percent of German white-collar workers were organized, which was a very high percentage by international standards; and in the early Republic, even low-ranking officials and public manual workers, groups that had not been strongly unionized before World War I, made important strides in forming associations that represented their economic interests.[7] Such evidence fails to speak to the issues of participation or effectiveness in pursuing group aims, but it does suggest a high or increasing level of formal organization.

Critics argued that associational life had become a fetish, an object of obsessive devotion, particularly for the lower middle classes who supposedly valued joining *per se* more than they valued the public responsibilities ostensibly attached to association membership. Association fetishism *(Vereinsmeierei)* was said to isolate the lower middle classes from public life or distort their views of public obligations by promoting a narrow vocabulary of group interest. The issue of fetishism was taken up in a particularly scathing way by Kurt Tucholsky, a brilliant observer of social life in twentieth-century Germany, in "Das Mitglied," a 1926 poem satirizing the world of the joiner. "Here I live / and here one day they'll bury me / in my *Verein*" said the associational patriot of Tucholsky's rhyme.[8] Tucholsky focused on the splintering of public life into solipsistic voluntary groups, an obsessive devotion to the rituals of those groups, and an irrational preoccupation with the power gained by holding associational office. His critical view had already become widespread among "literary activists" such as Heinrich Mann, who wrote a still-powerful account of a petit-bourgeois bigot's involvement in small-town associational life in the novel *The Straw Man*.[9] So widespread was this notion of *Vereinsmeierei* that Germans coined variations of the word that spoke to the conditions of specific associations, as when late-nineteenth-century critics of the Tübingen Academic Glee Club *(Akademische Liedertafel)* accused that group of promoting a selfish *Liedertafelei*.[10] Social Democratic leaders realized that the supposed cult of associations also had an impact on the daily life of the organized working class; they thought that many leisure-time clubs of the socialist movement diverted workers from political goals and borrowed too directly from bourgeois and petit-bourgeois cultural models.[11] Anthropological literature has focused on the language of associations *(Vereinsprache)* and the use of symbolic flags, buildings, and other devices to promote loyalties to both social clubs and interest groups,[12] thus lending credence to the image of associational solipsism.

In responding to the argument, a number of points need to be mentioned. First, it is important to remember that only a large minority of individuals participated in organizational life, even after the roster of *Vereine* became larger and more diverse at the turn of the century. Sociological evidence suggests that this is a general characteristic of associational life in advanced capitalist societies. There is enough evidence to suggest, moreover, that enthusiasm for and real loyalty to associations were hard to come by, and that participation in club events, subscription to the publications of associations, and other forms of involvement were gained only with considerable prodding and pleading.[13] Hans Fallada's well-known 1933 novel *Little Man, What Now?* made the point that joining could be a very empty affair for some members of the lower middle classes.[14] The salesman Johannes Pinneberg dutifully defends the policies of the employees' union he belongs to when confronted by his future father-in-law, a Social Democrat, but he finds his association dues galling and realizes how little he benefits from membership. Later, he rejects the opportunity to become a member of a very different group—a Berlin nudist club. His subsequent retreat into family life may have been just as typical as compulsive joining was for some white-collar workers. All this suggests that voluntary associations never reached as many people or engaged as much of their memberships as the argument of *Verein* fetishism suggested. They were thus never uniformly representative of the larger populations they tried to organize.[15]

When the lower middle classes did become involved in associational life, they interacted with groups that they would not necessarily meet in the home or workplace. The rigid class boundaries of twentieth-century Germany were perhaps never uniformly reproduced at the level of associational life, even when voluntary groups played an important role in reinforcing class differences. The lower middle classes could be found in relatively prestigious civic associations and sharpshooting clubs in small or medium-size towns just as they could be found in choral groups or tourist associations in which wage-earning craft workers and even members of the socialist movement were members. This social interaction with workers is worth stressing, because it is possible to mistake the relative isolation of Social Democratic networks from the wider society for the complete isolation of the German working classes from the middle and upper classes.[16] If this local, or horizontal, interaction took place in specific communities, then vertical interaction also took place through the vehicle of branch leadership of voluntary groups. The officials of most large national voluntary associations usually came from the upper and upper middle classes, as did the leaders of branch associations in major urban centers; but in medium-size cities or smaller towns the *Kleinbürgertum* and some workers could also be found in the ranks of nonsocialist associational officers. Through leadership of such branch associations, the lower middle classes also came into contact with their "betters" in regional and national posts.

If the lower middle classes were preoccupied with the power and ritual of voluntary organizations, then most evidence suggests that this was a general feature of German social life rather than a typically petit-bourgeois characteristic. Indeed, the bickering, infighting, and resultant proliferation of functions and competing associations—all allegedly characteristic of the jealous, resentful *Kleinbürgertum*—also could be found among the upper middle classes and elites. One can find abundant proof of this in the political sphere, where leading bourgeois party leaders in the Weimar Republic spent more time fighting one another than trying to defend democracy. Here the associational fetishism of German elites had particularly disastrous consequences. But this tendency ran deeper, permeating elite practices in economic and cultural associations. In 1932 in Düsseldorf, for instance, a new historic preservation society, the *Düsseldorfer Jonges,* was formed when five individuals—an architect, a city archivist, a lawyer, a liqueur manufacturer, and a medical doctor—broke away from the established society, the *Bürgergesellschaft Alde Düsseldorfer,* formed in 1920, in a disagreement over the latter group's policies.[17] Historic preservation in a major urban center was often the project of local notables, especially when it came to central leadership positions of either exclusive or more plebeian clubs, and the proliferation of associations in this area could be attributed to upper-middle-class jealousies.[18] None of this should be startling to close observers of German culture or of group interaction in the contemporary world. Nonetheless, so many authors have stressed the pointless bickering of a notionally *lower-middle-class* associational life, that the counterexamples are worth mentioning. Indeed, the evidence suggests that the fractiousness of German voluntary groups resulted, not from petit-bourgeois selfishness, but from the penetration of elite models and practices throughout everyday communications networks.

More than a fetishistic pursuit of associational offices and titles, the lower middle classes' involvement in many different voluntary groups paved the way for political participation insofar as membership in an artisans' association, sharpshooting club, or religious *Verein* could be used to build contacts and shape opinion. The politicizing effects of nationalist associations or economic pressure groups are well known for the era before World War I.[19] But many different associations, even those ostensibly removed from political conflict, contributed to the political education of the German people.[20] In the Weimar period, the relation between politics and social or cultural organizations was even more direct. The Republic was established in a wave of grass-roots political activity not just by parties but by older social and economic organizations and newly created groups as well. When the Republic was temporarily stabilized, voluntary associations in some communities entered local politics directly by contesting political offices. In the Swabian village of Hausen, for instance, where political parties were not yet developed enough in 1931 to shape local power struggles, a gymnasts' club ran its own list of candidates for the town council elections.[21] But even in larger communities, municipal elections featured the proliferation of special-interest slates through which all kinds of organizations, from homeowners' associations to sports clubs, were directly represented.[22] In one respect, this reflects a general tendency in Germany toward the displacement of social, economic, and even cultural concerns onto the political sphere, a process dramatically furthered by the opening of municipal politics to universal suffrage in 1919 and the general escalation of political struggle in the Republic.[23] But politicization would have been less rapid and dramatic had large parts of the German population not already received an indirect political education in the everyday life of voluntary groups. In short, associational life was political, if by that term we refer to all ideas, structures, and practices that involve people in basic questions of who has the right and capability to rule.

The question of who has the right to rule became more contested than ever before in Germany after 1880, when intense industrial and urban growth, increased state activity in social life, rapid mobilization of the Social Democratic movement, and increased national organization of all socioeconomic groups took place.[24] The lower middle classes were no strangers to the new age of organization and mobilization. They established small retailers' associations that cried for help against allegedly greedy consumers, white-collar employees' unions that agitated for social legislation that set employees off from the manual laboring classes, and Catholic artisans' groups that pressed the Center party to demand economic policies more favorable to small producers.[25] This general voicing of sectional demands was also part of a growing clash over how the national polity was to be organized. Thus, once the lower middle classes trod the national political stage, they became entangled in an intense ideological conflict in which bourgeois leaders tried to capture and maintain petit-bourgeois loyalties. But from 1880 until 1933 no single ideological formation carried the day for German bourgeois groups in the national sphere. Instead, radical nationalism, liberalism, political Catholicism, christian socialism, populist anti-Semitism, particularism, popular conservatism, and ultimately fascism appeared on the menu of nonsocialist political contenders.

These different ideological trajectories shared some features—sharp antisocialism being of particular importance—but none of them could be used to exercise hegemony in a coalition of nonsocialist groups in the national parliament. This disunity was reinforced by a rigidified party system that originated before World War I and was extended in the Weimar Republic. The German party system consisted of three main blocs: the Marxist bloc consisted of the Social Democratic party and, after World War I, the Communist party; the Catholic bloc consisted of the Center party and its Bavarian affiliate, the Bavarian People's party; and the Protestant bourgeois bloc

consisted of liberal, conservative, splinter, and special-interest parties whose
names changed between the pre–1914 and post–1918 eras, but whose constituencies were consistently drawn from the Protestant working, middle,
and upper classes. Crystallized around these blocs were distinctive "social-
moral milieux" consisting of many different social networks, institutions,
and voluntary associations.[26] The lower middle classes split their votes
among all parties, but they gave their support most consistently to the
parties of the Protestant bourgeois and Catholic blocs.

Given such national political disunity, a part of the lower middle classes
found refuge in the local. Much of the literature, including several essays
in the present volume, refer to the localism of the lower middle classes,
their privileging of town, neighborhood, and family over wider public involvement. Mack Walker's deft analysis of German "home towns" suggests
that this localism, part of a long history of political fragmentation and
regional autonomy, was very deeply rooted in German social thought.[27]
Localism may also have gained influence from wider changes in the perception of space and time. Scholars have argued that, after roughly the middle
of the nineteenth century, small propertied identity depended more than
before on the status of ownership than on social obligations, thus altering
an earlier balance between possession and public responsibility.[28] In view
of this change, space came to be regarded in terms of "small kingdoms"
of private property defended from an undifferentiated outside world that
held countless dangers. Closely connected to this was a sense of time that
contrasted an unsettled present with a supposedly harmonious past that
must be recaptured in the near future if individualized small property was
not to disappear in a wave of criminality, immorality, disruptive social
change, and endless political conflict.[29] Such possessive thinking was reinforced not just by party rhetoric or the mass media but by concrete patterns
of everyday life, such as individual urban house gardens, which were very
important for the middle strata in Germany but less so for the working
classes, who in the 1920s had to rely on distant plots of land (Schrebergär-
ten) for extra produce.[30]

But localism was also a political construction, manipulated by power
brokers who wanted to enhance their own position in the community and
insulate their constituencies from class and party contention that raised
difficult questions of power, justice, and legitimacy. This was more than
a purely instrumental or self-serving notion, however. Many local elites
were convinced that their authority rested on social relations, values, and
institutions that were not only different than those of national political
life but morally superior to them. Local power arrangements were "unpolitical" in the sense that they originated in "natural" relations of personality, deference, and influence—in a historically substantiated way
of life—that had little to do with the notional artificiality and illegitimate

contemporaneity of political mobilization, interest groups, and parliamentary negotiations.[31]

One of the most important causes of grass-roots social conflict in the Weimar Republic was the removal of institutional safeguards of a political localism that had provided such strong common referents for the upper, middle, and nonsocialist working classes. The ending in 1919 of a three-class voting system that had been in effect in Prussian and most other German cities allowed the Social Democratic and Communist parties to penetrate local political spheres. Nonsocialist parties now were forced to resort to new modes of political mobilization in local politics, new coalitions, and new organizations.[32] They did so reluctantly, adapting the local polity to mass politics, but calling on "tradition" in the process. Thus, a broad mobilization of local culture occurred, an invigoration of the symbolism of the "homeland" *(Heimat)* that stretched from narrow party politics to history writing, architecture, and voluntary group activity.[33] What was lost or threatened in the clash of political interests could, they hoped, be absorbed or even regained in the heightening of local experience and feeling. None of this necessarily implied the rise of National Socialism; but part of the attraction of Nazism was that it offered national political expression to this *local* mobilization—not always or necessarily in municipal and provincial parliaments but certainly in voluntary clubs, churches, workplaces, families, and the streets.

Nationalism played a big role in this process. A part of German nationalism evoked very strong images of distinctive neighborhoods, towns, and regions. The championing of a vernacular architecture anchored in specific regional building styles was one of many expressions of this tendency.[34] Given the pronounced provincial elements of German nationalism, one way of defusing the effects of national political conflict was rhetorically to link supposedly unpolitical local structures or traditions to an imagined national community that somehow hovered above the complexities of parliamentary politics. In this way, disparate social locations such as a small grocer's shop in Königsberg, a sharpshooting club's meeting room in a Neuß tavern, and a local parliament meeting in the *Rathaus* of the Hessian village of Fronhausen could appear more "national" than the national parliament itself, which before 1914 became dominated by Social Democratic and Catholic mass parties, and after 1918 became shaped more than ever before by tense bargaining between big industry and socialist labor. In this respect, petit-bourgeois localism could issue easily into nationalist imagery and support for nationalist political causes.

But nationalism was not typically or exclusively a lower-middle-class attribute. The caveat is important given the habit of older arguments, discussed in the introduction and in some of the other contributions in this volume, to stress the reactionary quality of petit-bourgeois politics, of which intense and irrational nationalism seemed to be a natural component. It is undoubtedly true that one could find substantial support in the lower middle classes for nationalist and radical nationalist causes in Germany. But nationalism was a cross-class phenomenon rather than something for which the petite bourgeoisie had a unique and disproportionate attraction. Indeed, the middle and upper classes were in the forefront of nationalist movements in the first third of the twentieth century in Germany. Members of the educated and well-off classes organized and led German patriotic societies, some of which promoted integralist thinking that had little tolerance for the seemingly retrograde provincial loyalties of earlier forms of nationalism. University students, many from lower-middle-class homes but always identified with the middle classes proper, were among the most nationalist groups in German society.[35] Zokfa found that the Günzberg area elite, partly lower-middle-class from a national standpoint but not entirely so, was more nationalistic than the bulk of the local petite bourgeoisie. Hamilton also stresses the nationalism of the upper middle classes of big German cities.[36] If nationalism was a cross-class movement, then it is also necessary to point out that nationalism did not easily paper over the political, social, and economic differences that caused class and intraclass tensions. In fact, nationalism was itself the source of a dynamic fragmentation and reconsolidation of coalitions in which various groups appropriated nationalist language to pursue their interests. These differences were most obviously present in the conflict between "elite" and "popular" forms of nationalist mobilization.[37]

Contained in all versions of nonsocialist, grass-roots nationalism after World War I in Germany was a moral critique of the Weimar state. For their part, petit-bourgeois opponents of Weimar revered the national state and argued that it should act as a moral beacon and organizer of a general social, or even racial, interest. But the Weimar state appeared to routinize pressure-group conflict and open public life to endless compromise rather than decisive leadership. For many members of the independent lower middle classes, interest-group conflict had led to a privileging of labor and industry; this was the political core of the argument that small enterprise was exposed to "unfair competition" in so many areas.[38] Significantly, criticism of the state found expression in a language that extended private values into public discourse. The speaker for a Hamburg pressure group of property owners criticized "papa state" for policies that allegedly hurt homeowners, reflecting the importance of metaphors derived from patriarchal family life.[39] Through the use of such language the lower middle classes tried to derive meaning from their vulnerable position in a long-term process of growing state power and simultaneous extension of public authority into nationally organized pressure groups.[40]

In comparison to nationalism and anti-state sentiment, popular anti-

Semitism, which characterized Jews as either rapacious capitalists or communist agitators, was uneven and often unconvincing as a focus of political
resentment in the lower middle classes. Anti-Semitism was a persistent element of German politics and everyday life in the Weimar Republic, but
the evidence does not seem to support the argument, held by numerous
scholars, that hatred against Jews was especially virulent among the lower
middle classes.[41] A classic text in this regard is Allen's study of Nordheim,
a town whose social structure was dominated by craftsmen, officials, and
shopowners. Dislike of Jews, who themselves were usually small businessmen integrated into the thriving club life of the town, was expressed in
"jokes and slight feelings of generalized distaste" but was not organized
at the political level until after the Nazi party came to power.[42] One may
contrast this to the Hessian university town of Marburg, where the presence
of the university and local traditions of political experimentation did establish anti-Semitism as an important theme of local political language. However, in Marburg the right-wing German National People's party was a
chief promoter of anti-Semitism after the war, and it gained only part
of its following in the lower middle classes. Equally important to the party
were local elites and especially the Protestant church.[43] Numerous studies
have stressed the variable social locations and unevenness of anti-Semitism
throughout Germany before 1933. It thus comes as no surprise that popular
responses to Nazi racial persecution and the annihilation of European Jews
in the dictatorship varied widely.[44] The political use of anti-Semitism was
therefore dependent on specific local and national conditions, and cannot
be taken as an *a priori* element of the language of which some members
of the lower middle classes were prisoners.

In one respect, *Vereinsmeierei* can be viewed as part of a tangle of associational networks and symbols that absorbed political strife and facilitated
general ideological unity for upper, middle, and nonsocialist working classes
at the grass roots. It was a complex of practices that countered political
dissidence with an imagery of consensus, potential and real. But this statement requires some qualification. In times of relative political calm, local
group life could foster political participation and simultaneously temper
bourgeois political disunity. But in periods of intense conflict, grass-roots
voluntary associations could appear to be living negations of ideological
coherence. This was true in the middle and late 1920s. For many scholars,
these were the supposedly calm years of the Weimar Republic between
the revolutionary upheavals of the early postwar period and the Depression
of late 1929. But these years were anything but calm.[45] The growing dissolution of the national state forced a realignment of class and political loyalties
in these years, which culminated subsequently in the complete breakdown
of Protestant bourgeois parties,[46] the splintering and reorganization of many
voluntary associations, and the rise of the Nazi movement. The contradic-

tions of *Vereinsmeierei* multiplied in the middle Republic, and, in Protestant groups especially, local bourgeois associational networks produced the ideological ammunition for their own downfall. The local bourgeoisie criticized national interest-group politics, but for many Germans, local associations had become integral elements of that narrowly focused politics. Bourgeois spokesmen called for a new sense of national loyalty and reorganization of the German state, but their authority appeared antiquated and selfishly provincial. Older associational leaders joined younger members in trying to keep *Vereine* "above" party politics, but those older leaders failed to see that the younger generation still wanted some form of national political commitment, not a retreat into the local polity.

Catholic associational life developed in a context of greater political stability. The Catholic Center party experienced some electoral slippage in the Weimar Republic, but Catholic constituencies generally remained loyal to their party in elections to the national parliament (Reichstag). In the representative bodies of mainly Catholic cities such as Trier, the Catholic Center also remained stable. Thus Catholic voluntary associations could still look to an intact ideological center, an advantage that Protestant groups did not possess. Nonetheless, Center party supporters and members of Catholic social organizations were not immune to political malaise, disaffection with parliamentary government, antisocialist anxieties, and growing divisiveness. The Center party also contributed significantly to the development of a political language that the Nazis would exploit. In the 1920s it made frequent use of the notion of the "national community" *(Volksgemeinschaft),* the integrated, popular, and mobilized nation. This was to replace what was regarded as a more passive and conservative metaphor of the nation that obtained before World War I.[47] Nazi agitators used such imagery also, tying it to a racist conception of the state.

Economic hardships sharpened the tensions of social and political life. It is impossible to give full credit to the complexities of the situation here, but it is important to note general developments. As for the traditional lower middle classes, the economic history of the Republic should be seen against the wider background of trends that had begun before 1914. There was a decline in the absolute number of artisans and an increase in the number of retail outlets, processes that varied in scope and timing for specific branches. The inflation of 1916 to 1923 and the Depression of 1929 caused much hardship, but no universal decline of self-employed artisans and retailers took place. As Winkler has noted, economic branches with inelastic demand did better than those with elastic demand or those that relied on substantial investment activity. In 1932, less than one percent of small retail businesses went bankrupt. Overall, the proportion of the independent lower middle classes in the working population declined, but the economic situation of the group was partially consolidated. The situation of white-collar workers, who would be significantly overrepresented in the membership of the Nazi party, was extremely variable, which is unsurprising given the tremendous social differentiation of *Angestellten*. However, Speier's detailed study of white-collar workers before Hitler's rise to power demonstrated that "the average white-collar worker was more likely able to keep his job than the average worker" during the world economic crisis. Deflationary government policies cut civil service salaries, but overall, the comparative job security of officials enabled them to withstand the crisis more ably than white-collar workers. This of course did not prevent many minor officials from joining or voting for the Nazi party. Finally, local differences in cost of living and levels of industrialization or urbanization further modified the impact of economic troubles.[48]

One consequence of this accumulation of tensions was "progressive social disgregation," to use Enzo Mingione's term for the contemporary era. This refers to a general societal crisis in which "class confrontations explode in a very diffused area but on a strictly local basis, so that it becomes more and more difficult to connect and organize them in general terms."[49] In Germany between the national political upheavals of 1918 to 1923 and the decisive widening of Nazi electoral power in 1932, the partial breakdown of the state and uneven economic hardship dispersed conflicts in such a way that no political contender could organize conflicts in general terms. This was related partly to the social-political bloc system of Germany inherited from the pre–World War I era, but partly also to specific conditions of the period. This decentralization of conflict, harmful to elites or socialist workers seeking to organize politically at the national level, benefited groups, including parts of the lower middle classes, who were most critical of the Weimar system. Decentralization of conflict allowed critics of Weimar to exert pressure on political stage more decisively than before. Given the often-local focus of petit-bourgeois politics, disgregation was an opportunity rather than a threat. Yet this pressure could find effective political expression only when many dispersed clashes could be reorganized in a national strategy that could defeat the Republic. Only the Nazi party, with great difficulty and uncertainty, "accomplished" this reorganization long enough to end Weimar democracy for good. This was the major difference between the 1970s discussed by Mingione and the Weimar years: in the last-mentioned period, progressive social disgregation led to a confused but general political strategy of Nazism, which claimed that it had found a way out of the crisis by rejecting both socialism and capitalism in an authoritarian, hypernationalist dictatorship.

Despite Hitler's pose of going it alone in the struggle for power, Nazism was a result of coalition-building both in national politics and in many different geographical settings. The lower middle classes played a varying role in this heated mobilization of political resentments. Hamilton has argued that only a minority of the big-city lower middle classes voted for the NSDAP *(Nationalsozialistische Deutsche Arbeiterpartei)*, whereas there was majority support for National Socialism among Protestant farmers and a vote against Nazism in the Catholic farm population. Childers' study also suggests variability and an extremely unstable and fluctuating constituency for Nazism. The Nazi party benefited from only shifting support among white-collar and civil service groups; collectively these groups were not good predicters of the Nazi vote "even after the calamities of the world economic crisis descended on the Republic." On the other hand, artisans and storeowners made up the nucleus of the Nazi electorate. The Nazi party also relied on very large groups of voters outside both the old and new middle classes, including elites and perhaps as many as 3.5 million workers in the July 1932 Reichstag elections.[50]

Evidence for Nazi party membership makes a similar point. Kershaw has pointed out that most members of the petite bourgeoisie did not join the NSDAP and probably feared what they perceived to be radicalism and hooliganism in the party.[51] Obvious though it may be, the remark is significant, given an older historiography that saw a panic-stricken, heavily Nazified lower middle class. As for the groups that did become organized in the Nazi party, it is true that the lower middle classes joined in proportions that exceeded their share of the labor force.[52] However, the level of lower-middle-class participation in the Nazi party varied considerably by community and region, an unsurprising qualification for a country with tremendous regional differences, but one that is usually overlooked. More generally, the fluidity of party membership, emphasized by numerous scholars, suggests that Nazism's hold on its following was variable and at times very provisional.[53] The lower middle classes may have been even more inconsistent than other groups in committing themselves fully to the Nazi cause, given their often-grudging attitude toward national politics and electioneering. In this light, the dedicated local agitators, many of them lower-middle-class "new men"[54] of the provinces who built the grass-roots Nazi party, were hardly typical representatives of the petite bourgeoisie.

The meaning of party membership could vary by class and region also, and thus national party statistics must always be read against the backdrop of diverse local perceptions of the interests and goals represented by the Nazi movement in particular and party political involvement in general. The NSDAP could appear to be a force for nationalizing the working classes, for defending small property interests against the assaults of big labor and capital, or for protecting bourgeois respectability against the inroads of a developing welfare state. Not all members of the lower middle classes who supported the Nazi party may have thought of themselves as "Nazis" in the sense that they fully endorsed the party platform, however that was perceived. They may have been attracted to the party because of Hitler, whose popularity remained very durable even during the period of the dictatorship in spite of widespread disgruntlement with state and party policies.[55] However, several authors have argued against placing undue emphasis on the popularity of Hitler, at least for the years before 1933, stressing that the dictator was appealing because his party was.[56] Still other party members may have thought of themselves simply as part of the everyday consensus—shared by groups on the Right and Left—that felt that the Weimar political system could not go on as it had and that something had to change.[57] For these individuals, the Nazi party represented the latest, but by no means the final or exclusive, vehicle for change; it was not the culmination of decades of petit-bourgeois reaction but the historically specific vehicle of interests and traditions that assumed new urgency in the violent politics of the interwar era.

Nazism captured resources set free in the decentralization and dispersal of political conflict that marked the Weimar system. It did not necessarily wrest individuals and groups from their previous loyalties but responded to the dissolution of the national state, bourgeois parties, voluntary organizations, social networks, neighborhoods, and families. In the early stages of mobilization, Nazism could do nothing more than increase disengagement of groups from the national polity, further the decentralization of conflict, and assist in the process of social dissolution. The dynamic of party and pressure-group splintering has been richly documented, but the everyday experiences of social clubs in specific locales are less widely known. We need to know much more about the process—suggested in the recollections of members of the Hamburg gymnastics society, *Turnerschaft 1816*—whereby "*Verein* comrades went their separate ways, [and] friendships broke up in the 1930s" over political matters.[58] The Nazis operated on many different fronts in such situations, trying to capitalize on any opportunity to further the process of sociopolitical dissolution. They were helped not by some linear process of political mesmerization but by the efforts of clubs and institutions to use the growing power of the Nazi movement to ensure their own survival. For instance, the Hamburg *Turnerschaft* changed the language of club leadership, substituting "Leader" (*Führer*) for more neutral terms such as president in 1932,[59] before the real *Führer* came to power. This was a sign of the influence that new forms of authoritarianism had in everyday life and of the anticipation with which voluntary groups viewed the Nazi movement. Only after Hitler gained the Chancellorship would his party face the impossible task of reassembling this mobilized, fragmented social life in a national whole.

Nazism used capitalist marketing principles to appeal to particular groups.[60] One cannot quickly dispense with this point, for Nazi marketing techniques were more than mere "ecological" effects: some groups may have supported National Socialism precisely because of its successful marketing strategies and use of the latest technique of design and advertising. This applies as well to parts of the lower middle classes, whose attraction to Nazism could be seen as a parallel to their responsiveness to the blandishments of mass culture.[61] Party agitators identified target audiences, tailored their propaganda to each audience, and then followed no other strategy than flooding the market with as many messages as time, financial resources, and human endurance allowed. Local party functionaries may have gradually lost their independence in targeting groups and identifying issues by the early 1930s, but even in 1932 Nazi agitators had some discretion in these matters.[62] The frantic nature of propaganda reflected the condition of a latecomer that had to break into the social fields occupied by other parties.[63] Violence, wild language, extravagant promises—all this was necessary to attract paying customers to party assemblies, to increase the visibility of the organization, and to distinguish it from other competitors. The party incorporated many of the rituals of German associational and political life, inscribing Nazi symbolism in public life through the use of flags, uniforms, colorful posters, banners, and salutes. It incorporated authoritarian forms of sociability based on male fears and fantasies.[64] Its ideology was eclectic and confused, combining elements from biological racism, populist anti-Semitism, socialism, radical and moderate nationalism, and many other sources. Its agitators were heterogeneous, coming from all social classes and regions. The party's ideological confusion and social heterogeneity reflected the confusion and splintering of the political marketplace over which Nazism sought dominance.

German elites were implicated in this process from the start. This applies most obviously to the business, military, and government elites in Bavaria who helped the Nazi party gain its first national visibility; to Paul von Hindenburg, president of the Republic after 1925, and his advisers, who made it possible for Hitler to gain the chancellorship; and to the elite members and voters of the party. But it also applies more broadly to elites who openly criticized Weimar democracy or withheld their support from it without supporting the Nazi party. This is a wide array of individuals, too variegated in its internal makeup to be discussed in a brief essay.[65] There was much to criticize about the Weimar state, as much of the preceding argument has suggested. Yet without necessarily foreseeing the outcomes of their actions, elites contributed mightily to Nazism's success because they furthered the process of social disgregation and political deconstruction that the Nazi movement benefited from so completely. They helped to create a collective need for precisely the kind of movement that Hitler's party represented. Finally, one cannot overlook the role of numerous public officials, who differed in their outlooks on Nazism but who in the months after January 1933 had a "stabilizing function" during the chaos of Nazi "coordination" of government and social life.[66] These individuals performed a traditional function of the modern state, namely social control; but they did so in service to a movement that would eventually atomize the state and replace it with a fragmented but unprecedentedly powerful authoritarian rule.

"Those who want everything to stay as it is vote for Hindenburg," the Nazi party claimed in the presidential campaign of spring 1932, and "those who want everything changed vote for Hitler."[67] After Hitler came to power, the promise of complete change seemed to come true in the brutal destruction of Germany's socialist trade unions, the persecution of political opponents on both the Right and the Left, the growing regimentation and fearfulness of public life, war, and the eventual annihilation of most of European Jewry. Party agitators predicted no-less-sweeping changes for the middle strata who either supported the Nazi movement or at least were not identified with its enemies. Party radicals argued that they would eradicate the solipsism of grass-roots social life, disengage individuals from their narrow local loyalties, and envelop them in a new state based quite possibly on much older dreams of the coming of a "third age."[68] All this would supposedly make possible a new morality of race rather than the immorality of interest-group bargaining. Such a radical vision engaged uneasily with the provincial perspectives of much of petit-bourgeois politics; the vision could be a direct challenge not only to the power brokers of associational life but to many Nazi party members who remained active in *Vereine* after they joined the National Socialist movement.[69] Research on local *Vereine* in the dictatorship is not as highly developed as it is for previous periods, partly because there has been a tendency to take Nazi claims of totalization at face value, even after the publication of Schoenbaum's influential study in 1966 of German social life in the dictatorship. But recent work has begun to take seriously a central implication of Schoenbaum's research; namely, that everyday life and its social stresses did not come to a halt in the dictatorship.[70]

One result of this social tension was that Nazi totality was muted. For the lower middle classes, there were significant changes in the level and form of interest groups, the symbolic importance of particular groups to the regime, and the status and economic well-being of particular occupations. On the basis of current scholarship, it is difficult to argue definitively about which parts of the middle strata gained or lost most from the social and economic policies of the Nazi dictatorship.[71] If this evidence remains ambiguous, the information we have on local social life suggests that the template of *Verein* ritual fashioned by local bourgeois leaders was damaged but still intact after the first wave of Nazi "coordination" ended in late 1935, even if many formal group networks had dissolved or been destroyed.[72] This applies above all to ostensibly unpolitical social clubs. The

Nazi official Martin Bormann remarked in late 1936 that "the number of choral, rabbit breeders', and stamp collectors' clubs, etc., etc., are legion," and that "the individual feels he need not worry about the future of Germany, and that he can once again pursue his tastes undisturbed." In 1943 Bormann once again referred to leisure-time clubs, saying somewhat resignedly that "there is little purpose in cursing the habit of compulsive joining (Vereinsmeierei). It is better to persuade voluntary groups to use their activities and interests to provide something of value for the whole community."[73] The power of this tradition of social interaction was evident not only in the inability of the state and party to capture and regiment such groups but in the fact that some of the worst features of Vereinsmeierei—solipsism, group jealousies, compulsive hoarding of offices and titles—found abundant expression inside the Nazi movement itself. If the Nazi party tried to envelop German social life in a new totalitarian state, it was victim to many of the same problems that it had attacked so violently in the Republic. Unsurprisingly, a reflorescence of leisure-time clubs occurred in West Germany after the dictatorship crumbled under the blows of Allied and Soviet armies.[74] The mundane, changing world of the joiners—along with the lower-middle-class groups that populated a part of it—outlived yet another political regime.

It is no longer possible to maintain, as many theorists of Anglo-American pluralism once did, that a dense network of secondary associations insulates democratic institutions from political attack. Indeed, as the preceding pages and numerous other studies have demonstrated, Germany in the 1920s is a powerful example of how heightened associational activity facilitated rightist assaults on a bourgeois democracy that was the site of a unique concatenation of tensions common to all modern capitalist systems.[75] But the central theme of this article deals less with the fact of widespread participation in voluntary groups than with varied *perceptions* of that participation. I have argued that academic critiques of German associational life were exaggerated, vague about the exact social location of certain *Verein* practices, and insufficiently aware of particular useful attributes of local communications networks based on voluntary groups. *Vereinsmeierei* was not a typically lower-middle-class phenomenon, but a general characteristic of German associational life. Its causes thus can be found not only in the specific conditions of the petite bourgeoisie, but in broader processes of ideological conflict, political change, and state formation in Germany. From the point of view of proponents, *Vereinsmeierei* had some positive features. Although it entangled lower-middle-class groups in a ritualized world of narrow social practices, compulsive joining also created numerous opportunities for lower-middle-class interaction with the upper middle and working classes and for the construction of specific ideological referents in grass-roots politics. Compulsive joining could indeed lead to civic irresponsibility and reaction, as many observers realized. But it could also provide a web of defense for individuals who wanted to protect family, workplace, neighborhood, and local polity from modern Germany's fractious politics—a politics that in the Weimar period failed to provide workable models of power and legitimacy for either the Right or the Left. There was a cult of associations, a complex of social practices and language that created unusually strong loyalties to voluntary groups. Yet the political implications of such loyalties were not always those presumed by cultural critics, social theorists, or political activists. Compulsive joining offered no home for democracy; but even when it led to Nazism, it was never fully engaged for the racist destruction that gave the Third Reich its unique character. Between the pluralist utopia of concerned, balanced voluntary group activists and the "mass society" nightmare of lockstep, hypernationalist irrationality, there were many complex alternatives. One of the goals of future research on the dynamic interaction of social forms and political conflict should be to suggest what these alternatives were.

It is easier today than it was just thirty years ago to emphasize the nuances or even positive features of local associational life in interwar Germany. This does not stem from a trivializing "relativization" of the Nazi experience; the unprecedented horrors of that period must remain deeply etched in postwar history writing. It stems rather from changed political conditions. The attempt to diminish state and capitalist "colonization" of grass-roots systems of communication has become a defining characteristic of many political conflicts in West Europe and North America in the last quarter of the twentieth century, and hence some features of petit-bourgeois survival, for all their contradictions, seem to offer hope for the possibility of partial identity, relative autonomy, and potential democratic change in the future.

Notes

1. Lothar Kettenacker, "Sozialpsychologische Aspekte der Führer-Herrschaft," in *Der 'Führerstaat': Mythos und Realität: Studien zur Struktur und Politik des Dritten Reiches*, ed. Gerhard Hirschfeld and Lothar Kettenacker (Stuttgart, 1981), 112; for a similar argument, see Kettenacker, "Hitler's Impact on the Lower Middle Class," in *Nazi Propaganda: The Power and the Limitations*, ed. David Welch (London, 1983). The view has a long heritage, of which Hermann Glaser, *Spießer-Ideologie: Von der Zerstörung des deutschen Geistes im 19. und 20. Jahrhundert* (Freiburg, 1964) is an influential example. Insofar as Jürgen Kocka stressed the persistence of "pre-bourgeois" values in particular German white-collar associations and their susceptibility to right-wing radicalism, his work is also compatible with Kettenacker's view. Nonetheless, whatever the problems of his argument for Germany, Kocka's comparative perspective also leads

him to argue that not all white-collar groups were prone to political reaction. See *White Collar Workers in America, 1890–1940: A Social-Political History in International Perspective,* trans. Maura Kealey (London, Beverly Hills, 1980). See also the reference to Kocka in note 7, below.

For the nineteenth-century background of German associational life, see the articles in *Vereinswesen und bürgerliche Gesellschaft in Deutschland.* Ed. Otto Dann. Beiheft 9 (Neue Folge): *Historische Zeitschrift* (München, 1984); and the suggestive piece by Thomas Nipperdey, "Verein als soziale Struktur in Deutschland im späten 18. und frühen 19. Jahrhundert. Eine Fallstudie zur Modernisierung I" in idem, *Gesellschaft, Kultur, Theorie: Gesammelte Aufsätze zur neueren Geschichte* (Göttingen, 1976). More recently, see Wolfgang Kaschuba, "Deutsche Bürgerlichkeit nach 1800: Kultur als symbolische Praxis," in *Bürgertum im 19. Jahrhundert. Deutschland im europäischen Vergleich,* eds. Jürgen Kocka and Ute Frevert, 3 vols. (Munich, 1988), 3:9–44, *passim.*

2. Richard Hamilton, *Who Voted for Hitler?* (Princeton, 1982), 122.

3. For the heterogeneous quality of the lower middle classes, see David Blackbourn's discussion of the German term *Mittelstand,* which may be approximately translated as "middle strata," in his "The *Mittelstand* in German Society and Politics, 1871–1914," *Social History* 4 (Jan. 1977): 409–33. On the allegorical nature of history writing, see Hans Kellner, *Language and Historical Representation: Getting the Story Crooked* (Madison, Wis., 1989), esp. 285–93, which on p. 287 refers to Nancy Partner's notion of overplotting. (See her "Making Up Lost Time: Writing on the Writing of History," *Speculum* 61, 1 [1986]: 102.)

4. Hamilton, *Who Voted for Hitler?* 46.

5. Hans Speier, *Die Angestellten vor dem Nationalsozialismus: Ein Beitrag zum Verständnis der deutschen Sozialstruktur, 1918–1933* (Göttingen, 1977), 15.

6. "NSDAP, Deutsche Arbeitsfront, Verbände, Innungen, Vereine und Kassen," *Einwohnerbuch der Stadt und des Landkreises Gießen* (Gießen, 1933): 29; "Verzeichnis der Gesellschaften und Vereine," in *Einwohnerbuch der Universitätsstadt Tübingen* (Tübingen, 1928): 214; Heimatverein Düsseldorfer Jonges, *50 Jahre Heimatverein Düsseldorfer Jonges* (Düsseldorf, 1932); Wilhelm Ewald, *Die Rheinischen Schützengesellschaften* (Düsseldorf, 1933), viii.

7. Heinz-Gerhard Haupt, "Mittelstand und Kleinbürgertum in der Weimarer Republik. Zu Problemen und Perspektiven ihrer Erforschung," *Archiv für Sozialgeschichte* 26 (1986): 235; Jürgen Kocka, "Soziale Entwicklung und politische Orientierung der Angestellten im Ersten Weltkrieg und in der Weimarer Republik (1918–1933)" in *Die Angestellten in der deutschen Geschichte 1850–1980* (Göttingen, 1981), 159; Andreas Kunz, "Arbeitsbeziehungen und Arbeitskonflikte im öffentlichen Sektor: Deutschland und Großbritannien im Vergleich" *Geschichte und Gesellschaft* 12 (1986): 59–60. More generally on officials in the early Republic, see Kunz, *Civil Servants and the Politics of Inflation in Germany, 1914–1924* (Berlin, 1986).

8. Kurt Tucholsky, "Das Mitglied," *Gesammelte Werke,* ed. Mary-Gerold Tucholsky and Fritz J. Raddatz, 3 vols. (Frankfurt/Main, 1960), 2:457–58.

9. On the literary activists, see Iain Boyd Whyte, *Bruno Taut and the Architecture of Activism* (Cambridge, 1982), 16, 64; Mann's novel was originally published as *Der Untertan* (Berlin, 1918).

10. "Die akademische Liedertafel (1829–1904)," *Tübinger Chronik,* Jubiläums-Ausgabe, 1927.

11. Dieter Kramer, "Arbeiter als Touristen: Ein Privileg wird gebrochen" in *Mit uns zieht die neue Zeit. Die Naturfreunde. Zur Geschichte eines alternativen Verbandes in der Arbeiterkulturbewegung,* ed. Jochen Zimmer (Cologne, 1984), 54. But for discussion of a local Social Democratic leadership that, despite having doubts about workers'

cultural pursuits, seemed to harness the political potential of social clubs, see Mary T. Nolan, *Social Democracy and Society: Working-Class Radicalism in Düsseldorf, 1880–1920* (Cambridge, Mass., 1981), 134–45, *passim.*

12. See, for example, Hermann Bausinger, *Volkskultur in der technischen Welt,* reprint ed. (Frankfurt, New York, 1986), chap. II, *passim;* Herbert Freudenthal, *Vereine in Hamburg* (Hamburg, 1968); Heinz Schmitt, *Das Vereinsleben der Stadt Weinheim an der Bergstraße* (Weinheim, 1963); Günter Wiegelmann, Matthias Zender, Gerhard Heilfurth, *Volkskunde: Eine Einführung* (Berlin, 1977), 180–97, *passim.*

13. Rudy Koshar, *Social Life, Local Politics, and Nazism: Marburg, 1880–1935* (Chapel Hill, N.C. and London, 1986), 104–5.

14. Hans Fallada, *Little Man, What Now?* trans. Eric Sutton (New York, 1933).

15. The issue of the relationship between formal organization and popular petit-bourgeois attitudes is taken up in David Blackbourn, "Between Resignation and Volatility: The German Petite Bourgeoisie in the Nineteenth Century," in *Shopkeepers and Master Artisans in Nineteenth-Century Europe,* ed. Geoffrey Crossick and Heinz-Gerhard Haupt (London, New York, 1984), 53–54; and Haupt, "Mittelstand und Kleinbürgertum in der Weimarer Republik," 235.

16. For the point on the lower middle classes and bourgeois associations, see the evidence cited in Koshar, *Social Life,* 103–4, 109; on socialist workers and nonsocialist clubs, see Vernon Lidtke, *The Alternative Culture: Socialist Labor in Imperial Germany* (New York, Oxford, 1985), 44–45.

17. *50 Jahre Heimatverein Düsseldorfer Jonges,* 5–6.

18. This was certainly true in the case of historic buildings. See for example the membership roster for the national conference of conservators in *Zweiter Tag für Denkmalpflege. Freiburg i.Br. 23.–24. September 1901* (Karlsruhe, 1901), 3–5. However, if the lower middle classes did not lead historic preservation societies, they did join them: see Celia Applegate, "A Nation of Provincials: The German Idea of Homeland in the Rhenish Pfalz, 1870–1955" (Ph.D. diss., Stanford University, 1987), 137. My thanks to the author for sending me the relevant parts of her thesis.

19. For nationalist clubs, see Roger Chickering, *We Men Who Feel Most German: A Cultural Study of the Pan-German League, 1886–1914* (Boston, 1984); Geoff Eley, *Reshaping the German Right: Radical Nationalism and Political Change After Bismarck* (New Haven, London, 1980). For economic pressure groups of the traditional petite bourgeoisie: Robert Gellately, *The Politics of Economic Despair: Shopkeepers and German Politics 1890–1914* (London, Beverly Hills, 1974); Shulamit Volkov, *The Rise of Popular Antimodernism in Germany: The Urban Master Artisans, 1873–1896* (Princeton, 1978).

20. Henning Dunckelmann, *Lokale Öffentlichkeit. Eine gemeindesoziologische Untersuchung* (Stuttgart, 1975).

21. Albert Ilien and Utz Jeggle, *Leben auf dem Dorf: Zur Sozialgeschichte des Dorfes und Sozialpsychologie seiner Bewohner* (Opladen, 1978), 134.

22. See Koshar, *Social Life,* 55–59.

23. A compelling discussion of the issue of political displacement can be found in David Blackbourn, "The Politics of Demagogy in Imperial Germany," *Past and Present* 113 (Nov. 1986): 160–61. For some broader implications of the politicization of municipal affairs in the Republic and beyond, see Jürgen Reulecke, *Geschichte der Urbanisierung in Deutschland* (Frankfurt/Main, 1985), 152.

24. The most insightful discussion of this period is David Blackbourn and Geoff Eley, *The Peculiarities of German History: Bourgeois Society and Politics in Nineteenth-Century Germany* (Oxford, New York, 1984).

25. Gellately, *Politics of Economic Despair;* Iris Hamel, *Völkischer Verband und Na-*

tionale Gewerkschaft. Der Deutsch-nationale Handlungsgehilfen-Verband, 1893– 1933 (Frankfurt/Main, 1967); David Blackbourn, *Class, Religion, and Local Politics in Wilhelmine Germany: The Centre Party in Württemberg before 1914* (New Haven, London, 1980).

26. The phrase "social-moral milieux" derives from Rainer Lepsius' influential work. See his "Parteiensystem und Sozialstruktur: Zum Problem der Demokratisierung der deutschen Gesellschaft" in *Die deutschen Parteien vor 1918*, ed. Gerhard A. Ritter (Cologne, 1973). One can accept that such political subcultures existed without accepting Lepsius' argument that they reflect Germany's inability to develop a modern political system. Eley criticizes Lepsius' argument in Blackbourn, Eley, *Peculiarities*, 72–74. For discussion of German electoral patterns, see Stanley Suval, *Electoral Politics in Wilhelmine Germany* (Chapel Hill, N.C. and London, 1985).

27. Mack Walker, *German Home Towns: Community, Estate, and General Estate, 1648–1871* (Ithaca, N.Y., 1971). For a most recent statement on local politics in Germany, see Peter Fritzsche, *Rehearsals for Fascism: Populism and Political Mobilization in Weimar Germany* (New York, 1990).

28. The point is taken up in Geoffrey Crossick, "The Petite Bourgeoisie in Nineteenth-Century Europe: Problems and Research," in *Arbeiter und Arbeiterbewegung im Vergleich: Berichte zur internationalen historischen Forschung*, ed. Klaus Tenfelde (Munich, 1986), 269, in reference to William Sewell, *Work and Revolution in France: The Language of Labor from the Ancien Regime to 1848* (Cambridge, 1981), 112.

29. Christian Lalive d'Épinay, "Time, Space and Socio-Cultural Identity: The Ethos of the Proletariat, Small Owners and Peasantry in an Aged Population," *International Social Science Journal* 107 (1986): 97–100.

30. Roman Heiligenthal, *Deutscher Städtebau: Ein Handbuch für Architekten, Ingenieure, Verwaltungsbeamte und Volkswirtschaftler* (Heidelberg, 1921), 119.

31. James J. Sheehan, *German Liberalism in the 19th Century*, 2nd ed. (Chicago, 1983), has many examples and references.

32. Koshar, *Social Life*, 81–86; for Communist advances in municipal politics in Ruhr cities, see Beatrix Herlemann, *Kommunalpolitik der KPD im Ruhrgebiet, 1924– 1933* (Wuppertal, 1977).

33. Gert Zang, "Subjektive Reflexionen über ein Projekt und seine organisatorische, methodische und inhaltliche Entwicklung: Überlegungen zu einer kritischen Regionalgeschichtsschreibung für das 19. und 20. Jahrhundert," in *Provinzialisierung einer Region*, ed. idem (Frankfurt/Main, 1978), 499; Ina-Maria Greverus, *Auf der Suche nach Heimat* (Munich, 1979), 68–69; Dorothea Trittel, "Geschichtswerkstätten—auch eine 'Heimatbewegung'?" *Geschichtswerkstatt No. 6: Schwierigkeiten beim Entdecken der Heimat* (May 1985), 27–28. For an argument that links small propertied interests and perceptions of *Heimat*, see Günther Lange, *Heimat: Realität und Aufgabe. Zur marxistischen Auffassung des Heimatbegriffs* (East Berlin, 1973), 88.

34. One of the most visible promoters of vernacular building styles was Paul Schultze-Naumburg. For an example, see his *Die Gestaltung der Landschaft durch den Menschen*, 3rd ed. (Munich, 1928), 3:37–147.

35. Chickering, *We Men Who Feel Most German*, 102–8; Konrad Jarausch, *Students, Society and Politics in Imperial Germany: The Rise of Academic Illiberalism* (Princeton, 1982).

36. Zdenek Zofka, *Die Ausbreitung des Nationalsozialismus auf dem Lande* (Munich, 1979), 154–56; Hamilton, *Who Voted for Hitler?*

37. See Eley, *Reshaping the German Right*, and Sheehan, *German Liberalism*, 278–83.

38. Ursula Büttner, *Hamburg in der Staats- und Wirtschaftskrise, 1928–1931* (Hamburg, 1982), 370.

39. For the general point on the relation between public and private spheres, see Blackbourn, "Between Resignation and Volatility," 51; on "papa state," see Büttner, *Hamburg,* 379.

40. The general perspective on state power and the public sphere derives of course from Jürgen Habermas, *Strukturwandel der Öffentlichkeit. Untersuchungen zu einer Kategorie der bürgerlichen Gesellschaft* (Neuwied, Berlin, 1972).

41. I take issue here with Michael Kater, "Everyday Anti-Semitism in Prewar Nazi Germany: The Popular Bases," *Yad Vashem Studies* 16 (1984): 136–37.

42. William S. Allen, *The Nazi Seizure of Power: The Experience of a Single German Town, 1922–1945,* rev. ed. (New York, 1984), 218.

43. Koshar, *Social Life,* 79–81.

44. Detlev J. K. Peukert, *Inside Nazi Germany: Conformity, Opposition and Racism in Everyday Life,* trans. Richard Deveson (New Haven, 1987), 58–60.

45. Thomas Childers, *The Nazi Voter: Social Foundations of German Fascism, 1919– 1933* (Chapel Hill, N.C., 1983), 79–80.

46. See Larry Eugene Jones, *German Liberalism and the Dissolution of the Weimar Party System, 1918–1933* (Chapel Hill, N.C., 1988).

47. Herbert Kühr, *Parteien und Wahlen im Stadt- und Landkreis Essen in der Zeit der Weimarer Republik* (Bonn, 1973); Emil Zenz, *Die Stadt Trier im 20. Jahrhundert. 1. Hälfte 1900–1950* (Trier, 1981), 251–83, *passim.* On *Volksgemeinschaft* and the Center party: Jane Caplan, "Speaking the Right Language: The Nazi Party and the Civil Service Vote in the Weimar Republic," in *The Formation of the Nazi Constituency, 1919–1933,* ed. Thomas Childers (London, 1986), 192.

48. Haupt, "Mittelstand und Kleinbürgertum in der Weimarer Republik," 220; Winkler, *Mittelstand, Demokratie und Nationalsozialismus,* 31–34, 39; Speier, *Die Angestellten vor dem Nationalsozialismus,* 71; Childers, *Nazi Voter,* 228–33. See also the contribution by Haupt and Niermann in this volume.

49. Enzo Mingione, *Social Conflict and the City* (New York, 1981), 38–39.

50. Hamilton, *Who Voted for Hitler?* 49–50; Childers, *Nazi Voter,* 172; and for the Nazi vote among working-class Germans, Tim Mason, "National Socialism and the Working Class, 1925–May, 1933," *New German Critique* 11 (Spring 1977): 65; and more recently, Jürgen W. Falter and Dirk Hänisch, "Die Anfälligkeit von Arbeitern gegenüber der NSDAP bei den Reichstagswahlen, 1928–1933" *Archiv für Sozialgeschichte* 26 (1986): 179–216.

51. Kershaw, *Popular Opinion and Political Dissent in the Third Reich: Bavaria 1933–45* (New York, 1983), 115.

52. Michael Kater, *The Nazi Party: A Social Profile of Members and Leaders, 1919–1945* (Oxford, 1983).

53. Ibid., 34; Mathilde Jamin, *Zwischen den Klassen: Zur Sozialstruktur der SA-Führerschaft* (Wuppertal, 1984), 2–3.

54. Rainer Hambrecht, *Der Aufstieg der NSDAP in Mittel- und Oberfranken, 1925– 33* (Nuremberg, 1976), 136–42.

55. Ian Kershaw, *The Nazi Dictatorship: Problems and Perspectives of Interpretation,* 2nd ed. (London, 1989), 76; Kershaw offers a fine discussion of a very large literature on the subject of Hitler's popularity and power in Chapter 4 of this source.

56. Koshar, *Social Life,* 204; Zofka, *Ausbreitung des Nationalsozialismus,* 84.

57. Peukert, *Inside Nazi Germany,* 38–42.

58. Gerhard Seehase and Hans Reip, "Anatomie eines Vereins: Hamburger Turnerschaft von 1816—der Weg durch fünf Generationen," in *Der Verein: Standort, Aufgabe, Funktion in Sport und Gesellschaft,* ed. Hamburger Turnerschaft 1816 e.V. (Schorndorf bei Stuttgart, 1967), 52.

59. Ibid.

60. Hans-Ulrich Thamer, *Verführung und Gewalt: Deutschland, 1933–1945* (Berlin, 1986), 157.

61. See the introduction, note 72, on mass culture and the German lower middle classes.

62. Detlef Mühlberger, "Central Control versus Regional Autonomy: A Case Study of Nazi Propaganda in Westphalia, 1925–1932," in *Formation of the Nazi Constituency*, 63–103.

63. See Juan J. Linz, "Political Space and Fascism as a Late-Comer: Conditions Conducive to the Success or Failure of Fascism as a Mass Movement in Inter-War Europe," in *Who Were the Fascists. Social Roots of European Fascism*, eds. Stein Ugelvik Larsen, Bernt Hagtvet, Jan Petter Myklebust (Bergen, 1980).

64. For provocative examples: Klaus Theweleit, *Männerphantasien*, 2 vols. (Frankfurt/Main, 1977).

65. Still very suggestive in this regard is Walter Struve, *Elites against Democracy: Leadership Ideals in Bourgeois Political Thought in Germany, 1890–1933* (Princeton, 1973).

66. Thamer, *Verführung und Gewalt*, 233.

67. Nazi Reich Propaganda Department directives for March–April 1932 excerpted in *Documents on Nazism, 1919–1945*, eds. Jeremy Noakes and Geoffrey Pridham (New York, 1975), 103.

68. For a fascinating commentary on the ideology of a "third age," see Ernst Bloch, *Erbschaft dieser Zeit*, rev. ed. (Frankfurt/Main, 1962), 126–28.

69. I have tried to deal with this point in "From *Stammtisch* to Party: Nazi Joiners and the Contradictions of Grass Roots Fascism in Weimar Germany," *Journal of Modern History* 57, 1 (March 1987): 1–24.

70. David Schoenbaum, *Hitler's Social Revolution: Class and Status in Nazi Germany, 1933–1939* (New York, 1966). The extraordinary outpouring of literature on daily life in the Nazi dictatorship is reflected in the review essay by Detlev J. K. Peukert, "Das 'Dritte Reich' aus der 'Alltags'-Perspektive," *Archiv für Sozialgeschichte* 26 (1986): 533–56.

71. Von Saldern argues that the Nazi dictatorship realized many of the major goals of the artisanate in particular, whereas Winkler takes the position that the old middle strata were disadvantaged by Nazi social and economic policy. For von Saldern's argument, see Adelheid von Saldern, *Mittelstand im 'Dritten Reich,': Handwerker—Einzelhändler—Bauern* (Frankfurt/Main, 1979); idem, "'Alter Mittelstand' im Dritten Reich," *Geschichte und Gesellschaft* 12 (1986): 235–43. For Winkler's position, see *Mittelstand, Demokratie, Nationalsozialismus;* "Der entbehrliche Stand: Zur Mittelstandspolitik im 'Dritten Reich'" *Archiv für Sozialgeschichte* 17 (1977): 1–40. And for a recent interesting view of the debate that deals with white-collar workers, see Michael Prinz, "Der unerwünschte Stand: Lage und Status der Angestellten im 'Dritten Reich'," *Historische Zeitschrift* 242, 2 (April 1986): 327–59; for Prinz's full argument, see Michael Prinz, *Vom neuen Mittelstand zum Volksgenossen: Die Entwicklung des Sozialen Status der Angestellten von der Weimarer Republik bis zum Ende der NS-Zeit* (Munich, 1986).

72. For the background, see Peukert, *Inside Nazi Germany*.

73. For the first quote, Martin Bormann to *Brigadeführer* Schaub, "Denkschrift betreffend Einrichtung und Stellung von Reichsluftsportkorps und Staatsjugend," 13 Nov. 1936, in *Akten der Partei-Kanzlei der NSDAP*, ed. Institut für Zeitgeschichte/Munich (New York, 1984), microfiche ed., pt. 1, vol. 1, 124 00229-124 00249; for the second, Martin Bormann, "Klopt an das deutsche Herz!" *Kulturpolitische Mitteilungsblatt der Reichspropagandaleitung der NSDAP* 2, 1 (Jan. 1943): 1–6 in *Akten der Partei-Kanzlei*, pt. 1, vol. 2, 117 06004-117 06009.

74. For one local example, see Horst Morgenbrod, "Die Liebe zur Heimat war unge-

brochen: Das Wiederwachen der Brauchtums- und Heimatvereine," in *1946—Neuanfang: Leben in Düsseldorf,* ed. Stadtmuseum Düsseldorf (Düsseldorf, 1986), 343–51.

75. For discussion of a part of the theoretical literature, see Bernt Hagtvet, "The Theory of Mass Society and the Collapse of the Weimar Republic: A Re-Examination," in *Who Were the Fascists,* 66–117. On the Weimar Republic and the tensions of sociopolitical modernity, see Detlev J. K. Peukert, *Die Weimarer Republik. Krisenjahre der Klassischen Moderne* (Frankfurt/Main, 1987).

3

Between Solidarity and Splintering: Bremen Shopkeepers in the Weimar Republic

HEINZ-GERHARD HAUPT
and
CHARLOTTE NIERMANN

One of the central tasks of this volume is to focus attention on features of interwar petit-bourgeois politics in Europe that have been insufficiently discussed previously. Bremen offers an excellent base from which to do this.

The politics of Bremen retail trade organizations before 1914 departed considerably from what scholars, dealing mainly with north German examples, have established as the characteristic policies of the old *Mittelstand,* which may be somewhat imprecisely translated as the traditional "middle strata" or "middle classes."[1] Not a system of state guarantees and reinsurance, but independence; not protectionist and reactionary "politics of concentration" *(Sammlungspolitik),* but reliance on liberal big commerce and overseas trade *(Großhandel)* characterized shopkeepers' associations in Bremen. Retailers were organized in three major voluntary groups: the Association of Bremen Shopkeepers *(Verein Bremen Ladeninhaber,* VBL), which originated in shopkeepers' involvement in debates over the implementation of Sunday vacation laws for employees; the Discount Savings' Association *Brema,* which after 1900 tried to appeal to established, stable businesses by offering standardized discounts to cash-paying customers; and finally, after 1907, the Chamber for Small Retail Trade *(Kleinhandelskammer),* in whose elections all shopkeepers and textile traders could participate as long as they possessed Bremen citizenship, which entailed meeting a minimum income requirement. All these organizations reached only a minority of Bremen retailers, but one should not underestimate

---

This essay was translated from the German by Rudy Koshar.

the influence these groups had on the behavior and attitudes of small shop-owners.[2]

Bremen shopkeepers' associations promoted mainly liberal and non-protectionist policies. Although the associations as well as the Chamber united in opposition to the short-term, small enterprises often run by manual laborers or their spouses (or *Eintagsfliegen,* as the economic historian Werner Sombart wrote), and the VBL refused membership to Jewish retailers, their attitudes and policies placed them more on the left wing than on the right wing of German retail organizations. Thus Eberhard Neddermann, a member of the Bremen Chamber for Small Retail Trade, also sat on the retail trade commission for the *Hansa Bund,* which strove for cooperation between big commerce, industry, and the *Mittelstand.* Additionally, in Bremen anti-Semitic proposals were rarely heard in retailers' associations, and the department store tax, which elsewhere was praised and implemented as an excellent defense against major commercial competition, was of little public concern.[3]

By studying Bremen shopkeepers in the Weimar Republic, we can look at persistence and change in the organizational forms and political outlooks of shop-owners' associations. What effects did the Revolution of 1918, inflation, and the world economic crisis have on the political orientation of Bremen retail trade? Were these major economic processes more important in determining the actions of Bremen shopkeepers than were debates within voluntary associations, the constellation of political parties, and the influence of National Socialism? Finally, does it suffice to speak of the "Nazification" of Bremen retailers or of a "panic in the *Mittelstand*"?[4]

From Political Solidarity to Splintering

After the revolution of 1918–1919, which established Germany's first parliamentary democracy, Bremen shopkeepers' associations developed partly on the basis of pre–World War I outlines. The Fruit and Vegetable Dealers' Association, founded on 17 May 1917, thus relied on the tradition of the Association of Fruit and Vegetable Wholesalers and Shopkeepers, founded in 1912, even though the new organization excluded big dealers.[5] Besides such efforts to continue prewar traditions, retailers founded completely new organizations and dissolved old ones. In 1917, for instance, grocers founded a new association that was listed in the Bremen Association Register *(Vereinsregister),* making the group a juridical person,[6] whereas on 30 August 1921, the VBL dissolved and was incorporated in the Provincial Association of Bremen Retail Trade.[7]

Abundance and variety characterized shopkeepers' professional associations. Dividing associations according to levels of social exclusivity, we can identify two general types. The Grocers' Association is paradigmatic of the first type. It stated in 1917: "Only Bremen residents who are owners of professionally run grocery stores and specialty shops may be members of the association. . . . The principal requirement for eligibility is that the candidate has acquired satisfactory knowledge of the business in question or has demonstrated the ability to manage a business in an orderly and efficient fashion."[8] Many small, temporary shops that were often run by women whose husbands had other jobs were thus excluded from association membership. Moreover, these requirements presupposed and furthered the professionalization of small-scale commerce.

The second type of association aimed for a wider audience. The best example of this type was the Fruit and Vegetable Dealers' Association, whose bylaws read in part: "All [male and female] self-employed fruit and vegetable dealers who run a public vegetable business and who possess full citizenship rights may be members of the association."[9] Bourgeois respectability was still the criterion of membership, and women played no leadership role in the association. Nonetheless, groups like the Fruit and Vegetable Dealers' Association emphasized quantity more than quality. It is possible that these contrasting structures and goals explain trends in the membership of each association. Based on attendance at regular monthly meetings, the Grocers' Association had over 500 members in January 1920, only about 300 in January 1922, and only 270 in June 1933. Only 62 members of the 270 who belonged to the group in June 1933 could be mobilized to attend an important assembly that year.[10] In contrast, the only evidence for membership of the Fruit and Vegetable Dealers' Association suggests that 300 people belonged to that association, which is astounding, given traditional arguments claiming that precisely this branch of shopkeepers was difficult to organize.[11]

Above all, the prewar situation contrasted with the Republic mainly because of the strengthened position of the *Kleinhandelskammer* and the federation of all retailers in a provincial branch *(Landesverband)*. After 1918 the Chamber received legal recognition, which it had longed for and demanded for some time. This gave the Chamber equal standing with various other official organs representing the interests of commerce, business, white-collar workers, and blue-collar workers. It also gave small retailers the opportunity to review and issue opinions on legislation that affected them, to elect representatives in the Chamber, and to nominate candidates for commercial judges *(Handelsrichter)*. The Chamber bylaw of 17 July 1921 laid down guidelines whereby the organization was financed through revenues from Bremen business and sales surtaxes, thereby integrating the *Kleinhandelskammer* in the constitutional and institutional structures of the city and codifying its legal position.[12]

The Provincial Association of Bremen Retail Trade was founded in November 1918 by about 1,200 retailers, who announced their "struggle against the regulation of the economy begun during World War I *(Zwang-swirtschaft)* and the attacks on and efforts to eliminate retail trade."[13] The *Landesverband* was part of the nationwide Federation of German Retailers *(Hauptgemeinschaft des deutschen Einzelhandels),* a link symbolized in the person of Bremen city senator Franz May, who for a long time was chair of the Provincial Association and a member of the executive board of the national Federation. The Provincial Association tried to document and reconcile the interests of its member organizations largely by publishing the magazine "The Small Retailer" *(Der Einzelhändler),* which in 1924 was published by the Provincial Association itself and thereafter by the Chamber. At the same time, the Provincial Association worked to create adequate political representation for small retailers and textile dealers.

Although the association encouraged its members to join the political party of their choice in 1919, disillusionment over political matters soon became widespread.[14] In February of 1919 an "anonymous member" wrote: "The hopes of many have been dashed. Although the association has grown tremendously since its birth in November, and although it has stood its ground in many conflicts, it has now capitulated to the big political parties. Instead of calling its members together and courageously steeling them for battle, it has accepted the fool's paradise offered by the political parties—in the form of guaranteed seats on party tickets—and thereby sold itself to the parties." The author then formulated a maxim that would gradually gain widespread acceptance in the *Landesverband:* "If parties are necessary for Germany, then the representation of economic interests is important for Bremen."[15] Small retail traders had gained no adequate representation on the left-liberal Democratic party (DDP) ticket in Bremen, and the *Kleinhandelskammer* member Neddermann, who sat on the executive board of the right-liberal German People's party (DVP), had been able to offer small retailers little in the way of concrete promises.[16] Thus the Provincial Association decided either to put together a list of representatives from small retail and artisanal groups, or, if artisans were not willing to go along, to enter elections with a ticket consisting solely of retailers. After artisans rejected a joint list, thirty representatives of small retail trade put together a ticket for the National Assembly elections in Bremen. Their goal was to protect free trade, gain the "right of co-determination" *(Mit-bestimmungsrecht)* in parliament, and fight against socialization and the bureaucratic state. These demands clearly put distance between the candidates and the Social Democratic party, and therefore it was not surprising that, much to the regret of many Association members, Social Democratic shopkeepers were not on the ticket.[17]

Substantial "Bremen merchants and restaurant owners" had considerable influence on the ticket, as revealed by the occupations of the candidates.

These include, besides owners of a milk business and a shoestore, eleven other merchants, a counsellor for the Chamber of Small Retail Trade, and an engineer. It is reasonable to assume that the evidence distinguishes between better-off merchants and small shopkeepers, given the practice of observing such differences in Bremen since the nineteenth century, and thus we can conclude that local shopkeepers were willing to be represented by the commercial and professional middle and upper-middle classes.[18] Individuals whose political and economic interests differed from those of shopkeepers thus sometimes represented small retail trade. But shopkeepers were not the only group whose political representation failed to reflect perfectly its social makeup; nor were they alone in allowing women to be underrepresented as political candidates. The fruit and vegetable dealer Minna Wobbe occupied the lowly twenty-first position on the ticket, and was thus not among the seven candidates who were elected with 5,728 votes. These candidates included three merchants and the counsellor of the Chamber of Small Retail Trade.[19]

As the 1920 elections to the Bremen City Assembly (Bürgerschaft) approached, however, the unity of the Provincial Association unraveled. One faction, headed by the chair May, argued that the Association should make its demands felt within the existing parties, while the opposed—and eventually successful—faction spoke for the creation of a corporate ticket. Representatives of the latter argued that "if small retailers split their votes between separate parties, they would become utterly dependent on outside forces."[20] Twenty candidates gained 6,263 votes in the City Assembly elections. Although restaurateurs and innkeepers were now absent from the ticket, thirteen members of the list had already stood as candidates in the 1919 elections. Four representatives now entered the Bürgerschaft in order to have "real specialists" rather than "political commentators" organize local economic life, as the candidates' campaign literature stated.[21] In 1921 still another corporate list for small shop owners was organized, but this time it received only 5,218 votes and three seats.[22] In response to this electoral slide, the Provincial Association shifted to the view that negotiations with the existing parties rather than separate lists would best serve the interests of small shop owners. This shift marked out a party political development that Heinrich August Winkler and others have already discussed for the national level and various regions.[23] The organized group of small shop owners who in 1918 and 1919 had sought contact with the Democratic party and, at least rhetorically, with the Social Democratic party had in the meantime moved to the Right. In 1924 the representatives of shop owners in the Bremen City Assembly included Hans de la Roche of the right-wing German National People's party (DNVP), Wilhelm Hermann and Otto Hillebrecht of the right-liberal German People's party, and Dietrich Allerheiligen of the left-liberal Democratic party.[24]

With the victory of those who advocated splitting votes between the parties came a major break in the internal politics of the Provincial Association. In 1927 six Bremen branch organizations demanded that the Provincial Association leave the Chamber and establish an executive board at the head of an independent organization.[25] The branch groups argued that it was difficult to fight against department stores and consumers' cooperatives because these very establishments qualified as retail businesses and were therefore members in the Chamber. Because Chamber policy on this issue matched that of the national *Hauptgemeinschaft*, to which the Provincial Association belonged, the Association repulsed the critics' argument all the more decisively. At a joint assembly of the provincial group and the Guilds' Union attended by about two thousand people, the Provincial Association chair, Senator May, faced intense criticism from his own ranks, who accused him of not being combative enough when it came to fighting for Association interests.[26] The debate ultimately led to a reformulation of the Association bylaws that made substantial concessions to the opposition. The bylaws now stated that department stores and consumer cooperatives should not belong to the Provincial Association, but that in all its deliberations the Association would continue to seek the counsel of the Chamber.[27] Reflecting a real willingness to compromise, this break with previous Association policy was not enough to calm the opposition. Six major associations of Bremen retail trade—including the Grocers' Association, the local branch of the Reich Association of Textile Retailers, and the Specialty Foods Shop Owners' Association—left the *Landesverband*.

The Provincial Association lost some of its vitality due to the withdrawal of these large groups, who exacerbated the Association's difficulties even more by forming the Federation of Bremen Shopkeepers. The coming world economic crisis and the national government's emergency policies lessened the attractiveness of the program of the Provincial Association executive board, which had always stressed the diversity of retail trade, the legitimacy of all shopkeepers' interests, and the need for self-help. The Association's defensiveness was clearly reflected in the language of the 1928 yearly report: "Whoever thinks that shopkeepers' associations exist simply to save their members from competition, whoever considers the building of a new department store to be a sign of the failure of local shopkeepers' groups or the national federation, they are still in the dark about the sense and limits of such organizations."[28] In February of 1929 the Provincial Association organized a "demonstration of the commercial and industrial *Mittelstand*" to which it invited the Guilds' Union, other artisans' associations, and innkeepers' groups. Significantly, none of the leading members of the Provincial Association spoke at the rally, which passed a resolution that signaled the Association's renunciation of liberal self-help in favor of protectionist policies.

The resolution demanded "protection . . . from big capitalist concerns and trusts; from the government machinery of Reich, province, and town; from misuse of the system for granting contracts on communal projects; from the infringements of department stores and consumers' cooperatives." This protection was to be achieved by revising the Versailles treaty, lowering public spending, balancing government budgets, and reducing social benefits for workers.[29] In light of the passage of this protectionist-corporate program, which included all the arguments of the conservative parties, the Provincial Association executive board's remaining in office proved to be a Pyrrhic victory. The Association persisted, electing officers for the last time in the Weimar Republic in 1929,[30] but more and more toeing the line of the renegade Federation of Bremen Shopkeepers. This was evident in the rally of 4 February 1932, which the Association held in the assembly hall of the Bremen "Union." The rally featured a speech by Joachim Neßler, who after the "National Socialist" party came to power in 1933 would become vice-president of the Association. Neßler praised his listeners and "expressed . . . his satisfaction that the Federation and Association had united."[31] But this reunification was cemented by a program of social protectionism and oriented toward the right-wing parties. Organized shopkeepers in Bremen were now united behind a nationalistic program that attacked monopoly power and state fiscal and social policies. By turning away from the internal problems of retail trade, by eschewing self-help policies that stressed the unique qualities of individual branches, shopkeepers were to achieve solidarity.

Nazification of Bremen Shopkeepers in the Weimar Republic?

Whether they refer to a "panic in the *Mittelstand*" or "extremism of the middle,"[32] scholars routinely argue that in the second half of the 1920s, shopkeepers and artisans prepared the way ideologically and politically for the end of the Weimar Republic, although they did not anticipate the Nazi seizure of power. Therefore it is hardly coincidental, the argument goes, that they were overrepresented in the ranks of voters and members of the "National Socialist German Workers' party" (NSDAP).

"National Socialists" tried to gain support in the old *Mittelstand* before 1933 in Bremen just as they did throughout Germany. For instance, one of their members became chair of the Sharpshooters' Club *Wildschütz*, to which mainly shopkeepers belonged.[33] Commercial employees, who apparently considered the NSDAP to be a vehicle of job advancement, were mentioned most frequently in police reports on Nazi party members, but a druggist, the owner of a linen goods store, and two other traders also gained mention because of their visibility in the "National Socialist" movement.[34] The *Bremen National Socialist Newspaper (BZ)* featured regular advertisements by a porcelain and glass store whose owner became a member of the *Kleinhandelskammer* in 1933.[35] A cigar store on the Obernstraße, the busiest commercial street in the city, ostentatiously displayed a picture of the burial of a member of the paramilitary arm of the Nazi party, the SA.[36]

In addition to these activities, the Nazis tried to appeal to shop owners by staging assemblies such as the one held in March of 1930 in the main hall of the "Casino" restaurant, where 2,000 people listened to the SA chief Herzog speak on "self-defense of the productive *Mittelstand* and new ways to fight the department stores and consumers' cooperatives."[37] Above all, the party tried to expand and strengthen its appeal by interrupting speeches at meetings of the Economic party *(Wirtschaftspartei,* also called *Reichspartei des deutschen Mittelstandes),* which sought to mobilize the *Mittelstand* in a single political party. Police reported that on one occasion thirty Nazi party members harassed an Economic party assembly attended by 320 people.[38] On 5 November 1931 the NSDAP was able to break up an Economic party meeting whose main theme was "Why the Economic Party Voted for Chancellor Brüning's Government." Three hundred members of the NSDAP and of the nationalist, paramilitary veterans' association, the Steel Helmet, attended that meeting.[39]

Terror in the form of abuse and beatings of individual people on the street accompanied these rather limited Nazi propaganda activities. These attacks began in 1928 and, if the documents are reliable, were especially widespread before 1930. Terror against individuals usually did not include the raiding of stores or the smashing of windows, equipment, and furniture. It was usually directed against Jewish store owners.[40] Typical of such action was the assault on Hans Blumenthal, who owned a sporting goods store, and who at midnight on one of Bremen's well-known business streets was beaten severely about the face and head by a shop clerk who had been an NSDAP member since 1922.[41] Shop clerks were overrepresented in the ranks of Nazi terrorists, but shopkeepers' associations failed to react to the violence. Whereas documentation of shopkeepers' solidarity on other issues is often absent, we have evidence showing that in some cases store owners appeared in court to defend fellow merchants who were accused of violent assaults.[42] In general, indifference was the dominant attitude.

Despite all these examples of "National Socialist" activities in Bremen, Nazi influence over shopkeepers was limited. Neither the Fighting League Against Department Stores and Consumer Cooperatives nor its successor, the Fighting League of the Productive *Mittelstand,* both Nazi groups, gained much influence before 1933. Part of the reason for this was that Bremen retailers were not overly concerned about department stores, of which there were six in the Hansa city, according to the 1933 census.[43] Although both the NSDAP and Economic party had tried on numerous occasions to have a department store tax passed, they were unable to gain much support for the cause. In both 1931 and 1932 the "National Socialist" city deputy Wegener proposed a department store tax in the *Bürgerschaft*, only to have his proposals either turned down immediately or tabled.[44] The department store tax earned no mention at all in the publications of Bremen shopkeepers' associations, and until 1933 neither the Chamber nor the Provincial Association demanded it. This seems to contradict our earlier discussion, which demonstrated that the Provincial Association was torn apart over the issue of membership of department stores in the organization. However, the debate within the Association did not touch directly on the problem of competition from department stores but on their role in the activities and policies of the Association. As the 1932 commentary of the Chamber of Small Retail Trade indicated, local economic hardship would hardly be lessened by prohibiting department stores in Bremen because there were so few of them,[45] and so direct economic competition from these big commercial enterprises appeared slight for small shops. One of the important themes of "National Socialist" agitation went up in smoke with that realization.

Evidence for 1933 also supports the argument that "National Socialist" influence over shopkeepers was limited. Euphoric telegrams congratulating Hitler's accession to power on 30 January and stressing the "National Socialist" convictions of shopkeepers in general and Chamber members in particular[46] appear in stark contradiction to the statements of the Fighting League of the Productive *Mittelstand*, which complained that store owners showed little interest in its membership drive in August 1933.[47] The Fighting League also found it necessary to rely on the authority of the Chamber to induce less active shopkeepers to attend assemblies.[48] To speak of a seizure of power in the "National Socialist" sense of the term is impossible in the light of this evidence, but to speak of resistance is equally impossible.

Before 1933 the Chamber of Small Retail Trade expressed opinions that were in no way protectionist or hostile to the state. These provide one measure of how insubstantial Nazi influence was in this organization prior to Hitler's gaining of the Chancellorship. But the lack of Nazi influence can also be elucidated by reference to the NSDAP's attempts to gain personal influence in the Chamber. Seventy percent of the individuals who, after a period of transition, found themselves holding high office in the Chamber in August 1933 had not been elected to a leadership post in the last regular election of 1932. Two of the fifteen had previously been active in the Chamber, but the other thirteen did not belong to the traditional group of functionaries who had been active either in the Provincial Association or the branch associations of Bremen shopkeepers.[49] One can interpret this—as Martin Broszat does—as a reflection of how "National Socialism" expressed a widespread longing for renewal. But it is also a sign of the limited Nazification of the leadership strata of Bremen shopkeepers before 1933.

Such fragmentary evidence requires fuller development, to be sure, but it does allow one to conclude that the ongoing controversy between protectionist and antiprotectionist wings of organized shopkeepers hardly went hand in hand with a Nazification of retail trade. The number of activist shopkeepers in the NSDAP was too small, Nazi influence in retail trade organizations too weak, and support for the standard themes of "National Socialist" propaganda too limited to enable the NSDAP to gain real dominance. It is true that internal fissures led the Provincial Association to adopt much of the language of right-wing political slogans. But the Grocers' Association, one of the main opponents of previous Provincial Association policy, favored political candidates from the German People's party and Economic party in 1930.[50] And opponents of consumer cooperatives at a 29 September 1932 Provincial Association meeting fell far short of NSDAP demagogy when they formulated a moderate resolution that read: "Private business is the fundament of our state and the source of revenues that the state has at its disposal. Consumer cooperatives purposely try to destroy private business, however, and therefore they have no right to state monies."[51]

Why did shopkeepers increasingly rely on the slogans of the right-wing parties during the Weimar Republic? The most important reason was that shopkeepers were convinced that they were overlooked by the parties in particular and the German polity in general. The Provincial Association expressed this feeling as early as 1920, when it said that postrevolutionary conflict was among the causes "of a growing desire among shopkeepers and their organizations, including the Provincial Association, to make a real contribution at the highest levels of authority and for once not to be looked at or treated as the fifth wheel of the wagon."[52] But negotiations to get secure places for shopkeepers on the Democratic party fell through, as did attempts to incorporate a separate list of elected shopkeepers in the Social Democratic parliamentary delegation. These failures reflected the rejection rather than acceptance of shopkeepers' claims by the Weimar Coalition (Social Democrats, Democrats, and Catholic Center), the parties that established the Weimar Republic, and when shopkeepers gravitated to the German People's party and Economic party their disillusionment with the Coalition could not have been made clearer.

Shopkeepers' associations also felt alienated by state policies. This was true not only in the matter of the communalization of trade, much discussed after 1918, but also in legislation dealing with usury, taxes, and prices. Indeed, a fully developed conspiracy theory seems to have characterized the view of the Grocers' Association when it commented in 1931 on the Depression-induced emergency legislation of the previous year: "If we are trying to avoid a breakdown in the eleventh hour, then it must be asked if emergency decrees are the proper means for doing so; after all, it always depends on which political powers are dictating the decrees. These powers do not seem to be very friendly toward the self-employed *Mittelstand,* as we learned at the end of last year when Bremen passed emergency legislation that levied a fifth payment of the business and sales tax and of the property tax. In the meantime the emergency decree that lowered prices for name-brand goods has demonstrated that behind the scenes there are forces whose wage policies and socialist goals make them want to eliminate the small shopkeeper."[53] Conspiracy theory and a personal view of politics combined with the opacity of large-scale organizations to produce this outlook. Small shopkeepers complained that the regime paid little attention to their concerns and continually hurt retail trade by lowering prices and reducing incomes. For shopkeepers, therefore, the watchword was tax cuts, which were deemed absolutely necessary "if even larger numbers of Bremen stores were not to collapse immediately."[54]

One of the effects of state regulation of prices was that consumers thought it was possible to bring about general and mass price reductions, which the big firms probably could absorb, but not the small retailer. At the same time store owners engaged in an increasingly bitter competition with one another, using preventative price reductions as well as gifts to drum up more customers. In the 1920s various shopkeepers' associations had spoken out repeatedly against discounts and gifts without getting the support of all their members.[55] But this opposition and the prohibition of gifts in the emergency decree of March 1932 had little effect on shop owners, who continued to use various devices in the competition for business. Of little effect also were the so-called arbitration offices *(Einigungsäm-ter),* introduced in 1932 and designed to handle shopkeepers' complaints about unfair competition not by litigation but by consent; their impact was diminished by a similar, albeit private office formed in 1924 by the Chamber of Small Retail Trade.[56]

We have so far discussed legislation that had no or only a negative impact so far as shopkeepers were concerned. But in other legislation small retailers recognized how little their specific interests mattered when it came to formulating state policy. A good example is the von Papen regime's tax voucher decree of September 1932, which provided for the issuing of vouchers for tax payments and the employment of additional workers. However, special sales, clearances, inventory sales, and the Christmas season were excluded by the decree—precisely the times when small stores had their highest turnover rates and hence the best opportunity to earn the vouchers.[57] In response to the decree, the Chamber for Small Retail Trade wrote: "We believe that the Reich Labor Ministry will have to decide immediately what it wants to do once the many hundreds thousands of stores begin agitating after seeing how they will be excluded from the advantages that other, less burdened economic groups enjoy." Addressing this protest, the government changed the decree on 31 October 1932 to suit the needs of shopkeepers.[58]

A peculiarity of the organizations of the lower middle classes (Kleinbürgertum) in the Weimar Republic was that their protest against neglect and the favoring of big pressure groups could not be expressed in political language derived from the democratic and socialist parties. On the Right of the political spectrum only the NSDAP, the Economic party, and the German National People's party strove for support from shopkeepers whereas on the Left it was the Communist party. The Social Democratic party thought an alliance with the "old Mittelstand" was unattractive; the Center party concentrated on the Catholic population; the Democratic party was soon too weak to serve as an effective political vehicle; and the German People's party was too closely tied to big industrial groups. The Communists courted shopkeepers repeatedly, if not thoroughly. By the start of the 1930s, Communist agitators were appearing at numerous assemblies of the Mittelstand, but they failed to represent their position effectively.[59] A passage from the Workers' News (Arbeiter-Zeitung) of 9 January 1932 captured the gist of the Communist message: "Industrial capital, cartels, syndicates, and trusts are destroying the Mittelstand. Capitalism is the ruin of the Mittelstand. . . . Bolshevism [Communism] would not think of expropriating the working Mittelstand. Has Bolshevism in the Soviet Union expropriated the Mittelstand? No! It has expropriated the banks, big industry, department stores, and big landowners—but not artisans, shopkeepers, and innkeepers." Of most interest to the Communists was the great array of small, unstable, and short-lived stores, stalls, and workshops that were dependent on big wholesalers and suppliers. Without prejudging the results of a more complete social-historical analysis, we may reasonably assume that the Communist party gained a foothold among the unorganized and most unstable shopkeepers. Yet this agitation was too unsuccessful to cause much concern among the Bremen political police, who on 15 September 1923—in the midst of the inflation—reported that "twenty-six people attended a Communist assembly for self-employed artisans and retailers" and that "the Communists' plan to use the evening to build a subgroup for artisans and retailers failed."[60]

Most organized, established store owners found the Communist party unattractive, partly because of its program and orientation toward the Soviet Union, but especially because the Communists could easily be lumped together with groups that threatened to plunder local shops. Shop owners were especially traumatized by the "cherry riots" of June 1920, in which hungry, working-class men and women plundered local grocery stores while unconcerned or powerless police stood by.[61] During times of economic crisis, shopkeepers always became preoccupied with the possibility of such self-help actions by the needy. On 8 October 1923, for instance, the vegetable dealer Frau Decker told police that "three young people had told her that this was the evening [for plundering]. The Communists have held numerous secret assemblies to organize the action."[62] Shopkeepers had no specific examples of plundering to point to during the world economic crisis, but the growing numbers of unemployed increased their anxiety, nonetheless.[63]

Having made socialist terminology taboo, shopkeepers had only the slogans and the example of the right-wing parties to express their aims and demands, and thus shopkeepers' dissatisfaction was transferred from one level of argumentation to another. Opposition to a fusion of city senate adminstration and Provincial Association leadership (personified by Senator May), as well as to the cooperation of the Association and Chamber, issued into rabid attacks on department stores, whose economic influence was small in Bremen. Dissatisfaction with the privileged position of major pressure groups could also be expressed through such arguments. Finally, Martin Broszat argues that such protests questioned the legitimacy of traditional notables and leadership strata.[64] The evidence makes it clear that the pronouncements of associations of the lower middle classes should not be read exclusively as documents of protofascism but should be decoded in the context of their unique and highly complex social meaning.

Notes

1. See Heinrich August Winkler, *Mittelstand, Demokratie und Nationalsozialismus: Die politische Entwicklung von Handwerk und Kleinhandel in der Weimarer Republik* (Cologne, Berlin, 1972); Shulamit Volkov, *The Rise of Popular Antimodernism in Germany: The Urban Master Artisans, 1873–1896* (Princeton, 1978). See also the discussion in the introduction to this volume.

2. Heinz-Gerhard Haupt, "Der Bremen Kleinhandel zwischen 1890 und 1914: Binnenstruktur, Einfluß und Politik," *Beiträge zur Sozialgeschichte Bremens* (hereafter, BSB) 4 (1982): 7–40; Achim Saur, "Die Organisationen der Bremen Kleinhändler vor 1914 und ihre soziale Basis" in BSB 4 (1982): 41–84.

3. For example, until 1928, representatives of large department stores sat on the board of directors of the Provincial Association of Bremen Retail Trade *(Landesverband des Bremischen Einzelhandels e.V.).* See *Der Einzelhändler: Mitteilungen des Landesverbandes des Bremischen Einzelhandels e.V.* (after 1924: *Der Einzelhändler: Amtliches Organ der Kleinhandelskammer zu Bremen;* hereafter cited as *Der Einzelhändler*), special ed. no. 2 (15 Jan. 1933): 9. See also Verhandlungen der Bremischen Bürgerschaft (1931 and 1932), regarding department and branch store taxes, and Handelskammerarchiv Bremen (hereafter, HkABr) Z.V.72.

4. See Theodor Geiger, "Panik im Mittelstand," *Die Arbeit* 10 (1930): 638ff.; Arthur Schweitzer, *Die Nazifierung des Mittelstandes* (Stuttgart, 1970).

5. Compare Staatsarchiv Bremen (hereafter, StAB), 4,75/7 - VR 191.

6. StAB 4,75/7 - VR 235.

7. *Der Einzelhändler* 19 (Oct. 1921): 383.

8. StAB 4, 75/7 - VR 235.

9. StAB 4,75/7 - VR 191.

10. Compare the reports in *Der Einzelhändler* 3 (Feb. 1920): 56; ibid., vol. 5 (May 1922): 70.

11. StAB 4,75/7 - VR 251; *Der Einzelhändler* 9 (May 1929): 119. Calculations are based on the statutes of the *Landesverband des Bremischen Einzelhandels* and the number of elected representatives from the *Verein der Obst- und Gemüsehändler*. Based on their total number, the largest part of Bremen fruit and vegetable dealers may have been organized. According to Statistisches Landesamt Bremen, *Volks-, Berufs- und Betriebszählung vom 16. 6. 1933* (Bremen, 1936), there were 5,809 retail stores in the city, of which 1,525 were grocery stores and 555 were vegetable and fruit shops. We assume, however, that numerous tiny shops selling fruits and vegetables slipped through the censor's mesh.

12. *Bremer Nachrichten,* 5 March 1932; see also *Der Einzelhändler* 11 (1920): 247.

13. *Der Einzelhändler* 23 (Dec. 1920): 501f.; ibid., 1 (Jan. 1919): 2ff.

14. Ibid., 2 (Feb. 1919): 16.

15. Ibid., 16f.

16. Ibid., 3/4 (March 1919): 33. DDP=Deutsche Demokratische Partei; DVP=-Deutsche Volkspartei.

17. *Der Einzelhändler* 3/4 (March 1919): 36.

18. This precise difference was expressed in debates over the scope of activities and franchise of the Chamber of Commerce. Besides Saur, "Die Organisationen der Bremer Kleinhändler," see Robert Gellately, *The Politics of Economic Despair: Shopkeeepers and German Politics, 1890–1914* (Beverly Hills, London, 1974).

19. *Der Einzelhändler* 3/4 (March 1919): 25f.; ibid., 5/6 (April 1919): 41f.

20. Ibid., 10 (May 1920): 222.

21. Ibid., 11 (June 1920): 246.

22. Ibid., 5 (March 1921): 88.

23. See Winkler, *Mittelstand, Demokratie und Nationalsozialismus;* Peter Wulf, *Die politische Haltung des schleswig-holsteinischen Handwerks, 1928–1932* (Cologne, 1969); but compare also Heinz-Gerhard Haupt, "Mittelstand und Kleinbürgertum in der Weimarer Republik: Zu Problemen und Perspektiven ihrer Erforschung," *Archiv für Sozialgeschichte* 26 (1986): 217–38, which suggests some of the shortcomings of the traditional view and calls for a more expansive perspective of the political life of the *Kleinbürgertum.*

24. DNVP=Deutschnationale Volkspartei. *Der Einzelhändler* 1 (Feb. 1924): 6.

25. Ibid., 23 (Dec. 1928): 353.

26. *Bremer Nachrichten,* 16 March 1928; see also StAB 4,65 - II.A.7.g.

27. StAB 4,75/7 - VR 251.

28. *Der Einzelhändler* 9 (May 1929): 120ff.

29. Ibid., 5 (March 1929): 65ff.

30. Ibid., 9 (May 1929): 119; StAB 4,75/7 - VR 251.

31. *Der Einzelhändler* 4 (Feb. 1932): 41f.

32. See note 4.

33. StAB 4,65 - II.k.1.b.3.

34. StAB 4,65 - II.A.9.b. vols. 2–3; StAB 4,65 - IV.1.c. vol. 10.

35. StAB 4,65 - II.A.9.b. vol. 2.

36. StAB 4,65 - II.A.7.g.

37. StAB 4,65 - IV.1.c. vol. 10.

38. StAB 4,65 - II.A.7.g.

39. Ibid. Heinrich Brüning, of the Catholic Center party, was Chancellor of the Weimar Republic from 28 March 1930 to 30 May 1932.

40. Compare StAB 4,65 - II.A.9.b.4. vols. 1–2.

41. StAB 4,65 - II.A.9.b.4. vol. 2.

42. Compare StAB 4,65 - II.A.9.b.4. vol. 2.

43. Statistisches Landesamt Bremen, *Die Volks-, Berufs- und Betriebszählungen vom 16.6.1933.*

44. Verhandlungen der Bremischen Bürgerschaft (1931), 382; (1932), III, 145.

45. *Der Einzelhändler* 6 (March 1932), 65f.; ibid., special ed. no. 2 (15 Jan. 1933): 9.

46. StAB 6,12 - I.k.10.

47. HkABr C 47.

48. Ibid.

49. *Bremer Nationalsozialistische Zeitung,* 24 Sept. 1933; *Bremer Adressbuch* (Bremen, 1932).

50. *Der Einzelhändler* 23 (Dec. 1930): 277.

51. Ibid., 20 (Oct. 1932): 214.

52. Ibid., 10 (May 1920): 222.

53. Ibid., 5 (March 1931): 63.

54. *Bremer Nachrichten,* 10 Jan. 1932.

55. *Der Einzelhändler* 24 (Dec. 1927): 369; ibid., 14 (July 1928): 14; ibid., 9 (May 1929): 122; ibid., 7 (April 1931): 87f.; ibid., 22 (Nov. 1931): 256f.; ibid., 23 (Dec. 1931): 267.

56. Ibid., 4 (Feb. 1931): 1.

57. Ibid., 23 (Dec. 1932): 241. Franz von Papen succeeded Brüning (see note 39) to the Chancellorship in late May of 1932.

58. *Der Einzelhändler* 23 (Dec. 1932): 241.

59. StAB 4,65 - II.A.7.g.

60. StAB 4,65 - II.U.1. vol. 3.

61. StAB 4,14/1 - XII.D.4 and StAB 4,65 - VI.83; *Der Einzelhändler* 14 (July 1920): 317–21; Ute and Eckhard Brockhaus, "Die Lebensmittelunruhen in Bremen Ende Juni 1920," *Autonomie* 2 (1976); Doris Bollinger, "Bezahlt wird nicht! Die Lebensmittelunruhen im Bremen am 24./25. Juni 1920," BSB vol. 2: *Arme Leute,* pt. 1: *Armut und ihre Verwaltung, 1875–1920* (Bremen, 1981).

62. StAB 4,65 - II.U.1. vol. 3.

63. Ibid.

64. Martin Broszat, "Zur Struktur der NS-Massenbewegung," *Vierteljahrshefte für Zeitgeschichte* 31 (1983): 52–76.

4

A Place in the Nation: The Lower Middle Class in England

TOM JEFFERY

I belong to the lower middle class. From the financial consideration I should limit this to income ranges of about £200–£300 per annum. . . . In a word, the middle-class man must be a "blackcoated worker. . . ." Although I belong to the "blackcoated" middle class, I do not think this classification is very hard and fast. For I belong to another division of the middle class, what I may call the "technologically educated" class.

This division I consider very important—and interesting from a historical point of view. Soon after the Industrial Revolution when Marx made his classical analysis, the "skilled artisan" class was losing ground, and it appeared as though society would divide in the main between the rich capitalist class and the poor, uneducated, unskilled, machine-minding proletariat. But there has been an increasing growth of this "technological class," university or technical college trained; chemists, engineers and so on, as well as the clerical classes, accountants and the like. This technical class does show differences from the working class, and also from the purely "black-coated" section of the middle class. Its members are highly trained specialists, with or without (generally without) wide cultural interests. It is more independent than the "blackcoated" section . . . but it has not the independence and social solidarity of the almost defunct "skilled artisan" class. And it has less power, and more opportunities for power, than any other class in the modern world.

Volunteer Mass-Observer and industrial chemist, aged twenty-four, June 1939[1]

In the last thirty years . . . the demands of modern industry, and the technical schools and provincial universities, have brought into being a new kind of man, middle-class in income and to some extent in habits, but not much interested in his own social status. People like radio engineers and industrial chemists. . . . They are an important section of society, because their numbers are constantly growing . . . and the characteristic outlook of the technicians is already spreading among the older strata of the middle class.

George Orwell, "The English People," 1944[2]

The young industrial chemist was one of hundreds of lower-middle-class men and women who, in the late 1930s, volunteered to describe their lives and opinions for the pioneering social research organization, Mass-Observation. Few adopted quite so analytical an approach when responding to the June 1939 questionnaire on "class"; indeed, many declared that they rarely thought about the issue. But many of those whom we would, by common judgement, place in a "new lower middle class," explicitly and without prompting chose such a description themselves. In so doing, some showed that they were aware of, but uninhibited by, the contemptuous image of the lower middle class as mean little people, languishing between the collective strength of the working classes and the saving graces of their supposed betters. Some, consciously or otherwise, demonstrated such truth as lies in that image; others revealed how partial and distorting the image can be. For they chose the description that best suited their circumstances, citing as indices the factors that most directly impinged upon their lives and drew them apart from the working classes on the one hand and from the established middle class on the other: their work, their incomes, their modest homes in the suburbs, and their educational histories. While conscious of their marginal status, they tended to be more wary of the consequences of rising than fearful of falling in the social scale. And few expressed resentment, still less hostility, to the working class: most felt more ill at ease with "the type of person who . . . goes on talking about 'when I was at Varsity'," or the "yak, yaks," as one termed them. These Mass-Observers occupied a particular social world, that of the lower middle class.

At one level, the Observers had volunteered their services because, in the words of one young bank clerk, they wanted "to help a movement that seemed likely to spread to all classes of people knowledge of how the other classes lived." But in the circumstances of the late 1930s, their involvement in Mass-Observation, like their reading of Penguin Books and the *News Chronicle* and their frequent membership of the Left Book Club (LBC), had a vital political dimension.[3] In the main they had not previously been involved in political activity; most were quite comfortably situated. But in the crisis of the coming of war, many in the lower middle class came to resent the isolated and acquiescent role assigned to them by the National Government of 1931 as the price of social stability, and sought instead to understand the crisis through which they were living and to lay claim to a more active role in political affairs. The majority of the lower middle classes (and a large proportion—probably the majority—of the working class) remained loyal to conservatism throughout the 1930s. But these lower-middle-class Mass-Observers were representative of a resurgence in lower-middle-class radicalism as war approached, clearly demonstrating that the government and subsequent historians could not take lower-middle-class conservatism for granted.

A self-contained essay might be written on historians' treatment of the lower middle class. It would note in passing the recurrent strain of writing that, at times of inflation and labor unrest, has bewailed the imminent demise of the respectable classes;[4] it would pay considerable attention to the ever more sophisticated Weberianism of the 1950s and 1960s;[5] and, while acknowledging occasional challenges, it might conclude that the derogatory image of the lower middle class has been among the most resilient of all social stereotypes, surviving not only over time but in quite different political quarters. Historians' guiding principles have tended to inhibit or promote recourse to this image. A concern with status-consciousness inevitably focusses attention on aspirations and anxieties. Similarly, attempts to identify defining class cultures tend to conjure up a uniform lower middle class often in conformity with the image, and thus to enforce an equation between culture and conservatism. Thus Geoffrey Crossick, in his important work on the Victorian and Edwardian lower middle class, the parents and grandparents of the Mass-Observers, found an individualistic lower middle class, moving under labor market pressures to an acute status-consciousness. That consciousness was in turn consonant with a reactionary but inchoate conservatism. Contained but isolated, presented with political ideologies they played no part in formulating, uncourted by the major political parties, the lower middle class were "offered no foothold on the wider political and social tradition."[6] But while Crossick's account was carefully qualified, others have been less circumspect. Writing on the interwar period, Raphael Samuel found a "grotesque" middle-class culture, fissured by "exquisitely graded status orders" but united by "an acute sense of social deficiency." For Samuel the roots of conservative dominance in the period were to be found in the "cult of gentility" of which the Conservative party was merely the "institutionalized expression."[7] Eric Hobsbawm could quickly dismiss the lower middle class as "pinching and resentful . . . a sullen army of the suburbs and massive supporters of right-wing and anti-labor newspapers and politicians."[8]

The identification of a uniform culture, especially a culture informed by the contemptuous image of the lower middle class, tends, necessarily, to obscure complexities, or, at best, to marginalize contradictory characteristics as deviant. It suggests also the existence of equally uniform but contrasting working-class and established middle-class cultures. There is, moreover, an assumption that structural factors have dictated cultural patterns, which themselves give rise to political reactions (and reaction) in a relatively unproblematic and unmediated process. Thus the political becomes an afterthought, the mere expression of a debilitating culture. Political change must be explained by structural and cultural change. Short-term political change, often incapable of explanation in these terms, must be ignored. In an era of relative cultural and social stability, such as in Britain in the later 1930s, the cultural approach must decline the challenge of explaining the rapidly changing politics of the lower middle class.

That structural changes, in, for example, labor markets, have had a bearing on the politics of the lower middle class, is undeniable. But such changes have always been variously interpretable both by those affected and by politicians: the resultant class "interests" have been constructed—inferred rather than implied. Similarly, cultural considerations—questions, for example, of localism—have influenced the modes of political practice adopted by the lower middle class but have not dictated the content of that practice. It is not the influence of these factors, structural or cultural, that should be questioned, but their predictive capacity. They have framed the agenda on which political forces have worked, not predetermined the outcome of the debate. Moreover, "if the politics of class is not determined solely by circumstance, it is in part the result of choice. Where there is choice, argument counts."[9] In England in the interwar period, the choices made by the middle classes varied over time and at any one time. The nature of these choices must be understood by reference to the political context, particularly the degree of stability in political structures; the always limited range of options realistically available in constantly changing national and international circumstances; and by reference to the ways those options were presented to the lower middle class.

Yet the lower middle class was never addressed in isolation. If the interests of social groups were constructed rather than given, the very nature of politics dictated that those interests should be constructed alongside those of a host of other groups in a wider context: that of the formation of electoral coalitions, of regions and classes, which were a precondition of the formation of parliamentary majorities. After the turmoil of 1918 to 1922, all parties, the Conservatives struggling to contain Labour, the Liberals struggling to survive, and Labour struggling to counteract Conservative party success among the working class, needed to attract cross-class electoral support. To that end, they fashioned coalitional rhetorics in which policies could cohere and the politically constructed interests of their full range of potential support could be drawn together in a wider community of interest. For all parties, but for Labour with varying degrees of conviction, the rhetorical embodiment of that wider community was "the nation": the politics of the interwar period consisted of the presentation by political parties of competing and mutually antagonistic versions of the nation. Meanwhile, lower-middle-class politics, even more subsumed within the politics of the nation than working-class politics, took the form of identifying alternative places for the lower middle class in those nations. In the consonance of those different places with lower-middle-class experience of social change, in their resonance in lower-middle-class lives, in the plausibility of their interpretation of lower-middle-class interests—here are the keys to understanding lower-middle-class politics in the age of fascism, which, in England, was the age of fascism's conservative antithesis, Stanley Baldwin, three-time Prime Minister in the 1920s and 1930s.

In describing the politics of the lower middle class I must, necessarily, allude, elide, and omit in the attempt to set the framework for Susan Pennybacker's case study of a particular group of lower-middle-class activist workers. I shall say something very briefly about the material circumstances of the class. I shall then discuss the reaction of the lower middle class in the period of economic and political confusion following the first world war; the relationship eventually established between the National Government and the lower middle class; and attempts, from the Right, but more important, from the Left, to articulate new, more participative roles for the lower middle class in national political life. In so doing, I shall devote particular attention to the role of the popular press. For if the lower middle class was but one concern among many for political parties, it was the main market target for popular national daily newspapers, which, in the interwar period, were an increasingly important force in the delivery of political rhetoric. Such newspapers, building their own versions of the nation, played a crucial role in identifying roles for the lower middle class in the politics of the nation. Newspapers spoke both more directly and more frequently to the lower middle class than did the political parties: yet here, too, we shall find variety, for the lower middle class never favored one particular title, one newspaper-created place in the nation, to the exclusion of all others.

There was, of course, a basic unity to the lower middle class. In lighting upon income and occupation and their consequences for education and housing, the Mass-Observers identified the nexus of inequalities that defined a core "new" lower middle class of public servants, teachers, bank and insurance officials, technicians and draughtsmen, and many, if not all, clerical workers in private industry and commerce. That core, with incrementally growing incomes, could expect to earn between £250 and £500 a year (when a university professor earned about £1,000 a year and a skilled worker perhaps £4 to £5 a week) and to receive pensions, sick benefits, and holidays with pay in generally secure posts.[10] In the main they were educated at, and sent their children to, secondary schools, which most left at sixteen. Fees at the elite public (that is, private) schools were far beyond the reach of the lower middle class, as were the premiums demanded by the established professions: there was some mobility from the skilled working class to the lower middle class, but the latter was locked into a reproductive mechanism with little opportunity to advance into the established middle class.[11] Yet secure blackcoated (or white-collar) employment did allow the lower middle class to become the major beneficiary of the expansion of consumer industries of the 1930s. In 1938, 66 percent of schoolteachers and public officials earning between £250 and £500 a year owned or were buying their homes, compared to only 18 percent of all those earning less than £250. But once again there were distinctions on both sides: if the core lower middle class had three times as much disposable income after subsistence items were accounted for than the working class, the established middle class spent far more on domestic service and on education, and, on the consumption luxury of the 1930s—motoring—spent five times as much as the lower middle class.[12]

These distinctions were reflected in the lives of the Mass-Observers. If some had lost fathers in the war or savings in the slump, by the end of the 1930s most worked short hours in small offices and lived with parents, in lodgings or in houses they were buying in the suburbs. Few employed domestic servants or owned cars. Summer evenings were spent in the garden as friends came and went freely; summer weekends and holidays walking or cycling in the countryside, drinking in pubs, and staying in youth hostels.[13] Some working-class Observers had adopted such aspects of this lower-middle-class life-style as they could afford. But the lives of the established middle-class Observers were much wider in scope, with university education, foreign travel, more exotic food, a wider range of friends, and a more confident, if not always better informed, acquaintance with high culture.

In these material respects lower-middle-class Observers were representative of the lower middle class as a whole. Politically, on the other hand, they were representative of only a particular section. For the political responses of this core lower middle class, living, by and large, the quiet, comfortable, local lives of the Mass-Observers, were very rarely uniform. Most were not actively involved in politics. Many always voted Conservative, and most declined to support Labour. A very few, very briefly, were attracted by fascism. But before the war the Liberal government and the Progressives on the London County Council (LCC) had relied upon substantial lower-middle-class support, while lower-middle-class individuals had been at the heart of the development of socialism.[14] In the 1920s this lower-middle-class progressivism continued, to be eclipsed in the period of unchallenged "National" dominance from 1931 to 1935, only to re-emerge with renewed vigor in the crisis of the coming of war. To explain this varied pattern of lower-middle-class politics, we must turn to the place of the lower middle class in the politics of the nation.

If the politics of the lower middle class was, in general, shaped by and contained within wider political structures, it should not be surprising that, when those structures were broken apart and reconstructed during the First World War and its immediate aftermath, the politics of the lower middle class should assume an unusual prominence and take on a brief and limited independence. For the middle class as a whole, the first years of peace were a period of unprecedented and unrepeated difficulty and instability. They had suffered a huge and disproportionate toll on the battlefield. After 1918, with the turning point in the summer of 1920, rapid inflation was followed by drastic deflation, full employment by chronic unemployment, and concessions to militant labor by the repression of the labor movement, as the promise of a world fit for middle-class and working-class heroes was revoked.

All the while, parliamentary power rested with a coalition, overwhelmingly elected in 1918, led by the Liberal Lloyd George, and supported by Conservatives toying with the establishment of a new antisocialist bloc. The coalition was opposed by Liberal party followers of Herbert Asquith, former Prime Minister; by the Labour party; by maverick antisocialist press lords; and, increasingly, by diehard and dissident Tories. Within and beyond Parliament, with an enlarged electorate and a greatly expanded trade union movement, the nature of the state, the shape and ambition of political parties, the relative positions of social classes, the role of trade unions, and the influence of both manual and nonmanual workers within their enterprises, were all centrally contested issues. The collective actors in this confusion of forces, maneuvering for position in the attempt to dictate the postwar settlement, sought to enroll the support of the lower middle class, while elements in the lower middle class asserted their own claims to political and industrial recognition. If, as we must suppose, the majority did not directly participate in this struggle for control, those who did took widely different paths.

In part seeking defense against inflation, in part also seeking to gain control over their working lives, hundreds of thousands of nonmanual workers were ready to join trade unions. Disparate and generally weak before the First World War, nonmanual unionism had been boosted by the propitious conditions of the war itself, by organizations that gained strength in the munitions industry, such as the draughtsmen, and by newly formed bodies such as those of the bank clerks and insurance officials. The various approaches they took and the various success they achieved in the postwar period were dictated by the degree of government involvement in a particular industry or service and its often concurrent and consequent rationalization; the attitude of employers; and, quite simply, timing. Those who moved before the summer of 1920 met with some success; those who waited did not.[15] Thus the civil servants, teachers, and railway clerks, encouraged by government involvement and seizing upon the recommendations of the Whitley Committee for partnership in industry,[16] achieved cooperative, rationalized, and national bargaining arrangements by 1920, which ensured relatively stable conditions for those workers throughout the interwar period. The attempts of local government workers and bank and insurance officials to secure similar arrangements foundered on employer hostility: the case of the LCC clerks was the exception rather than the rule. A quite different approach was taken by draughtsmen and clerks in private industry, who, rejecting Whitleyism under the influence of guild socialism, sought direct control in industry. They achieved limited success while employers were on the defensive, but crumbled when the economic tide turned. By 1922, the National Union of Clerks was close to bankruptcy.

Yet the guild socialist unions did contribute to the establishment of the one broad grouping of nonmanual workers to survive the interwar period: the National Federation of Professional Workers (NFPW). By the close of the war the employed lower middle class had become a central concern of the leading theorist of guild socialism, G. D. H. Cole. He had influenced the drafting of the Whitley Report, which, as a guildsman, he publicly rejected.[17] In February 1920, through the Labour Research Department, he brought together nonmanual unions with the object of facilitating the cooperation of workers of "hand and brain" (and thus to prevent any separatist "third party" tactics on the part of nonmanual workers) and of promoting the cause of workers' control. As he told the inaugural conference, if "the technical and administrative skills of our particular class of workers" could be "fully utilized," there was "an amazing chance of making industry and service a really efficient thing . . . of changing the industrial order."[18] Weathering the collapse of guild socialism and of its sister organization in the public sector, the Professional Workers Federation, to which the LCC Staff Association had been affiliated, the NFPW struggled into the 1930s. From mid-decade, as we shall see, it led a revival in nonmanual union activity, reopening, in changed circumstances, questions of the participation of the lower middle class in the efficient management of a planned economy.

Issues of control, and Cole's influence, were central also to the Labour party's attitude to the middle class. The new constitution adopted in 1918, with its appeals to workers by hand and brain and its commitment to common ownership and popular control (the latter being inserted at Cole's insistence), was designed quite explicitly to appeal to the middle classes, expressing their functional importance to any socialist society. Yet this bold departure, drawing on both Fabian and guild socialist concerns, and expressing Labour's ambition to win vital middle-class support, was loaded with irony. For a constitution designed to present Labour as a bulwark against Bolshevism and as an ally of the middle classes strengthened the power of the trade unions at the expense of the Independent Labour Party (ILP), then still a constituent part of the much larger Labour party, and presented antisocialists with a ready target.[19] They seized upon Labour's self-proclaimed socialism, equated it with Bolshevism, and drew large sections of the middle classes into the antisocialist camp. For while so many of the lower middle classes turned to trade unionism in an attempt to gain a purchase on the postwar settlement, many also enrolled in the antisocialist nation that emerged.

From early in 1919, journalists and politicians, particularly but not exclusively dissident antisocialists, conjured up a middle class that, both powerless and apathetic, the victim of its own inaction, was being "harassed out of existence by the after consequences of the war."[20] This sense of middle-class crisis was given most coherent expression by the newspapers of the Harmsworth brothers, Lords Northcliffe and Rothermere, and particularly by the *Daily Mail*, orchestrating reaction against rampant trade unionism and profligate plutocracy, against both the coalition of 1918 and socialism, and promoting the organized expression of middle-class discontent through support for the Middle Classes Union (MCU), the one, short-lived example of middle-class self-organization to emerge in the interwar period. In 1919 and 1920, claiming to speak for the voiceless, for those who suffered while capital and labor prospered, the MCU attacked a web of what it saw as connected evils. It campaigned against anticonstitutional trade unions led by Kaiser Smillie of the miners, against all forms of public expenditure, against nationalism in Ireland, against aliens in England, and against Bolshevism worldwide. By December 1921 there were 330 branches nationally; in a corner of suburban southeast London, six separate branches were established in twelve months, holding regular and well-attended meetings. Little is known about the membership of the MCU, but while some in the lower middle class may have supported its policies, its tone and activities smack far more of established middle-class renegades from the major political parties. However that may be, the MCU probably achieved greater success among the middle class, broadly defined, than any extreme right-wing organization of the interwar period, not excluding the British Union of Fascists (BUF). The organizations' respective relative success and abject failure must be attributed in some part to the very different political contexts in which they operated.

The MCU flourished both before and after the turn from inflation to deflation. It was political change, the break from the coalition, and Stanley Baldwin's reestablishment of Conservative independence that took the wind from the populist sails and opened the way to the incorporation of substantial sections of the lower middle class in a more securely based antisocialist nation. Yet Baldwin's strategy of controlling the reactionary elements in his own party, dividing Labour and crushing the Liberals, was only partially successful. Local Conservative associations, dominated by the established middle class, remained vigorously antisocialist; the Labour party continued to gain ground among the working class, often led, particularly in London, by lower-middle-class activists; the structures if not the strength of non-manual unionism survived; Liberal causes, particularly internationalism, attracted much, especially middle-class, attention; and the Liberal party, reunited under Lloyd George, reemerged as a significant electoral force, splitting the antisocialist vote in many middle-class as well as working-class constituencies in the election of 1929. The resultant minority Labour government collapsed in the financial crisis of 1931. It was only then that the antisocialist nation was fully established. At the October election the National Government led by MacDonald and Baldwin and containing most elements of Liberalism, reduced Labour to a rump of fifty-five MPs. The antisocialist vote in constituencies with large middle-class electorates soared; the great majority of the middle classes were enrolled in the antisocialist nation.

The rhetoric of that election was remorselessly exclusionist. As one southeast London suburban Tory put it, "the alternative to the National Government was the Anti-National Socialist Party, who were divided among themselves except when the questions of damaging the interests and welfare of their country were concerned. Shouting hatred, malice and evil were the only things that bound them together."[21] But we should not assume that, in supporting the National Government, the middle classes shared the bitterness of its rhetoricians. Given Labour's failures and divisions, antisocialist unanimity, and the complete identification of the Government with a coherent version of the nation, the place of the middle classes in that antisocialist nation seemed self-evident. The new coalition was very different from that of 1918 to 1922. It was born of socialist failure, not antisocialist fear. It was presented in rigorously democratic if exclusionist terms. Parties to the extreme right and left made no impact. The choice was, as a suburban newspaper put it, between "National" and "Anti-National" candidates. And if, in supporting the former, the middle classes showed an unusual unity, they were not united in isolation: a clear majority of the working class made the same choice.

Moreover, the nation that emerged from the 1931 election was far from extreme. Laying claim to a place above the merely political, the Government presented itself as the true expression of national consensus and the guarantor of democracy, standing foursquare with other great institutional representations of stability: the Monarchy, the Church, and the British Broadcasting Corporation (BBC). Exuding security, it was a Government that repudiated all messianism and zealotry. It assumed that the middle classes felt the same and wanted little more than to be left in peace. The government demanded no action of the lower middle class and offered no more than security after relatively mild sacrifice. Neither the government nor the Conservative party that underpinned it encouraged lower-middle-class participation in political life. Despite some democratization and the important role played by women fund-raisers, local conservatism remained oligarchical, its leadership dominated by the suburban gentry of substantial traders, successful professionals, and people from the City (in London: the financial center of Britain). But it was closed to the lower middle class. The critical assumption, reflecting, as we have seen, long-held views of the lower middle classes, was that they were politically quiescent and unassertive, that they had no desire to participate directly in the nation's affairs: the middle classes, particularly the lower middle class, were offered a place in the nation on those terms. Looking back from 1936, just as the worm began to turn, the NFPW's President lamented that the "blackcoated worker" had "been taken for granted and regarded as a reliable and pliant supporter of the possessive and non-progressive classes, as one who could be safely utilized or exploited at election times and ignored at others. Unfortunately, there had been too much justification for this view."[22]

Yet if this statement of the middle classes as a political reserve army gave the government strength, it was also, eventually, to contribute to its downfall. The government undertook to provide domestic stability and, from 1934, international security. Should it be seen to break the terms of this contract, the government ran the risk that sections of the middle class would come to resent their supposedly benign neglect. While it seems clear that the government retained the allegiance of the majority of the middle classes—and of the lower middle class—throughout the 1930s, significant groups did challenge the assumption of their quiescence. It is to those challenges that I now turn; first to the quickly contained challenge of fascism, then to the much more important challenges from the Left, which began to prise open the antisocialist definition of the nation and to articulate a version of a nation in which the lower middle class, the blackcoated and the technical elements, would have a far more prominent and participatory role.

Fascism was never a serious electoral option in Britain between the wars. In the 1920s, fascist groups attracted only minimal numbers from the eccentric Right. Sir Oswald Mosley's British Union of Fascists (BUF), founded in 1932 out of the remnants of the New Party, which had been devasted at the 1931 election, made rather more of an impression but never contested a general election. Educated guesswork[23] suggests that the BUF may have attracted about 50,000 supporters from across the social scale at its high point in the first six months of 1934; that it declined rapidly immediately thereafter; regained ground through anti-Semitic campaigns in the East End of London in 1936 and 1937; and, in a further change of complexion, lost working-class support but made progress among the established middle classes in the southeast, campaigning for peace with Germany, as war approached. The leadership seems to have been drawn disproportionately from rootless and disillusioned men and women with military and imperial connections, the disappointed black sheep of Orwell's "lower upper middle class." But at no stage did the BUF command the support of any more than a small minority of any social group, including the lower middle class.

The political fortunes of the BUF must be explained in political terms: mere reference to the relative prosperity of the lower middle class would beg all the questions, not least implying that they were inherently disposed to turn to extreme solutions. Beyond issues of timing, the emergence of the BUF just as economic prospects improved, and the absence of any threat from the Left or any crisis of political structures, we must take into account the political confidence of the higher grade petite bourgeoisie, organized in effective trade associations,[24] and the contract between the National Government and the middle class as a whole. Only when the government was distracted, as in 1934, or wavered, as in 1939, was there a glimmer of middle-class support for fascism. In 1939 the failure of government appeasement of Hitler's demands gave Mosley an opening. In the first six months of 1934 many factors combined temporarily to undermine the government's position: dissent within its own ranks over India; uncertainty over the future of the National coalition; the absence of any centrally organized government publicity; apathy and abstention in the middle-class suburban electorate in the London County Council elections of March 1934 (in part contributing to Labour's victory); a thoroughgoing loss of morale in constituency associations;[25] and the enhanced political prominence of blackcoated unemployment with the passage of the Unemployment Insurance Act (although there is nothing to suggest any actual increase in redundancies). Mosley, supported from January 1934 by Rothermere and the *Daily Mail*,[26] took the opportunity to present the BUF as a party of youth and dynamism ranged against the inadequacies of "old gang" politicians and their enfeebled polity. For six months Mosley and Rothermere threatened to occupy an apparent vacuum on the Right. Yet when a mass rally in Olympia in London in June 1934 broke up in well-publicized violence, Rothermere withdrew his support. Thereafter, Baldwin reasserted himself, government publicity was stepped up, local Conservative associations revived, and the National Government retained power at the election of 1935 with Mosley in his tent, offering only the slogan "Fascism Next Time."

Insofar as the *Mail*, which had done so much to orchestrate the reactionary postwar settlement among the middle class, also played some part in Mosley's brief success, its history and the nature of its readership may, we speculate, tell us something about the politics of the middle class in general and about the impact of the BUF. Even in its heyday—before and immediately after the first war, when it held unchallenged preeminence among popular papers—the *Mail* in no sense encompassed the political views of the lower middle class.[27] By the early 1930s its circulation was in relative decline. By mid-decade that decline had become absolute. In 1934 the *Mail*'s lead in the lower middle class was confined to the provinces, and its greatest impact, at the time of its support for fascism, was on the established middle class in the north and northwest. By 1939 the *Daily Telegraph* had secured a greater share of the established middle-class market: so far from expressing the political outlook of the lower middle class as a whole, the *Mail*'s continuing claim to leadership was confined to its success among elderly, provincial, established middle-class women.

The *Mail*'s support for fascism was a symptom of its more general decline. The paper had lost plausibility, retaining the rhetoric of 1920 in the quite changed circumstances of 1934; praising Germany, which had hitherto been presented as the national enemy; and advocating a hard, violent politics just as the National Government began to set itself up as the guarantor of democracy threatened by alien fascism. Lower-middle-class readers could more easily recognize the worlds of the *Express* and the *News Chronicle*, which played more acutely on their divergent concerns in the late 1930s: the *Express* emphasizing consumerism and escapism in a light, attractive style, the *News Chronicle* articulating lower-middle-class concern about the threat of fascism and war. Both papers had overtaken the *Mail* among the London lower middle class by 1934. By 1939, when the *Mail* reached 15 percent of London lower-middle-class readers, the *Telegraph* and the *News Chronicle* each reached 20 percent, and the *Express* 28 percent.[28]

For at least five years the Left was no more effective than the Right in threatening the National Government's hold on the lower middle class. Labour's internal preoccupations precluded the development of any sophisticated approach to the middle classes,[29] whose future received more attention from the Communist party, particularly in the light of the dominant assumption on the Left that an unstable middle class had contributed most to Hitler's accession. The idea that, beset by mechanization, rationalization, and unemployment, the lower middle class was being remorselessly driven back into the proletariat, had an influence, albeit briefly, beyond the Communist party, reaching many nonmanual unions, including the NFPW. But it was debatable whether it was the middle classes or the Left theorists who evolved "a belief in direct contradiction to reality" and acted "upon it to their own detriment." To the Communist Party, "for the mass of clerks and small administrators under imperialist capitalism," there was "a future blanker and blanker, a cramping life as workers of office machinery, automata"; and only by "taking the path towards Communism" would "the masses of the middle class" be "freed from what is spiritual ruination."[30] Yet, frustrated proponents of the proletarianization thesis could not help but recognize the bond that held the middle class to Baldwin's nation: as one put it, "the middle class man presents in caricature the traditional 'national' characteristics of capitalist Britain; he sums up in himself the narrow, pettifogging outlook, the 'respectability,' the cant, humbug and hypocrisy, the insularity and chauvinism, the combination of practical energy with disgraceful intellectual indolence." As the Communist party later recognized, this facile contempt damagingly underestimated the intellectual aspirations of the wider audience they wished to address,[31] even if it served as a palliative to those few lower-middle-class individuals who in the early 1930s were recruited to the Communist party, inserting them into the proletariat and allowing them to adopt its aspirations as their own.

Lower-middle-class workers did not escape unscathed from the recession of the early 1930s, but they were less severely affected than many manual workers and were well aware of their relative advantage. While there were, of course, marked sectorial differences within blackcoated employment, in general salaries held up better than wages;[32] salary cuts imposed in 1931–1932 were restored by mid-decade and were in any event offset by falling prices. There was some mechanization and rationalization, but most offices, where most clerks worked, remained small and unaffected.[33] There was a further influx of women into routine clerical labor, but this often served to buttress the position of the core, usually male, lower-middle-class worker. Most important, perhaps, opportunities for promotion, particularly in the railways and in the banks, were severely curtailed.[34] Some lower-middle-class young people, including some Mass-Observers, had difficulty finding work in the early 1930s. But lower-middle-class workers in the public sector, in banks, and on the railways, were wholly secure. There were some redundancies among clerks in private industry and in small-scale commercial concerns, but, contrary to the impression created at the time, such unemployment was not new.[35] Perhaps 5 percent of lower-middle-class workers were unemployed in 1931, compared with 14 percent of the skilled and semiskilled, and 30 percent of the unskilled.[36] It was the impact, as much as the incidence, of lower-middle-class unemployment that attracted attention and concern. For salaried workers earning more than £250 a year were ineligible for unemployment benefits: they were left to their own, often meager, resources.[37]

The main focus of the NFPW's work in the 1930s was the campaign to extend social insurance to cover core lower-middle-class workers. Accepting the main tenets, if not all the ideological impediments, of the proletarianization thesis and representing vulnerable workers in the staple industries, the Federation naturally concentrated in the early 1930s on the supposed ill effects of industrial rationalization. But the NFPW was also severely weakened, by the aftereffects of the General Strike of 1926, by the recession, and by the loss of parliamentary spokesmen in 1931. Giving evidence to, and campaigning around, two official enquiries, by a Royal Commission of 1930 to 1932 and a Statutory Committee in 1935–1936,[38] allowed the Federation access to the political stage. Over time, the NFPW turned defense into attack and, abandoning the proletarianization thesis, began to challenge the Government's approach to the lower middle class. For the social insurance system, by excluding the core lower middle class from medical as well as unemployment benefits, expressed and ratified the assumption of a self-sufficient lower middle class, with neither the need nor the desire to participate in collective provision and whose only privilege was exclusion. For lower-middle-class workers were asked to make no contribution to the insurance of others. The system therefore promoted divisions not only between the core lower middle class and other workers earning less than £250 (manual and nonmanual), but also, within the lower middle class, between the secure and the insecure, divisions the Government was quick to exploit.

Some middle-class organizations, like the Over Forty-fives Association, endorsed the principle of self-help.[39] Others, representing secure workers, argued that the extension of unemployment insurance would constitute a further tax on their members.[40] Only the teachers suggested that inclusion would amount to a slur on their professional status. But as the decade developed, the NFPW, working alongside the Trades Union Congress (TUC), secured a broad range of tacit support for an increasingly effective campaign. Government opposition came, not from the Ministry of Labor which, grudgingly, saw the justice of the claim, but from the Ministry of Health, which was conscious that extended unemployment insurance would lead to pressure for the extension of medical benefits and was fearful not only of the financial but also of the political consequences. For the extension of coverage to the employed middle classes would arouse the opposition of doctors and the self-employed and would undermine the vital notion of middle-class self-sufficiency. With Kingsley Wood, Minister of Health and leading Conservative spokesman among the suburban middle classes, to the fore, the Government adopted a strategy of delay and diversion. They equivocated over the recommendations of the Royal Commission; referred the issue to Beveridge's Statutory Committee; incorporated the principle of self-help into the 1935 Manifesto by promising a voluntary pensions scheme for the self-employed, which was brought forward the moment Beveridge recommended extension;[41] and thereafter claimed that any extension would jeopardize the success of the voluntary scheme.

The NFPW's immediate objectives were secured with the change of government in 1940; its wider aspirations, with the implementation of Beveridge's 1942 report. But in the meantime, while the NFPW and its affiliates regained confidence, there had been a more general change in the tenor of the Left's approach to the lower middle class. Socialists as diverse as George Orwell and Evan Durbin insisted that the lower middle class would not recognize themselves as the automata depicted in the proletarianization thesis. Orwell felt socialism had failed to "capture the exploited middle class . . . because of the 'proletarian' cant with which socialist propaganda is mixed up."[42] The Labour party, dominated by Hugh Dalton, began to tailor its propaganda to middle-class concerns.[43] In the light of the apparent success of Soviet planning and in the context of the growing strength of "middle opinion" at home, the proletarianization thesis was jettisoned, and the potential benefits rather than the dangers of technical change were emphasized. The Fabians turned once again to the employed managerial middle class.[44] Individuals such as Herbert Morrison and Lancelot Hogben urged the Labour party to speak to the blackcoated and technical class, whose "numbers and influence" were "steadily increasing . . . contrary to Marxist prophecy" and to command "the cooperation of chemists, agri-culturalists, and engineers; men who have a vision of what human life could be if scientific knowledge were used to the benefit of mankind as a whole."[45] For the NFPW's secretary, "the professional, technical and administrative staffs . . . produced through the secondary and technical schools, the polytechnics and the modern universities . . . are everywhere the key men."[46] Thus the ideas of the early Independent Labour Party (ILP) and the guild socialists were recast in the changed circumstances of the late 1930s, emphasizing the functional importance of a lower middle class as directive workers in a planned, efficient economy. It was not only the industrial chemist and Mass-Observer who recognized that such work-ers had "less power and more opportunities for power than any other class in the modern world."

But the majority of Mass-Observers and of those who participated in the upsurge of radicalism in the late 1930s were drawn in not only by domestic politics but also by urgent issues in foreign affairs and the politics of other countries, the rise of fascism and the threat of war. In 1931, as the National Government was formed, the publisher Victor Gollancz of the Left Book Club had written that "the most tragic thing about the whole business is that the public doesn't appear to want to know."[47] Later in the decade, bewildered not only by the government's inaction but also by rumors of trials in the Soviet Union and the suppression of radical opposition in Spain, many in the lower middle class felt an urgent need to know and to make their voices heard. The relationship between the government and significant sections, if not the majority, of the lower middle class began to break down as many came to resent the assumption that they were not interested, and to reject the government's anodyne reassur-ances and the orchestrated optimism of the press.

The organizations that both met and fomented this concern afforded the lower middle class a politics of knowledge, a sense of participation, and an assurance that their views were widely shared and valued. The radicalism of the late 1930s was certainly shaped by the material and cultural conditions of lower-middle-class young people. Their modest spending power, their educational histories, and their aspirations to, but lack of confidence in, wider cultural and political involvement, predisposed them to a certain form of politics. But there was no proletarianization, no status panic, inducing political involvement. And if leading proponents were on occasion disingenuous, even duplicitous, and their followers naïve, there was nothing "sullen," at least until the shades began to fall in 1939, about the lower-middle-class radicalism of the late 1930s. Many years later, Tom Harrison, co-founder of Mass-Observation, recalled: "In that time of European squalor, 1937–39, M-O at least did throb and felt undefeated. Perhaps this was its peculiar contribution—and why so many people who were young and tortured then think kindly of it today."[48] The same could be said of all the radical cultural organizations.

Like many new industries of the 1930s, those organizations discovered, and exploited with conspicuous success, a new market in the lower middle class. *Picture Post,* for example, sold 1.35 million copies a week in 1939, surpassing even the *Radio Times* among the middle classes in the prosperous southeast.[49] Each nonfiction Pelican book sold on average 40,000 copies over twelve months, while sales of the almost invariably radical Penguin Specials could exceed 100,000. But the relationship between these organizations and their very largely lower-middle-class audiences went beyond the market. These organizations, challenging the government's central assumption of lower-middle-class lack of interest, presented facts and knowledge as inherently radical. They discovered in the lower-middle-class young who, leaving secondary school at sixteen, had been introduced to academic interests and just as soon excluded, a readiness, indeed desperation to go on learning, to gain some understanding of the crisis that was shaping their lives. They discovered, too, a willingness to defer to cultural authority, a readiness to accept the position of the taught. Gollancz saw the Left Book Club as "a Left Wing University";[50] Pelican Books were edited by university teachers and by W. E. Williams, a former secretary of the British Institute of Adult Education. The tone of many correspondents writing to Mass-Observation was that of the diffident student addressing the eminent professor.

But the radical organizations did not, with occasional exceptions, condescend to their audiences.[51] They found value in the lives of "ordinary people of goodwill"; they attacked the ventriloquism of the press, its claim to reproduce the voice of the nation; and they challenged, in a new rhetoric of the nation, the Government's claim to be truly "National." Mass-Observation's most successful published work, a study of popular reaction to the Munich crisis, recognized "the urgency of fact and the voicelessness of everyman" and aimed "to give both ear and voice to what the millions are feeling and doing under the shadow of these terrific events."[52] The *News Chronicle* was the first British paper to carry the results of opinion polls, declaring that "probably the greatest weakness of the democratic form of government is the difficulty of the people in making their voices heard."[53] Beyond this, cultural radicalism also allowed the previously apolitical lower middle class access to new and congenial forms of political involvement, distinct from those offered by the established parties and closer to an older radicalism, if closer also to the opportunistic concerns of the Communist party. Over 1,000 local Left Book Club groups were established, particularly in the suburbs and at lower-middle-class workplaces (including the LCC), offering a full social life as well as discussion of the monthly book choice.[54] Frequently such groups led campaigns, usually unsuccessful, for the formation of local popular fronts. More than 2,000 groups, Aid Committees, Foodships Committees, Basque Children's Committees, again notably strong in the suburbs, adopted every conceivable means of raising relief for Spain.[55] In 1937 and 1938 the London suburbs hummed with the activity of these groups.[56]

Contributing to Mass-Observation was a rather more private commitment to this public cause. But many of the Observers were fully representative of the "men and women of goodwill" whose political outlook was molded by the constellation of radical movements of the late 1930s.[57] Only a few had been actively involved in politics: some were trade unionists, one or two members of the Communist party. The low-church pacifist element was strong, as it had been in the pre-1914 radical lower middle class. Most were deeply concerned at the threat of war. Some, like Orwell's George Bowling, dreamt of air raids, one imagining himself "escaping from an enemy air raid attack over the City . . . avoiding the vulnerable points likely to be targets"; another dreamt that the laboratories at which she worked "were razed to the ground . . . by Japanese bombers—who came over in great swarms flying low." Most tried to follow events in Spain and China but could not trust all they heard. An office worker explained that his views were "those of the *Daily Chronicle,* i.e., I am keenly internationalist and generally speaking liberal (non-politically) in outlook. I don't however believe all they say on Spain." The laboratory worker, describing herself as "violently anti-fascist," despaired at new advances "by the Rebels" but could not "believe anything one reads in the paper." But she, like others, was a member of the Left Book Club, visiting the Soviet Union under its auspices and recording her excitement when the monthly choice arrived.[58] All Mass-Observers read widely, some collecting Penguins and a large proportion taking the *News Chronicle* and *New Statesman.* Their reports record, with a remarkable unanimity of language, tone, and reference, the feelings of a radical lower middle class coming to political involvement as war approached.

This resurgent radicalism began to prise open the relationship between the government and the lower middle class. Yet up to and beyond Munich, many, probably most, placed their faith in Chamberlain and appeasement. Equally important, the radical challenge, seeking to create an alternative to antisocialist national unity, was not itself united. By the late 1930s the Labour party was, without question, the only political force capable of overturning the antisocialist nation. Yet to do so, it required the support of liberal and radical forces to its Left and Right. It was offered that support but on terms that, with reason, it could not accept. For while Penguin Books, *Picture Post,* and Mass-Observation had no formal political ties and were regarded by many in the Labour party as merely "diversionary," the most directly political groups among the radical organizations, the Left Book Club and some of the Spanish Aid Committees, were influenced, often to the extent of complete control, by the Communist party. For the Communist party, "unity" was no innocent aspiration. It had always been a key word: its meaning had however constantly shifted, from the unity of class against class (when, as we have seen, the party's spokesmen so derided the middle class), to the unity of socialists against reaction in a United Front, to the unity of progressive forces (including quite explicitly, the radical lower middle class), in a Popular Front. The politics of the suburbs, in which the Labour party was not, contrary to some subsequent suggestions, wholly inactive, was the site of a sometimes merely implicit, but often bitter battle for the leadership of the lower middle class.[59] It was not a struggle in which Herbert Morrison in particular, Labour's leading strategist in the search for middle-class support and strongest opponent of Communist approaches since the 1920s, was likely to give ground, despite appeals from Stafford Cripps, Harold Laski and others on the Left. For Morrison the Left Book Club was "the cleverest innocents' club yet devised," a jibe not without truth in its ambiguity.[60] The Communist party and its satellites gave impetus and temporary strength to the radical movement in the suburbs but vitiated sustained success: the advocates of unity stood in the way of united action.[61] Even in the 1930s Labour was unable fully to incorporate lower-middle-class radicalism.

Moreover—gradually after Munich, more swiftly after the invasion of Czechoslovakia—the structure of politics began to fissure on both the Right and the Left, in the former case encouraging the reemergence of Mosley, in the latter, ironically, allowing Labour to gain dominance over the Communist-influenced Left, although not without cost in the short-term. Mass-Observation found that, as the real danger of war increased, so large numbers turned to escapism and superstition, anxious to believe the 1939 slogan of the *Daily Express,* "No War This Year or Next."[62] As appeasement failed, so pacifism and (a different matter) groups seeking peace with Germany gained ground: it was in these circumstances that Mosley made some impression on the established middle classes in the southeast.[63] On the Left an outburst of intense activity was followed by growing despair, Gollancz noting in May 1939 "a widespread feeling of apathy, weariness and disillusion."[64] Gollancz himself began to move away from the Communist party. Stafford Cripps and others advocating a Popular Front were expelled from the Labour party. The Communist party began to distance itself from the radical movement, turning its attention to rent strikes, often vilifying Labour council landlords.[65] In the summer, Communists who had taken root in constituency Labour parties renounced their assumed allegiance.[66] The Nazi-Soviet Pact of 1939, war, and the Communist party's reaction merely confirmed the split.

In 1939 Mass-Observation recruited a new group of volunteers, who were, in political terms, more representative of the lower middle class as a whole than their 1937 forerunners. But while there had been a certain confidence in the latter's political comments, by the summer of 1939 all confidence had gone. As one civil servant put it: "I do feel that my generation is growing up bewildered by present day affairs. I know I am. We were brought up to feel safe, to feel that Britain was on top of the world, that her enemies had been finally 'vanquished' in 1918 and that Versailles had settled them once and for all. Now we see things in a different light. The oppressed have become the oppressors."[67]

On the evidence of by-elections, the National Government would have been returned at the general election due by 1940. It was the war itself that saw the dissolution of the antisocialist nation. The appeasers came to be seen as the "guilty men." Cultural radicalism spread across the press, onto the bookstalls, into the BBC and the armed forces.[68] By 1945, after senior party figures had held key domestic offices in Churchill's wartime coalition, and with the Communist party confined to a supportive role after its self-induced marginalization of 1939 to 1941, only Labour could draw together the disparate radical voices that had addressed the lower middle class since the mid-1930s. It has long been recognized that the policies of the wartime coalition and the postwar Labour government owed much to the work of pioneering individuals and groups in the 1930s, some within, many outside the Labour party. It should also be recognized that developments in popular politics, including the rejection of Conservatism by a substantial proportion of the lower middle class, also had roots, again within and beyond the Labour party, in the late 1930s.

In 1945 Herbert Morrison moved to the southeast London suburban constituency of East Lewisham, the home, from 1937, of a particularly active Left Book Club group and, coincidentally, of Mass-Observation. He did so, he said, out of his conviction that if Labour was "ever to secure an independent, stable parliamentary majority, it must gain and keep the support not only of the politically conscious organized workers, but also of large numbers of professional, technical and administrative workers, of whom there are many in East Lewisham."[69] Morrison appealed to "all men and women of goodwill and intelligence and progressive outlook ... to get together on the only genuine basis of national unity, which is ... the Labour Party's basis."[70] The rhetorical tables of the 1930s had been turned. Morrison transformed a National Conservative majority of 6,000 into a Labour majority of more than 15,000, securing some 33 percent of the vote in established middle-class areas of the constituency, about 45 percent in lower-middle-class areas, figures that closely reflected the best available estimates of the national middle-class vote for Labour.[71]

This essay has presented only a schematic account of lower-middle-class politics. It has concentrated on the employed lower middle class, although it is probable that many of the self-employed, for example, the more comfortable small shopkeepers, shared the same patterns of inequality and were subject to many of the same relative advantages and exclusions as the employed. It has ignored regional differences between occupations, although it is worth remembering that the Mass-Observers came from all areas of England (if not, importantly, from Scotland and Northern Ireland) and from all middle-class occupational groups.[72] And it has paid little attention to distinctions between the experiences and outlook of men and women: the contribution of middle-class women and the degree of involvement of lower-middle-class women in fund-raising, political education, and electoral organization in the constituencies, and in Conservative associations perhaps even more than in the Labour party, calls for further study.

Yet a picture has emerged of a lower middle class gaining confidence in the mid-century. Conservative forces had long assumed that quiescence was the inherent political disposition of the lower middle class, which would be naturally supportive of a party offering security and stability. Labour, slowly recognizing the political importance of the lower middle class and assisted in the long run by extra-party forces it eventually subsumed, sought to identify and give political expression to more positive aspirations within the class.

The eclipse and eventual secession of the ILP after 1918 saw the removal of a distinctive lower-middle-class radicalism from the heart of the party. But even in the 1920s there began a gradual process whereby lower-middle-class individuals assumed prominence as activists, candidates, and leaders, and policies were developed that, by 1945, offered the lower middle class a plausible place in a Labour nation. That, in turn, prompted significant change in Conservatism, which, recovering from the trauma of 1945, began to speak directly to the lower middle class as participants in a "property owning democracy." By the mid-1950s, Weberian sociologists of the middle class could conclude that the "new middle class," the class of the administrator, technician, and industrial chemist, possessed a "very substantial measure" of economic and political power.[73]

As the sociologists also stressed, that power was always put to diverse, never uniform ends. It was, of course, limited and, in the era of the postwar consensus, sometimes invisible. It was also exercised to ends not envisaged by the Labour party—as, for example, the lower middle class emerged as the major beneficiaries, as both consumers and producers, of the welfare state. With the collapse of the postwar consensus, lower-middle-class political self-assertion became ever more apparent. But diversity remained: lower-middle-class individuals and groups emerged as driving forces on the Left of the Labour party, in the short-lived but significant Liberal-Social Democratic Alliance of the 1980s and in the dominant form of post-consensus politics, Margaret Thatcher's Conservatism.

Notes

1. Class directive, June 1939. Mass-Observation Archive, University of Sussex. I am most grateful to Dorothy Sheridan and the trustees of the Mass-Observation Archive for permission to quote this and other extracts. I am also particularly grateful to Susan Pennybacker for her help in the preparation of this essay and in the wider work that underpins it: see my forthcoming thesis, "The Lower Middle Class Between the Wars," University of Birmingham.

2. Sonia Orwell and Ian Angus, eds., *The Collected Essays, Journalism and Letters of George Orwell* (Harmondsworth, 1970), vol. 3, *As I Please, 1943–1945*, 36.

3. For the background to Mass-Observation, see my "Mass-Observation. A Short History" (Centre for Contemporary Cultural Studies, stencilled paper no. 77, Birmingham, 1978).

4. See R. Dimsdale Stocker, *What's Wrong with the Middle Classes* (London, 1919); Roy Lewis and Angus Maude, *The English Middle Classes* (London, 1949); Patrick Hutber, *The Decline and Fall of the Middle Class* (Harmondsworth, 1977).

5. David Lockwood, *The Blackcoated Worker* (London, 1958); W. G. Runciman, *Relative Deprivation and Social Justice* (London, 1966).

6. Geoffrey Crossick, "The Emergence of the Lower Middle Class in Britain," in *The Lower Middle Class in Britain,* ed. G. Crossick (London, 1977), 44.

7. Raphael Samuel, "Middle Class Between the Wars," *New Socialist* 9, 10, 11 (Jan.–June 1983).

8. E. J. Hobsbawm, *Industry and Empire* (Harmondsworth, 1969), 277. Hobsbawm has since emphasized the contribution of significant elements of the lower middle class to antifascist movements across Europe; see, for example, "Rebuilding the Left for a New Europe," *Guardian,* 27 Sept. 1982.

9. Charles F. Sabel, "Ambiguities of Class and the Possibility of Politics," in *The Future of Socialism in Europe?* ed. Andre Liebich (Montreal, 1979), 257–79.

10. Sources on the pay and conditions of nonmanual workers are vast and diffuse, but see Joan G. Marley and H. Campion, "Changes in Salaries in Great Britain, 1924–1939," *Journal of the Royal Statistical Society,* Part IV (1940): 524–33. For condi-

tions see Lockwood, *Blackcoated Worker,* and F. D. Klingender, *The Blackcoated Worker in London,* (D.Phil., University of London, 1934), which is both more detailed and more reliable than Klingender's polemical book, *The Condition of Clerical Labour in Britain* (London, 1935), for which see below, note 30.

11. See, for example, Olive Banks, *Parity and Prestige in English Secondary Education* (London, 1955); Kenneth Lindsay, *Social Progress and Educational Waste* (London, 1926); Jean Floud, "Educational Opportunity and Social Mobility" in *The Year Book of Education, 1950* (London, 1950) 117–35; and "The Educational Experience of the Adult Population of England and Wales as at July 1949," in *Social Mobility in Britain,* ed. D. V. Glass (London, 1954). For public schools, see David V. Glass and J. L. Gray, "Opportunity and the Older Universities," in *Political Arithmetic: A Symposium in Population Studies,* ed. Lancelot Hogben (London, 1938). The most exclusive public boarding schools charged £150 per annum, while average fees at county secondary were £11 per annum.

12. Philip Massey, "The Expenditure of 1,360 Middle-Class Households in 1938–39," *Journal of the Royal Statistical Society,* Part III (1942). Massey's study afforded interesting comparisons with the position of the middle class in the mid-1920s: the proportion of the middle-class income devoted to food, housing, and clothing had fallen, while more went to fuel and light (the result of increased use of electricity in the middle-class home) and other items. D. Caradog Jones, "The Cost of Living of a Sample of Middle-Class Families," *Journal of the Royal Statistical Society,* Part IV (1928).

13. For a young Communist clerk's observations on the rites of weekend cycling, see Mass-Observation, Day Survey, 1937, no. 363.

14. See Henry Pelling's comments on the gap between lower-middle-class socialists and the great bulk of the working class in *Popular Politics and Society in Late Victorian Britain,* second edition (London, 1979), 13–14, 126–29. Stanley Pierson noted that the ILP "drew a significant number of recruits . . . from the lower middle class or the 'professional proletariat'," *British Socialists: The Journey from Fantasy to Politics* (Cambridge, Mass., 1979), 18; while in 1910, Keir Hardie wrote, "There are in the ranks of the ILP thousands of what, without offence, I may describe as the lower middle class and a fair sprinkling of the middle class itself." *My Confession of Faith in the Labour Alliance* (London, 1910), 7. See also Susan Pennybacker, "The Labor Question and the London County Council 1889–1914" (D.Phil., Cambridge University, 1984).

15. George S. Bain, *The Growth of White-Collar Unionism* (Oxford, 1970); George S. Bain, David Coates, and Valerie Ellis, *Social Stratification and Trade Unionism* (London, 1973).

16. The Reconstruction Sub-Committee on the Relations of Employers and the Employed, chaired by the deputy speaker, J. H. Whitley, was set up in November 1916 and issued an interim report in 1917, recommending the establishment of Joint Industrial Councils, a recommendation accepted by the Government in October 1917. A second report in 1918 stressed that state involvement should vary inversely with the degree of organization on both sides of industry. Whitley Councils, as they came to be known, "composed of representatives of employers and workers in each industry were intended to discuss everything—not just wages and conditions but participation, job security, technical education, and the improvement of management—'affecting the progress and well-being of the trade from the point of view of those engaged in it, as far as this is consistent with the general interest of the community'." K. Middlemas, *Politics in Industrial Society* (London, 1979), 137. Such councils failed in the staple industries, largely because of union hostility; they made greatest progress in services with large nonmanual work forces, and also on the railways.

17. J. M. Winter, *Socialism and the Challenge of War* (London, 1974), 136–37. Cole

believed that Whitley Councils might provide a training ground for more complete workers' control, disenfranchise nonunionists, and exclude the state from industrial affairs.

18. Cole's address to the founding conference of the NFPW, February 1920. NFPW papers, Modern Records Centre, University of Warwick.

19. For differing views on the 1918 Constitution, see Winter, *Socialism;* and Ross Mckibbin, *The Evolution of the Labour Party, 1910–1924* (Oxford, 1974).

20. C. F. G. Masterman, *England After the War* (London, 1922), 68.

21. Sir Philip Dawson, MP for West Lewisham, speaking in his constituency. *Lewisham Borough News,* 14 Oct. 1931. For a fuller account of southeast London suburban politics, see Tom Jeffery, "The Suburban Nation: Politics and Class in Lewisham," in *Metropolis: London Histories and Representations Since 1800,* eds. David Feldman and Gareth Stedman Jones (London, 1989).

22. George Latham, assistant secretary of the Railway Clerks' Association and president of the NFPW from 1921–1937, at the 1936 Annual Conference of the NFPW, *The Times,* 3 Feb. 1936.

23. Richard Thurlow, *Fascism in Britain, 1918–1985* (Oxford, 1987); Gerry Webber, "Patterns of Membership and Support for the British Union of Fascists," *Journal of Contemporary History* 19 (1984): 576–606.

24. This point is made strongly in Neil Killingback, "The Retail Trade and Cooperative Societies: Some Attitudes and Aspects of the British Petite Bourgeoisie" (M.A. thesis, University of Sussex, 1976).

25. For the torpor of Conservatism in 1934, see John Ramsden, *The Age of Balfour and Baldwin* (London, 1978), 343–44; and Tom Stannage, *Baldwin Thwarts the Opposition: The British General Election of 1935* (London, 1980), 40–45.

26. Lord Rothermere, "Hurrah for the Blackshirts," *Daily Mail,* 15 Jan. 1934.

27. These remarks are based on newspaper readership surveys, undertaken for advertising purposes, of the 1920s and 1930s. See Tom Jeffery and Keith McClelland, "A World Fit to Live In: The *Daily Mail* and the Middle Classes, 1918–1939," in *Impacts and Influences: Essays in Media Power in the Twentieth Century,* ed. J. Curran, A. Smith, and P. Wingate (London, 1987).

28. The Institute of Incorporated Practitioners in Advertising, *A Survey of Press Readership* (1939). The established middle class, Class A, were defined as those earning over £500 a year, with a house in the more expensive suburbs, sending children to private or good secondary schools, employing domestic servants, and owning a telephone and a car; the lower middle class, Class B, earned between £250 and £500 a year, were buying a house on a mortgage, sent their children to secondary school, employed only occasional domestic help, and may or may not have owned a telephone and a car.

29. The most likely advocates of such an approach among the party's younger leadership, Dalton and Morrison, lost their seats in 1931 and did not return to Parliament until 1935, Morrison in the meantime devoting himself to the LCC, which was won for Labour in 1934.

30. Alec Brown, *The Fate of the Middle Classes* (London, 1936), 105, 175–77; see also F. D. Klingender, *The Condition of Clerical Labour.*

31. Allen Hutt, *The Condition of the Working Class in Britain* (London, 1933), 232.

32. Joan G. Marley and H. Campion, "Changes in Salaries."

33. Lockwood, *Blackcoated Worker,* 75.

34. See J. R. Winton, *Lloyd's Bank, 1918–1969* (Oxford, 1982).

35. Thus, before 1914, "clerks were still much better off than unskilled or casual workers in terms of security of employment but they were by no means absolutely

certain of their jobs. In some trades such as cotton, which were liable to sudden changes in trade conditions, clerks were as susceptible to unemployment as other workers." Gregory Anderson, "Clerical Labour in Liverpool and Manchester, 1851–1914" (D.Phil., University of Lancaster, 1974); see also Anderson, "The Social Economy of Late Victorian Clerks," in Crossick, *Lower Middle Class in Britain,* 113–33. Nor was blackcoated unemployment during the interwar period confined to the slump of the early 1930s. For the NFPW's general secretary, writing of 1921, "the most marked problem of the year has been unemployment"; in 1922 he referred to "the scourge of unemployment among non-manual workers." But unemployment among blackcoated workers remained, throughout the period, far less severe than among manual workers.

36. Colin Clark, *National Income and Outlay* (London, 1937), 45–46.

37. Newspaper correspondence columns of the mid-1930s frequently contained accounts of the distress of the nonmanual unemployed, who, "ineligible for the dole, health insurance or transitional benefit . . . their homes gone, their clothes either in pawn, sold or worn out . . . able and willing to work, educated, sensitive, feeling their position terribly . . . sink lower and lower as their means become less, from one boarding house to another, from one furnished room in a decent neighbourhood to a small backroom in the slums." *The Times,* 12 Sept. 1935. For a graphic account of a lower-middle-class worker in such a condition, see Winifred Holtby's novel *South Riding* (London, 1936).

38. Royal Commission on Unemployment Insurance. Final Report. Cmd. 4185, 1932; Report of the Unemployment Insurance Statutary Committee on the Remuneration Limit for Insurance of Non-Manual Workers, Ministry of Labour, 1936.

39. The Over Forty-fives Association saw "no radical difference between State Insurance and the operation of the Poor Law; *inter alia,* inasmuch as whenever a person becomes entitled to a penny more than he himself contributes for, he is thereby to that extent pauperised." *The Spectator,* 24 April 1936.

40. Even the railway clerks took this view, creating considerable tension with the TUC, to which the RCA was generally the most staunchly loyal of all nonmanual organizations. But they, and others, saw their members as pressured from both sides—by their insecure counterparts and by the economizers in government. The May Committee, established in March 1931 to recommend reductions in public expenditure, had recommended that unemployment insurance should encompass the secure purely on financial grounds, so as to bring the insurance fund into balance. Given that they had already accepted pay cuts and taxation increases, it is hardly surprising that some nonmanual organizations saw extended unemployment insurance as a further "sacrifice" imposed on them by the Government rather than as a call for help from their less fortunate colleagues.

41. Enacted as the Widows, Orphans and Old Age Pensions (Voluntary Contributions) Act, 1937. Introducing the bill, Wood emphasized "that this scheme is essentially a contributory one. It is a voluntary scheme. It encourages self-help. The State will be helping those who are helping themselves . . ."; it would, he hoped, "bring a further measure of happiness and contentment to many British homes." Official Report, Vol. 321, col. 399, 22 March 1937, and Vol. 323, col. 1332, 27 April 1937.

42. George Orwell, *The Road to Wigan Pier* (Harmondsworth, 1972), 199. For Durbin, see *The Politics of Democratic Socialism* (London, 1940).

43. Ben Pimlott, *Hugh Dalton* (London, 1985), 238.

44. One week of the 1936 Fabian Summer School concentrated on "The professional middle classes and their political interests." Stephen Smith, secretary of the NFPW, and Evan Durbin were among the speakers; Smith returned to the 1937 school. The Fabians, in cooperation with the NFPW, also organized two London conferences for

professional workers in 1936 and 1938. Speakers included Harold Macmillan, the great proponent within "middle opinion," of planning, as well as Smith, Dalton, and a host of LCC Fabians, Susan Lawrence, Somerville Hastings, Emil Davies, and Barbara Drake.

45. Lancelot Hogben, "Marxism and the Middle Classes," in *Dangerous Thoughts* (London, 1939).

46. Stephen Smith, "The Place and Function of the Administrative and Technical Workers in the New Forms of Economic Structure" (Paper delivered at the British Association for the Advancement of Science, Blackpool, 1936). NFPW paper.

47. Quoted in Ruth Dudley Edwards, *Victor Gollancz: A Biography* (London, 1987), 208–9.

48. Tom Harrison, *The World Within* (London, 1959), 162.

49. IIPA, "A Survey of Press Readership." See also Tom Hopkinson, *Of This Our Time: A Journalist's Story, 1905–1950* (London, 1982); and Stuart Hall, "The Social Eye of Picture Post," *Working Papers in Cultural Studies 2* (Birmingham, 1972):71–120.

50. Gollancz, *Left News*, Sept. 1937, 495.

51. Samuel Hynes, *The Auden Generation* (London, 1976), 264.

52. *Britain by Mass-Observation* (Harmondsworth, 1939), 9.

53. British Institute of Public Opinion, *What Britain Thinks* (London, 1939), 16.

54. See John Lewis, *The Left Book Club: An Historical Record* (London, 1970); and for necessary balance, Stuart Samuels, "The Left Book Club," *Journal of Contemporary History* 1 (1966): 65–86; Ruth Dudley Edwards, *Victor Gollancz;* and the Club journal, *Left News*, distributed to all members.

55. Jim Fyrth, *The Signal Was Spain: The Aid Spain Movement in Britain, 1936–39* (London and New York), 1987.

56. J. E. Morpurgo, *Allen Lane: King Penguin* (London, 1979), 117–18.

57. Some were, as Hynes has suggested "the lonely bored livers of unexciting lives," and turned to M-O for emotional relief: Hynes, *The Auden Generation*, 282. But the Mass-Observers as a whole, and the wider movement of which they were a part, should not be dismissed in this way.

58. Mass-Observation, Day Surveys, 1937, Men Nos. 291 and 263; Women No. 179.

59. John Saville, "May Day 1937," in *Essays in Labour History, 1918–1939*, ed. Asa Briggs and John Saville (London, 1977); Kenneth Newton, *The Sociology of British Communism* (London, 1969), Chap. 6, "Communism and the Middle Class."

60. Bernard Donoughue and G. W. Jones, *Herbert Morrison: Portrait of a Politician* (London, 1973), 238.

61. Ben Pimlott argued that not only did the Left Book Club "not produce a Popular Front it almost certainly reduced the possibility of a progressive alliance being achieved by others," and, taking a wider frame, that "if the idea of a progressive alliance had not been identified as the 'Popular Front' and a central aim of the Communist Party, the chances that it might have been achieved would have been far greater." See *Labour and the Left in the 1930s* (Cambridge, 1977), 161, 202.

62. *Britain by M-O*. M-O estimated that when Eden resigned as foreign secretary in February 1938, 34 percent expected war, while by August 1939, only 18 percent did so. Bob Willcock, "Polls Apart," unpublished typescript, Mass-Observation Archive.

63. Webber, "Patterns of Membership and Support for the British Union of Fascists," 597–98.

64. Gollancz, *Left News*, May 1939.

65. Phil Piratin, *Our Flag Stays Red*, new edition (London, 1979), 41–49.

66. Henry Pelling, *The British Communist Party: An Historical Profile* (London, 1958), 106.

96

67. Mass-Observation, Self-Reports, 1939, Men C191.

68. "Guilty Men" by "Cato" lambasted the appeasers. Cato was Michael Foot, editor of the then-radical *London Evening Standard* from 1942–1944 and later leader of the Labour party. One of the prime conduits for the flow of radicalism into the armed forces was the officially sponsored Army Bureau of Current Affairs, directed by the former teacher, adult educator, and editor of Pelican Books, W. E. Williams. See Paul Addison, *The Road to 1945* (London, 1977), 127–64.

69. Donoughue and Jones, *Herbert Morrison,* 337.

70. *Kentish Mercury,* 16 Feb. 1945.

71. Figures for East Lewisham calculated from estimates prepared by the East Lewisham Labour Party, 1946, London Labour Party Constituency Files, 1946–1949, East and West Lewisham. John Bonhan calculated that, nationally, Labour secured 31 percent of the middle-class vote and 44 percent of the lower middle-class vote: *The Middle Class Vote* (London, 1954).

72. While the influence of the workplace itself should not, of course, be underestimated, it should not be assumed for the interwar period, as may be more plausible for the postwar period, that occupational choice—as between the private and public sectors—reflected political predisposition: before the war middle-class occupational choice was a good deal more constricted and opportunities for public service employment rather more restricted than in the later period.

73. R. K. Kelsall, D. Lockwood, A. Tropp, "The New Middle Class in the Power Structure of Great Britain," *Transactions of the Third World Congress of Sociology,* III, Part 3 (1956): 320–26.

5

Changing Convictions: London County Council Blackcoated Activism between the Wars

SUSAN PENNYBACKER

In 1937, the Left Book Club group of the London County Council (LCC) staff met to consider the position of the middle classes:

> . . . the main attention of the club was turned to the importance of the middle classes in the struggle for the preservation of peace and democracy against the barbaric forces of fascism. It is widely held that fascism has a peculiar appeal to members of the middle classes, but that it was not necessarily so was amply shown in the discussion. Many members of the middle classes have grown up in the old radical tradition and it is only when no alternative to fascism is offered that they will accept that doctrine. Therefore it is up to the anti-fascist forces to show them the alternative, and that can only be done with a united anti-fascist movement based primarily on working-class unity. This has been amply demonstrated in Spain and France. . . .[1]

The "lower-middle-class" Londoner seldom figures as a symbol of inter-war Britain, and rarely in the guise of a Left Book Club reader, earnestly committed to the antifascist struggle. The better-known Oxbridge Spain volunteers or the radical intelligentsia who trekked to European peace congresses bore little resemblance to the activist clerks employed by the London County Council. A few hundred lower-middle-class radicals were part of

I am grateful to Tom Jeffery for his invaluable assistance in the preparation of this essay and in the wider project of which it forms a part. John Mason, Steve Zdatny, Gloria Clifton, and Ian Patterson assisted in the completion of the piece. I thank them and Rudy Koshar for the investment of time and effort. This research was funded in part by an NEH summer stipend, 1985, and by Trinity College, Hartford, Connecticut. LCC archival sources are held in the Greater London Record Office. I thank the Mass-Observation archive, Sussex University, for permission to quote from its holdings.

a work force numbering in the thousands, public servants of the Empire's premier municipal body.[2]

But as Tom Jeffery suggests in the previous essay, in order to explain the underlying dynamic of British politics in the period, we must understand the divided nature of that stratum from which the great majority of LCC white-collar staff were recruited.[3] This essay explores the commitments of a single group within the interwar London lower middle class—those LCC employees involved in several forms of political and organizational activism. Their experiences are interpreted with reference to the period before the Great War. Interwar staff activism exhibited continuities with this earlier period and was at the same time influenced by the particular pressures of Council employment. As the nation's largest municipal employer, seated near Crown and Parliament, the LCC provided a useful laboratory for those of its staff who felt a sense of social mission and conscience, just as it served as a nursery for future parliamentarians. LCC activists were in the avant-garde of lower-middle-class political mobilization between the wars.

Those who purposefully forged, as one of them put it, "changes . . . in their convictions or way of life," were part of an inspired minority, more active and vocal than their political opponents but only occasionally able to muster large audiences.[4] Whereas the exceptional case must lead us to question any monolithic presentation of lower-middle-class life and aspirations, it should not foster new, suspect generalizations. Economic circumstances widely shared among blackcoated workers clearly did not prompt a unified political response. Nor did doctrines of radical Right or Left call forth a mass lower-middle-class following. The political crisis of Jeffery's "nation" was caused in part by the inability of any single creed—labourism, Baldwinite conservatism, the BUF, or the Communist party—to offer a convincing strategy for the avoidance of military conflict and the preservation of democracy.[5]

The assumption held by many across the political spectrum that the lower middle class could and would act virtually homogeneously, according to a Pavlovian notion of political and economic reward, formed a crucial element in the dynamic of this protracted crisis, a crisis only resolved (or postponed) by rearmament, war, and death. The 1945 government offered little consolation to many. However naïve and in some ways banal the English experience may appear in the light of the desperate circumstances faced by activists on the Continent, it formed an inextricable part of the wider European dilemma. And lower-middle-class radicalism in public-sector employment in England and on the Continent shared some common origins. A radical municipal creed of international significance, influential in Munich as well as in London and Paris, formed a part of the pre-1914 social democratic canon.[6]

Prelude, 1888–1919

The London County Council was created in 1888 as the first popularly elected municipal government authority for London. Between 1889 and 1907 the Council was controlled by the London Progressives. Though liberalism was the dominant force within progressivism, socialists also participated in the movement. Fabian Sidney Webb and John Burns, the socialist trade union leader of the 1889 London Dock Strike, both held seats as Progressive councillors. The Progressive program called for radical intervention into some sectors of the London economy—what some dubbed "gas and water socialism" offered relief from the miseries of Victorian poverty still engulfing much of the metropolis. The hope of converting this great city into an enlightened civic realm, free of the worst aspects of *laissez-faire*, of lavishing upon it the benefits of municipalization and a reformed government structure, inspired some of the young recruits to early Council employment to see themselves as junior emissaries of social change.[7] But the Progressives were trounced in 1907 in the largest electoral poll in London's municipal history. A fierce antisocialist rhetoric employed by a revitalized Conservative party machine helped to bring the "Municipal Reform" party to power, and the Conservatives held the LCC until 1934, when Herbert Morrison's London Labour party took over.[8]

The rapid growth of the LCC white-collar staff under the Progressives mirrored the rise in clerical employment across the capital. London was inundated with hopeful clerks and typists, often refugees from provincial areas where pay was lower, the cultural milieux more restrictive, and opportunities less common. Though some lower-middle-class men and women did find respectable positions at the LCC, they faced competitive entrance examinations and a more rigorous recruitment policy than that of most other employers. Those finally hired by the Council were privileged over the bulk of clerks in what was now a severely glutted labor market—too many had come to town for too few openings despite the accretion of jobs that accompanied late Victorian imperial, commercial, and financial expansion.

LCC labor policy, like all of the work of the Council, was subject to parliamentary mandate, and though employees enjoyed a coveted degree of job security, they were dependent on the state and to some extent the electoral process for the realization of better conditions, greater decision-making powers, and "meaningful work." From the 1880s, women were hired within the state sector to fill posts in newly created areas of work. This was not a process of "proletarianization," but the creation of a separate tier of women's employment, often in new clerical posts, manifestly those requiring typewriting skills. Eventually, higher positions were created, and were often construed as requiring special feminine skills.

The proliferation of "routine work," boy labor, cheap women's work, and the regrading of strata that lay below the hierarchy of Council official-dom, all inevitably affected the "quality" of staff recruits. Now fewer public school and university graduates would enter municipal service, while some posts would become exclusively open to them. A more typical male recruit was a grammar school graduate with several years' work experience in business who had spent many leisure hours cramming for an examination that might require him to write on subjects such as: "Is war inevitable?" "the effect of science on literature," or "methods for dealing with the unemployed." In 1906 a marriage bar, already imposed on typists, was extended to other categories of women's employment at the LCC.

The position of male clerks was further reduced by the imposition of a barrier beyond which no automatic promotion took place. The Conserva-tive party that came to power in 1907 instituted this bitterly resented block to mobility; the "£200 barrier" subsequently served as the single greatest spur to staff collective organization before the war. By 1909 the LCC Staff Association had 2,000 members, a third of its roster in 1939. The Associa-tion's activities were recorded in an independent journal, first called the *Staff Gazette* and then *London Town*. A branch of the National Union of Clerks (NUC) was formed, whose greatest success was among the "Minor establishment" men, the bottom tier of the two-tiered clerical ladder and lower-middle-class in composition. These structural and organizational de-velopments became endemic to life at County Hall—the men and women employees of the interwar period faced essentially the same conditions of work.[9]

The frustration induced by the terms of Council employment combined with the radical influences available in London's wider political culture at the turn of the century to shape the first generation of staff activists. But most staff did not indulge the radical Fabians, suffragists, or NUC members. They were more likely to join athletic clubs, the horticultural society, the Christian union, the camera club, the cycling club, or perhaps the Ling club for physical training. Men worried over being able to afford to dress appropriately; women sought an eligible colleague to marry. But even the less political clerks complained of wanting housing nearer the center of London. They found the mediocrity and barrenness of a commuter existence unpalatable.

The day-to-day job routine fostered a sensitivity to social concerns. Tasks like copying minutes of sanitary and housing committees, or carrying out the administrative legwork of social and cultural policy, engendered an acute awareness of social conditions in London and a detailed knowledge of local politics. Those who chose the activist route were more likely to identify with the Left than with the Right, and while on the job many staff members could acquire the raw data with which to substantiate their

convictions. Even lower-ranking clerks were employed to assist in the amel-
ioration of the conditions of London's working class, and their marginal
social superiority over their charges was accentuated by their proximity
to institutional and legislative power. These were all provocative influences.
Among the daily commuters to County Hall intent upon eventually reading
for a university degree and moving a growing family to Surrey or Sussex,
sat the brooding atheist vegetarian who considered himself or herself a
socialist, or the weekend Territorial volunteer who would leave LCC service
in order to bring "enlightened" local government to an African colony.
Single women sought out Council careers in social work, as lodging house
inspectors, guarantors of the Infant Life Protection Act, the Children Act,
the Midwives Act.[10]

A broadly based debating society was formed before the war, in which
Fabian Society members played leading roles. Topics of interest included
the family, poor-law revision, free trade, and various imperial and colonial
issues. Meetings addressed questions like, "Is socialism inevitable?" and
debated the validity of "votes for women." One Fabian staff member spoke
in favor of the creation of an international police force, "combined with
the promotion of international working-class solidarity and the gradual
overthrow of the capitalist system . . . [as] the best means in our power
of fighting and finally destroying the red demon of militarism." By 1914,
almost 4,000 staff had joined the Association, while three hundred participated in the socialist NUC branch. Most white-collar LCC employees, then,
were lower-echelon, upwardly mobile "brainworkers" without decisive
links to the external trade union or socialist movements; but, like Hobsbawm's *nouvelle couche sociale,* many were sympathetic to a broadly defined collectivism implying support for elements of state intervention in
urban life.[11]

The Great War subjected the LCC to widening central government control and prerogative in matters formerly under greater Council purview.
One-tenth of the ten thousand LCC employees serving at the front (including the blue-collar work force) were killed. Those at home struggled to
complete heavy work assignments with fewer resources at their disposal.
Grievances in both private and public employment and the general advantage afforded trade unionism as a result of wartime concessions were reflected in the doubling of the membership of white-collar unions between
1913 and 1920. Trade union density nationally rose from 20 to 48 percent.
The acquisition of conciliation rights by the civil service unions in particular
crucially influenced the bargaining position of the LCC Staff Association.[12]

The issue of army pay was a contentious one both in Whitehall and
in County Hall. When emergency legislation forced the Council into arbitration before a government body, war bonuses were awarded to those like
the thousands of school teacher enlistees who were not earning enough

to support their dependents. But the awards made to those at the front and at home did not allow the many temporary women employees of the LCC to receive the equivalent pay of men. "Equal pay for equal work" was gratuitously invoked as a rationale for discrepancies in pay. No standards of comparability were established.

Staff expectations were only heightened by the Armistice and by the establishment of Joint Industrial Councils in the civil service and in local government—a watershed in the history of white-collar unionism. These were the result of recommendations made by the Whitley Commission, which also proposed a subsistence wage, maternity benefits, and mothers' pensions—the ubiquitous call for the endowment of motherhood was extended and refined in the aftermath of the war. A natalist, family-centered social program was articulated among white-collar organizations, in consonance with the Whitley spirit.[13]

The Twenties

Unlike the civil service unions, the Association was never given representation on the Whitley Joint Industrial Council for local government employees. The LCC sat on the Council without its own employees' being represented! But a "Joint Committee" of the LCC and the Association did negotiate a new pay agreement granting the 10 percent war bonuses, 20 percent salary increases, the abolition of the barrier to promotion at £200, and new wage and salary minimums with bonuses linked to rises in the cost of living. Not all white-collar workers chose this route. Some unions, like the teachers', negotiated absolute, rather than linked, increases. When prices fell, LCC employees, like civil servants, paid harshly for the sliding scale. With the passing of the Whitley ideal and incidents like the dismissal of guild socialists, followers of G. D. H. Cole, by an insurance firm, clerical militancy and national organization increased. Nevertheless, the Association still found a motion against blackleg labor in the coal-mining districts highly controversial, and it possessed no ties to the TUC or the Labour party. While the struggle for a national minimum for public sector workers had been lost, there was as yet little desire to marry the movement for rights and better terms at work to the concerns of the wider labor movement or the Left. And the attitudes displayed by men on the staff toward the equal pay debate of the early twenties showed a marked conservatism in many instances. Women were paid five-sixths the rates of men under the new agreements, a practice justified, many thought, by men's presumed role as breadwinners. And on the 1926 General Strike, the staff remained silent, in noted distinction from many better-off middle-class supporters of trade unionism and the vocal Left intelligentsia.[14]

But a perceptible shift in interests occurred in the late twenties, partly encouraged by national political developments. Women of the LCC staff participated in a Peacemakers' Pilgrimage in Hyde Park, where groups of marchers from all over Britain rallied; an LCC typist was one of the platform speakers. A League of Nations Union (LNU) branch was formed at County Hall, whose purpose was to encourage interest in the League and its goals. Meantime, the government had moved to quell dissent in the civil service by restricting the Civil Service Clerical Association from Labour party and TUC affiliation under the 1927 Trades Disputes Act, reaffirming the ban on party-political activity imposed by the state on its servants.[15]

Given the similar strictures upon activity borne by Council employees in this period, it is perhaps not surprising that sharper debates first ensued on a more "domestic issue," that of the endowment of motherhood. Did the tide turning against war propel women into a more important position in society? Had the abandonment of physical force as a solution to international problems eliminated, at least symbolically, one of the most tangible elements of sexual difference? The conflicting theories of over- and under-population, then sparking national concern and debate, were given expression at County Hall: "Is not the problem of surplus population a fruitful source of war? . . . It is generally agreed that a falling birthrate is not desirable, having regard to the fertility of rival peoples and Empire." Put another way, childbearing could be seen as protecting the nation: "until we have a universal agreement on birth control and armaments, we must regard the child as an asset."

The language of racial superiority and of eugenicism persisted, carried over from a late-nineteenth-century discourse on motherhood. But the recurrent discussion among interwar staff of the "family wage" and family allowance centered on whether innate differences between men and women, signified by childbearing, ought to find recognition in state policy through payments issued for children. The division in attitudes between those who continued to regard women as innately equal if different, or innately different and thus unequal, was slowly superseding a more rudimentary exchange over the nature and fact of women's presumed inferiority.[16]

Anxiety about diminishing incomes was a predominant theme of the twenties in *London Town*. Family allowances represented one strategy for coping with the war's aftermath and the slump, but others included the removal of the sliding scale agreements on wage and salary bonuses, thereby making employees less vulnerable to the Government's calculation of the cost of living, based only upon a putative "working class budget." But the fear of sinking into the proletariat or the fear of women's undercutting men's wages, certainly prompted rather than discouraged some members' organizational zeal. And given a hierarchical pay structure, those men and women in the lower echelon, now called the General Grade, were struggling to meet basic living costs while their more privileged colleagues worried over wages for domestic servants, holidays, and their children's school bills.[17]

Faint references to the international political scene are discernible in the pages of *London Town* in the 1920s. Most of the journal's reportage concerned public sector employment. But in a series on the Italian government, one writer ventured a critique of Italian fascist reforms in local government, while a portrait of the German civil service praised Weimar's creativity and penchant for state interventionism, deeming the Republic perhaps more sophisticated in these matters than England. This admiration for German methods echoed the sentiment of the years before the war when the international commerce of ideas was reflected in activities like an athletic exchange between the Art Workers' Guild and municipal employees in Cologne, abruptly canceled in August 1914.[18]

The Early Thirties

> Not since 1914 have the months of August and September been so crowded with incident nor the social fabric so deeply shaken. . . . Economy has entered our homes. . . . The working of economic forces has already transformed old political issues. Our view is not limited to these islands. It ranges from state to state and takes in dictatorships actual and potential, nationwide planning, and, perhaps, we wonder, whether our day to day interests may not be affected.[19]

In this way *London Town* issued its first condemnation of the serious cuts affecting the public sector in the wake of the election of the National Government of 1931. Before Labour wrested control of County Hall from the Conservatives, the staff challenged the credibility of the "model employer" reputation cultivated by the LCC since its inception. Now the staff journal altered its policy on the coverage of international news, a decision marked especially by the publication in 1934 of "Fascism and the Public Service," featuring a German antifascist political cartoon: "Fascism has been described as capitalism with its back to the wall; when democratic forms of government no longer suffice to insure the dominance of the possessing class, it resorts to methods of violence to protect its interests."[20] Significantly, the article attempts to win the reader to an antifascist view by lamenting the fate of public servants in Germany and Italy, not through a general condemnation of fascist society. The writer cited public service salary cuts, the exclusion of Jews from service, and the establishment of propaganda organizations among employees, emphasizing the invasion of private life by the state and the reduction of permanent staff effected in order to create a lower-paid and insecure work force.

This practice of linking the day-to-day concerns of white-collar workers in England to the European political conflicts was the chief rhetorical device of the debates and calls to action aimed at County Hall employees in the thirties. No longer were issues of promotion, recruitment, education, equal pay, or the marriage bar discussed in hermetic isolation from those of fascism, the Soviet Union, Spain, the Unity movement, or the Popular Front. A sea change in the mode of argumentation and in the urgency of approach employed by activists stimulated an excited response. Each new international event was woven into the language in which domestic issues were voiced.

The preoccupations of the twenties were rephrased in the changed terms of the thirties. When the House of Commons debated equal pay for equal work, the LCC staff once again debated family allowances and the marriage bar. The presence of a Labour Council (after 1934) helped to push these and the equal pay issue to the fore. But an international sensitivity was now evident, illustrated by one staff member's comments on her visits to the unemployed. She had been convinced that women's work supplied the only income available to many families:

> The penalization of such women as want to work has only a flea bite effect on unemployment—Hitler and his like use it speciously to cover their reaction against the women's movement, which is anti-militarist and international. . . . Equal pay . . . has . . . the advantage of being a liberating and democratic measure instead of a repressive one. . . . It may be that my arguments have failed to move you and you will reply by Nordic arguments about Woman and the Home.[21]

Advocates of birth control invoked similar imagery: "Were Britain's billions to be added to Hitler's hordes and Mussolini's millions, competition for places in the sun might become even more acute." Though the welfare of their "own race" remained a concern voiced by all sides, the plea for "free men" and "free women" challenged any portrait of motherhood and the domestic sphere that implied feminine weakness.[22] This altering of political language had many causes. In the early thirties, the LNU branch at County Hall participated in the arms limitations movement, while a woman staff member, Phillipa Fawcett, daughter of militant suffrage leader Millicent Fawcett, served as secretary for the declaration committee of the National Peace Ballot. Sympathy for the Soviet Union was more readily expressed, with returning travellers offering talks. Finally, the presence of a fascist threat at home became a constituent element of this new language. The rights of public servants seemed threatened by Special Branch surveillance and telephone taps. When Mosley's British Union of Fascists was permitted to use the Albert Hall, London Town reported that similar privileges had been denied "to perfectly legitimate meetings of working-class and anti-fascist organizations whilst Conservative, fascist and religious bodies are allowed to continue their harangues unhindered."[23]

The Late Thirties

The LCC branch of the LNU and the Left Book Club group (LBC) were the two political organizations of greatest staff activism during the critical closing years of the decade. Each was characteristic of the patterns of liberal and Left activism developing in the lower middle class nationally, as Jeffery shows. The LNU had members of all parties in its ranks (the Clerk of the Council, G. H. Gater, served as its president), while the LBC was altogether more left-wing in tone and mode of recruitment. Though strongly directed by the Communist party, it was perhaps more catholic in its local operations than that tie might have implied. A third sphere of activism remained in the persistent campaigns around promotion issues, equal pay, benefit structures, and the like. This "internal" activity, as we have seen, ceased to have an existence independent of the motion around peace and the armaments issue, and most especially around Spain. Let us turn to look briefly first at the concerns of the LNU during the years 1936 to 1938; second, at the LBC during the same period; and third, at the efforts of the Staff Association, in order to understand the year of maximum activity and dénouement—1939.

The LNU branch sent delegates to the 1936 Brussels conference of the International Peace Campaign, who accompanied representatives of the English National Peace Council, the Society of Friends, the trade unions, cooperatives, the teachers, and several town councils. Conceived as a means to mobilize support for the League and international peace through "grassroots" organizations in thirty-five countries, the conference was an outgrowth of the heterogeneous movement of social and international conscience bred in the aftermath of the Great War. Enthusiastic participants attempted to inspire those at home:

> On the wide terraces . . . overlooking Brussels, in the crowded lobbies and dining halls, miners, aviators, doctors, writers, textile workers, businessmen, peasants and ex-servicemen jostled one another. . . . Discussions in three languages could be heard at once. . . . Here were people representing millions . . . who were determined to carry that struggle through to the end no matter what changes its fulfillment might necessitate in their convictions or way of life.[24]

In solidarity with the conference, the County Hall LNU passed motions supporting the call for the nationalization of the armaments industry and for its submission to international control.

But of all the foreign policy issues taken up, none seems to have captured the interest and support of County Hall workers more than that of Spain, not least because it was presented as a conflict in which liberal legality had been abridged. A "record crowd" gathered in November 1936 to discuss "arms to Spain." The typical Spanish anarchist was pointedly described in the meeting as "a bitter opponent of Russian communism." Sir Peter Chalmers Mitchell stressed Spanish President Manuel Azaña's "moderate liberal" credentials, while John Langdon-Davies of the *News Chronicle* pointed to the "legal middle-class" acceptability of the Republican argument, emphasizing the illegal nature of Franco's loyalist rebellion. Even the fate of the Empire could be construed as resting in part on a democratic outcome of the conflict, "for if Spain fell to the fascist international, the fate of India would probably be settled by Hitler and Mussolini." This meeting overwhelmingly supported the reinstitution of arms sales to the Spanish government; antifascism was effectively linked to the destiny of the English state and empire.[25]

Practical efforts ensued. The National Joint Committee for Spanish Relief raised money for 4,000 Basque children rescued from the Bilbao area, and the staffs of various County Hall departments adopted particular children, pledging money each week, arranging visits to refugee houses: "After taking our little family of eight out to tea, we all returned, and the children were only too pleased to show us what they could do in the way of singing and dancing. [Of another group it was said] all are well, but would be glad of warm clothes and illustrated periodicals containing Spanish news."[26]

By late 1938, the call for assistance to victims of mass starvation dominated the Spanish relief efforts. There was fierce opposition to the government's proposals to afford Franco belligerent rights and promote a blockade of the Republic. The LNU called for support to the various relief organizations including the Spanish Medical Aid Committee, whose secretary was LCC councillor and physician Dr. Charles Brook. The committee's vice-chairman was the surgeon Somerville-Hastings of the LCC.[27]

Besides organizing for Spain, the LNU spent several weekends in Surrey; one such retreat in 1938 was devoted to the Czechoslovakian question. Referring to the demands of the "totalitarian governments," League supporters opposed proposals to dismiss leftward-leaning League officials, all the while clinging to the notion of a negotiated international peace.[28] They never forsook the defense of the "nation-state" and, indeed, entertained speakers whose opposition to fascism was inseparable from their hostility to the Soviet system. They strove to push the government away from conciliation with fascism and toward the forces of law and order in foreign policy. An eclectic and inclusive society of a few dozen stalwarts, the LNU at County Hall was nevertheless able to draw large crowds for its star-studded roster of mostly liberal-minded speakers. Despite its overlapping audience, the LBC group must, in comparison, have resembled a bolshevik propaganda cell in the making.

Victor Gollancz launched the Left Book Club in 1936 as a project to stimulate regular readings of critical, radical texts, which spawned the Club at County Hall. *London Town* also began to review books like Alec

Brown's *The Fate of the Middle Classes*. Brown's crude Marxist presentation of middle-class history was a revelation to his reviewer, who repeated
Brown's challenge: "You must then find yourself on one side or the other.
Which shall it be?" Pointing to the similar thrust of Klingender's *Clerical
Labour in Great Britain* (whose cover was reproduced in the review, strik-
ingly symbolizing the displacement of workers by machines), the reviewer
described the assault on middle-class and artisanal status in the later stages
of capitalist development, concluding: "Only a bureaucracy, a supreme
corps of administrators, is able to hold fast, as the leading functionaries
in the new marketing boards and corporations, in the civil service, as an
officer class in the police, and in the council's service as importees wearing
the old school tie."[29]

In late 1936, *London Town* also reported on a Fabian conference on
"The Political Needs of Blackcoated Workers," indicative of the growing
politicization of the white-collar trade union movement, particularly in
its left-wing sections. The head of the National Federation of Professional
Workers gave the keynote address bemoaning the decline in status faced
by two million nonmanual workers. Representatives from the NUC and
the Civil Service Clerical Association were among the participants, representing fifty such organizations, whose membership would have been overwhelmingly lower middle class. Refusing to confine itself to the problem
of "status decline," the conference moved the following: "No political
movement can satisfy the political needs of the professional and non-manual
workers without taking the initiative on the basis of the People's Front,
in opposing the foreign policy and rearmament program of the 'National'
Government, in organizing war resistance, to compel the nationalization
of armaments and a Pact of Mutual Assistance with all countries desirous
of securing peace."[30]

Left-wing clerical trade unionism closed the gap between a rhetoric appealing to the special needs of a victimized stratum of "brainworkers"
to that calling for the broader aims of a Popular Front movement throughout Europe, even as it disguised divisions and distinctions between groups
of workers. It is hardly surprising that the LBC found adherents in this
milieu. By early 1937 the LBC decided to meet biweekly instead of monthly
on the basis of its growing support. They learned from Gannes' and Repard's *Spain in Revolt* that the defense of the Republic against fascism
had required the unity of all working-class organizations "and many of
the middle class." Most LBC discussions were directed toward an appreciation of the inevitability of such a unifying strategy. Spain was put forward
as a model for the movement to preserve democracy at home. The group
struggled repeatedly with the problem of what role to assign themselves
in the impending transition to a new form of society, or even in the effort
to fortify the old. George Orwell's *Road to Wigan Pier* was too insistent

upon the presence of a gulf between middle and working classes, according to Vera West, who introduced the book to the group: "The absence of theory or strategy in Orwell had similarly rendered such movements as the Peace Ballot and the League of Nations Union unable to achieve their aim effectively and permanently. The predominance of emotion over understanding which weakens these movements is found also in Orwell's approach to socialism."[31]

Throughout the ensuing months the LBC had occasion to elaborate on its differences with the more moderate and liberal movements vying for lower-middle-class and middle-class leadership, countering accusations against it of being a profit-making enterprise, useless to people of idealistic motives.[32] The LBC became more and more preoccupied with forays into the vicissitudes of Left orthodoxy—pursued, for example, through reading Leo Huberman's *Man's Worldly Goods* and discussing the "materialist conception of history" it espoused, or on a weekend retreat in Surrey spent with the Indian novelist Mulk Raj Anand discussing "literature and politics" in conjunction with Wells' *Outline of History*. In these sessions Anand spoke of the British presence in India, and of "oppression harsher than that which any fascist state can boast"; of a proletariat "existing under conditions by comparison with which the circumstances of Stockton-on-Tees are luxurious." Here the reference is a pointed one: Conservative MP Harold Macmillan's charity relief scheme for the unemployed at Stockton was a project to which the County Hall staff had contributed for years.[33]

The LBC harshly criticized pacifism, appealing to confirmed adherents to abandon an absolutist stance. This discussion paralleled the national rearmament debate, the crisis in the Labour Party over parliamentary allocations for defense, and the dilemma posed for those on the Left already supporting a "just war" in Spain. Controversy also surrounded the perceptions of the Soviet Union. Trotskyist tracts were decried by the LBC nationally, and the County Hall group typically read pro-Soviet literature. Admiration for the Soviet way of life, and a recognition of the improvements in living standards still to come, prompted the assertion that if war were avoided, given the "forward direction of change in the USSR as compared with the unmistakable retrogression manifesting itself in so many ways in the West . . . in a generation's time the USSR may very well stand, in relation to the West as a civilization does to barbarism."[34]

While the Communist party's influence was obviously paramount in the group, that of Labour was noticeably weak. In late 1937, the group criticized Labour's position, its failure to achieve the aims of its rank and file, its social-democratic stance on militarism and fascism. The LBC then came out squarely for the "unity campaign," the Labour Left's latest policy, which called for the formation of a classic united front of the Labour

Party with "the more politically developed minority parties." Though the "unity campaign" was the focus of a weekend retreat, a participant admitted that "most of the time was spent walking in the Surrey hills, or playing billiards and table tennis."[35] This disjunction between political or intellectual urgency and the leisurely and pedagogical character of meeting and reading was not only the product of its supporters' perception of the LBC as a way of life; it also signified their relative organizational passivity in the face of political crisis.

Through a didactic process of study and exposure to living links with the various international events, LBC members had moved far beyond the staff journal's polite critique of Mussolini's and Hitler's contempt for advancement in the civil service. By late 1938, Langdon-Davies was lecturing for the LBC on the present state of warfare and London's vulnerability to air raids. John Lewis, Communist party member and a national organizer of local LBC groups, railed against the pacifists even more vehemently than his comrades had done in earlier years, citing pacifism's failure in both Spain and China: "sincerity of purpose was insufficient, and pacifism was now becoming a menace to those very values which it sought to defend."[36]

However much the nonpolitical or Conservative members of staff may have wished to eject the LBC or the LNU members from their midst, however much they may have attempted to separate work from politics by joining the apolitical or religious clubs of the day (even as their counterparts had done in the 1890s), international conflicts and the workaday grievances of many staff continued to converge in the later thirties. One Mass-Observer unwittingly captured the ironies of the day, writing in 1939 when he was a general grade clerk in the comptroller's office of the LCC. He had dropped out of both the London Armoured Car Corps of the Territorial Army and the local dramatic society in his home in Sutton in 1938: "Discontinued both owing to the necessity for study for examination for promotion to a higher grade. First opportunity, 1937, unsuccessful; ditto, second, 1938. Am now working for third attempt in June." He was engaged to a "fellow County Hall worker," and though a believer, he did not "approve of organized religion"; and of politics, stated, "Uninterested except as regards local government, which interests me deeply. Here I might be termed a socialist." The writer served as a Staff Association representative.[37]

Even the Association was involved in wider political debate, proposing a measure in 1938 for air raid and anti-gassing preparation for Council staff. It joined the Civil Liberties Union, which was leading a campaign against the further abridgement of the rights of civil servants under the Official Secrets Act and other legislation. As the Union put its case: "the rearmament program and air raid precautions are bound to affect public servants not only in their employment itself but in their private activities."

It warned local government officers that "especially with the examples of the fascist countries before our eyes . . . this narrowing of the liberty of the civil servant would not be long in spreading to other walks of life."[38]

In 1937, an opposition group within the Association offered an alternative slate of candidates for election, some of whom were successful in seeking office. The group called pointedly for a "united front" of several national white-collar unions, advocating a freely mixed service of men and women, equal salary scales for staff in comparable positions, equal pay for women employees, and better pay for many grades of workers. This was a wholly unprecedented development and a profound challenge to the Association's traditional leadership. One candidate, typist Maggie Tubbs, had joined the Fabian Women's Group in the 1910s, spoken before the staff debating society before the war, participated in the Peacemakers' Pilgrimage, and served as an official of the Help China Fund. Now the Left had decisively appeared even within the circles of the organization some had always thought of merely as a cricket club or an insurance society.[39]

From early 1939 the LNU strove to present themselves, in a new flurry of activity, as impeccably noncommunist and broadly based in membership. In thanking contributors to the all-London Aid Spain Council, the group welcomed "a response which has transcended the normal boundaries of opinion and party." Speakers came to describe the work of the International Brigades and to report on conditions that had forced women to bear children in order to use their milk to feed starving siblings. Mrs. Winifred Bates declared, "When the women of a nation are forced to do this, it is time for women of other nations to take action about it." With war an ominous possibility, the LNU called for negotiation and collective action and for the pooling of armaments by the league nations. A greater polarization among activists was evident: "Accusations of 'Leftism' and 'redness' scarcely lie well against the general council of the British League of Nations Union, which is largely composed of Conservatives and Liberals."[40]

As part of its effort to reach an even wider cross-section of staff, the League issued a questionnaire on foreign affairs, to which nearly 300 staff replied, two-thirds of these members of the LNU, and 87 nonmembers, one-third of whom wished to join. Those participating did not consider "sacrifices to aggression" as improving the international situation. While three-quarters felt that war would come from "claims against the British Empire," only 7 percent were willing to contemplate relinquishing the Empire to international control. In another clear statement against appeasement, only 13 percent were prepared to concede "democratic liberties and tolerance to avoid war"; only 6 percent felt it was appropriate to call for buying off the aggressors.

Sixty percent saw an alliance of the "non-aggressor" nations as the only hope for peace; less than one-quarter favored British armed isolation. Not surprisingly, the League was seen as the best vehicle for cooperation, though some favored "socialism" or "moral rearmament," a policy that would remove nations and politicians from the role of dictating solutions. The key alliance preferred was one including Britain, the U.S., the U.S.S.R, and France. Most interesting was the fact that 72 percent balloted in favor of "democratic social reform" as a means to prevent war and 74 percent for a nationalized armaments industry.[41]

As if upon a similar quest to reach as many fellow travelers as possible, the LBC presented a particularly useful speaker, Richard Acland, Liberal MP, lecturing on the "need for a popular front." Acland spoke of changing such a formation's name to the "national opposition . . . a movement which would embrace the millions of people of all parties and of no party who see in the policy of Mr. Chamberlain the active encouragement of fascism at home and find in it no hope of the elimination of war." Sir Stafford Cripps, former leader of the now-defunct Socialist League grouping within the Labour party, also spoke (which must have deeply angered LCC leader Herbert Morrison, who supported Cripps' expulsion from the party).[42] The group continued to encourage debate on the Labour Left opposition. Elwyn Jones delivered an attack on the government, pointing to its failure to stand up to fascist aggression: "The strength of fascism lay in the moral weakness and disunity of the democratic forces."[43]

Willie Gallacher, Communist MP, came to speak in a similar vein, for a democratic response to the National Government: "it was the National Government, as the representatives of the big financial houses, which had deliberately betrayed democracy in Europe, and it was imperative that all progressive people in Britain should unite to 'keep the road open'." Despite a new focus on unemployment at home, and the visit of a speaker from the National Unemployed Workers' Movement, who spoke of government failure to cope with the problem of retraining and benefits to those out of work, the LBC would never succeed in helping to foster a broad democratic front against the National Government. Even had their approach become more palatable, time had run out.[44]

Conclusion

When war was declared, *London Town* commented first on the multitude of services being rendered by staff and then on the need for the staff to protect its interests: "to preserve their communal life . . . they will not consent to the overthrow of autocracy abroad at the price of seeing it established at home . . . they will cherish in wartime those democratic organizations, of which the Staff association is our domestic example, which are the guarentee [sic] that freedom and reasonable living conditions shall be preserved."[45] The Association soberly continued to negotiate issues of wartime employment. As early as October 1939, the fear of a postwar slump and the need for vigilance in relation to the cost of living were acutely felt.

The obvious change in tone adopted by the Association between 1914 and 1939 tempts us to conclude that general attitudes among this group of lower-middle-class Londoners had changed decisively in the same period; moved to the Left, experienced a radicalization. But the weight of the argument rests in the lines of continuity that flow from the 1890s through the 1930s. Promotion issues, pay issues, recruitment issues, issues of women's work and pay—all these were raised before the Great War, and none had been resolved in a comprehensive way when World War II broke out, despite the leap that the Whitley machinery had been designed to assist. New layers of lower-paid employees, both men and women, had been added to the staff, and a general rationalization of LCC labor had occurred. But grievances, in the main, still were essentially those common in the earlier period. Public sector work seems to have played a distinctive role in informing employees' struggles, and as time wore on, these campaigns were more firmly articulated in a rhetoric increasingly preoccupied with international affairs. This was a noticeable change, and it came in the aftermath of the war, though it was fueled in the harsh years of the later twenties when the assumptions of returning heroes and those who had waited for them had finally proven far too optimistic.

Staff liberals and radicals and Communists unfurled their banners, and their audiences became increasingly exposed to a language of social reform, women's rights, peace, and democratic values. These issues were seen by the far Left, here the LBC group, increasingly in terms of a class struggle in which the lower middle class would embrace the proletariat. Yet this study reveals the vantage point of the casual readers of *London Town,* the men and women who worked alongside the activists, whose exposure to a myriad of meetings, discussions, reviews, and debates would not necessarily have induced them to abandon the sporting clubs, the Christian Union, or the horticultural society. Nor would the difference between the Popular Front and the unity movement have been clear to the average County Hall worker. But the drift toward war and the urgency of the demands for peace being tossed about surely came across. Widespread sympathies were apparent in a workforce now numbering over six thousand.

The few hundred who passed through the inner circle of organizers and propagandists, who spent precious leisure hours collecting for Spain or preparing polemics on the Kuomintang, formed another layer of lower-middle-class life in the period. What is evident is that few were themselves leaders. These came, especially in London, from the outside, from the intelligentsia and the politicians who came to speak and to guide, or to indoctrinate, as some would interpret it. The optimism and the naïveté, the distance from the trade union movement and the North, all come into focus. Ironically, given the prescripts of the day, framed as "which side they will take in the evermore intense class struggles of present-day Britain," those in the ranks never did take a side so much as they began to form a side of their own.[46]

With the Labour party in transition, and even the Communist party hegemony in the LBC breaking down from 1937; with the League program obliterated by the realities of military conquest; the agitation of this sector of concerned activists grew in intensity, far removed from alliances with a larger-than-life proletariat whose encounters with them had been practically nil. (In fact, the polarization at County Hall was between groups of lower-middle-class people, not between classes.) This essay offers some proof of the potential strength of the lower middle class, the political force that remained unharnessed while the major actors and parties moved ineptly toward war. It further suggests that other case studies of the English lower middle class would be likely to reveal the widespread nature of this kind of activity.

There can be no *a priori* assumption of a uniform lower-middle-class conservatism. But in order to discover how ideas and options were conveyed to those who rejected conservatism, it is especially necessary to give close attention to unheralded collective and individual experience. Members of the intelligentsia and the monied, highly educated middle- and upper-class leaders of the period cannot stand proxy for the interwar lower-middle-class activists any more than William Morris or Sylvia Pankhurst can replace their Edwardian counterparts. John Cornford and Beatrice Webb cannot stand in for the Mass-Observers, or Fabian clerks, or first-time LBC readers. When figures like these are substituted for more anonymous participants, the picture of the period becomes distorted. We are left marching with university students and coal miners from Jarrow to London, with hardly a clue as to where all the shillings for Spain came from.

But once the picture is clearer, other questions remain unresolved. There is, for example, scant reference in *London Town* to anti-Semitism, yet Wickham Steed, one of many popular LNU guest speakers, wrote of German Jews, after all, being too close to Bolshevism for comfort.[47] Did the emphasis on the "nation," even as it was reconstituted in competing versions and visions, be they Liberal or Left, suggest another set of continuities? Were these those of race and Empire, of goodness and goodwill, seen as exclusively English and Christian qualities, drawn nostalgically from an Edwardian chimera? Was the slipperiness of much of even the most progressive language not an element in the failure to reply more urgently to the unmistakable signals beamed across the Channel? These and other questions lie at the heart of a thorough investigation of lower-middle-class attitudes over the long duration. Antifascism was not strong enough in any group in society to allow us comfortably to evade these issues. At the same moment, such investigation allows us to understand the outpouring of social-democratic sentiment in 1945, and the spirit of the electoral alliance underlying Labour's episodic leadership since. The prolific postwar white-collar unionism (which enveloped County Hall as well as many other workplaces), the minority political activism of the 1950s, the Fabian summer schools, early C.N.D.—these, too, share this common legacy.

Notes

1. "Left Book Club Circle," *London Town* (1937): 187. Hereafter, *LT*.

2. See, e.g., Vera Brittain, *Testament of Youth* (London, 1978), 556–60, for her visit with Winfred Holtby to the League of Nations summer school at Geneva, 1922, and 623–47 for her subsequent tour of Europe. The fixed staff of the LCC numbered 3,902 in 1920; 5,026 in 1930; and 6,066 in 1937. (LCC Annual Reports, 1920, 1930, 1937.) These figures do not include, e.g., the teachers, of whom there were 18,150 in 1937, or the staffs of hospitals, asylums, or the fire brigade. As they include only those working at County Hall on the south bank of the Thames near the Westminster Bridge, most members of the "blue-collar" LCC workforce are excluded from these data.

3. "A Place in the Nation: The Lower Middle Class in England," this volume. Jeffery discusses lower-middle-class incomes on page 74: the core "could expect to earn between £250 and £500 a year" during the interwar period. Before the Great War, only those earning more than £150 a year paid income tax; "middle class" incomes generally lay above this line. Maximum male wages in the LCC minor establishment (replaced by the general grade) stood at £156 a year before the war, rising to £208 in 1921, and to £318 in 1929. Women received five-sixths the pay of men in the general grade, while women typists were on a separate pay scale. By 1930, for example, Maggie Tubbs, activist typist, who started at the LCC in 1910, was earning £290 a year. These are approximate figures that mask the barriers to promotion and the benefits that came over time from negotiation. The LCC reported that the "higher clerical class" within the general grade were earning between £255–375 (men) and £200–320 (women) on the eve of World War II. (See LCC, "Services and Staff," 1920–21, 1930; and LCC, "Staff and General Services," 1 April 1939.)

4. "The Brussels Peace Congress," *LT* (1936), 319.

5. BUF is the British Union of Fascists, led by Oswald Mosley.

6. For a useful comparison of certain features of urban life see Anthony Sutcliffe, *Towards the Planned City: Germany, Britain, the United States and France, 1780–1914* (Oxford, 1987). See also Joan Wallach Scott, "Social History and the History of Socialism: French Socialist Municipalities in the 1890s," in *Le Mouvement social* 3 (1980): 145–53. Stephen Spender wrote: "Will the English socialists, flattered into somnolescence by hearing the Tories explain how different conditions are in England from the Continent, learn their lesson only from a punishment which is the English equivalent of fascism?" See *Forward From Liberalism* (London, 1937), 238. This was a popular selection for the Left Book Clubs, read by the County Hall circle.

7. On the history of the LCC, see Sir Gwilym Gibbon and Reginald W. Bell, *History of the London County Council* (London, 1939); Ken Young, *Local Politics and the Rise of Party* (Leicester, 1975); Ken Young and Patricia Garside, *Metropolitan London*

(New York, 1982); and *LCC Centenary History*, ed. Andrew Saint (1990). For the general history of pre-1919 LCC clerical employees, see Susan D. Pennybacker, "The 'Labour Question' and the London County Council, 1889–1919" (D.Phil., Cambridge, 1984), Chaps. I, V. See also Pennybacker, "'The Millennium by Return of Post': Reconsidering London Progressivism" in *Metropolis: London Histories and Representations Since 1800*, eds. David Feldman and Gareth Stedman Jones (London, 1989).

8. See Pennybacker, "The Millennium"; Young, *Local Politics;* and John Davis in *LCC Centenary*, for the history of progressivism and the 1907 election. See also Avner Offer, *Property and Politics* (Cambridge, 1981), for the overall political-economic context in which progressivism developed. See Bernard Donaghue and G. W. Jones, *Herbert Morrison: Portrait of a Politician* (London, 1973); James Gillespie, "Economic and Political Change in the East End of London During the 1920s" (D.Phil, Cambridge, 1983), chap. 8, for a discussion of Morrison's early London Labour party; and Mark Clapson, "Localism, the London Labour Party and the LCC, 1920–39," in *LCC Centenary*.

9. See Pennybacker, "The 'Labour Question'," Chap. I, *passim;* Meta Zimmeck, "Jobs for Girls: The Expansion of Clerical Work for Women, 1850–1914" in *Unequal Opportunities*, ed. Angela John (London, 1986), 154–77; and Zimmeck, "Strategies and Stratagems for the Employment of Women in the Civil Service, 1919–39," *Historical Journal* 27, no. 4 (1984): 901–924, though Zemmick relies heavily on the "proletarianization thesis" in her discussion of the pre-1914 period. See also LCC, Department of the Clerk, "Examination Papers, Clerkships, January, 1905"; for a general study of examination structures, see John Roach, *Public Examination in England* (Cambridge, 1971).

10. See Pennybacker, "The 'Labour Question'," and idem, "The Millennium." The crucial studies of pre-1914 white-collar workers and the lower middle class in England are: Geoffrey Crossick, ed., *The Lower Middle Class in Britain* (London, 1977); G. L. Anderson, *Victorian Clerks* (Manchester, 1976); George Sayers Bain, *The Growth of White Collar Unionism* (Oxford, 1970); David Lockwood, *The Black-Coated Worker* (London, 1966). See also Patricia Hollis, *Women in Public* (London, 1980); Lee Holcombe, *Victorian Ladies at Work* (Hamden, 1973); and Patricia Hollis, *Ladies Elect* (Oxford, 1988).

11. The speaker was Eric Noel Makeham, who was killed in the Great War. See *Staff Gazette* (Nov. 1909), 145, hereafter *SG;* Pennybacker, "The 'Labour Question'," Chap. I; Eric J. Hobsbawm, "The Fabians Reconsidered," *Labouring Men* (London, 1964).

12. See Pennybacker, "The 'Labour Question'," Chaps. IV, V; Bain, *The Growth of White-Collar Unionism;* B. V. Humphreys, *Clerical Unions in the Civil Service* (Oxford, 1958); Alec Spoor, *White Collar Union—Sixty Years of NALGO* (London, 1967); W. J. Brown, *So Far . . .* (London, 1943); LCC Staff Association, *Progress Report, 1909–59* (London, 1959); George Willmot, "The LCC Staff Association: The Story of Its Inception and Progress" (London, n.d., circa 1938).

13. Pennybacker, "The 'Labour Question'," Chap. V; "A Whitley Council for Local Government Bodies," *SG* (Nov. 1919), 151.

14. "£200 Barrier Abolished, Staff Wins in Historic Fight," *SG* (June 1920), 99–101; "Equal Pay for Men and Women," *SG* (Aug. 1920), 139; "Industrial Disputes," *SG* (Sept. 1921), 143; "Whitleyism—A Review and a Warning," *SG* (May 1922), 87–88; "Pay and Equality," *SG* (Oct. 1926), 267–68; LCC Staff Association, *Progress Report,* 34–56; G. D. H. Cole, "Guild Socialism," Fabian Tract no. 192 (London, 1920).

15. "Place Aux Dames," *SG* (July 1926), 187; W. J. Brown, general secretary of the Civil Service Clerical Association, "The Attack on the Service," *SG* (Sept. 1926), 228–29.

16. "Pay and Equality Again: A Reply by P.M." *SG* (Oct. 1926), 286; "Pay and Equality Yet Once More," *SG* (Dec. 1926), 324–25; "Pay and Equality, C.E.D. replies," *SG* (Mar. 1927), 49–50. For the history of the "endowment of motherhood" notion, see Deborah Thom, "The Ideology of Women's Work, 1914–24," (D.Phil., Thames Polytechnic, 1982); John Macnicol, "Family Allowances," in *The Origins of British Social Policy*, ed. Pat Thane (London, 1978); Jane Lewis, *The Politics of Motherhood*, (London, 1978). Lewis points out that in 1938 and 1939, the Conservatives led in the call for allowances as a solution to the problem of low wages and large families. It is certainly the case that LCC staff Conservatives joined in this debate and in the "equal pay" and "marriage bar" debates, as the staff journal correspondence columns suggest.

17. "Letters to the Editor: The Common Cause," *SG* (1928), 90; "Women's Work and Wages," *SG* (1928), 91–92; "Middle-Class Cost of Living," *SG* (1928), 241, re-printed from the *New Civilian*, 19 Sept. 1928; Ellen Wilkinson, MP, "The Office Robot: How the White Collar Brigade Is Exploited," *SG* (1928), 252–53.

18. "The Government of Italy: II. Local Government," *SG* (1929), 269–270. This piece was signed "L.W.," probably Laurence Welsh, editor of the *Gazette* and Staff Association activist. See Herman Finer, "The German Municipal Service," *SG* (1929), 277–80; a preface reprinted from Mulert, "The Training and Examinations of Municipal Officers in Prussia," read to a conference of the Institute of Public Administration, *SG* (1929), 277; "The Staff Visit to Cologne," *SG* (1914), 175, reporting on the recreational exchange between the Art Workers' Guild and the Werkbund Fussball-Vereinigung, planned for 17–24 August, 1914. (The Guild had attracted several socialist LCC architects.) Brigitte Granzow maintains that before 1930, the British press had little to say about the Nazis. See *A Mirror of Nazism: British Opinion and the Emergence of Hitler* (London, 1964), 28.

19. "Economy," *LT* (Oct. 1931), 259; see also "The Axe Falls," *LT* (Jan. 1932), 2.

20. "The Axe Falls," *LT* (Jan. 1932), 176. The cartoon displayed Hitler's body in the shape of a swastika, fleeing several arrows pointed at him. The caption read, "Down with fascism!" ("Nieder mit dem Faschismus!").

21. Patricia Knox, "Equal Pay," *LT* (1935), 241; "Equal Pay and Family Allowances: The Objections Examined," *LT* (1935), 309–10; E. Watts, "The Marriage Bar—Is There an Economic Justification?" *LT* (1935), 313–14; "The Marriage Bar: Lively Debate at County Hall," *LT* (1935), 337–38; citation from letter of D. Ibberson, *LT* (1935), 244. For the history of the equal pay dispute in Parliament, see Harold Smith, "The Problem of Equal Pay," *Journal of Modern History* 53 (Dec. 1981): 652–72. The Staff Association held a referendum in 1935 on the marriage bar and on equal pay, though the former was viewed as more contentious. 1,165 members voted for retaining the bar while 617 voted for scrapping it. Significantly, 305 women wanted it abolished while only 247 wanted it retained. 1,643 voted for instituting equal pay, while 505 opposed it (LCC Staff Association, *Progress Report*, 93). Some claimed the wording of the questionnaire had prejudiced the vote. The civil service referendum on the marriage bar had produced a similar result.

22. *LT* (1935), 337.

23. See, e.g., the review of Archibald Lyall, *Russian Roundabout: A Non-political Pilgrimage* (London, 1933) entitled, "A Holiday in Russia," *LT* (1933), 293; "Letter to the Editor, Where the Workers Rule," *LT* (1935), 334–35; "League of Nations Union, National Declaration," *LT* (1934), 390; Citation from "Letters to the Editor, This Freedom," *LT* (1935), 335.

24. "The Brussels Peace Congress," *LT* (1936), 318–19.

25. "Arms for Spain?" *LT* (1936), 381–82. Sir Peter Chalmers-Mitchell, biologist and zoologist, reshaped the Regent's Park Zoo before his retirement to Malaga; he was released by the "insurgents" on the promise he would not speak of Spain in England, where he instead published several books of memoirs. During the Second World War he was associated with the Joint Committee for Soviet Aid. His works included a translation of Ramón José Sender's *The War in Spain* (1937) and *My Fill of Days, Reminiscences* (1937). See obituary, *Times,* 3 July 1945. Langdon-Davies was a popular writer on anthropology and medical science, as well as a combatant on the Loyalist side in Spain, from 1936–1938. See obituary, *Times,* 6 December 1971. For a detailed account of the Spanish Aid movement, see Jim Fyrth, *The Signal Was Spain* (London, 1986).

26. "League of Nations Union: Spanish Relief," *LT* (1937), 317; "League of Nations Union: Basque Children," *LT* (1937), 414; "League of Nations Union: Basque Children," *LT* (1938), 71.

27. See Fyrth, *The Signal Was Spain,* esp. 46–47. Somerville Hastings represented Mile End in the LCC from 1932–1946 as a Labour member, and was Labour MP for Barking from 1945–1959. He chaired the LCC from 1944–1945 and was president of the Socialist Medical Association. He was an early National Health Service advocate. See obituary, *Times,* 8 July 1967. Brook was also active in the Socialist Medical Association, as were Eleanor Rathbone, Julian Huxley, and Ben Tillet, who had once served as an LCC alderman in the Progressive period. See Fyrth, *The Signal Was Spain,* 47.

28. "League of Nations Union: Week-end at Surrey Crest," *LT* (1938), 267.

29. "The Little Victims Play: The Doom of the Middle Classes," *LT* (1936), 123–24. See Stuart Samuels, "The Left Book Club," *Journal of Contemporary History* I (1966): 65–86.

30. "A Gathering of Blackcoats," *LT* (1936), 349. The PWF was a mass organization of public servants, a product of the early days of Whitleyism, to which the LCC Staff Association was affiliated.

31. "Left Book Club Circle, the Road to Wigan Pier," *LT* (1937), 187. Harry Gannes and Theodore Repard (pseud., Theodore Draper), *Spain in Revolt* (London, 1936); discussion of this text appears in *LT* (1937), 71.

32. "Left Book Club Circle," *LT* (1937), 188.

33. "Left Book Club Circle, Man's Worldly Goods," and "Week-end at Treetops," *LT* (1937), 264–65, which states "the party included a number of members of the LNU County Hall branch." See also "Relief of Distress, Stockton Community Centre," *LT* (1936), 261; "Relief of Distress, Stockton Scheme, Clothing Needed Now," *LT* (1936), 10.

34. "Left Book Club Circle," *LT* (1937), 291.

35. "Left Book Club Circle," *LT* (1937), 414. Stuart MacIntyre offers an analysis of some of the writings of leading Communist party member and theoretician, Palme Dutt, which provides insight into his and other Communists' method in the period: "Particular phrases and sentences are marked to appear, frequently out of context, in future 'Notes of the Month' (a column). Dutt could discern an underlying rationale in the most fragmentary bits of evidence, for in his world there were no coincidences or random events, only tendencies and plots." See *A Proletarian Science: Marxism in Britain, 1917–1933* (Cambridge, 1980), 54. Dutt spoke before the County Hall LBC on "The World in Crisis," *LT* (1938), 205.

36. "Left Book Club," *LT* (1938), 396.

37. Mass-Observation Archive, Life History 1939, H 616.

38. "Staff Association News, Air Raid Precautions," *LT* (1938), 218; Neil Lawson (Executive Committee, National Council for Civil Liberties), "The Rights of Public Servants," *LT* (1938), 227. In 1950, the Policy Committee of the LCC met to discuss

security issues: "Mr. Daines stated that he felt we should have to 'vet' anyone who would receive secret information. He inquired whether it was automatic that all the Architect's Dept. would go over to heavy rescue service, as in the last war, as there were certain architects whom he would not like to go over to work involving security. The Leader stated that he was of opinion that anyone undesirable was well-known to the authorities and would be put under lock and key immediately on the outbreak of hostilities." 6 November 1950 (Policy Committee only), MI5, 1950. I am indebted to John Mason for this reference, illustrating continuing security practices of the sort objected to in the thirties.

39. For a description of the "ginger group," see LCC Staff Association, *Progress Report*, 72; see also "An Election Manifesto," in Ellen Leopold, "In the Service of London" (Industry and Employment Branch, Greater London Council, 1985), 38.

40. "League of Nations Union: Famine in Spain," *LT* (1939), 43. Winifred Bates was living in Spain when the war broke out, and became a journalist, broadcaster, and personnel officer of the nurses, writing *A Woman's Work in Wartime* about her experience. See Fyrth, *The Signal Was Spain*, 104–5; "Foreign Affairs Are Our Affairs," *LT* (1939), 67.

41. *LT* (1939), 185–86.

42. For Acland's talk, see *LT* (1939), 43. Acland assisted in the work of the Aid Spain committee; see Fyrth, *The Signal Was Spain*, 256. He was a one-time pacifist and Liberal MP, and the leader of the Commonwealth Party from 1942–1945. For a recent editorial statement of his, see "How to Be a Party of Natural Government," *Guardian* (17 Aug. 1987). For a lengthy discussion of the Unity campaign, see Ben Pimlott, *Labour and the Left in the 1930s* (London, 1977). Though Morrison was active in the London Foodship Committee to Aid Spain (see Fyrth, *The Signal Was Spain*, 260), he attacked the LBC in January 1939, stating that it had "become a political movement with substantial money behind it" and had gone "in the direction of manipulation and controlling local Labour parties" (quoted in Samuels, "The Left Book Club," 77, citing the London Labour party's *London News*). A bitter opponent of the Unity campaign, he forbade LCC councillors to contribute to the CP press (Pimlott, *Labour and the Left,* 102). Pimlott further notes that Strauss, Morrison's former private secretary, was stripped of LCC leadership posts because of having been a Unity signator and a recipient of Communist party electoral assistance (*Labour and the Left,* fn. 27, p. 225). A. J. P. Taylor concluded: "Now the LBC was diverting highminded school teachers into reading Communist tracts when they ought to have been joining the Labour Party and working for it." *English History 1914–45* (New York, 1965), 398.

43. "Left Book Club," *LT* (1939), 186. Jones later served as a Labour Lord Chancellor and was a prosecutor at Nuremberg.

44. Ibid. Gallacher was the first Communist MP, serving for West Fife from 1935–1950. In 1924 and 1935 he served on the executive of the Communist International. He visited Spain during the Civil War.

45. "The Staff and the War," *LT* (Oct. 1930), 346.

46. See S. D. Klingender, *Clerical Labour in Britain* (London, 1936), 100. MacIntyre wrote of the Communist party: "By the 1930s there was an increasing demarcation of the role of the theorist from that of the organizer, and the principal theorists were those university-trained intellectuals who were fully conversant with Soviet Marxism." See *A Proletarian Science*, 181.

47. See "Foreign Affairs Are Our Affairs," *LT* (1939), for notice of Steed's talk, "The International Situation." In Steed's *Hitler, Whence and Whither* (London, 1934), he stated, "On many points this Jewish defense is cogent . . . in recalling the services to Germany of men like Walter Rathenau . . . doubtless this issue is complicated by

the fact that many Jews have been prominently associated with Russian bolshevism. . . . Indeed, not a few Jews have seemed disposed to turn their backs upon the principles of Western liberal civilization in the name of which they were emancipated during the nineteenth century and to have allied themselves with systems or doctrines inspired by political or economic intolerance. Notable among such doctrines are those of 'class warfare' and of the 'dictatorship of the proletariat'" (pp. 141, 144–46). Steed edited the *London Times* in the early twenties, was active in the League, and was an anti-appeaser. He lectured at King's College, London, from 1925 to 1938 (obituary, *Times*, 14 Jan. 1956).

48. C. N. D. signifies the Campaign for Nuclear Disarmament.

6

The Class That Didn't Bark: French Artisans in an Age of Fascism

STEVEN ZDATNY

It is scarcely possible to deduce certain political opinions from socioeconomic structures. But it is useful to understand a class's political options which flow from its social and economic experiences.

Heinz-Gerhard Haupt[1]

One of the more persistent sociological images of this century is that of the "losers of industrialization," those "little guys"—in farming, petty production, or small retailing—caught in the economic maw of capital and labor concentration, socially *déclassés,* politically casting about for some elusive answer to a desperate situation. They turn away from the liberals, who offer only the "invisible hand" that already has them by the throat, and from a Marxist Left that promises to finish them off for their own good. The fascists, however, vowing to secure the world of small property, seduce them.

Compelling as this image may be in some cases, it fits poorly with experience of France, where fascism failed to sink its roots very broadly or deeply in the political soil. The ground would have seemed fertile enough in a country where the nineteenth century had not eliminated the older social forms, where small farmers, small shopkeepers, and artisans continued to weigh so heavily both in the economy and in the national self-image. Klaus-Jürgen Müller implicitly offered one explanation for fascism's lack of success in France: its strongly modernist content.[2] That is (as expounded by, for example, Georges Valois), fascism was not the reactionary and retrogressive program that would have attracted the put-upon petite bourgeoisie. Müller's idea is logical and fits with the evidence as we have it. But therein lies the problem, for the state of the evidence makes it impossible

121

to specify the appeal—or lack of appeal—of fascism in France. Absent is the documentation about who joined the *Francistes,* the *Cagoulards,* the *Jeunesses Patriotes,* and the other *ligues* and parties; absent too are the kind of reliable statistical and electoral data that have facilitated quantitative study of the social bases of National Socialism. Consequently, work on the radical Right in France, much of it very good, has focused on the persons and the ideas of its leaders: Valois, Drieu de la Rochelle, Charles Maurras.[3] There exists as yet no sociology of French fascism.

I cannot present that sociology here. Instead I propose to approach the question from a different angle. Somewhere in the mysteries of Sherlock Holmes the solution to a crime rests on an inverted piece of evidence: a dog that did not bark. Pursuing that Holmesian insight, this essay will look at a group that elsewhere was grist for the fascist mill, artisans. To be more specific, I am not concerned with skilled workers in an industrial setting or with apprentices and journeymen. Nor will I consider the small capitalist businessman. An artisan is defined as an independent, skilled craftsman, one who combines skill and small property, who works with his hands but owns his own tools and workshop. Between the world wars these tradesmen found themselves increasingly pressed by a "modernizing" economy, most immediately represented by competition from factories and department stores, on the one side, and a series of short-term crises, the most serious of which was the Depression of 1929, on the other. How did France's artisans understand their historical predicament, and how did they propose to get out of it? This essay will look first at artisans' peculiar social vision and subsequently at some of the plans for political reform that sprang from this. We will see that artisans' perspective on France's troubles was not unique. Their proposals often resembled those coming from the extreme Right. In the end, I will argue, the differences counted for more than the similarities.

"The despair of the middle classes," wrote Henri Mougin in 1939, "is already an old story."[4] This despair, however—if that is what it was—had bred not inaction but political mobilization. Geoffrey Crossick points out the existence of a "petit-bourgeois international" even before the first world war. The French *Association de Défense des Classes Moyennes* was founded in 1907.[5] It was therefore not without precedent that in March 1922 representatives of several dozen artisanal groups convened in Paris in order to put together the General Confederation of French Artisans (CGAF). "En avant!" cheered the Lyon journal, *L'Artisan:* "We have the numbers, we have the strength."[6] The militants saw their activism as the beginning of an artisanal renaissance in France. To be sure, skilled tradesmen such as tailors, carpenters, glass-blowers, blacksmiths, masons, cobblers, etc., had long recognized their differences both with unskilled workers and with capitalist employers and had joined together in unions *(syndicats)* and federations. The creation of the CGAF, however, signaled an important shift in perspective from Trade to Class, and reflected the new idea that all those who shared the facts of productive skill and limited property—the Artisanat, as it came to be called—had a common social interest transcending the differences between, say, a plumber in Lille and a wheelwright in the back country of the Dordogne.

The second CGAF congress in Bordeaux, in the spring of 1923, laid out the program of the new Confederation in its so-called Artisanal Charter. The Charter presented the Artisanat as a *tampon social,* a social buffer in a troubled, tumultuous time, as a group based on the quality of work, on individualism, and on regional diversity.[7] The Charter was general enough and rhetorical enough to please all the parties to the CGAF; but this unity was deceptive. Despite the headiness of the initial congress in 1922 and of the even bigger one in Bordeaux, a political and organizational fault ran through the middle of the new Confederation. On one side of the movement was a corporatist and regionalist tendency, defended by the Chamber of Trades of the recently returned province of Alsace. On the other, a syndicalist and centralizing approach to artisanal politics found its champions in the Shoemakers' Federation *(Fédération de la Petite Industrie de Chaussure),* based in Paris and led by two militant syndicalists, Robert Tailledet and Georges Grandadam, who hoped to make the CGAF an artisanal analogue of the General Confederation of Labor (CGT), the most important trade-union organization. Leaders of the two wings had managed to find enough common ground to launch the artisanal movement in 1922, yet deep divisions over style and tactics (which will become clear) soon caused the movement to fracture, and continuing efforts to reunite it were unsuccessful. Nevertheless, throughout the twenties the movement continued to grow in membership and influence. By the mid-1930s it had attracted some half-million artisans and been accorded representation in many of the key councils and commissions of the French administration— the National Economic Council, for example.

Despite the multiplication of groups and the frequent quarrels between corporatists and syndicalists, regionalists and centralizers, the world view of the artisanal movement was remarkably homogeneous. At its center was the Profession, "the human activity . . . productive as opposed to speculative . . . manual, full of personality, as opposed to anonymous, mechanical, and schematized."[8] For corporatists, who believed in the possibility of complete social harmony, the profession—the shared skill and holistic labor experience—was the glue of the artisanat; the social fluidity leading from apprentice to journeyman to master meant the absence of fixed boundaries necessary to class formation. It bound employers to workers and united masters of vastly different means. At the same time it erected a barrier between artisans and the proletarians and nonlaboring bourgeois of industrial capitalism. The syndicalists also placed the profession at the hub of their political sociology. "When a man exercises a profession for a long time," claimed Tailledet, "it gives him a certain turn of the spirit, a manner of being and of feeling that situates him, that classifies him, that places him definitively in the world."[9]

Defense of the profession always went hand in hand with that of the family, "an island of order in our world in disarray; a 'land of liberty' closed to directed and aggressive proletarianization." Ask a shoemaker, carpenter, or mechanic why he wanted to be an artisan, suggested the *Artisan de l'Ouest,* and he would reply: "Because I have to live and make a living for my family."[10] It was not always true that the artisanal workshop was primarily a family enterprise, with the wife keeping the books and minding the store, the children sweeping up and collecting bits of loose material while they learned their skills at their father's side. In some trades—baking, for instance—the family did form a productive unit; in others it did not. The size of a business mattered, too. Small businesses depended more on family labor than those with a greater number of journeymen.[11] The movement nonetheless identified the interests of the artisanat with those of the family, both practically and morally. "The artisan works at home," wrote Jean Delage. "He has his shop, his hearth. Marriage for him is the foundation of his trade. His wife will be his helpmate; his children, too. The more children, the more *compagnons,* and the more his enterprise will prosper."[12] Given this emphasis on home and family, it is clear why several of the movement's leaders involved themselves in the crusade to increase French natality. In 1937 a group of mostly Breton artisans, led by Pierre Manoury and with the support of the Church, launched the *Confédération de l'Artisanat familiale* (CAF). In Normandy, Albert Dupuis, goldsmith, president of the Chamber of Trades of the Seine-Inférieure and of the Assembly of Presidents of Chambers of Trades (APCMF), was at the same time, chairman of the *Ligue des familles nombreuses* of Rouen. Dupuis saw the family not only as the basis of a "healthy and happy existence," but also "still the best guarantee against revolution."[13]

As artisans' support for the family was socially conservative it was also patriarchal. Tens of thousands of *artisanes* might work in hatmaking, dressmaking, and the other so-called "professions féminines." A wife might support her husband in the shop, or a widow continue to run the business when her husband was called to the Eternal Workshop, but her role always remained subordinate. Though Delage claimed, "We must defend the female artisanat," he also counseled that, "women must develop aptitudes consistent with the direction of their nature without seeking to imitate men. Their role in the progress of civilization is higher than the men's. They

must not abandon it."[14] Similarly, "Grand'mère," frequent columnist for
L'Artisan (Le Puy), wrote: "The role of the wife is of great importance.
She is the soul of the household." Behind a successful business, she continued, is a home, well-run—not necessarily in luxury, but efficiently and
"even with a bit of *coquetterie*."[15] Conversely, she observed, "Nothing is
more grotesque than a business about which it can be said vulgarly: 'It's
the woman who wears the pants.'"[16] For women, accordingly, "Grand'-
mère" came down firmly for obedience and against the vote.[17]

Perceiving that the survival of the artisanat depended on the strength
of the family and the traditional "duties" of its members, artisans were
led to denounce as immoral or decadent whatever threatened this delicate
sexual division of labor. Fear of immorality and decadence often translated
into concern about the "crise rurale" and demonization of the city, with
its "influence délátaire" on the nation[18]—a center, not only of factories,
but of "cinemas, dancing, and other dens of germs and diversions."[19] Lucien
Gelly, a longtime ally of the artisanal movement and one of Vichy's philoso-
phers of rusticism, deplored the tendency for young women to leave the
countryside for the towns where they would be tempted by consumer goods
and by the "possibility of an easier promiscuity." Naturally enough, he
pined in a brief venture into sexual demography, "The young girls having
left, the young men follow them."[20] Artisanal commentators looked with
horror on the prospect that wives and daughters might leave the home
to become factory workers, salesgirls in department stores, or office secretaries, for this implied the disintegration of the most fundamental of artisanal institutions.

The novels and journals of the artisanal movement were filled with a
romantic portrayal of the "true" artisan: independent, honest, hard working, disdainful of the materialism of urban industrial culture—a French
version of the cowboy. In Isabelle Dudit's didactic novel, *Marbréry: Maître-
Artisan*, for example, the hero, Jean Marbréry, son of Antoine, a carpenter,
inherits his father's small workshop. Diligent, talented, devoted to his family
and community, Jean soon finds himself with five assistants and three apprentices. A friend suggests to Jean that he ought to expand his business
and become a genuine entrepreneur instead of an artisan-patron, but Jean
demurs: "What?! A factory? So it won't matter how the work is done
or who does it? No. I love my trade, and I love my responsibilities. I
leave to others the profits of mass production. Me, I'm satisfied with a
job well done."[21]

The transition from workshop to small factory, in effect from artisan
to small capitalist, was more than a matter of the number of workers
and the division of labor. It implied the use of machinery, and this presented
artisans with a dilemma. As far as the success of the individual craftsman
rested on manual skill, a measured suspicion of the machine made sense.

"The triumph of the machine will lead to worldwide disaster," wrote one commentator.[22] This was a minority view within the movement, yet the issue of mechanization always left artisans ambivalent.

This wariness of technology is nicely conveyed by a story told in Adelaïde Blasquez' *Gaston Lucas, sérrurier: chronique de l'anti-héro*. Gaston remembers how his grandfather, a gardener, reacted to the installation of electricity in his house: "Never! I don't want anything to do with your so-called progress. Progress is going to kill you all. It will cut off your arms; you won't be able to work anymore. Machines will do everything. They'll replace you and you'll be worthless." And later, when Gaston tells his father that he wants to begin an apprenticeship as an electrician, Dad expresses his skepticism: "Electricity? Why, that's no profession. . . . Don't you realize what wonderful opportunities there are for locksmiths? Now that's a secure trade. The world will always need locksmiths, but as for electricity. . . ."[23]

In the real economic world, however, a too-sincere traditionalism was a recipe for disaster. For if technological change had historically brought with it the degradation of skill and the centralization of production, innovations such as electricity and the internal combustion engine—to take only the two prime examples—allowed the workshop to increase its productivity markedly, if not necessarily to compete with the factory. Thus the leaders of the artisanat, while they might have longed for the preindustrial past, also took care to recommend modern business and production methods. *L'Artisan* of Lyon, which began as the organ of blacksmiths, farriers, and wheelwrights in the southeast, encouraged its readers to use gasoline engines and electricity in their work and to keep careful account books. Indeed, it remarked, the blacksmith already practices Taylorism; he just calls it "economy of time."[24] The CGAF showed particular concern with the technological development of the artisanat. At its offices in Paris, the "Cité Clémentel" (named for the Confederation's early patron, former commerce minister and senator Étienne Clémentel), the Confederation installed "model workshops," and in 1931 set up the *Institut National des Métiers* (INM), with the aim of promoting collaboration between technicians and workers, between men of the liberal professions and men of trades.[25] Both the CGAF's biweekly *Artisan Français* and the INM's monthly *Cahiers de l'Artisanat* published regular articles with suggestions about improving techniques and bookkeeping. The journals and congresses of the other artisanal organizations likewise directed their attention to the modernization of petty production. Within the artisanat, therefore, the workshop of the future coexisted uneasily with the workshop of the past.

It was inevitable that artisans' social conservatism and moralism would spill over into their political philosophy, the kernel of which was a longing for a past in which the tradesman was better trained, professionally secure, and more respected. The artisanal movement conceived of itself as the defender of class under attack. Its ideology and politics were in large part a self-conscious opposition to the progress of industrialism and to the political economies of liberalism and Marxism, both of which, the artisanal press never tired of reminding its readers, assumed the imminent disappearance of the small, independent producer. What had these modern philosophies brought France, and what were they likely to bring in the future? Social atomization and economic anarchy: a world of "professional incompetence," with "tailors who can't sew and masons [who can't] build."[26]

It has been said that behind every economic theory is a metaphysic, and for the artisanal movement it was the so-called moral economy. In a characteristically artisanal fashion Tailledet equated public and private finances: "Public finances are only the reflection of the situation of private finances." The financial health of a country, he added, rests on savings and on the "multiplicity of personally run businesses."[27] Artisans claimed not to be anticapitalist. The workshop as well as the factory lived by private property and profits, but by reasonable profits, honestly earned. What artisans condemned, rather, was capitalism without morality and production without humanity. They therefore distinguished between "productive" and "speculative" capital. Speaking at an artisanal congress in 1936, Prosper Convert offered this comparison: "[Artisanal enterprises] are subject to and follow the . . . natural law of supply and demand. Their profit is but the legitimate remuneration of the work of transformation carried out on the merchandise, [whereas] big businesses, organized in trusts, form a consortium powerful enough to affect prices. Their profit is always speculative."[28]

In a similar vein, assessing responsibility for the economic crisis of the mid-twenties, the *Artisan Français* pointed the finger at "the money merchants who make their livings by so inflating the economy." Wrote Tailledet:

> Circulation, it is said, creates wealth. But this circulation re-creates always the same wealth—a ruinous parasitism for the [real] producers. It is thus of the greatest urgency that we get rid of the web of finance capital in which we struggle and that we eliminate it from all areas of national activity. We must then turn to all those who work and produce, for it is through them and through them alone that the financial stabilization of our country can be achieved.[29]

Responsibility for moral and social decline lay chiefly with industrialization—not simply the machine, but the complete division of labor and mass production that the worker felt as the "amputation de sa personne morale." In its journals and monographs, and in its appeal to the public authorities, the movement elaborated a theory of alienation, based on the psychological effects of the factory. What does modern production mean? asked Georges Chaudieu, president of the butchers' federation and later Vichy functionary.

"Monotony, standardized taste . . . lack of human contact." So unlike the artisan, he continued, who works with "a grain of friendliness, a smile, expressions of humanity and the joy of living."[30] This was where artisans found the germ of class conflict—in the profoundly unsatisfying nature of pure machine-work, on the one hand, and in ownership without social responsibility, on the other. In response, they offered their own situations as the model of social harmony and national salvation: "If the spirit of France can be regenerated, it will be by the Artisan, by the petty patron, united with his worker."[31]

From its beginnings, therefore, the artisanal movement had insisted on the material and spiritual bankruptcy of industrial capitalism. "Despite all the victories of modern man in the domain of science and technology," wrote Fernand Peter, president of the Alsace Chamber of Trades, "the century of aviation, of radio, of statistics, and of rationalization finds humanity in an indescribable anarchy . . . at the same time moral, social and economic."[32] And as artisans looked around in the early thirties they were almost gratified to see that the Depression seemed to signal the "twilight of the gods of mechanization and technology," a "divine judgment" on a century of economic development. Accordingly, the movement tried to seize the occasion to enable the artisanat once more "to fulfil a function of the highest order" in the nation's economy.[33]

The precise impact of the economic crisis on petty producton is hard to measure. In general it added a conjunctural squeeze to the already considerable difficulties of small, independent producers in an industrializing economy. Their old markets dried up in the wider drought, a situation aggravated by sharpened competition for those customers who remained. Artisanal businesses saw themselves menaced by the "bolshevization" of retailing: that is, by cheaper, factory-made goods and by the spread of department stores and "prisunics" ("five and tens"). Competition also took the form of *travail noir,* "unauthorized work." Between 1931 and 1935, while the numbers of employees in large-scale industry dropped sharply, those involved in commerce and small-scale production rose, evidently as underemployed and underpaid blue-collar workers augmented their incomes with odd, and traditionally artisanal, jobs. On the whole, it was a matter of old customers being lost and new competitors found.[34]

Artisans quickly made the connection between their old diagnosis and their new troubles: economic crisis followed inevitably from modernization. "We must recognize," wrote Peter in the Strasbourg journal, the *Gazette des Métiers,* "that our [liberal-capitalist] economic regime . . . has gone awry in putting technical progress at the service of a purely quantitative civilization and in favoring industrial concentration and over-mechanization, abandoning in the name of individual liberty small and medium-sized producers in a battle of murderous competition, and in tolerating class war and professional anarchy." He called for a regime "free from class egotism" and for a socio-professional system that would tie the present to "a past in which order and discipline reigned."[35]

At the time, Peter and his artisan colleagues were far from alone in this analysis. The history of interwar France was widely perceived as a woeful tale of *immobilisme,* marked by economic stagnation, demographic decline, irrelevant parliamentary maneuvering, and class war. Schemes for fundamental reform appeared therefore from across the political spectrum: from the fascists, from the CGT, and even from the General Confederation of French Production (CGPF, the employers' group). Each sought to cure the present crisis and to prevent its recurrence.[36] Most schemes hinged on some abandonment of liberal political economy, a step away from the free play of the market and the institution of a more rationally conceived and executed economic policy.[37]

As this debate developed, the artisanal movement staked out its position—or rather positions, for the antimodernist consensus within the movement had always obscured sharp disagreements, which became sharper under the pressure of economic and political crisis. The corporatist and regionalist elements of the artisanal movement had left the CGAF in the mid-twenties, unhappy generally with the Confederation's moderately leftist orientation, but more immediately with its insistence on dictating to its regional federations. These elements had remained the more amorphous half of the movement until 1933, when they united to form the Committee for Artisanal Entente and Action (CEAA), dominated by the Alsatians and dedicated to a corporatist and regionalist solution to the artisanat's problems. Evidence about the professional compositions of the CGAF and the CEAA, while not conclusive, suggests that political discord between the Confederation and the Committee owed as much to the divergent interests of their constituencies as to different ideological temperaments. The Confederation seems to have attracted masters from the so-called "contemptible trades,"[38] such as shoemakers and tailors, and those of more modest property. Hence its vaguely leftist politics and its equation of artisan with "petit." Hence also its refusal to admit the food trades, composed usually of larger and more prosperous businesses. The CEAA, reflecting the jurisprudence in the recovered provinces, considered the size of an enterprise irrelevant; more important were the skill of the patron and the absence of a division of labor. It drew its most important support from the local corporations in Alsace-Lorraine and the "métiers d'alimentation" shut out of the CGAF. The Committee thus represented a section of the artisanat with a history of corporatist and regionalist sympathies, comprising more substantial workshops and more stable trades. Its organizational structure also left more room for the autonomy of its regional federations.

Opinion in the artisanal movement blew with the prevailing winds. Within French politics by the early 1930s corporatism and syndicalism had emerged as the leading challengers to classical political economy. The two orientations had markedly different origins, however. Though they shared common themes, they led in opposing directions. Corporatism in its modern guise grew out of Catholic social thought of the previous century. It aimed to ease social suffering while protecting property by restoring discipline and morality to economic activity.[39] More practically, it sought to diffuse social conflict by reorganizing society "vertically." Hubert Ley, general secretary of both the CEAA and the Alsace Chamber of Trades, explained: "In opposition to the 'social class' in the Marxist sense, that divides society into horizontal groups, the corporation erects a vertical division of society according to one's trade; for the class struggle it substitutes professional solidarity.[40]

Syndicalism, on the contrary, had its roots in the labor movement, and its chief support between the world wars came from the reformist wing of the CGT, for whom syndicalism meant economic planning and labor-management co-determination. The CGT saw this as a way, first, of avoiding the cyclical crises of market capitalism, and, second, of giving labor some influence over the direction of the economy. In 1925, under a coalition of Left and Center-Left parties (Cartel des Gauches), syndicalists had gained some satisfaction with the creation of the National Economic Council (CNE), a kind of economic parliament composed of the syndical representatives of major economic and social groups.[41] Such tinkering with political economy, however, especially one emanating from the Left, met widespread opposition. And the CNE remained peripheral to the political process, at least until its renovation in 1936.

Consistent, then, with its corporatist traditions, the Alsatian-led CEAA searched for a socio-professional regime that would "tie an anarchic present to a past in which order and discipline reigned. . . ." Accordingly, the CEAA elaborated a number of schemes aimed at returning to "a disciplined and directed economy" and restoring the "healthy regulation of the profession." It envisioned a reconstruction of French society, where all the members of a corporation—workers, management, technical people—would meet and make economic policy through discussion and compromise instead of through confrontation. The artisanat would constitute one corporation among several, beside those for industry, commerce, agriculture, and other sectors. Each corporation would further be divided into its constituent professions (in the artisanat, for example: shoemaking, metalworking, construction, woodworking, etc.) and organized up from the local and regional level. At the top of this structure the CEAA envisioned a sort of corporative parliament, coordinating intercorporate affairs at the national level and advising the National Assembly on social and economic legislation. The result, the CEAA believed, would be an end to strikes, lockouts, and social conflict: an economic policy in the "general interest."[42]

The CGAF also interpreted the Depression as the collapse of industrial capitalism. "The underlying cause of the crisis," wrote Tailledet, "is industrial concentration and all the processes that flow from it: standardization, rationalization—words as barbarous as the things they describe."[43] As he had in 1925, Tailledet laid economic disorder at the door of finance capital, the notorious "two hundred families," whose peculations constrained the free circulation of money and produced a consequent crisis of underconsumption.

Like the CEAA, the CGAF expressed its dissatisfaction with the existing political system, especially with the economic policies—or rather the lack of these—produced by the parliament. It similarly imagined a new structure for making national economic decisions. The Confederation's model for this was syndicalist. Naturally, artisanal syndicalism differed from the CGT plans, taking as its measure the interests of small, independent producers and not those of industrial workers. But the CGAF shared the CGT's commitment to politics-as-conflict and to the trade union as the vehicle of particular interests. For Tailledet, the artisanat was a homogeneous class of independent tradesmen of modest means, bound together and made an effective political force by the development of a class consciousness conditioned by the "labor process," by which he meant "professional activity and the exercise of a trade."[44] Homogeneity was a key factor in artisanal solidarity; for how, Tailledet wondered, could a cobbler, working with his wife, his children, and an apprentice have the same consciousness and, ultimately, the same interests as a master shoemaker with a shop employing thirty workers and several foremen? Because, in the syndicalists' view, classes always developed in a pluralist society, because they inevitably organized to defend their interests, and because these always clashed with those of other classes, conflict became an immutable law of politics. Institutions might aggravate conflict or facilitate its resolution, but no arrangement—and this is the crux of their disagreement with the corporatists—could eliminate it. "Our design," wrote Tailledet,

> is not only to establish the effective existence of classes, but even more to prove that it is in the interest of all to proclaim loudly the precise divergences of interest that separate the classes, to finish not with civil or social war, but with the best solutions to social and economic problems in order to guarantee the legitimate interests of every class while respecting the intangible rights of the working class.[45]

"We ask simply," wrote the Cahiers de l'Artisanat, "that our democracy adapt itself to the necessities created by the evolution of the economy and the social transformation [that] has accompanied it." The CGAF therefore planned to put a reconstructed National Economic Council at the center of economic policy-making. Here the syndical representatives of various interest groups, along with a leavening of so-called experts, could confront each other directly. The Council would then present the parliament with a prenegotiated and rational economic program, sparing the deputies and senators a task they had proved unable to perform effectively. The Confederation proposed only two major alterations in the existing Council: investing it with more power and giving artisans a greater voice within it. Such a system, the CGAF believed, would produce a more coherent and efficacious policy, while shielding artisans from the ravages of the free market.[46]

As a practical matter, the Confederation's schemes had several advantages over the Committee's, as indeed syndicalism had over corporatism in general. First, syndicalism rested on an amalgamation of interest groups such as already existed. It did not require the unlikely professional reorganization implied by corporatism. Second, syndicalism began with a more realistic view of the political process. While corporatists searched for an elusive harmony among diverse interests, the syndicalists left each group free to defend itself as it thought best. Even so, syndicalists and corporatists shared a characteristic artisanal blind spot, which forced them, in the end, to fall back on two dubious, and as it turned out incorrect, assumptions: that artisans would ever be accorded a significant role among more powerful economic and social forces, and that, apart from these forces, the state could function as a neutral guardian of the "general interest." After a decade of complaints about the neglect of the "little guy" by the state administration, artisans failed to see that the kind of rationalization of political economy they entertained would strengthen precisely the forces artisans feared most: big capital and big labor.[47]

The appearance of these comprehensive programs for reform hint at a decisive turn for the artisanal movement. From the first rumblings after the war the movement had been scrupulous in declaring its distance from both capitalists and proletarians. If anything, artisans in the twenties had consistently placed greater responsibility for what they saw as incipient class war on the "feudal lords of finance" and the "oligarchy of trusts." As a rule they stood behind progressive social legislation—more equitable taxation and a system of family allowances, for example—asking only that artisans, as "petits," be included. If the workers were being won to Marxism, the movement believed, it was because they were being exploited and deprived of their "humanness" and "good sense" by mechanization. Yet artisans had not for all this denied the social utility of profits, only of "speculation." They merely condemned the system that encouraged the latter at the expense of the former. This amalgam, mixing support for profits and distaste for speculation, sympathy for the working classes and horror of Marxism, however unrealistic or romantic, had meshed nicely with artisans' notions of historical decadence and their strategy of the *tam-*

pon social. The worsening crises of the thirties, though, broke down this perhaps ingenuous neutralism and flushed out the politics concealed in the ideology.

Such partisanship was already visible in the debate between artisanal syndicalism and corporatism. Half the movement emphasized economic "order," and thus the protection of property and profits, while the other stressed the maintenance of organizational and tactical freedom. Until 1936 the contradictions between these orientations and their political implications remained murky; both corporatists and syndicalists could continue to insist on their position between workers and employers, assigning to one "fair" wages and to the other "fair" profits. The events of the spring of 1936—the factory occupations, the election of Léon Blum as France's first socialist prime minister, the signing of the Matignon Accords regulating labor and economic conditions—forced artisans to declare themselves.

In the artisanal movement's initial responses to the Popular Front, which stretched from middle-class Radical Socialists to Communists, the political lines were already drawn. The CGAF, though it was disappointed at having been left out of the Matignon discussions, took care to couch its criticisms so as not to appear "des esprits rétrogrades."[48] Its attitude is best characterized as, "Yes, but. . . ." In principle it supported a new deal for French workers and in practice wanted it applied only to industry. Independent artisans, it argued, simply did not possess the resources to bear the pay raises, forty-hour weeks, and paid vacations for their employees provided in the new legislation. The Popular Front, yes—but with dispensations for artisans.

The corporatist half of the movement displayed no similar ambivalence. The artisanal right wing responded to what it perceived as a working class "powerfully organized, installed in power, and determined to realize its ends by any means possible, legal or not." Blum understands, wrote the *Artisan de l'Ouest,* that the concentration of production is a necessary prelude to socialization, and his government intends to fulfill the prophesies of the *Communist Manifesto.* The journal roundly denounced this "syndicalisme révolutionnaire" and called instead for the reinforcement of "corporative liberty."[49] Hubert Ley, of the CEAA, blasted the collective conventions for the artisanat signed in September 1936 by the CGAF and CGT, seeing them as a ruse to separate artisans from their real allies: "to divide the patronal world in order to finish it off more quickly."[50] Indeed, Ley feared that France had reached the moment of the "final conflict between collective and private property."[51] And he called for the constitution of a "Bloc des classes moyennes": "Today, at least, the artisan knows who he is. He is a *small* employer. But he is an *employer* . . ." (italics mine).[52] The CEAA thus tossed off the cloak of the "social buffer" and scrambled to its place on the barricades.

For the artisanal elements that agreed with Ley it was a short and predict-
able step outside the artisanal movement proper and into the growing organization of the "middle classes."[53] The contemporary "mouvement des
classes moyennes" had gotten its modest start in 1934 when Armand Pugi,
a vice-president of the Beziers Chamber of Commerce, in order to battle
"the planned economy, nationalizations, and state monopolies," set up the
Bloc du Petit Commerce.[54] But it was the Popular Front that gave the movement a new impetus.

As a matter of form, the various "middle-class" groups proclaimed their
political neutrality, by which they meant their antipathy to social conflict
and their faith in class collaboration. Most subscribed to a vaguely corporatist program of reform. The rhetoric of much of the "classes moyennes"
was obsessively anti-Marxist, their practical policy a point-by-point opposition to extended benefits for employees and support for the retrenchment
begun under the government of the Radical Socialist Camille Chautemps
in 1937 and thrown into high gear under the regimes of Édouard Daladier
and Paul Reynaud thereafter.

Several of the prominent figures in the artisanal movement directly associated themselves with this new movement of the "middle classes." Pierre
Manoury, president of the *Confédération de l'Artisanat familiale* (CAF),
and Henri Huguet, Peter's successor as president of the CEAA, sat on
the "Study Commission" of the *Confédération générale des syndicats des
classes moyennes* (CGSCM); Huguet was chairman of its Artisanal Section.
George Chaudieu, president of the national butchers' federation, member
of the CEAA's National Council, and future functionary in the wartime
Vichy regime, was a CGSCM secretary. Dejeante, president of the Union
of French Artisans (UAF), served as vice-president of the *Confédération
des Classes Moyennes* (CGCM).[55]

Artisans' participation in the movement of the "middle classes" was not
surprising. Craftsmen had traditionally belonged to associations for safeguarding the interests of small business stretching beyond the borders of
the artisanat. Much of what had become the artisanal movement could
trace its origins to these *Associations des commerçants et industriels* and
syndicats mixtes.[56] The CEAA had always presented the artisan as both
worker and proprietor, merely emphasizing the latter connection. The nov-
elty of the late 1930s lay, first, in the breadth of this "middle-class" organization and, second, in its frankly conservative appeal. Only after 1936
did Marxism and the working class become the chief threat to small property, to the virtual exclusion of "trusts" and "big finance." The CEAA's
concern with the need for "loyalty in production and order in society"
and with the "moral" interests of France then became its special mission
to protect artisans from the "Marxist doctrine" supposedly preached by
the CGAF.[57]

The CGAF for its part accepted the concept of the "middle classes" with reservations. "The defense of the middle classes is the order of the day," wrote Tailledet.[58] Yet the Confederation abstained from the new movement. Its syndicalist leadership felt that, despite impressive numbers and high-placed sponsors, the movement of the "middle classes" would achieve few concrete results. That is, they believed that the "classes moyennes" were not the proper category for conceiving or implementing policy. Their various parts were too diverse and their interests too often at odds. Artisans should defend artisans.[59] The CGAF perceived, moreover, in this politics of the "middle classes," as it had all along in corporatism, a naïveté and a species of demagoguery aimed at manipulating small producers for ends that were ultimately not their own. In the balance between artisan-worker and artisan-owner, the Confederation had always tipped toward the former.

In his 1940 analysis of corporatism, Henri Colliard offered this judgment:

> The petite bourgeoisie, brusquely dispossessed or merely impoverished, will become angry. Its reaction will be like that of a spoiled child. Understanding that the banks and big business are responsible for its situation, its revolt will be anti-capitalist; but at the same time, attached to its past contentment and desirous of carefully marking itself off from the proletariat, to which it refuses to be assimilated, it will also be reactionary.[60]

This survey of the ideology and the politics of the artisanal movement indicates that this is but a partial truth—and maybe not the most important part.

Economic conditions within the artisanat varied, as did organizational and political orientations. The artisanal movement between the world wars nevertheless developed a relatively coherent world view in reaction against the industrializing and capitalist French economy. To the thousands of artisans affiliated with the CGAF, the CEAA, the CAF, and the UAF—and many more who were not so affiliated, I suspect—the modern economy raised the specter of dehumanizing factory work and class war. In a more personal sense, it meant bankruptcy or unemployment. The movement responded by articulating a vision of a society in which the "middle classes" would no longer be the victims of economic concentration but rather the "dorsal fin" of the nation, steering a course of moderate change, moderate prosperity, and moderate happiness. Artisans imagined a kind of "trades-Gemeinschaft," a world of "moral" economy where skill would count more than productivity, and where "le bon sens" and not utility would be the measure of value. They dreamed of a stable society based on a loving, dutiful household and an ordered professional life—the smith at his anvil or the cobbler at his workbench, nurturing his compagnons (the CGAF saw him with one or two, the CEAA with ten or twenty) and tutoring his apprentices, while his wife tended the account books, the cash register, and the hearth; his relations with his customers comprising more than the "cash nexus." They longed for a return to a time when, as it was told in the Faubourg Saint-Antoine, "Furniture-makers were considered artists, [and] many women had the ambition to marry one."[61] Altogether a seductive "image d'Epinal."

As with so many "utopias," this one had only an incidental relation to fact. Above all, the notion of social harmony within the artisanat, so central to this tableau, will not stand up under the evidence of the personal testimony of so many workers,[62] of the more decisive record of *compagnons'* continuing hostility to the Chambers of Trades, or of the strikes and disputes over collective work contracts. Moreover, since factory production was increasingly the condition of material prosperity, the idyll of the workshop was not likely to have a broad appeal. The *Artisan* could write, in a moment of romantic excess, that "one can live very well without pleasure trips, without cinemas, without dance halls and cafés, without silk stockings."[63] But few were likely to agree. Indeed, it is difficult to imagine that even the blacksmiths, wheelwrights, and farriers who read the *Artisan* would agree.

All this has been said before and represents little more than a restatement of Marx's old observation that, in their world views, classes tend to universalize their particular interests. The idealization of the artisanal experience, then, is less important for its own contradictions than for the way that it points to the limits of artisanal politics.[64] That is to say, artisanal versions of corporatism and syndicalism were not merely impractical, they were absurd. The parliamentary anarchy of the Third Republic, which had incubated small property, could not resolve the economic crisis; yet any of the remedies the artisanal movement proposed were bound to make the situation worse. Simply put, there was no nonindustrial solution to the problems of industrial society, and a more effective national economic policy would inevitably bury a substantial part of the artisanat.

The moralistic and romantic nature of so much of artisanal ideology pointed no way out of this cul de sac. Instead, the politics of the movement were burdened by a fundamental misunderstanding of the sources and the functions of power. Liberalism could prescribe a system in which capital would reign and where the political dominance of the capitalists would follow their possession of the real sources of wealth. Marxism could envision a politics dominated by a working class likewise in control of industrial production. Both these ideologies posited the relation of political power to the domination of the production and distribution of wealth. Artisanal ideology displayed no similar sophistication. Artisans were able to mourn the disappearance of traditional social virtues and preach the superiority of the family workshop over the factory. But, in the end, neither syndicalists nor corporatists within the artisanat could conjure a system in which petty production would predominate. Each consistently refused to come to terms with basic issues of power, and each fell back on the ingenuous notion of the "general interest."

The rejection of liberal political economy, the conservative social vision, and the language of the general interest were the core of the fascist appeal to the lower middle classes. Even during the 1920s, as their ideology began to take shape, artisans took their distance from the Third Republic and expressed their dissatisfaction with a system that they thought favored the factory over the workshop and the "big guys" over the "petits." The crises of the thirties did not so much create this process of alienation as accelerate it. The Depression ground on, social divisions deepened, the political system appeared incapable of decisive action, and the artisanal movement began to look for a way to stanch the tide of concentration and protect *petites situations.*

Artisans' diagnoses of social ills and prescriptions for recovery resembled those of the Right in general and of the fascists in particular. The *Jeunesses Patriotes,* under a banner of "Order, Hierarchy, and Discipline," promised a war against the "forces of disorder" threatening the family and other "French traditions." The *Parti Populaire Français,* in its Manifesto of 1932, wrote: "[France's] shopkeepers and artisans are driven to the wall by misery. The middle classes are being ruined." And the *Croix de Feu* called for "Class reconciliation and collaboration. Restoration of national morality. A controlled economy . . . and parliamentary reform."[65] The fascists saved their heaviest salvos for the Marxists.

None of this would have sounded out of place at a CEAA congress or in a policy statement by one of the "middle-class" organizations. It was all part of the language of the middle classes "enragées." The artisanal world view in its details reflected the specific experience of small craftsmen. But in a larger sense it belonged to a generic populism. This was the ideology of a distraught lower middle class, characterized by a rejection of an economic and political structure that succored "big business," but also by a refusal to follow the working class into collectivist socialism. It is important to stress, however, that middle-class disaffection was a necessary but not a sufficient condition of fascism. Between Adam Smith and Karl Marx many kinds of politics were possible.[66]

As we have seen, the artisanal movement in France, whatever ideological affinities it might have had with the radical Right, never slipped over into the authoritarianism that is the *sine qua non* of fascism. The CGAF pursued a leftish populism, suspicious of the authorities, full of respect for the virtue and the good sense of the "français moyen," with a constant eye to democracy and social justice. It frankly rejected "any authoritarian solution which would sacrifice the individual to a state bureaucracy."[67] The corporatists, led by the Alsace Chamber of Trades, with its Wilhelmine pedigree and more substantial constituency, with its intense concern for "discipline," sometimes slipped away from democracy, as when they flirted with the idea of "compulsory" corporations. And some of the CEAA partisans later drifted smoothly from the movement of the "middle classes" to Marshal Philippe Pétain's National Revolution of 1940. Throughout the thirties, however, while the CEAA steered closer to the authoritarian edge, it did not fall off.

As a result, French fascism, unable to attract even such likely recruits as disgruntled artisans, never found a mass base of support. This failure of authoritarian politics in the Third Republic seems (briefly) to be the product of several conditions. First, the economic crisis in France, buffered by the country's large nonindustrial sector, never attained the proportions that it did in Germany or the United States. At its worst, French unemployment did not much surpass one million.[68] The effect of the Depression in France, moreover, was regressive. It struck large, highly capitalized producers harder than it did small. The economic and psychological threat to middle-class property and status in France was therefore comparatively moderate. Second, the Chamber of Deputies, for all its "immobility," continued to patronize small property. It preserved, despite its budget difficulties, the tax advantages granted to artisans in the early twenties. It restricted foreign and industrial competition for small producers and gave artisanal organizations representation on all the major administrative bodies. And, finally—an inchoate but to my mind decisive factor—French artisans operated within the democratic political culture embedded in both syndical and national traditions. Exasperated with the operation of the Republic, artisans demanded not a "Führer" or a "Duce," but a new "Estates-General."

Notes

1. Heinz-Gerhard Haupt, "La petite bourgeoisie: une classe inconnue," *Mouvement social* 108 (July–Sept. 1979): 20.

2. Klaus-Jürgen Müller, "French Fascism and Modernization," *Journal of Contemporary History* 11 (1976): 78–82.

3. See, for example, Yves Guichet, *George Valois: L'Action francaise—le Faisceau—la république syndicale* (Paris, 1975); Jean Plumyène and Raymond Lasierra, *Les fascismes français, 1923–1963* (Paris, 1963); Robert Soucy, *Fascist Intellectual: Drieu la Rochelle* (Berkeley, 1979); Edward Tannenbaum, *The Action Française: Die-Hard Reactionaries in Twentieth-Century France* (New York, 1962); Eugen Weber, *Action Français: Royalism and Reaction in Twentieth-Century France* (Stanford, 1962); Zeev Sternhell, *La droite révolutionnaire* (Paris, 1978); and *Neither Left nor Right: Fascist Ideology in France*, David Maisel, trans. (Berkeley, 1986).

4. Henri Mougin, "Un projet d'enquête sur les classes moyennes en France," in Raymond Aron et al., *Inventaires III: Classes Moyennes* (Paris, 1939), 288.

5. Geoffrey Crossick, "The Petite Bourgeoisie in Nineteenth-Century Europe: Problems and Research," in *Arbeiter und Arbeiterbewegung im Vergleich: Berichte zur internationalen historischen Forschung,* ed. Klaus Tenfelde (Munich, 1986), 227n. See also François Gresle, "Indépendants et Petits Patrons: perrenité et transformations d'une classe sociale" (thèse, Paris V, 1980), 76.

6. *L'Artisan* (Lyon) 34 (June 1922).

7. For summaries of the Bordeaux congress, see *Gazette des Métiers* (hereafter cited as *Gazette*) 26 (29 June 1923): 418–19; ibid., 27 (6 July 1923): 435–36; ibid., 28 (13 July 1923): 452. *Artisan Français* (cited hereafter as *AF*) 6 (June 1923) published a copy of the Artisanal Charter.

8. *L'Artisan* (Lyon) 72–73 (Oct.–Nov. 1925).

9. For the corporatist position see Hubert Ley, *L'Artisanat: Entité Corporative* (Paris, 1938), 33. For the syndicalists, the quote is from *Cahiers de l'Artisanat* (hereafter cited as *Cahiers*) 4 (Jan. 1935): 6.

10. *L'Artisan de l'Ouest* 22 (March 1937).

11. Bernard Zarca, "Survivance ou transformation de l'artisanat dans la France d'aujourd'hui" (thèse en sociologie, Institut d'Études Politiques de Paris, 1983), 22 and 391.

12. Quoted in *AF* 1 (Jan.–Feb. 1926).

13. René Dumontier, *Un apôtre de l'artisanat et de la famille: Albert Dupuis, artisan-maître, 1873–1937. Sa vie et son oeuvre* (Yvetot, 1946), 196–99. Ironically, according to Henri Mourier, artisans did not always practice the fertility they preached: "L'artisanat, sa structure et son intégration dans l'économie moderne" (thèse en droit, Paris, 1952), 108.

14. The quotation is in a review of *L'Homme: Cet Inconnue* by Dr. Alex Carrel in *Cahiers* 16 (Feb. 1936): 31.

15. *L'Artisan* (Le Puy) 10 (Oct. 1931).

16. *L'Artisan* (Lyon) 2 (Nov. 1919).

17. *L'Artisan* (Le Puy) 7 (July 1932).

18. *L'Artisan* (Lyon) 59 (Aug.–Sept. 1924).

19. Mougin, "Un Projet d'enquête," 338.

20. Lucien Gelly, *L'artisanat rural: ses problèmes actuels* (Joigny, 1944), 38–39.

21. Isabelle Dudit, *Marbréry: Maître-Artisan* (Paris, 1930), 4.

22. *L'Artisan* (Le Puy) 2 (Feb. 1932).

23. Adelaïde Blasquez, *Gaston Lucas, sérrurier: chronique de l'anti-hero* (Paris, 1976), 24–25.

24. *L'Artisan* (Lyon) 2 (Nov. 1919); ibid., 3 (Dec. 1919); ibid., 23 (July 1921); ibid., 95–96 (Sept.–Oct. 1927).

25. *Cahiers* 4 (Jan. 1935): 27.

26. *L'Artisan* (Le Puy) 1 (Jan.–Feb. 1936).

27. *AF* 102 (June 1931).

28. See Convert's report on the milling industry, Compte-rendu du Congrès de l'Artisanat National, CEAA (Saint-Étienne, 1936), 73.

29. *AF* 2 (March 1926).

30. Georges Chaudieu, *Artisans et commerçants* (Paris, 1982), 24.

31. *L'Artisan* (Lyon) 9 (June 1920).

32. See Peter's report, "Why a CEAA?" in Compte-rendu du Congrès de l'Artisanat National, CEAA (Lille, 1934), 103.

33. *AF* 155 (28 Feb. 1934).

34. See Alfred Sauvy, *Histoire économique de la France entre les deux guerres,* vol. 2 (1931–1939) (Paris, 1967), 116; also J.-J. Carré, P. Dubois, and E. Malinvaud, *French Economic Growth,* trans. John P. Hartfield (Stanford, 1975), 162–63. See also the report, "Situation du travail à fin avril 1932," in *AF* 118 (May 1932). The crisis naturally struck the artisanat unevenly; that is, some trades suffered more dramatically than others. For some, current troubles merely exacerbated a long-term decline. Paradoxically, several of the more dynamic sectors of the artisanat, especially the construction trades, experienced a more precipitous slump in their fortunes as the economy ground to a halt.

35. *Gazette* 16 (20 April 1934): 272.

36. For the plans cooked up by the Radical-Socialist Party see Serge Berstein, "Le Parti Républicain Radical et Radical-Socialiste en France de 1919 à 1939" (thèse, Université de Paris-Nanterre, 1976), 683–706 *passim;* Peter J. Larmour, *The French Radical Party in the Thirties* (Stanford, 1964), 63–64; Jean-Thomas Nordmann, *Histoire des Radicaux, 1820–1973* (Paris, 1974), 237–42. For a general discussion of these programs of reconstruction, see Georges Dubost, *Le Conseil National Économique: ses origines, son institution et son organisation. Son oeuvre et son avenir* (Paris, 1936), 353–60; Richard F. Kuisel, *Capitalism and the State in Modern France: Renovation and Economic Management in the Twentieth Century* (New York, 1981), 98–118 *passim.*

37. Dubost, *Conseil National Economiqué,* 317; Herbert van Liesen, *Explication du Fascisme* (Paris: 1926), 28–33.

38. The phrase is from Jacques Rancière, "The Myth of the Artisan: Critical Reflections on a Category of Social History," *International Labor and Working Class History* 24 (Fall 1983): 2.

39. For an overview of corporatism see Mathew Elbow, *French Corporative Theory: A Chapter in the History of Ideas* (New York, 1953); Henry Laufenburger, *L'intervention de l'état en matière économique* (Paris, 1939); Jean-Philippe Parrot, *La représentation des intérêts dans le mouvement des idées politiques* (Paris, 1974).

40. *Gazette* 39 (28 Sept. 1934): 697.

41. Parrot, *La représentation des intérêts,* 143, 148; see also Dubost, *Conseil National Économique,* 59–63; Kuisel, *Capitalism and the State,* 109–11. For an examination of specific CGT plans see Georges Lefranc, *Le mouvement syndical sous la Troisième République* (Paris, 1967), 287. On the opposition of the "patronat" see Henry Ehrmann, *Organized Business in France* (Princeton, 1957), 3.

42. *Gazette* 16 (20 April 1934): 272; Ley, *L'Artisanat: Entité Corporatif,* 196; Compte-rendu du Congrès de l'Artisanat National, CEAA (Toulouse, 1935), 35.

43. *AF* 103 (July 1931).

44. See the series of essays by Tailledet in the *Cahiers,* "Doctrine," which were later edited and published as Robert Tailledet, *La doctrine de classe de l'artisanat moderne* (Paris, 1937).

45. *Cahiers* 1 (Oct. 1934): 8.

46. For example, see the "Declaration of the CGAF," from the XIᵉ Congrès, CGAF (Chaumont, 1934), reproduced in *AF* 161 (30 June–31 July 1934).

47. Armand Kopp, *Le rôle de groupements professionnels dans l'organisation de la profession* (Nancy, 1937), 108.

48. *AF* 209 (20 July–Aug. 1936).

49. *L'Artisan de l'Ouest* 16–17 (Aug.–Sept. 1936).

50. *AF* 208 (10 July 1936).

51. *Gazette* 43 (23 Oct. 1936): 726.

52. *L'Artisan de France* (CAF) 24 (May 1937).

53. Discussions of the development of the organizations of the "middle classes" appear in Berstein, "Le Parti Républicain," 1162, 1197; André Desqueyrat, *Classes moyennes*

françaises: crise, programme, organisation (Paris, 1939), *passim;* Mougin, "Un projet d'enquête," *passim.* Mougin writes that the first Association de Défense des Classes Moyennes, based on Belgian models, was actually founded in 1907: 329.

54. Archives Nationales F12 9505: report from the Prefect of Police to the Minister of Commerce and Industry, 18 July 1938, on the Bloc du Petit Commerce.

55. The record of artisanal participation is in Desqueyrat, *Classes moyennes françaises,* 205, 247; *Gazette* 47 (19 Nov. 1937): 811–12; ibid., 26 (1 July 1938): 464; and ibid., 36 (9 Sept. 1938): 635.

56. Compte-rendu du Congrès de l'Artisanat National, CEAA (Lille, 1934), 113, 119.

57. See, for example, the survey of professional organizations in France done by the Ministry of Labor, beginning with Archives Nationales F12 21.

58. *AF* 226 (1 Feb. 1937).

59. *AF* 228 (20 Feb. 1937).

60. Henri Colliard, *Le corporatisme et la lutte des classes* (Rive-de-Gier, 1940), 59. See also Richard Scase, "The Petite Bourgeoisie and Modern Capitalism: A Consideration of Recent Theories," in Anthony Giddens and Gavin Mackensie, eds., *Social Class and the Division of Labor: Essays in Honour of Ilya Neustadt* (Cambridge, 1982).

61. Laurent Azzano, *Mes joyeuses années au faubourg: souvenirs du faubourg Saint-Antoine* (Paris, 1985), 34.

62. See Azzano, *Mes joyeuses années, passim;* Zarca, "Survivance ou transformation," vol. 2, *passim.*

63. *L'Artisan* (Le Puy) 11 (November 1931).

64. See B. Elliot, "Petty Property: The Survival of a Moral Economy," in F. Bechhoffer and B. Elliot, eds., *The Petite Bourgeoisie: Comparative Studies of the Uneasy Stratum* (New York, 1981).

65. See the pamphlets in the Bibliothèque Nationale, Paris: Croix de Feu, Parti Social Français, "Tracts politiques, 1934–1939"; Parti Populaire Français, "Tracts politiques, 1932–1938"; Jeunesses Patriotes, "Tracts politiques, 1928–1935."

66. Tom Bottomore writes: "Structural causality, in this view, is something less than the rigorous determination of a specific effect; instead, it is conceived as the production of conditions and constraints within which diverse, but not unlimited, alternative courses of political action [and ideology] and development are possible." *Political Sociology* (New York, 1979), 96. See also E. P. Thompson, *The Poverty of Theory and Other Essays* (New York, 1978), who says that class only "determines" in the sense of "setting limits and exerting pressures" and of defining a "law of motion" as a "logic of process": 351. Raymond Williams, *Problems in Materialism and Culture* (London, 1980), 32, essentially agrees.

67. *AF* 242 (1 Sept. 1937). See also "La création et le fonctionnement d'une représentation professionnelle et économique devant l'état," *Cahiers* 3 (Dec. 1934): 137; and *AF* 142 (15 Aug. 1933).

68. Julian Jackson, *The Politics of Depression, 1932–1936* (Cambridge, 1985), 29–30.

7 Created Constituencies: The Italian Middle Classes and Fascism

MABEL BEREZIN

The Italian Middle Classes as an Historical Problem

In the years following the first world war, contemporary social analysts established the boundaries that have dominated subsequent discussions of the political inclinations of the Italian middle classes. Historian Luigi Salvatorelli labeled the Italian middle classes "literate illiterates"; Antonio Gramsci, a founder of the Italian Communist party, used the term "monkey people" to describe this social group. Both characterizations suggest intrinsic collective defects that propel the middle classes towards fascist politics.

Salvatorelli identified a "humanistic lower middle class" that could be found in "bureaucratic offices, scholastic halls and . . . petty [mean] professional activities" as enthusiastic supporters of fascism.[1] The "humanistic lower middle classes" were half educated. They possessed a "smattering" of "grammatical and formulaic" culture, the "illiteracy of the literate," but they lacked the critical and synthetic abilities to use their knowledge to evaluate the contemporary political scene. The "humanistic lower middle classes" were frequently "totally misplaced and unemployed." According to Salvatorelli, the combination of some claim to education and the lack of a corresponding social status made them particularly susceptible to the rhetorical appeals of the fascist movement and regime.

I would like to thank Douglas Forsyth, Rudy Koshar, and Steven Perlmutter for critical readings of earlier versions of this article. Roger Gould, Cheryl Zollars, and other members of the Workshop of the Center for Research on Politics and Social Organization (CROPSO), Sociology Department, Harvard University, provided an evening of commentary and debate that aided the revision process.

142

Gramsci compared the lower middle classes to the monkeys in Rudyard Kipling's *Jungle Book,* who viewed themselves as superior to everyone else in the jungle, and he described fascism as the "urban petty bourgeoisie's latest 'performance' in the theater of national political life."[2] Gramsci warned that "monkey people supply daily news, they do not create history, they leave traces in the newspapers, they do not offer materials to write books."[3] No books have been written. In the sixty-five years that have passed since Gramsci wrote, no historical study has emerged that has either explored or challenged his assertion.

The Italian middle class of the early twentieth century is a class "without history." Their lack of a chronicler points to an anomaly in the historiography of Italian fascism. From the earliest days of the fascist movement, analysts such as Salvatorelli and Gramsci identified middle-class support as crucial to the success of Italian fascism. Subsequent studies by historians and social scientists have viewed the connection between the lower middle classes and fascism as axiomatic.[4] Adrian Lyttelton acknowledges the connection—"the middle classes . . . were the backbone of fascism"—while pointing to an obvious lacuna: "Until we have studied their structure, their income levels and the effect of inflation, and their previous political allegiances, the analysis of fascism will lack an important dimension. The study of particular occupational groups and their professional organizations (artisans, shopkeepers, bank clerks, urban landowners) might also be revealing."[5] Emilio Gentile strikes a similar note in a recent review of the historiography of Italian fascism: "It appears increasingly obvious . . . that the success of fascism derived decisively from its ability to gather together various components of the middle classes, which it then provided with an elite experienced in mass politics, with an efficient organization, and with an ideology which . . . extolled the political values, functions, interests, and ambitions of the middle classes."[6] Yet, Gentile adds, "We still possess only vague and inadequate data on the role of the middle classes during the Fascist regime and on the extent and magnitude of their 'seizure of power'. . . ."[7]

Why do we still know relatively little of the social history of the group whose initial and ongoing support was presumably crucial to the success of Italian fascism?[8] Why has the small renaissance in Italian fascist studies appearing in the 1980s produced nothing similar to Jeffrey Herf's *Reactionary Modernism,* a study of the attraction to and involvement of German engineers in nazism?[9] Political economy models, which analyze group interests and conflict management in response to macroeconomic change, have dominated the literature. In this type of analysis, group interests tend to be defined in purely economic terms, and groups emerge not in their own terms but only in relation to other groups.[10] Social history as a genre has come late to modern Italian studies. Where it does exist, it tends to focus on the working classes.[11]

The support that the Italian middle classes gave to fascism is not altogether puzzling, nor is it altogether straightforward. In a country that to that point had only one political class, it is not surprising that other groups would seek to enter the political arena.[12] But in what way? What kind of enfranchisement did these groups seek? What was the nature of support for fascism among the middle classes? The meaning of the evidence that we have is ambiguous. In any discussion of Italian fascism, it is crucial to differentiate between fascism in its movement and in its regime phases. Were the early fascist squads cadres of shopkeepers' sons? Were the numbers that swelled the ranks of the Fascist party in the thirties until the regime had to limit membership disproportionately members of middle-class groups?

The class origins of those who were involved in the early fascist movement are largely unknown. Participation in the city-based fascist movement should not be confused with membership in the country-based fascist squads. The fascist movement that Mussolini founded in Milan in 1919 was a mass-produced copy of the futurist arditist movement. *Arditismo,* which tried to fuse free-lance political activity with an avant-garde aesthetic, claimed Filippo Tommaso Marinetti, founder of Italian futurism, and novelist and dramatist Gabriel D'Annunzio as its leaders.[13] Although *Arditismo* may have attracted members of less than upper-class origin, its orientations were decidedly elite; and "for the numerous journalists, would-be poets or dramatists and out-of-work publicists, the *fasci* offered the chance of a career and the recognition which had eluded them."[14]

On the second question, we have old evidence suggesting that fascist party members and elites were largely middle class.[15] Renzo De Felice cites a 1921 survey of the local secretaries of the *Fasci di Combattimento* (Fighting Fascists) and concludes that the ". . . middle class forms about ninety percent of the party members enrolled, even in essentially rural areas where the landowners and many simple peasants and day laborers belonged to the party."[16] What is striking about De Felice's claim is that the statistics he uses to support it can bear another interpretation. Reclassifying the data he presents yields a different class distribution: 40 percent workers; 13 percent students; 12 percent land-owning farmers; and only 35 percent members of middle-class occupational groups. Party membership alone cannot be used to measure support for the regime. In the 1930s, party membership was required for entry to many of the employment opportunities the regime created for the middle classes, and they rushed to join.[17] For example, in 1931, the regime asked all university professors in their role as state employees to swear a "loyalty oath" to the regime; of 1,200 eligible university professors, only 11 refused to take the oath. Adrian Lyttelton, commenting on the oath, notes that "if wholehearted commitment to Fascism was comparatively rare among university professors, so, clearly, was active opposition."[18]

Redrawing the Boundaries of Italian Middle-Class Political Alliances

In order to understand fully the political coalitions that the middle classes were willing to support, we need to study in detail the historical trajectories of different occupational groups within the middle classes, which would include an occupation's political economy, cultural traditions, and place within the Italian labor-market structure. Although this essay does not provide such a study, it does draw upon existing studies as well as Fascist policy and propaganda documents to explore a series of propositions about the political propensities of the Italian middle classes. Its central argument is that the Italian middle classes of the early twentieth century were classes without a defined political ideology, and that their lack of a coherent ideology tended towards volatile rather than fixed capacities for political action. This implies that the Italian middle classes were equally capable of supporting either a socialist or a fascist movement, should either one have managed to acquire state power.

This interpretation requires the redrawing of the boundaries in which previous discussions of the middle classes have been cast. First, the time frame for analyzing the political participation of the Italian middle classes must be expanded to include the pre–World War I period. Limiting the analysis of the Italian middle classes to the immediate post–World War I period leads to the well-worn explanation that members of this class flocked to fascism as a result of the psychological despair they experienced as the postwar Depression eroded their hard-won social and economic gains and the working class threatened them from below.[19] An analysis that takes into account the political enthusiasms of this class from the late 1800s through the fascist period, however, suggests that the Italian middle classes were not predisposed to any particular ideological orientation.

Second, the highly disparate nature of the groups constituting the Italian middle classes and the political implications of this diversity must be taken into account. A critical reading of certain aspects of fascist policies suggests that support among the middle classes was based on a very fragile consensus that had to be continually re-created. One reason for this fragility is that the middle class, composed of widely varying subcultures, had no coherent set of interests to draw them together. For example, the Italian shopkeeper had little in common with the unemployed or underemployed lawyer.

This essay addresses these isues. The first part attempts to establish the political volatility of the Italian middle classes, and the second part examines the plurality of strategies and rhetorics which the fascist regime used to stabilize the support of the middle classes. The essay concludes by examining the political ideology of the Italian middle classes within the system of cultural and social closure that the Italian education system supported.

Salvatorelli's "humanistic lower middle classes" are indeed crucial to understanding the relation of the class as a whole to fascism. The "humanistic lower middle classes" stood on particularly shaky ground, not because of their inadequate education but because of the inadequacy of the Italian education system itself. Italy had simultaneously one of the highest rates of illiteracy and the largest oversupply of university graduates of any country in western Europe.[20] This suggests that a large percentage of those who managed to obtain a primary and secondary education went on to university. The labor market imbalance that resulted from this oversupply of "intellectual" workers meant that advanced education could not secure social mobility for groups that desired it.

The cultural claims of the fascist policy of corporativism and the importance that the regime assigned to placating professional middle-class labor is central to understanding the regime's perceptions of the political proclivities of the middle classes as a group. The fascist regime wrote extensively about the middle classes—both praising their participation in bringing fascism to power and speculating about their place in the new fascist order. Regime publications are useful for understanding the middle classes, not for their truthfulness but for what they convey about what the regime would have wanted the public to think.

The extent and nature of the rhetorical claims that the regime made about this group suggest that support for the fascist regime among the middle classes was conditional. In order to assure the consent of this group, the regime had to supply it continually with both bread and circuses: bread in the form of tax incentives and state regulation of all forms of competition; and circuses in the form of a vast apparatus of cultural enrichment programs that had the function of providing employment for the large numbers of unemployed university graduates who were both the producers and the beneficiaries of these programs.[21]

Who Were the Italian Middle Classes?

As a general analytic category, the term *middle class* is virtually useless.[22] In Italy, as elsewhere, the term aggregates a group of occupations with different historical trajectories and different (to borrow from Max Weber) "material and ideal" interests.[23] While the demarcation of the boundaries of this group was in dispute, in Italy it generally includes: proprietors of small farms, shopkeepers *(commercianti)*, lower-level white-collar workers in the public and private sector *(impiegati)*, artisans, and both low-level and high-level professionals, such as doctors and lawyers.[24] These groups were both internally and externally competitive. Internally, they fought over limited markets for their services; and externally, they competed with a vocal Italian working-class movement for public and private resources.

But even this is too global a statement for this group. For example, the Socialist Cooperative societies threatened the markets of small shop-keepers. The growing industrialization of northern Italy threatened artisanal production. Between 1881 and 1901, the number of artisans in Italy decreased by 50 percent, although it has remained remarkably stable from that point to the present day.[25] The small merchants had only contractual interests in common, whereas the professionals and artisans shared an occupational community with particular traditions that they could invoke in negotiating with the state.[26] Professionals, artisans, and shopkeepers preferred to limit the encroachment of the state upon their autonomy and favored a restricted state. In contrast to these groups, white-collar workers of various educational levels in Italy were largely dependent on the growth of the state for their continued material well-being.

While the process of group formation may sometimes be in dispute, no theory of social movement exists that does not argue that perceived common interests among social actors are necessary for effective mobilization.[27] It is difficult to imagine the disparate set of occupational groups that constituted the Italian middle classes mobilizing around any set of common interests in the advent of fascism. The only definitive aspect of this group was that its political orientations were historically "unstable." As Italian sociologist Paolo Sylos Labini has pointed out, the different strata of the lower middle classes have the potential to move toward either Left or Right at different historical conjunctures.[28]

Italian Middle Classes as Contested Terrain

Salvatorelli describes the "humanistic lower middle classes" as "socialis-toide"—socialists until they realized that the true benefits of socialism would accrue to the Italian working classes at their expense.[29] Whether or not these groups were true or false socialists, if such distinctions can be made, there is much evidence to suggest that there had been an early mutual attraction between socialism and all strata of the educated middle classes. In 1899, two British historians described the middle classes' attraction to socialism as based on a combination of idealism and pragmatism:

> To the best and most thoughtful of the educated middle classes it [socialism] appeals through its high idealism, its call to intellect, its protest against the barrenness of public life, its splendid campaign against evil in high places. . . . Smaller of the educated middle class are drawn to socialism, partly because they are poor themselves and sympathize with the poor, partly because discontent finds a natural home among the educated unemployed, the multitude of young university men without work—doctors, lawyers, civil engineers, would-be civil servants.[30]

The "university men without work" were a peculiar feature of the Italian social landscape. Although intellectual unemployment was not unique to Italy, it posed a greater problem there than elsewhere in Europe because the numbers of unemployed were larger and the government kept expanding, rather than contracting, the university system to deal with the problem.[31] This oversupply produced a radicalized intellectual middle class that was always vulnerable to appeals to better their situation. Improving their situation was not restricted to economic improvement, that is, finding a job with a living wage attached to it. They also sought the social power to have their own voice in politics. The educated middle classes were active participants in the *Risorgimento* and had done much to set the course of modern Italian history.[32] The expansion of this group in the late nineteenth- and early twentieth century weakened their position as leaders in Italian society. Italy at the turn of the century was essentially an agrarian society with high illiteracy rates.[33] While there may have been a social need for teachers, engineers, doctors, and lawyers, the social and economic resources to support them in large numbers were lacking. Italian Reformist Socialism emerged as compatible with middle-class goals of cultural, social, and political participation.[34]

Socialism provided a set of voluntary organizations whose purposes were to serve the working classes but that actually benefited the middle classes. The *Societa Umanitaria,* a Milanese benevolent society designed along English models, is an example of one such organization. Founded in 1892 by a prosperous Milanese industrialist, the Commune of Milan with its socialist administration took over the *Umanitaria*'s funding in 1893. The *Umanitaria* ran job enrichment programs for workers—providing lessons in arts and crafts such as woodworking, jewelry making, and printing. It had women's programs on home economics, fashion design, and nutrition. In 1914, it instituted a Children's House where it experimented with the educational methods of Maria Montessori. It also sponsored a People's Theater and Concert series that was intended to introduce workers to elite culture. In practice, the audience for the cultural programs were the educated middle classes whose limited incomes restricted their participation in privately sponsored cultural events.[35] This educated but impecunious middle class was the same group that benefited from fascist cultural policies.

The Italian middle classes' abandoning of socialism in the post–World War I years is frequently cited to explain their attraction to fascism: as Italian socialism became less reformist and more militant and pro-worker in orientation, the Italian middle classes drifted towards fascism. But this account neglects to distinguish between the educated middle classes and small merchant groups, and it fails to explore the growing presence of alternative groups within the middle class itself that began to compete for the allegiance of the class. Lastly, it fails to capture the historical volatility of the political alignments of the middle classes.

Nationalism, which had not been a force before World War I, began to assert itself strongly. Nationalism in Italy was never a mass-based political movement. The Italian Nationalist Association founded in 1910 by Enrico Corradini was principally a literary association.[36] It was a movement of elites for other cultural elites. The crisis over whether to intervene in World War I and the subsequent loss of Italian territory in the war provided the opportunity for nationalism to emerge as a mass political force. Nationalist syndical organizations began to compete with socialist organizations for members. The Socialist General Confederation of Labor (*Confederazione Generale del Lavoro*— CGIL), founded in 1906, whose membership had been increasing in the pre–World War I period, suddenly encountered Edmondo Rossoni's Italian Union of Labor (*Unione Italian del Lavoro–UIL*), founded in 1918, which sought to recruit members from the middle classes.[37] The emergence of nationalism as a popular ideology coupled with the nationalist syndical organizations, or labor unions, provided Mussolini with the opportunity to expand the base of the fascist movement. Between 1919 and 1922, he harnessed the rhetoric of nationalism to the organizational forces of fascism.[38] The Fascist party and the Nationalist Association merged in 1923, after fascism had come to power.

Rhetoric, Organization, and Shifting Alignments: The Case of the Milanese Actors

The shifting of a group of Milanese actors from socialism to fascism in 1921 provides an example of the process of realignment that occurred among the humanistic lower middle classes. The theater had a special place in the imagination and occupational aspirations of Italians. Guido Lopez, the son of a popular Italian dramatist of the period, notes in a memoir that among the petite bourgeoisie and working classes "aspiration to the stage" was common and that every family had a member or friend who belonged to an amateur theater group.[39]

While their numbers were not large compared to other occupational groups, acting was a highly visible cultural profession. Actors were typical of Salvatorelli's "humanistic lower middle classes," because their occupation combined cultural aspirations with poor job security.[40] In a letter to *Avanti*, the Socialist party newspaper, Domenico Gismano, head of the actors' union, wrote that the fortunate actors who become stars were the exception and that the majority of the "theatrical family" faced continual unemployment and woke up "as poor, tired and worried about their daily bread as the members of the manual working classes."[41]

In Italy, acting was an old and honored craft that was rapidly changing in the early years of the twentieth century. Acting as craft had been an inherited occupation. Its practitioners were called "children of art [*figli d'arte*]," and most actors were born into the occupation. In the late 1800s, acting began to become a profession with the corresponding prerequisite of academic training. The large number of amateur acting schools that had existed in Italy from the time of the unification were transforming, or attempting to transform, themselves into professional academies. Even with the development of the cinema, which provided new jobs for actors, the acting schools produced far more actors than the system could accommodate.[42]

On the eve of the 1922 March on Rome, which brought Mussolini to power, the Italian theater, like the rest of Italy, was wracked by labor conflicts. Beginning in 1919 and continuing until 1922, actors and theater personnel periodically waged strikes against theaters in large Italian cities. The League for the Betterment of Dramatic Actors (*Lega di Miglioramento degli Artisti Drammatici—[Lega]*), a socialist organization, represented the actors in these conflicts. Members of the theatrical community defined the League's role as necessary for bringing the organization of "class" to the theater.[43] In 1921, the League voted to become a member of the Italian General Confederation of Labor (*Confederazione General Italiana del Lavoro—CGIL*). The vote was controversial. Those in favor of the move argued that the actors had to learn to think of themselves as the "most important factor" of theatrical production. Dissidents within the organization claimed that artists represented the "free life" and should not band together with those who professed a definitive socialist ideology.[44] These dissenting elements gave birth to the Corporation of the Theater (*Corporazione del Teatro*) led by Gino Calza Bini, an acknowledged fascist actor and *squadrista*. All who "contribute[d] some activity or talent" to the theater were eligible for membership in the Corporation.[45]

Although the Corporation and the League were similar organizations, their rhetoric was different. The language of national solidarity replaced the language of class solidarity. The logo of the Corporation's newspaper proclaimed that it sought to "ennoble theatrical art according to the glorious Italian traditions and to elevate the conditions of those who live by art and who give their precious contribution of talent, will, and sacrifice."[46] The Corporation accused the League of "always waving the red badge of revolution."[47] The Corporation characterized itself as a band of fascists who would counter disorder in the theater.[48]

The contest between the League and the Corporation for the right to represent the actors centered around the actors' burgeoning consciousness of themselves as workers rather than artists and their ambivalence about that designation. The group that could represent their claims, or at least articulate their claims, as artists, won their allegiance. The wedding of rhetoric to organization was not enough. Opportunity was also needed. A strike in Milan in January of 1922 provided the opportunity for Calza Bini's Corporation to win the allegiance of the actors. Over one hundred and fifty actors and assorted theatrical personnel were involved in the strike.

Calza Bini's group initially consisted of only three actors. It eventually grew to include sixteen and managed to break the strike with the cooperation of the company heads and the authors' society. From that point, the socialist League lost its power as the chief representative of the actors, and the Corporation of Theater, which the fascist regime transformed into the Corporation of Spectacle, took its place.

Seventeen years after Calza Bini broke the strike, *Scenario*, the theatrical review sponsored by the Fascist regime, described the strike-breaking performance in Milan as the event firmly placing the theater among the "national forces" that "actively participated in the revolutionary and innovative work of Fascism."[49] What was the significance of Calza Bini's organization for the organization of the theater? While fascist elements were in the theater as elsewhere in Italy at this time, the strike gave them the upper hand and signaled the end of socialist dominance.[50] The fascists who saw national goals as coming before individual workers' goals appealed to the theater owners, company heads, and playwrights for whom actors who saw themselves as exploited were nothing but a nuisance. But, more importantly, they provided an organization that achieved the same work-related goals for the actors while appealing to them as artists. The Corporation of Theater managed to weaken both the market and status anxieties of the actors and placate the financial forces in the theater as well.

If one takes into account the entire period from 1892, the year in which the Italian Socialist party was founded, to 1922, the year in which Mussolini and fascism came to power, we can reformulate the question about the political persuasions of the Italian middle classes. Rather than ask why the middle classes were attracted to fascism, we might more profitably ask why the socialists were unable to hold on to their middle-class constituency. The middle classes, as in the case of the actors, responded to a rhetoric that fascism cleverly exploited and that the socialists were unable to exploit. When fascism came to power, it was confronted with the task of transforming some of its rhetoric into policy.

The Fascist Regime and the Italian Middle Classes: Corporativism and Class Collaboration

In 1927, the International Institute of the Middle Classes met in Rome. The Institute, founded in 1903 in Brussels, met annually to engage in the "discussion, documentation and popularization" of issues germane to the middle classes.[51] Giuseppe Bottai, Fascist Minister of Corporations, announced that the Fascist regime had solved the problem of the middle classes: "For us, in fact, gentlemen, the problem of the middle classes is definitively resolved . . . by our political and social system.[52] Bottai argued that the term *middle class* was not relevant in Fascist Italy, where the "corporativist order" had declared the equality of "all social classes"; however, the Italian middle classes were "called to a function of the first order to assure the social peace, the reorganization of production, and the just distribution of the material and moral goods of life."[53]

The "problem" solved by the regime concerned the social marginality of a large segment of the professional population. Order and stability are the only requirements that unite the small merchant class, and any party who achieves these objectives would receive their support. The other segments of the middle classes—the white-collar workers, the schoolteachers, the professionals—were far more disparate, and their interests not so easily collectivized. These segments of the middle classes could be either socialist or fascist and the Fascist movement at least temporarily captured them through its language of incorporation and its assignment of the explicit role of class mediator to unemployed intellectuals.

Corporativist doctrine was the central organizational and ideological vehicle for incorporating the middle classes into the Fascist regime. Private initiative drawn into the public sphere through the overarching presence of the Fascist state was the cornerstone of corporativist doctrine. The ideology found its organizational form in the Fascist unions (*sindicati*) and corporations. The regime organized industrial sectors in corporations. Each corporation consisted of suborganizations of members of a particular industry. It was through this series of interlocking and hierarchical organizations that the individual became an integral part of the Fascist state. Although corporativism is usually studied as an economic policy, it is also very much a cultural policy.[54] By *cultural*, I mean a policy that affects how a group interprets its social world. The doctrine of corporativism served as a metaphor for how one should live in Fascist society. It provided a language in which to frame everyday experience and reinterpret that experience in terms of fascist consciousness.

Corporativism was introduced in January of 1927 in the Labor Charter (*Carta del Lavoro*), a thirty-point document written in a series of aphoristic propositions that explained what the individual's relation to the state should be. Of the thirty propositions, the statements concerning the individual's relation to society, the function of unions and collective labor contracts, and the relation of the public and private sector are germane to this analysis. Giuseppe Bottai and Augusto Turati wrote the Charter, and Mussolini's Grand Council passed it immediately into law.[55] Turati was the secretary of the Fascist party. Bottai was the architect of the technocratic fascist state.

Corporativism as ideology and metaphor rethought the individual's relation to the public sphere. The Labor Charter proclaimed that it proposed a "new way for everyone to be part of the national society."[56] The good of the individual and the good of the nation were one. The nation was a moral collectivity, and it was the individual's duty somehow to find his appropriate place within that collectivity. All workers, including intellectuals and professionals, were obliged to organize in "free" unions and professional organizations that had to be legally recognized by the state. The collective labor contract was the "concrete expression of solidarity among the various factors of production."[57] The contracts were bogus, however, because there was no legitimate bargaining power.[58]

Private economic initiative and class collaboration were the central themes of corporativism. Because of the unifying nature of the state and the general goal of productivity there could be no conflict of interests between employers and employees. The Labor Charter declared that "the humblest employee, the interests of the contract of the clerk and those of the manual laborer, are placed on the same plane as the interests of the economic firm."[59] The union of interests between workers and their employees distinguished corporativism from socialism. In contrast to socialism, whose doctrine of "class struggle" tended to "suppress private property and individual initiative," Fascist syndicalism would emphasize "class collaboration." According to Mussolini, fascism "safeguards property—but elevates it to a social function—respecting the economic initiative of the nation."[60] In a single rhetorical stroke, the category of labor conflict was eliminated.

The Charter's position on economic activity was designed to accommodate the small merchant. The Charter exalted private initiative as "the most efficacious and useful instrument in the interests of the nation."[61] The fascist state would only intervene in collective production when ". . . private initiative is lacking or insufficient or when the political interests of the state are at stake. Such intervention can assume the form of control, encouragement, or direct management."[62]

In practice, "encouragement" translated into economic protection for the small merchant class. In a Fascist party publication entitled *Fascism and Commerce,* the author proclaimed that before the advent of fascism, Italian shopkeepers were treated as "specks of dust," but that the Fascist regime viewed them as "blocks of granite."[63] The author claimed that the Fascist Confederation of Shopkeepers (*Confederazione Fascista dei Commercianti*), which included shops as diverse as hotels, restaurants, and clothing stores, claimed 900,000 small businesses as members.[64] These businesses were reorganized in Corporations of wood, cereal, sugar, oil, textiles, chemicals, and hospitality.[65] The consent of these "blocks of granite" to the rule of the Fascist regime was not surprising. The agenda for the meeting of the Central Corporative Committee on 3 May 1930 listed the following items of business under the Corporation of Commerce: regulation of business contracts, a list of firms that could export vegetable oils, regulation of retail prices, hours of the opening and closing of shops, and protection of industrial property.[66] Despite a wide-ranging agenda, which included seven Corporations, the accomplishments of the 1930 Corporative Commit-tee were limited to regulation of the sale of milk in Rome and a new set of laws regulating the business activities of insurance agents.[67]

The Role of the Professional Middle Classes in the Corporativist State

Intellectuals had a special place in the fascist order. Since they were clearly not productive in the ordinary sense, they were to be guardians of fascist and corporativist morality. The duty of those who practiced a "free profes-sion" or "art" was to contribute ". . . to the guardianship of the interests of art, science, and letters, to the perfection of production, and to the attainment of the moral ends of the corporativist order."[68] The regime took to calling professionals and intellectuals the "third element" in society and argued that they were the group that the socialists neglected because they were frequently self-employed or "free professionals."

In 1925, the first National Fascist Corporation of Intellectual Professions was formed. This organization underwent various recombinations and name changes until 1934, when the Confederation of Professionals and Artists became the Corporation of Professions and the Arts.[69] Fascist party functionaries as well as practitioners of the various occupations sat on the Corporate Boards. The Corporation claimed 122,184 members. Physi-cians made up the largest category of membership, followed by lawyers. Fourteen hundred authors and writers and 3,000 journalists were enrolled.[70] Despite grandiose fascist rhetoric that placed professionals and artists in the vanguard of the fascist experiment, they were particularly difficult to organize, in part because of their attachment to their status.

At the first national meeting of the Corporation of Professionals and Artists, Mussolini said that the "representatives" of the individual intellec-tual activities in their respective syndicates—architects, lawyers, writers, doctors, musicians, engineers—would help to create a "personal act be-tween fascism and culture." Culture was not "cold erudition," and fascist culture creators had to disengage themselves from the "ivory towers," which often masked "aridity of spirit." Instead, intellectuals had to "live fully this life; to be men of their time, to avoid the isolation of a sterile egocen-trism. . . . With fascism for the first time in all the world professionals and artists enter in the State, come to be part of the State."[71]

What did Mussolini have in mind as constituting the intellectual's "per-sonal act between fascism and culture"? Mussolini's address to the first national meeting of the Physician's Syndicate provides a clue. He said that Italians were not having enough children and that doctors should instruct women on the value of fertility. In addition, Italians were becoming too thin and that doctors should inform their patients of the nutritional value of grapes and encourage patients to eat them. These were useful prescriptions for a regime that was waging a "demographic campaign" to increase the number of Italian births and an economic campaign to protect the marketability of Italian agricultural products. If a physician wished to leave this realm of pseudoscientific propaganda, Mussolini pointed out that he could also lecture his patients on the world depression and inform them that Italy was not suffering as much as other countries in the world—particularly if Italians ate the Italian grapes![72]

Physicians were typical of the underemployed intellectual.[73] The fascist Medical Federation frequently complained of the "plethora" of doctors. The situation was particularly acute in the large cities. According to Marzio Barbagli, "an attempt to estimate the existing relationship between demand and supply was made in 1932 by the National Fascist Union of Doctors. Estimating at 900 the annual demand for doctors and at 2,200 the supply, the union foresaw a surplus of over 8,000 doctors over the next six years."[74] The situation was much the same for lawyers, engineers, and architects. Yet the state-run universities did nothing to curtail the number of degrees granted.[75] The Fascist regime pursued a dual and self-defeating policy. It continued to use the university and the *laureato* as means to distribute social status while simultaneously using the pursuit of a degree to correct for labor-market inefficiencies.

In order to secure the support of professional groups, the regime did offer something besides rhetoric. The regime charged the Corporation of Professionals and Artists with the task of developing *albi,* official lists determining who had the proper credentials to practice a profession. The Corporation required its potential members to present their educational credentials and demonstrate that they had experience in their particular profession. This meant that noncertified practitioners could be excluded from practicing a profession. The development of the *albi* was a form of licensing, a standard procedure for any group trying to establish itself as a profession. The regime said that the creation of the *albi* was "delicate and complex" because "free professionals" had protected their freedom by reporting to no one. Nonetheless, the regime argued that it was reasonable to ask that professionals pass examinations before practicing their craft. Many Italian professional groups such as physicians already had such procedures. It is understandable that overpopulated professional occupations would welcome state-sponsored controls that could exclude members from their ranks.

When the Corporation presented its charter to Mussolini in January 1936, it claimed to represent the "indispensable element of culture and technique" in the corporative state.[76] The fascist *albi* were more than regime-sanctioned professionalization strategies. Like many activities in Fascist Italy, the *albi* had both a benign and a more questionable purpose. In addition to the possession of educational credentials, the regime required that professionals demonstrate "the necessary moral and disciplinary requisites."[77] The morals test would "avoid the abusive exercise of professions and give Public Boards the choice of professionals from those official lists, with criteria founded on faith, preferably to members of the National Fascist Party and members of the Fascist Syndicates."[78] The regime was at least as interested in assuring employment to its loyal supporters as it was in ensuring the purity of the individual professions.

Political Ideology and the Historical Construction of Social Class in Italy

The Italian middle classes suffered both status and market anxieties. Corporativism provided the ideological umbrella that permitted the Fascist regime to employ a number of different strategies to quell both types of anxiety. Because they required concrete state actions, market anxieties were more or less easy to satisfy once the regime came to power. The regime passed laws regulating competition and protecting the market position of small shopkeepers and artisans; it expanded the state bureaucracy to provide employment for the vast numbers of university graduates.[79] It is at this point that the distinction beween the "humanistic lower middle classes" and the shopkeepers and lower-level civil servants is crucial. Status anxieties were more difficult to resolve because they were related to the way social class was historically constructed and collectively understood in Italy. The alleviation of status anxieties required a total redesign of the social and political structures of Italy and their institutions. This is precisely what Italian fascism claimed to do; but it was also impossible to deliver on these claims.

The rigidity of pre-Fascist Italian social structure and the system of political and cultural closure it created suggests how fascism and the phenomenon of intellectual unemployment are linked. As previously noted, Italy had the largest oversupply of university graduates in western Europe. Two English scholars writing on the condition of the Italian educated classes noted as early as 1901: "Men, who in England would go into business . . . and be trained for it, here [Italy] swell the ranks of the educated unemployed. . . . Every successful tradesman hopes to see his son a lawyer or doctor or civil servant and spends 300 to 500 [lira] in educating him for a useless life. It is impossible for many men to make a living in the overcrowded professions."[80] Why were people, against all economic rationality, rushing into university educations and preparing for professional posts that they would never fill?

Social class in Italy was based on the possession of culture, not capital, although the two were frequently found together. Given these criteria, there were really only two classes in Italy—those who had culture and those who did not. Italian men of culture were the opposite of Salvatorelli's "literate illiterates." They possessed more than a superficial command of the literary and artistic heritage of the nation and the capacity to use that knowledge in a critical manner when evaluating current historical events. In short, they had what French sociologist Pierre Bourdieu identifies as "cultural capital"—a currency in the politics of everyday life.[81]

Because of the value that Italian elites attached to culture in this broad sense, culture became a powerful agent of social and political closure in Italy.[82] Italy had a long tradition of cultural exclusivity. The Italian *alta borghesia* (haute bourgeoisie) were always cultivated, and they kept a strict monopoly on the modes of cultural discourse. A common language, the cultural glue of modern nation-states, was the province of a few privileged elites. As Adrian Lyttelton notes, "For the 'cultured classes,' the sense of nationhood and the literary language were associated values of which they were the exclusive guardians; the masses, clerical or subversive, spoke dialect."[83] Literacy, until well after the unification, was confined to the north.[84] The public elementary education system was neglected, and teachers often went unpaid until the local government decided to allocate money to them.[85]

Italy stands in sharp contrast to England, where the bourgeoisie shared the high culture with other social groups. Although the British educational system was highly stratified and university attendance restricted, England did manage to create conditions that allowed for the possibility of democratic cultural participation. The proliferation of a mass reading public and the promotion of middle-class cultural leisure activities were measures of a relative cultural openness.[86] In England, culture was a free space that anyone might enter. Because the Italian bourgeoisie or "cultured classes" did not participate in the sharing of culture, culture became a barrier that had to be crossed and an area of contestation. In Italy, culture, or the claim to the possession of culture, became a scarce resource and a measure of social mobility. The Italian university was the only institution that could legitimate an individual's claim to culture and, by extension, full social empowerment—that is, the ability to have a directive voice in one's own future and the future of one's group and country. The competition over cultural goods and the struggle for social incorporation that it masked, rather than pure labor market inefficiency, contributed to the flight to the university. Instead of social power, it produced large numbers of dissatisfied "humanistic lower middle classes."

Salvatorelli's condescension is telling. It suggests that the same impetus that pushed Italian youth to the university may have pushed them toward fascism. The democratization of culture, which had occurred in England without the intervention of the state, never occurred in Italy. Socialism at first offered the middle classes cultural as well as political incorporation. Fascism was able to seize that offer and give the appearance of delivering it. The Fascist movement offered the illusion of proximity to elite cultural figures such as Marinetti and D'Annunzio; the Fascist regime, through its cultural policies and the employment of the "humanistic lower middle classes," appeared to bring cultural democratization.

Early in the Fascist regime, Antonio Gramsci recognized the link between the corporativist program and the educated and unemployed "humanistic middle classes": "In reality the corporative trend has operated to shore up the crumbling position of the middle classes and not to eliminate them. . . . the corporative trend is . . . dependent upon unemployment. It defends for the employed a certain minimum standard which, if there were free competition, would likewise collapse and thus provokes serious social disturbances; and it creates new forms of employment, organizational and not productive, for the unemployed of the middle classes."[87] For those unemployed intellectuals who did not easily fit into professional categories, the regime expanded the public bureaucracy. Between 1923 and 1943, the number of state jobs tripled.[88] These regime strategies did benefit certain segments of the "humanistic middle classes," but the well quickly ran dry. University graduates of the 1930s and early 1940s faced the same problems as earlier generations; and when the antifascist resistance emerged in the waning days of the war, the same university graduates flocked to join it.[89]

During the past hundred years, the Italian middle classes have been Socialists, Fascists, and democrats. They are a constituency perpetually waiting to be created. Different factions of the class have different requirements. To understand under what conditions and under what historical circumstances the middle classes decide to act, it is necessary to take individual segments of them seriously as groups and to examine their cultural requirements and structural position with regard to the political opportunities available to them in any given time. The Italian middle classes may consist of groups without fixed ideologies, but they all have occupational histories. If we are to understand fully their role as political actors during the interwar period, we must recover that history. In short, if we are to ascribe political motivation to the group, we must accord them more significance than "traces in the newspapers."

Notes

1. Luigi Salvatorelli, *Nazionalfascismo*, with a Preface by Giorgio Amendola (Turin, 1977), 15–16.

2. Antonio Gramsci, "Il popolo delle scimmie," *Sul fascismo,* ed. Enzo Santarelli, (Rome, 1978), 96.

3. Ibid., 99.

4. A classic American work on the general connection between class and authoritarian politics is Seymour Martin Lipset's *Political Man: The Social Bases of Politics* (New York, 1960; reprint, Baltimore, 1981). For specific discussions of the Italian case, see Gino Germani, "Fascism and Class," in *The Nature of Fascism,* ed. Stuart Woolf (London, 1968), 65–96; Renzo de Felice, "Italian Fascism and the Middle Classes," in *Who Were the Fascists: Social Roots of European Fascism,* ed. Stein Ugelvik Larsen et al. (Oslo, 1980), 312–17; and David D. Roberts, "Petty Bourgeois Fascism in Italy: Form and Content," in *Who Were the Fascists,* 337–47.

5. Adrian Lyttelton, "Italian Fascism," in *Fascism: A Reader's Guide,* ed. Walter Laqueur (Berkeley, 1976), 135.

6. Emilio Gentile, "Fascism in Italian Historiography: In Search of an Individual Historical Identity," *Journal of Contemporary History* 21 (1986): 194.

7. Ibid., 194–95.

8. In a review of recent studies of the lower middle classes published in an Italian historical journal, there was not one citation to a work on Italy. See Geoffrey Crossick, "Al di la della metafora: studi recenti sui ceti medi inferiori in Europa prima del 1914," *Quaderni Storici* 56 (Aug. 1984): 573–612.

9. While recent German historiography has focused on the lower middle classes, Jeffrey Herf's *Reactionary Modernism* (Cambridge, 1984) is particularly notable because it focuses on a professional middle-class group and attempts to demonstrate the interplay of ideology and occupational prerequisites. Recent studies of Italian fascism include Victoria De Grazia, *The Culture of Consent: Mass Organization of Leisure in Fascist Italy* (Cambridge, 1981); Donald Bell, *Sesto San Giovanni: Workers, Culture, and Politics in an Italian Town, 1880–1922* (New Brunswick, 1986); Alice Kelikian, *Town and Country Under Fascism: The Transformation of Brescia, 1915–1926* (Oxford, 1986); Tracy Koon, *Believe Fight Obey: Political Socialization of Youth in Fascist Italy, 1922–43* (Chapel Hill, 1985); Luisa Passerini, *Torino operaia e fascismo* (Rome, 1984).

10. Charles S. Maier, *Recasting Bourgeois Europe: Stabilization in France, Germany, and Italy in the Decade after World War I* (Princeton, 1975) is the major work in this mode. The studies drawn exclusively from the literature on Italian fascism are numerous. Kelikian, *Town and Country,* and Douglas Forsyth, "The Politics of Forced Accumulation: Monetary and Financial Policy in Italy, 1914–1922" (Ph.D. diss., Princeton University, 1987) are two recent and excellent examples of the approach.

11. See for example, De Grazia, *Culture of Consent;* Bell, *Sesto;* Passerini, *Torino operaia.*

12. For a concise discussion of fascism as an attempt to achieve political incorporation, see Juan J. Linz, "Political Space and Fascism as a Late-Comer: Conditions Conducive to the Success or Failure of Fascism as a Mass Movement in Inter-war Europe," in *Who Were the Fascists,* Larsen et al., particularly 153–65.

13. In *Making the Fascist State* (New York, 1928), Herbert W. Schneider lists among the candidates who ran in Milan in 1919 on the first Fascist party slate, "Mussolini, Marinetti (futurist), Podrecca (leading anti-clerical), Toscanini (the distinguished and popular musician), Bolzon (futurist), Macchi (an aviator and a futurist)": 61. When this slate went down in defeat, Mussolini decided to exclude artists from practical politics. The slate he assembled in 1921 lacked the futurists.

14. Adrian Lyttelton, *The Seizure of Power: Fascism in Italy, 1919–1929* (London, 1973; reprint, Princeton, 1987), 49 and 42–51 for a discussion of the distinction between a movement of elites and a movement that defined itself as elite.

15. There are no hard data on the social basis of Fascist party membership in the 1920s and 1930s. For an early discussion, see Herman Finer, *Mussolini's Italy* (London, 1935; reprint, Hamden, Conn., 1964), 371–74. The classic study of Fascist party elites is Harold D. Lasswell with Renzo Sereno, "The Fascists: The Changing Elite," *World Revolutionary Elites: Studies in Coercive Ideological Movements,* ed. Harold D. Lasswell and Daniel Lerner (Cambridge, Mass., 1965; reprint, Westport, Conn., 1980), 179–93.

16. "Italian Fascism and the Middle Classes," 314–15.

17. We shall know more about the meaning of Fascist party membership when William Brustein's work, which applies rational-choice theory to party membership, is completed. For preliminary findings, see William Brustein and Barry Markovsky, "The Rationality of Fascism: Interwar Party Membership in Italy and Germany," Paper presented to the American Sociological Association, Atlanta, Aug. 1988.

18. Lyttelton, *Seizure of Power,* 411-12.

19. See Germani, "Fascism and Class," 86–90, and Roberts, "Petty Bourgeois Fascism in Italy," 339–42.

20. Marzio Barbagli, *Educating for Unemployment: Politics, Labor Markets, and the School System—Italy, 1859–1973,* trans. Robert H. Ross (New York, 1982), 13–39. I am indebted to Barbagli's study, which does not explicitly draw the connection between fascism and intellectual unemployment, for much of my thinking on this subject.

21. DeGrazia felicitiously describes the bringing of culture to certain segments of the lower middle classes as "privileging the clerks": *Culture of Consent,* 127ff; for a discussion of fascist cultural programs, see Philip V. Cannistraro, *La fabbrica del consenso: fascismo e mass media* (Rome, 1975).

22. There is a large sociological and historical literature on this concept. For representative examples, see Arno J. Mayer, "The Lower Middle Class as Historical Problem," *Journal of Modern History* 47 (Sept. 1975): 409–36; Peter N. Stearns, "The Middle Class: Toward a Precise Definition," *Comparative Studies in Society and History* 21 (1979): 376–96; George Ross, "Marxism and the New Middle Class," *Theory and Society* 5 (1978): 163–90; and Val Burris, "The Discovery of the New Middle Class," *Theory and Society* 15 (1986): 317–49. For a collection of essays that discuss Italian class structure, see Massimo Paci, ed., *Capitalismo e classi sociali in Italia* (Bologna, 1978).

23. The Italian literature on social class written during and after the fascist period does not tend to distinguish between the various strata of the middle classes. *Ceti medi* (literally, middle layers) is the term most frequently used, although *piccola borghesia* appears occasionally.

24. For a description of the occupational distribution among the middle classes as of 1941 see Giuliano Pischel, *Il problema dei ceti medi* (Milan, 1945), 197–203.

25. Paolo Sylos Labini, *Saggio sulle classi sociali* (Rome, 1975), 155.

26. For a discussion of the role occupational traditions may play in political mobilization, see Craig Calhoun, "The Radicalism of Tradition: Community Strength or Venerable Disguise and Borrowed Language," *American Journal of Sociology* 88 (March 1983): 886–914.

27. For a summary of this literature, see Jean L. Cohen, "Strategy or Identity: New Theoretical Paradigms and Contemporary Social Movements," *Social Research* 52 (Winter 1985): 663–715; and Sidney Tarrow, "National Politics and Collective Action: Recent Theory and Research in Western Europe and the United States," *Annual Review of Sociology* 14 (1988): 421–40.

28. Sylos Labini, *Saggi,* 58, 61–62.

29. Salvatorelli, *Nazionalfascismo,* 17.

30. Bolton King and Thomas Okey, *Italy Today* (New York, 1901), 70–71.

31. Barbagli, *Educating for Unemployment*, 72.
32. See Clara M. Lovett, *The Democratic Movement in Italy, 1830–1876* (Cambridge, Mass., 1982).
33. Carlo M. Cipolla, *Literacy and Development in the West* (Harmondsworth, 1969), 127–28.
34. Carl Levy, "Socialism and the Educated Middle Classes in Western Europe, 1870–1914," *Intellectuals, Universities and the State in Western Modern Societies,* ed. Ron Eyerman, Lennart G. Svensson, and Thomas Soderqvist (Berkeley, 1987), 154–91.
35. For a fuller discussion of the Umanitaria and its programs, see Mabel Berezin, "Public Spectacles and Private Enterprises: Theater and Politics in Italy under Fascism, 1919–1940 (Ph.D. diss., Harvard University, 1987), 214–27.
36. For a discussion that focuses entirely on the Italian Nationalist Association, see Alexander J. De Grand, *The Italian Nationalist Association and the Rise of Fascism in Italy* (Lincoln, 1978), particularly 9–27.
37. For a history of the rhetoric and ideology of Italian syndicalism, see David B. Roberts, *The Syndicalist Tradition and Italian Fascism* (Chapel Hill, 1979), particularly 153–85; for a study of the relation between the national syndicates and fascist unions, see Ferdinando Cordova, *Le origini dei sindicati fascisti, 1918–1926* (Rome, 1974).
38. Franco Gaeta, *Il nazionalismo italiano* (Rome, 1981), 220–35.
39. See Guido Lopez, "Cartoline postali. In luogo di prefazione," *La cultura milanese e l'universita popolare negli anni 1901–1927,* ed. Guido Lopez (Milan, 1983), 10.
40. The Fascist regime was interested in the plight of unemployed actors. Gaetano Salvemini, the exiled anti-fascist, notes in *Under the Axe of Fascism* (London, 1936), 374: "An official communiqué of January 29th, 1935, stated that 1,500 actors were without employment."
41. Domenico Gismano, *L'Argante* (Milan), 7 Feb. 1918.
42. See Berezin, "Public Spectacles and Private Enterprises," 36–72.
43. "Sciopero degli artisti di prosa," *Giornale degli artisti* (Milan), 30 April 1919, p. 5.
44. "Un'altra magnifica vittoria della Confederazione dei Lavoratori del Teatro," *L'Argante* (Milan), 6 Jan. 1921, p. 1; Gaspare Di Martino, "Vannegiare e Soccombere," *L'Argante* (Milan), 16 Feb. 1921, p. 1.
45. Gino Calza Bini, "Chi siamo," *Tespi* (Milan), 5 April 1922, p. 1.
46. Ibid.
47. *Tespi* (Milan), 5 April 1922, p. 2.
48. Ibid.
49. Carlo Tamberlani, "Gli alberi del fascismo nel teatro," *Scenario* 7, 7 (1939): 328.
50. The League continued to exist, but in a weakened form, and finally identified itself as a fascist union in 1926.
51. M. Stevens, "L'Oeuvre de l'institut international des classes moyennes," *in Rapports et compte-rendu des séances de IVᵉ Congrès International des Classes Moyennes* held in Paris 2–4 June 1924 (Paris, 1925), 21. Its ideological position was that the middle classes were the "living force" of the nation and that "their [middle classes'] prosperity was essential to the economic prosperity of the country itself and equally important to the health of the social body (7)." Despite this global rhetoric, the organization's goals were narrowly economic and the shopkeepers and small merchants were the obvious beneficiaries of its international lobbying efforts.
52. Giuseppe Bottai, "Il sindicalismo fascista e le classi medie," in *Esperienza Corporativa* (Rome, 1928), 381.
53. Ibid., 383.

54. Writings on corporativism take its economic nature as implicit. See for example, Charles S. Maier, "The Economics of Fascism and Nazism," in *In Search of Stability: Explorations in Historical Political Economy* (Cambridge, 1987), 70–120; Lyttelton, *Seizure of Power*, 202–36, 308–64.

55. The Grand Council of Fascism (*Gran Cosiglio*) was a miniature parliament that aided Mussolini in governing Italy. Mussolini personally chose its members.

56. Giuseppe Bottai and Augusto Turati, *La carta del Lavoro* (Rome, 1929), 26.

57. Ibid., 36.

58. Adrian Lyttelton makes the point that while the Socialist unions were not outlawed, they were left with no power. See Lyttelton, *The Seizure of Power*, Chap. 12, and particularly 319, 322–24. The actors are a case in point.

59. Bottai and Turati, *Carta del Lavoro*, 31.

60. "Discorso di S. E. il capo del governo," in *Ministero delle Corporazioni, Atti dell'Assemblea Generale del Consiglio Nazionale delle Corporazioni* (Rome, 1931), 4.

61. Bottai and Turati, *Carta del Lavoro*, 37.

62. Ibid., 38.

63. Mario Racheli, *Il fascismo e il commercio, panorami di vita fascista* (Milan, 1938), 29.

64. Ibid., 30.

65. Ibid., 116–22.

66. Giuseppe Bottai, *Il Consiglio Nazionale delle Corporazioni* (Milan, 1933), 339.

67. Ibid., 387–402.

68. Bottai and Turati, *Carta del Lavoro*, 38.

69. Alessandro Pavolini, "I professionisti ed artisti nel primo decennale della Carta del Lavoro," in *Anni della Carta del Lavoro*, ed. Confederazione Fascista dei Lavoratori dell'Industria (Rome, 1937), 411–12.

70. Membership was distributed among groups whom are not always thought of as professional or artistic. Pavolini, op. cit., lists the following: 932 architects; 146 actuaries; 1,355 authors and writers; 15,072 lawyers; 11,373 fine arts, chemists, Bachelors of Arts, business consultants, pharmacists; 5,786 geometers; 2,999 journalists; 555 nurses with diplomas; 12,468 engineers; 1,331 private teachers; 11,175 midwives; 25,228 physicians; 2,822 musicians; 3,032 notaries; 476 legal defense counselors; 2,231 skilled business consultants; 2,653 skilled industrial consultants; 2,540 accountants; 209 directors and set designers; 3,658 agricultural technicians; 3,145 veterinarians; 3,400 artists and college graduates; and 716 inventors. The diversity of the groups suggests one reason why they had difficulty in understanding their common interests.

71. "Il discorso del Duce," *Le professioni e le arti: bollettino mensile della Confederazione Nazionale* 2 (Oct. 1932): 2.

72. [Benito Mussolini], "Discorso del capo del governo ai medici Italiani," *Le professioni e le arti: bollettino mensile della Confederazione Nazionale dei Sindicati Fascisti Professionisti ed Artisti* 2 (Jan. 1932): 3.

73. For a history of various professions in Italy that takes the Fascist period into account, see Willem Tousijn, ed., *Le libere professioni in Italia* (Bologna, 1987).

74. Barbagli, *Educating for Unemployment*, 183.

75. For a discussion of the labor market position of professionals during the Fascist period, see Barbagli, 142–86.

76. Ibid., 421.

77. *Confederazione Fascista dei Lavoratori dell'Industria, Le Corporazioni nel primo anno di vita* (Rome, 1936), 420.

78. Ibid., 421–22.

79. Sylos Labini, *Saggio*, 75–76.

80. King and Okey, *Italy Today* cited in Barbagli, *Educating for Unemployment*, 17.

81. For the most concise formulation of this concept, see Pierre Bourdieu, "Cultural Reproduction and Social Reproduction," in *Knowledge, Education and Cultural Change*, ed. R. Brown (London, 1973), 71–112.

82. Despite the unification and the establishment of the democracy in 1860, it was not until 1913 that Italy extended universal suffrage to males. Italy was the last country among the industrialized nations in western Europe to do this. See Eric Hobsbawm, "Mass-Producing Traditions: Europe, 1870–1914," in *The Invention of Tradition*, ed. Eric Hobsbawm and Terence Ranger (Cambridge, 1983), 267.

83. Lyttelton, *Seizure of Power*, 16.

84. Barbagli, *Educating for Unemployment*, 15.

85. Bolton and King *(Italy Today)* reported that teachers often had to wait months for their meager salaries, and "the arrears were often so serious, that many teachers had to live on charity": 242.

86. For a brief summary of this process, see Raymond Williams, *The Long Revolution* (London, 1961; reprint, 1965), particularly 145–236.

87. Antonio Gramsci, "Americanism and Fordism," in *Selections from the Prison Notebooks*, trans. and ed. Quintin Hoare and Geoffrey Nowell Smith (New York, 1971), 294.

88. Barbagli, *Educating for Unemployment*, 200–201.

89. See H. Stuart Hughes, *The United States and Italy*, revised ed. (Cambridge, Mass., 1965), 90–92.

8 Between State and Nation: Romanian Lower-Middle-Class Intellectuals in the Interwar Period[1]

IRINA LIVEZEANU

It keeps being said that we Romanians are erecting an unenduring house, that is only with base and roof, but without walls. The base would be the peasant estate, and the roof the leadership-intellectual class, while the walls, the artisans' estate, are missing! Yes, it is true, but in order to erect good walls good masons are needed. And where shall we seek the masons, if not in the intellectual class? Hence therefore from this too one can see that the leadership-intellectual estate must necessarily be expanded on the one hand to defend the peasant, on the other hand in order to nurture the artisans' estate.[2]

I. E. Torouțiu, 1911

If we include in the ranks of the petite bourgeoisie the small land-owning peasantry too, Romania is a petit-bourgeois country *par excellence*.[3]

Lucrețiu Pătrășcanu, 1945

In the interwar period Romania was generally characterized as an over-whelmingly peasant country. Yet just because of that, the transformation of a good part of the Romanian peasantry into an urban middle class was the strategy of both choice and necessity for the Romanian state as it moved to consolidate itself in territories greatly expanded in 1918. Since even the smallest step from village to town was socially a giant one, and since very few could step directly into the upper middle class, an expanded lower middle class arose with the help of nation-building policies. Despite new opportunities and state protection, this enlarged petite bourgeoisie was not a contented class. It was, rather, a class traumatized by the high expectations and mobility generated in the political effervescence of 1918 and the decades that followed.

In 1918, Romania more than doubled in size by adding the provinces of Transylvania, Bukovina, and Bessarabia, previously ruled by Hungary, Austria, and Russia, respectively. But these gains seemed precarious. Only the expansion of ethnically Romanian urban elites could solidify this new political creation. The state and majority nationality thus set out to replace the foreign minorities' elites in a process that could potentially turn into interethnic warfare over control of elite professional niches, urban areas, commerce, civil service, and cultural institutions. Established non-Romanian elites and aspiring Romanian elites were locked in bitter struggle. For the Romanians, the 1920s were both exhilarating and destabilizing. Although the process of Romanianization provided the newly promoted Romanian elites with important opportunities, it did not proceed as quickly and as thoroughly as expected. Paradoxically, the convergence on nationalist goals of the state and of the expanding Romanian lower middle class, and this class's disappointments with the state's performance, intensified lower-middle-class nationalism.

In Romania radical nationalist ideologies originated among groups of young intellectuals. Scholars generally agree on the importance of the intelligentsia in the vanguard of Romanian fascism. Eugen Weber has shown that the "legionary leadership came from the provincial only-just-urbanized intelligentsia: sons or grandsons of peasants, schoolteachers, and priests. . . . [T]heir bastion was in the schools, and . . . they soon attracted or at least affected an important portion of the country's youth and of the intellectuals."[4]

Given the importance of the lower middle class in Romania's nation-building strategies in the interwar period, and the prominence of the intellectuals in the formulation of extreme nationalist ideologies, let us look at the relationship between these two groups, and between them and the state.

Intellectuals and Petite Bourgeoisie

In most discussions of the European petite bourgeoisie the economic and social profile of this class is defined by its position between the two classes above and below it, the bourgeoisie and the proletariat, which are identified in relationship to each other and to the capitalist means of production. But in Romania the bourgeoisie and the proletariat developed late and timidly, in keeping with the country's predominantly agrarian character. In trying to locate Romania's lower middle class we come face to face with what has been called "the absence of a middle class in Romania."[5] Instead of a society polarized into bourgeoisie and proletariat with the mediating cushion of the lower middle class, in Romania the modern sector of the economy and society was dominated by the state. According to Henry Roberts, in the conspicuous absence of an urban bourgeoisie in Romania, the state alone could assume its functions.[6] But while the state thus supplanted the entrepreneurial bourgeoisie, the bureaucracy upon which the Romanian state rested became an enclave for a kind of bourgeoisie and petite bourgeoisie *de robe,* which overlapped with the intellectual class.

Intellectuals are not always included in the ranks of the middle classes. In some analyses of eastern Europe the intelligentsia are considered a class apart; nevertheless included there are professional categories of the lower middle class—white-collar workers, employees, office clerks.[7] It is perhaps the peculiarly East European phenomenon of intellectuals' involvement in the politics and state apparatuses of their countries that creates this semantic confusion. This involvement has been discussed by Zygmunt Bauman:

> The intellectual idiom as embraced in the East knew no division of labor between political and cultural leaders, between body politic and "civil society," between rights of the legislator and the duties of spiritual leadership. The separation between intellectual work and professionalized politics, the retreat of intellectuals into distinctly cultural institutions, the growing preoccupations of intellectuals with the autonomy of culture (which meant simultaneously their unconnectedness with politics, or, to put it bluntly, their political irrelevance)—all these processes which had been set in motion in the West soon after the Napoleonic wars and by the end of the nineteenth century reached their completion encapsulated in Weber's idea of *Wertfreiheit*—made little progress in East-Central Europe before the fulfillment of national aspirations in the wake of the Great War. . . .[8]

Debates among Romanian thinkers testify to the peculiarity of Romania's bourgeois development. While some questioned the very existence of a national bourgeoisie, even those who argued that Romania was following closely in the footsteps of the West along the path of bourgeois development observed basic differences from the classical pattern. The sociologist Ştefan Zeletin, for instance, argued that, unlike in the West, where the bourgeoisie was formed in opposition to the central political power, in Romania the bourgeoisie confounded itself with the ruling oligarchy and would not exercise a democratic, decentralizing influence.[9] Zeletin explained the oligarchic nature of the Romanian bourgeoisie by the fact that at an earlier stage in the country's development the ruling oligarchy had held only political power, while the economic power had been in the hands of "a small circle of foreigners, especially Jews."[10]

In the nineteenth century, Romania had come increasingly under the influence of capitalism and the West. Yet greater contact with western Europe did not result in a replica of Westernized market society.[11] While in the West capitalism rose with industrialization, in eastern Europe the initial effect of capitalist penetration had been to turn the area into a "bread basket" for the West. Local agriculture had been commercialized in response to opportunities for the profitable export of grain. In turn, the exploitation of peasant labor intensified, and the ability of the peasantry to be self-sufficient and to bargain for cash wages decreased.[12]

Class formation also differed from that in western Europe. In Moldavia and Wallachia, the two principalities that joined to form the Romanian Kingdom in the middle of the nineteenth century, the commercialization of agriculture and the opening up of foreign trade with western Europe had repercussions for the landed nobility, the boyars. While the big boyars profited and enlarged their estates and cash assets, the fortunes of the smaller boyars declined. In addition, the novel availability of luxury import goods from western Europe and exposure to Western political ideas and life styles made the lower gentry feel deprived compared to its West European counterpart. The *déclassé* nobles attempted to improve their position by studying at Western universities in preparation for professional and civil service positions back home.[13] The indigenous middle class originated from this lower landed gentry and became associated, not, by and large, with commercial, proto-industrial, and industrial activity, but with the state bureaucracy, on which it depended for status and income.

While the native middle class dominated the bureaucracy, foreigners dominated the manufacturing, commercial, and financial activities that swelled after the Treaty of Adrianople of 1829. The urban sector had historically had a large, ethnically foreign, component. In the nineteenth century, Greeks, Armenians, Jews, Germans, Russians, and Frenchmen made up the nonbureaucratic "old" petite bourgeoisie—craftsmen, artisans, merchants, shopkeepers, and middlemen. In Moldavia the foreigners were largely Jewish. Whereas in Wallachia commerce was concentrated in Bucharest, in Moldavia a more decentralized trade network in which Jews predominated was sprinkled throughout the little market towns.[14] Commenting on the Romanians' absence from lower-middle-class occupations, William Beatty-Kingston, a reporter for the *Daily Telegraph*, wrote in 1888 after several trips to Romania that:

[T]he Romanian would not mend a window, tile a roof, nor make a pair of breeches. All these trades, and a legion of others of the plainer, more merely mechanical sort, were exercised by the Jew and the German. The Romanian worked hard, from childhood to the tomb; his sole pleasure or amusements were the *hora*, or the raki-flask; his theater, lecture-room, picture-gallery, museum, and club was the roadside *krisma* [tavern] kept by the Jew who was his confidant, adviser, news-purveyor, agent, tradesman, money-lender, matchmaker, and, in a word, sole manager of his affairs and arbiter of his fate.[15]

Travelers were often struck by the concentration of Jews in middleman, trading, and artisanal occupations. Jews in Moldavia were involved in the retail, wholesale, and cattle trade. They were also estate managers, and they operated almost all the taverns leased to them by landlords who held the exclusive right to sell liquor on their property.[16] A paradoxical picture of the Jewish petite bourgeoisie emerges from descriptions of their squalid living quarters juxtaposed with judgments about their success in business. Writing in 1859, Eugène Poujade, French consul general in Bucharest from 1849 to 1856, described the Moldavian capital as "defaced by the Jewish quarter, where more than thirty thousand Israelites swarm in hideous hovels, surrounded sometimes by filthy mud and sometimes by thick dust. . . . Jassy offers a striking prospect, but one whose harmony is destroyed by this mass of miserable shacks through which one must pass to reach the city."[17] Yet, in the very next paragraph, Poujade declared that Jews had "immense advantages" in Romania, having "little by little" become "masters of all the [country's] business."[18]

The composition of Romania's middle classes in the nineteenth century is described more dispassionately by J. W. Ozanne, an Englishman who spent three years in Romania in the 1870s.[19] Noting that Romania was "the land of officialism *par excellence,*" having "more civil servants than either France or Prussia," Ozanne included in the middle classes the native bureaucrats and professionals alongside the foreign businessmen: "The middle class in the towns is composed . . . almost exclusively of the foreign element, of French and Germans and Jews—Polish, Austrian and Spanish. But there is also a small proportion of the native population which may come under this head. . . . The general run of the doctors, lawyers, officers of the line, and civil servants belong to this class."[20] Ozanne observed that most doctors and lawyers led "a struggling and a shabby existence," and that the lawyers and civil servants barely managed to keep out of debt.[21] These professionals clearly qualify as a lower-middle-class stratum.

By the end of the nineteenth century, Romania's lower middle classes were divided, as we have seen, between foreigners (a substantial proportion of whom were Jews) prevalent in the economic niches *per se,* and Romanians predominant in administrative and professional sectors. Ethnically, the addition of the new provinces in 1918 resulted in a considerable relative diminution of the Romanian urban middle classes, since in the new provinces the Romanians had been an overwhelmingly rural and oppressed population. Romanian peasants had generally experienced little upward mobility under foreign rule. Most of the civil servants and professionals in Bukovina, Transylvania, and Bessarabia had been non-Romanians, and many of the Romanians who had climbed against odds into the elite had become denationalized, thus leaving the rural profile of their original ethnic community almost unchanged. The economic lower middle classes—shop owners and artisans—of the new provinces were even less Romanian than in the Old Kingdom. Moreover, some of the political privileges of Romanian ethnicity that had existed in the Old Kingdom prior to 1918 had to be abandoned after the war. Mass enfranchisement of the Jews and other minorities were conditions of the treaties giving Romania sovereignty over its regained territories.

Peasants and Strangers

Greater Romania was an overwhelmingly rural and agricultural land: of eighteen million inhabitants in 1930 only one-fifth lived in towns; 72.3 percent of the population depended on agriculture. While only 9.5 percent of Romania's population worked in industry and mining, twice as many people were involved in trade, finance, communications, banking, transportation, public services, and the free professions.[22] Thus the nonagricultural population was much more oriented toward the white-collar than toward the blue-collar industrial sector, a fact that, along with others, suggests an important lower middle class.

In the new territories, Romania had acquired not only long-lost Romanians, but also large non-Romanian populations. The proportion of ethnic minorities grew from 8 to 28 percent of the population.[23] A large Hungarian minority lived in Transylvania, and smaller German, Jewish, Ukrainian, and Russian minorities lived throughout the new provinces. The Jews were a significant minority in both the old and the new territories. The minority populations were more urban than the Romanians. In the Old Kingdom, Romanians had made up three-quarters of the urban population, but in the new provinces they were only a third of the townspeople. Thus, while the Romanian nation was mostly one of peasants, the towns of the expanded state were largely foreign, a fact that portended conflict. The Romanian state based in Bucharest ruled politically and held ultimate coercive power, but in the newly annexed provinces it was not powerful in the urban milieu and civil society. Urban elites, networks, and institutions—remnants of previous political and social structures—were initially outside the reach of the Romanian state, and were viewed with enmity by ethnically Romanian elites.

In the new provinces the peasant Romanian population was the expanded state's main ally. To raise the social value of this ally, peasants were encouraged to become educated and urban, and to take up white-collar jobs. By so doing, they effectively strengthened the lower middle class and helped consolidate the Romanian nation. Country-to-city migration was also encouraged by the extensive postwar land reform that redistributed large estates among the country's peasants. Rather than promoting agricultural capitalism and rural prosperity, the reform had had a leveling effect. Furthermore, with limited credit available, the government invested primarily in industrialization and did not support the land reform by loans and pricing measures.[24] As a result, little class differentiation took place in the countryside. Instead, peasants' upward mobility took the form of an exodus of youth to institutions of secondary and higher education in towns. Beyond their schooling, these migrants also aspired to "gentlemanly" bureaucratic urban jobs.[25] The significant rates of urbanization in the interwar period[26] were thus the result of the country-to-city migration of an upwardly mobile peasantry joining the lower middle class.

Another migration, however, appeared to threaten the ethnic purity of Romania's core province. After 1918 the Old Kingdom, and especially its capital, Bucharest, received a stream of migrants from the new provinces. Bucharest became a capital for populations that had previously looked to Budapest, Vienna, and St. Petersburg for cultural, economic, financial, and political advancement. The composition of the capital's bourgeoisie and petite bourgeoisie began to change. Merchants from Bukovina and Transylvania opened shops in Bucharest, transforming the city's atmosphere. Romanian ethnologist Mihai Pop observed in 1937 that "today almost all the retail shops on the big boulevards and on Calea Victoriei [a fashionable avenue in Bucharest] are in the hands of Jews from Transylvania and Bukovina."[27] He warned that in the absence of a clear state policy and study of the problem, Romania was facing a possible surprise: an influx of a largely ethnically alien, central European bourgeoisie hailing from the annexed territories.[28]

Although Pop refered to the bourgeoisie as a whole, he drew particular attention to the petite bourgeoisie.[29] The lower middle classes were the most sizable segment of the commercial and professional elites affected by the union of the Romanian territories. Moreover, the Romanian state was most concerned with this second-level urban elite—doctors, professors, artisans, craftsmen, traders, lawyers, bureaucrats, journalists, teachers, and students. It wanted to control their development and to enlarge the ethnic Romanian component of the lower middle class. From the state's point of view, a Romanian lower middle class derived from ethnically pure peasant stock, and schooled in the growing educational institutions of Greater Romania, appeared to hold the salvation of the national structure weakened by multi-ethnicity, regionalism, and hostile elites. The native bureaucratic apparatus needed many new cadres with which to accomplish the unification, fulfill larger administrative and educational needs, and replace the bureaucracies of the previous ruling powers.

In addition to enlarging the Romanian bureaucracy, Liberal governments also wished to nurture an ethnically Romanian economic bourgeoisie. While Western observers were largely critical of the Liberals' autarchic economic policies, which aimed at nationalizing Romanian industry and finance and at eliminating much foreign capital and personnel,[30] some recognized that the Liberals were engaged in an *"oeuvre europeène"* inasmuch as "Romania had had no middle class and the Liberal Party was attempting to constitute one"[31] by means of autarchy.

Despite these measures, the younger generation of Romanian lower-middle-class intellectuals of the interwar period felt that the foreigners' economic power had not been overcome. This perception grew with Romania's addition of large new territories in which the urban elites were predominantly alien. The union of the new provinces to the Old Kingdom urgently posed the question of elites: ethnic Hungarians, Russians, Jews, and Germans were to be supplanted by Romanians. These elites consisted mostly of the old and new petite bourgeoisie—professionals, commercial clerks, civil servants, artisans, tradesmen, and intellectuals.

Elite politics took different shapes in each region of Greater Romania. Now we look in some depth at one province annexed to Romania in 1918—Transylvania. It was the largest of the new provinces, and it had more modern heavy and mining industry than the other regions. It was in many ways regarded as the most important addition to the Romanian Kingdom, while at the same time raising questions about the proper center of gravity of Greater Romania. Within Transylvania we focus on the ethnically Romanian lower-middle-class intellectuals. Although this group was not ideologically monolithic, it was dominated by the nationalist intelligentsia. We analyze the social origins of the post-1918 nationalist intelligentsia's political attitudes.

Intellectuals and the Faraway State

In the province of Transylvania the overhauling of the elite was particularly difficult because of tensions between an active and nationally conscious nucleus of Romanian patriots and the Hungarian and Magyarized urban elites, reluctant to renounce their traditional privileged positions. Ethnic conflict was sharper here because of the strength of both sets of contenders.

In 1910 Transylvania's population was 5,257,249, of which 54 percent were Romanians, 29 percent were Hungarians, and 11 percent were Germans.[32] Transylvania's cities were predominantly Hungarian and German. While almost 20 percent of the urban Transylvanian population was Romanian in 1910,[33] as a subordinate population, the Romanians had had little cultural impact on the region's urban environment. The Jews, although only 10.4 percent of Transylvania's urban population in 1930,[34] were largely assimilated to Hungarian culture. Since they effectively added to the Magyar presence in Transylvania, Romanian rule also tried to displace Jewish elites.

Of primary concern to Romanian authorities after 1918 were Transylvania's civil servants, whose loyalties were obviously crucial to the functioning of the Romanian state in that region. Following the National Assembly at Alba Iulia in December 1918, but before the signing of the Trianon Treaty—which formally transferred the territories of Transylvania, Banat, Crişana, and Maramureş from Hungary to Romania—in June of 1920, Romanian authorities demanded that civil servants of the previous regime pledge a loyalty oath to the Romanian king. If they refused to do so, they were fired and replaced with Romanian employees. While the German community of Transylvania made its peace with the Romanian state, the attempt to co-opt the Hungarian elite—which had consolidated its power since 1867—had very little chance of success. First of all, before the Treaty of Trianon was concluded, Hungarians were still hopeful that the Paris Peace Conference might rescue them from Romanian rule. Second, Hungarian elites could not conceive of subordinating themselves to a Romanian order, since they had until then prevailed unquestionably in the modern sectors of Transylvanian society: in cities, in political and cultural institutions, in industry and trade. To the Hungarian elite it appeared that the Romanian measures in 1919 were meant to change the absolute Hungarian majority of the towns, and that, by the destruction of the Magyar intellectual class, Romanian policies also intended to alter the Hungarians' "superior civilization."[35]

In fact, whether genuinely or not, Romanian authorities initially attempted to convince Hungarian employees to pledge the oath of allegiance and continue in their jobs by promising them better appointments and job security. But these attempts generally failed. The Hungarians who counted, "magistrates, functionaries, teachers, etc., took agricultural or industrial jobs or became unemployed giving up their plush residences rather than take the oath demanded by the Romanians."[36] Then, beginning in the late summer of 1919, Romanian authorities started expelling different categories of non-Romanians from Transylvania: aristocrats, intellectuals, civil servants who had refused to take the oath of allegiance, and store owners with businesses in the main squares and important streets in Transylvanian towns. While many were expelled from the country altogether,[37] others were only banished from urban to rural areas, or from their homes in the center of town to "miserable rooms at the outskirts,"[38] presumably to make room for their Romanian replacements. Inasmuch as Jews were assimilated to Hungarian elite society, they were subjected to the same measures.[39]

There followed the closing or nationalization of state institutions, schools, and Hungarian cultural institutions—museums, theaters, and universities. According to a French diplomatic report, as a consequence of such measures, for a time "the regular functioning of authority stopped," to the detriment of public welfare.[40] French observers did not think that the Romanians could provide more than one-quarter to one-half of the necessary public employees. They commented, too, on the persecution of the Hungarian middle class by the Romanians who had "pretended to combat bolshevism,"[41] presumably in their campaign against Béla Kun earlier in 1919. This remark reflects the fact that while directed at the middle class, Romanian measures were rooted in national rivalries—which is not to say that the national struggle was class-blind. After a brief (failed) attempt at co-optation it was the Hungarian elites, the upper and middle classes, whom the Romanian state tried to suppress despite its own insufficiently large elites.

Over time, ethnic Romanians replaced the Hungarian notables and became the main power-brokers of Transylvania. But Hungarian culture and its prestige persisted, together with a perceived inferiority of Romanian culture. This perceived inequality may in fact have been exacerbated by the political reversal. Observers sympathetic to the Romanian cause, such as the French diplomats who hoped that the Latinophile Romanians would serve as a vehicle for the penetration of French influence in Central Europe, were nevertheless critical of Romanian policies in Transylvania.[42] The French Legation reporting on the recently established Romanian University of Cluj, for instance, stated that "[t]his creation will evidently have for some time a slightly artificial character in a city where, in spite of everything, what counts from the intellectual point of view is still Hungarian or German."[43] Describing the Romanians' expropriation of Hungarian schools, the same report expressed a mixture of approval and disapproval:

> This policy of Romanianizing Transylvania by means of the school and the university derives from a just and great idea. We have an interest in supporting this expansion of Latin culture in this part of Central Europe. Nevertheless, it is no less true that there are many reservations to be made on the manner in which this work is being pursued and which is seeming that much more stupid [lourde] to the Hungarians since the Romanian teachers and their methods do not seem equal to [the Hungarians'] old teaching staff with its cadre made on the model of the German school.[44]

In spite of their sympathies, the French found the Romanian approach to *Kulturkampf* heavy-handed and a little embarrassing: "Expulsions, evacuations, schools closed down, attacks against the churches, all of these measures are destined to Romanianize Transylvania."[45]

Most Romanians did not share this French perception of the nationalization measures in Transylvania. In Transylvania itself the opinion prevalent among nationalist Romanian intellectual circles was that the Romanian state did not exercise *enough* determination in the struggle against the vestiges of Hungarian hegemony. These Transylvanian intellectuals had a definite sense of political mission. They were bureaucrats and professionals trained as lawyers, teachers, professors, journalists, and writers, or university students. As provincial patriots, they tended to find fault with the state for not being involved enough with the process of nationalization in their province. As members of an isolated vanguard, they wanted an unqualified commitment from the state they had helped bring to power.

In light of the Romanian government's interventions to displace Hungarian elites in the early years after union, the dissatisfactions expressed by Romanian nationalists from Transylvania in the mid-1920s may seem puzzling. While the nationalization of Transylvania after 1918 was ostensibly in support of Romanian elites and beneficial to those aspiring to rise into these elites, the processes of nationalization proved problematic to many Romanian intellectuals of that province. As a group they were closely involved with the program of Romanianization, and they stood to reap its benefits. Yet the transition from a persecuted opposition group within Hungarian society to one affiliated with the Romanian state provoked an identity crisis for them.

One of the periodicals that spoke out on this issue repeatedly was *Ţara noastră (Our Country)* directed by the nationalist poet and politician Octavian Goga. Following the poet's own political itinerary, *Ţara noastră* became the official paper of the National Agrarian party in 1932 and of the National Christian party—a "nationalistic and virulently anti-Semitic party of the conservative Right"[46]—in 1935. As the mouthpiece of the National Christian party, which, led by Goga together with the father of Romanian anti-Semitism, A. C. Cuza, *Ţara noastră* bore swastikas on its masthead.[47] But in the 1920s the publication was well within the mainstream of Transylvanian public opinion. Though outspoken against Transylvanian regionalism, and attacking the National, and then National-Peasant party on this issue,[48] *Ţara noastră* was not considered an extremist publication in the 1920s.

Articles published in *Ţara noastră* in the mid-twenties draw attention to the lower-middle-class intellectuals' discomfort with the process of Romanianizing their province. In a 1925 piece, "The Transylvanian Intellectuals After the Union," Petre Nemoianu conceptualized the position of these intellectuals (himself undoubtedly among them) as deriving from their "colonizing mission." The colonization of which he spoke was primarily a social process. Nemoianu compared the plight of the intellectuals with the happier fate of the peasantry who had "voted for the union, danced the *hora,* and then gone home." The intelligentsia, on the other hand, was "having to change [its] whole way of life" as a result of Transylvania's union with Romania.[49]

According to Nemoianu, Romanian intellectuals in Transylvania had formerly been the cadre of the peasantry. They had now become a distinct stratum whose function was to exercise the sovereignty of the Romanian state and to prepare the middle layer, of which they were themselves the seed, and which had until then been missing. The intellectuals had been transposed to a "new social continent," which involved moving to the cities and adopting radically different economic, political, and social goals. Whereas the peasantry had advanced in place, presumably benefiting from the land reform, the intellectuals had to undertake a traumatizing move within the province to an unfavorable "foreign domain." The intelligentsia was the vanguard of an embryonic Romanian urban class; they were pioneers into a social and cultural Hungarian territory, a "social continent" to be conquered: "In the framework of its new mission, our urban population is not awaiting the development of an already existing household . . . but rather its very creation. For this purpose it disposes of no support except for that of the official elements. . . . Aside from its own labors, [our urban population] is in need of the actual collaboration of the state, until such time as it will have become consolidated into a new social configuration."[50] In Nemoianu's view, the state had not done everything it could to strengthen the urban Romanian population in Transylvania. Nemoianu concluded that "the Romanians in the cities stood in a direct relationship to Romanian rule, which this population was liable to uphold if aided, but bring down if abandoned."[51]

While the task of Romanian intellectuals was now to initiate a new urban demography, their goals were also professional and economic—to replace the "foreign" class of professionals, engineers, administrators, and businessmen. In a 1924 article entitled "Transylvania's Economic Emancipation,"[52] Nemoianu complained that the state was not taking enough of an active role to protect "national intellectual capital," which he found even more in need of protection than financial capital. He argued that the state's passivity had negative implications for future Romanian generations; lacking encouragement, they would not be able to embrace anything other than the nonurban, non-middle-class careers they had traditionally practiced. The state's neutrality, he wrote, also left the door open to the onslaught of foreigners. Finally, the Romanian state itself might suffer from its own passivity: Romania, despite its political center in the Old Kingdom, might subordinate itself to the more industrially advanced Transylvania, the economy of which was still in the hands of minority elements.[53]

Nemoianu's articles proposed active state intervention in support of the Romanian urban intellectual and professional element in Transylvania. They reveal an intellectual's frustration with the insufficient presence of the state. They also signal the weakness of the professional, urban, and intellectual layers of Romanian society in Transylvania. A piece that appeared during the same period in *Țara noastră*, "The Crisis of the Legal Profession in Ordeal,"[54] suggests that Romanian lawyers also had an uneasy relationship with the Romanian state. Their identity crisis was provoked by the loss of the real calling the legal profession had represented for oppressed Romanians under the Hungarian regime. At that time, lawyers had been the "vanguard" of the Romanian urban intelligentsia. They had been forced toward this career by the regime, which allowed only Romanian intellectuals to practice the free professions, and by the desire to defend the rights of their co-nationals. Before 1918 they usually resided in little provincial towns close to their home villages, and had a secure, if not lavish, existence. They were "village emissaries of sorts, having the mission of maintaining contact with a foreign world which was hostile. . . , with which there was no mutual understanding, and which . . . [they] avoided."[55]

After union, many lawyers moved to larger cities. "The Crisis of the Legal Profession" describes them as troubled not only by their antiminority feelings (exacerbated now by their dwelling in the heart of resilient minority enclaves), but also by their loss of economic security. The Romanian regime, whose support they had counted on, was not sufficiently forthcoming. Under these conditions the lawyers felt that, while they were still intermediaries to the cities, they no longer knew between who and whom. Positions in the service of the state, as notaries, for example, were few in number and steeped in corrupt politics; this made them unattractive to idealistic nationalists. In any case, not enough such openings existed to allow for the consolidation of a true social group.[56]

Transylvania's Romanian lawyers were confused by the structural transformations underway. They had actively fought for these changes, but had not realisitically envisaged the practical results of success, least of all the effects of such success on themselves; they had just assumed that their lot would be substantially improved. Since the source of their dissatisfactions before 1918 had been the Hungarian state, they looked to its successor, the Romanian state, for improvement. The road was wide open for disappointment, because the expectations of this group were so formless and positive, so much based on the experience of the past under Hungarian rule, and so little geared to the realities of Greater Romania. The Romanian state itself was weak in the urban sphere and thus unable to provide the support the Transylvanians sought. Moreover, it was a state centralized under the aegis of the Old Kingdom and not always sensitive to the needs of the newly added regions.

The lawyers' case is one example of the crisis of an important group of the Transylvanian Romanian intelligentsia. As activists they questioned their role under the new regime they felt they had to represent. They were often repelled by the corrupt practices of this regime and disappointed in the neutral stance the state adopted with regard to themselves. In their minds, the only possible positive resolution to their dilemma could have come from a militant state that would carry on the nationalist revolutionary project they themselves had begun in opposition. Such a Greater Romanian state they could ethnically represent in Transylvania without feeling that they were betraying their beliefs and traditions. But the practices of the Bucharest-based government did not endow it with the revolutionary righteousness the Transylvanians favored. Most objectionable of all was the apparent lack of activism by this seemingly faraway state. These Transylvanians perceived themselves as "going it alone" in the difficult project of urbanizing the Romanians and of Romanianizing Transylvania. The dilemma they faced was to make them, along with other groups of lower-middle-class intellectuals, amenable to the ideological and political solutions offered by a growing fascist movement. The nationalist student movement was the breeding ground of Romanian fascism.

An Intellectual Proletariat?

Beginning in 1922 the nationalist student movement exploded with regularity into violent protest that demanded the exclusion of national minorities from universities and the professions. Parts of this student movement matured into an increasingly well-organized and visible radical Right. By 1927 it had spawned two extreme-Right political parties, the League of National Christian Defense, led by Iaşi law professor A. C. Cuza, and the League of the Archangel Michael, headed by the former student leader Corneliu Zelea Codreanu. The student movement's importance in setting the political tone in the interwar period can also be judged from the fact that the demands initially put forth by the student movement for the exclusion of non-Romanians from universities, high schools, and the professions were echoed not only by the radical Right, but also by the political propaganda of mainstream political parties.

While influential, the students active in the nationalist movement were feared by authorities as a volatile group capable of upsetting Romania's precarious political balance. There were those who characterized the inflated student population and dissatisfied young intellectuals as an "intellectual proletariat," and those who worried about intellectual unemployment. The solutions to these problems differed as much as their definition. The debate joined in the interwar decades on these issues expressed different views of Romania's lower middle class about itself.

The concept of an "intellectual proletariat" was not new in post–World War I Romania. Romania's nineteenth-century romantic poet Mihail Eminescu had written of a "proletariat of the pen," lower-gentry sons schooled in western Europe, who could not always find professional or administrative employment on coming home.[57] In the interwar period the intellectual-proletariat debate was sparked off by the dramatic increase in the secondary school and university student body, initially encouraged by government nationalization efforts. Overcrowded conditions coupled with insufficient facilities and a dismal faculty to student ratio politicized many youths. Ethnic Romanians who joined the nationalist student movement believed that the solution to their plight would be to exclude minorities, particularly Jews, from higher education and the professions.[58] Some educators believed that the number of students should be limited, but without an ethnic bias.

The pattern of educational development that Romania experienced in the interwar period also worried educators, who debated the possibility of limiting the number of students. Some argued that the universities were overpopulated, that intellectual careers were becoming proletarianized, and that "the intellectual market was saturated."[59] Constantin Kiriţescu, a prominent educator, thought that "[t]hose who had diplomas could only with difficulty find for themselves positions as public employees, in private enterprises, or in the free professions," and warned that "intellectual unemployment promised to be one of the most worrisome aspects of the general economic unemployment."[60] Dimitrie Gusti, the renowned sociologist and National Peasant Minister of Education from 1932 to 1933, wrote that the university had become "a diploma factory for professors without chairs, for lawyers without trials, for doctors without patients, for theologians without parishes,"[61] and favored more selectivity in order to limit access to the university,[62] and allow it to "become a true institution for the molding of the national spiritual elite."[63]

Romanian nationalist intellectuals from Transylvania were not well inclined toward such arguments.[64] Already displeased in the 1920s with what they saw as a somewhat remote, insufficiently militant state, many in the 1930s questioned the notion of an "intellectual proletariat" as it might apply to Romania. In May 1933 Petru Suciu wrote about the crisis of Romania's young intellectuals in the Transylvanian magazine Gând Românesc (Romanian Thought).[65] Echoing Nemoianu's arguments of a decade earlier, Suciu reproached the Romanian state with being "absent and indifferent" in the face of an "alarming crisis" wrongly diagnosed by general public opinion as the "peril of an intellectual proletariat." The solution of reducing educational capacity in order to reestablish social equilibrium by getting rid of discontented extremist elements was also wrong, according to Suciu. He identified the problem from a Transylvanian perspective:

> The problem cannot leave us cold. Especially not us Transylvanians. For, if the Old Kingdom has something of a plethora of intellectuals, we do not have it. If there the intellectual and middle classes are supersaturated, that is not the case with us. We do not have a social body with balanced classes. We are without Romanian cities, lacking a middle class and an ethnically homogeneous civil service, and we do not have a solid national culture. We are a people of peasants on the first step of its culturalization. We are at the beginning of conquests both in the economic and the cultural domains. And conquests are accomplished by trained people, by intellectuals. We need as well-trained and as many as possible of these.

Six months later, in an article entitled, "Do We Have Too Many Intellectuals?" Suciu argued the point from a slightly different angle; more schools were needed to enable Romania to advance by developing its industry and cities, which it gravely lacked:

> Especially here in Transylvania. The towns belonged until 1913 to other peoples. The process of penetration begun after that period has given us a larger proportion [of the urban population]; however, the cities are ours only peripherally. We are masters only over their political institutions, and not their economic ones. . . . A people dominates by means of economic and cultural forces, through its homogeneous and conscious urban element. Our urban element is insufficient in number and weak in its consciousness of race and in its material situation. . . . The city is the backbone in the socioeconomic structure of a state. We do not have . . . [the cities]. We shall have them, either by conquering those that exist, or by establishing new ones. The conquerors will be the educated elements. . . . The Romanian school of all levels is called upon to give us the army of elite fighters. For this reason we need as many [and] as good schools as possible.[66]

As these debates indicate, the issue of intellectual unemployment or proletarianization was not a purely objective one. It is not clear whether unemployment was a considerable problem at all in interwar Romania, and particularly among lower-middle-class intellectuals. At least in the early part of the twenties the government recruited many new people for bureaucratic and educational posts in the new provinces. A shortage of teachers, for example, is evident from the fact that teachers sent to the "cultural zone," the new areas where a special effort was exerted to establish Romanian language and culture, received a higher salary than those employed routinely in their home regions or in the Old Kingdom.[67]

After 1929, during the financial crisis and the Depression, we can assume that unemployment rose. In 1932 official statistics put the number of unemployed at 55,000, and estimates of "real" unemployment figures go as high as 300,000. Many small enterprises were ruined, and employees of financial institutions may have suffered more than others.[68] Even then, however, there were some who denied that the crisis had resulted in any additional unemployment. As the country recovered, unemployment fell in the official statistics to 17,253 in 1934, and 7,268 in 1938. Granting that much of the unemployment may have been statistically hidden by underemployment and by undeclared unemployment, it still appears that "the largest proportion [of unemployed] were factory workers,"[69] which in turn would mean that the lower middle class was relatively unaffected. According to the census of unemployed intellectuals taken by the Central Statistical Institute, there were only 6,090 unemployed intellectuals in March of 1937. Of these, only 652 qualified technically as intellectuals since the others did not have university degrees.[70]

Thus the issue of intellectual unemployment remains slippery: Romania's

Central Statistical Institute reported small absolute numbers, most of which seem to reflect the industrial work force rather than white-collar employees. Furthermore, the initial debates and outcry in student and university circles over intellectual unemployment did not coincide with the rise in the numbers of unemployed after 1929, but long preceded it. Lastly, legislation for the protection of national labor that implemented measures designed to satisfy nationalist public opinion and students' demands for limiting the competition from minority nationalities was passed for the first time in 1934 when the unemployment figures were on their way down again,[71] but when Romania's political atmosphere had become stridently nationalistic. The "intellectual proletariat" was an important subjective category in the ideology of disgruntled intellectuals, who viewed this category differently than establishment politicians and educators did.

Conclusion

Interwar Eastern Europe was a region of newly composed states, many of them re-created or enlarged after World War I and that much more socially and ethnically complicated for it. Right-wing nationalism became widespread in the area, not only because of the growth of fascist influences from abroad, but also for domestic reasons that had to do with the exigencies of nation-building, particularly with the nationalization of elites. We have focused on two lower-middle-class groups in interwar Romanian society and on their radicalization in nationalist and fascist directions. While other political tendencies existed among the lower middle class as well, ethnic Romanian professionals and intellectuals from Transylvania and university students from all provinces favored an integral nationalist ideology that prescribed the exclusion of ethnic minorities from elite positions. Transylvanian nationalists wanted the state to practice militant protectionism of ethnic Romanian lower-middle-class professionals and intellectuals. The demands of the student movement of 1922 anticipated the exclusivist nationalism and anti-Semitism later adopted by the Iron Guard. Both the Transylvanians and the students had had high hopes for their role in the process of nation-building undertaken at the conclusion of World War I. Unhappy with the slowness and awkwardness of this process, and with the continued competition of non-Romanian elites, many Romanians were drawn toward radical nationalist solutions.

The ideological profile of these lower-middle-class intellectuals seems to confirm older theories that saw fascism as a lower-middle-class phenomenon. An important distinction should be underscored, however: in the older scholarship, mainly treating German nazism, the petite bourgeoisie was typically described as having turned to the Right in reaction to its downward mobility. The Romanian petit bourgeois groups we have looked at became radicalized for opposite reasons; namely, because of the opportunities for advancement offered by their state's expansion and because of their rising—if unmet—expectations of upward mobility. The state was then accused of failing to create a fully Romanianized society with an elite expurgated of foreigners, and the minorities were blamed for illegitimately persisting in elite positions that rightly belonged to Romanians. The articulation of the Romanian intelligentsia's social aspirations gave rise to the political programs of the extreme Right, including the Iron Guard's. Given the integral nationalism of these groups, it would have been impossible for the non-Romanian petite bourgeoisie to join them. An analysis of the Center and Left of the lower middle class in Romania remains to be done.

Notes

1. Research for this essay was made possible by a grant from the International Research and Exchanges Board and by a Mellon Postdoctoral fellowship from the Center for Slavic and East European Studies at the University of California, Berkeley.

2. I. E. Torouţiu, Românii şi clasa intelectuală din Bucovina: Note statistice (Czernowitz, 1911), 47.

3. Lucreţiu Pătrăşcanu, Sub trei dictaturi (Bucharest, 1945), 194.

4. Eugen Weber, "The Men of the Archangel," Journal of Contemporary History 1 (1966), 107.

5. Henry L. Roberts, Rumania: Political Problems of an Agrarian State (New Haven, 1951), 109.

6. Ibid.

7. See, for example, Janusz Żarnowski, "East-Central European Societies, 1918–1939: The Polish Example," in Polska Akademia Nauk; Komitet Nauk Historycznych; Instytut Historii, Poland at the Fourteenth International Congress of Historical Sciences in San Francisco (Wrocław, 1975), 244.

8. Zygmunt Bauman, "Intellectuals in East-Central Europe: Continuity and Change," Eastern European Politics and Societies 1, 2 (Spring 1987): 168–69.

9. See Ştefan Zeletin, Burghezia română: Origina şi rolul ei istoric (Bucharest, 1925), 81; and Kenneth Jowitt, "The Sociocultural Bases of National Dependency in Peasant Countries," in Social Change in Romania, 1860–1940: A Debate on Development in a European Nation, ed. Kenneth Jowitt (Berkeley, 1978), 15.

10. Zeletin, Burghezia română, 84.

11. Jowitt, "The Sociocultural Bases," 15.

12. Daniel Chirot, Social Change in a Peripheral Society: The Creation of a Balkan Colony (New York, 1976), 9, 10.

13. See Andrew Janos, "Modernization and Decay in Historical Perspective: The Case of Romania," in Social Change in Romania, 1860–1940, 76–81.

14. Félix Colson, De L'État présent et de l'avenir des Principautés de Moldavie et de Valachie (1839), cited in Contrasts in Emerging Societies, ed. Doreen Warriner (London, 1965), 170.

15. W. Beatty-Kingston, *A Wanderer's Notes* 2 (1888), cited in Warriner, *Contrasts*, 193.

16. Elias Schwarzfeld, *Aşezămintele evreilor din Moldova în veacul al XVIII şi jumăta-tea veacului al XIX* (n.p., 1885), 19, 23, 24.

17. Eugène Poujade, *Chrétiens et Turcs* (1859), cited in Warriner, *Contrasts*, 159.

18. Ibid.

19. Ibid.

20. J. W. Ozanne, *Three Years in Roumania* (1878), cited in Warriner, *Contrasts*, 158.

21. Ibid.

22. Institutul Central de Statistică, *Anuarul Statistic al României 1937 şi 1938* (Bucharest, 1939), 44; and Joseph Rothschild, *East Central Europe between the Two World Wars* (Seattle, 1977), 285.

23. Rothschild, *East Central Europe*, 284.

24. Katherine Verdery, "Social Differentiation in the Transylvanian Countryside Between the Two World Wars," *Rumanian Studies: An International Annual of the Humanities and Social Sciences* 5 (1980–1986): 90–93.

25. Katherine Verdery, *Transylvanian Villagers: Three Generations of Political, Economic, and Ethnic Change* (Berkeley and Los Angeles, 1983), 292–97.

26. From 1900 to 1930 Romanian cities of over 100,000 people grew by 100–400 percent. After 1930 these cities grew even faster. See Lucreţiu Pătrăşcanu, *Sub trei dictaturi* (Bucharest, 1945), 195–96.

27. Mihai Pop, "Semnele formării unei noi burghezii bucureştene," *Sociologie Românească* 2, 1 (Jan. 1937): 27–28.

28. Ibid.

29. Ibid., 27.

30. For the French perspective, see Ministère des Affaires Étrangères, Archives Diplomatiques, Paris, Quai d'Orsay, Série Z (QD) 28/135-139r (27 March 1923); QD 28/142-146R (12 April 1923); QD 28/153-154rv (10 May 1923).

31. QD 29/132rv (28 March 1926).

32. Barbara Jelavich, *History of the Balkans: Twentieth Century* 2 (Cambridge, 1983): 73.

33. Sabin Manuilă, *Aspects démographiques de la Transylvanie*, Extrait de "La Transylvanie" (Bucharest, 1938), 15.

34. Ibid.

35. QD 41/81r-86.

36. Ibid.

37. QD 41/75rv (28 Oct. 1919); QD 27/220–222r (26 Aug. 1920).

38. QD 41/148rv-149 (10 Sept. 1920); QD 41/81r–86.

39. *Mântuirea* (29 Oct. 1919), Alliance Israélite Universelle, Paris, Archives, Roumanie, (AIU) VIII 53.

40. QD 41/81r-86.

41. Ibid.

42. QD 41/150-152rv.

43. Ibid.

44. Ibid.

45. Ibid.

46. Paul A. Shapiro, "Prelude to Dictatorship in Romania: The National Christian Party in Power, December 1937–February 1938," *Canadian-American Slavic Studies* 8 (Spring 1974): 45.

47. A Goga-Cuza government was in power for 44 days, from December 1937 until February 1938.

48. *Politics and Political Parties in Roumania* (London, 1936), 369–70.

49. *Ţara noastră*, 18 Oct. 1925.

50. Ibid.

51. Ibid.

52. Ibid., 27 Jan. 1924.

53. Ibid.

54. Ibid., 3 Feb. 1924.

55. Ibid.

56. Ibid.

57. Janos, "Modernization," 80–81. In a statistical essay on Bukovina's Romanian middle class published in 1912, I. E. Torouţiu pleaded against the "overproduction of intellectuals" thesis, which, he said, was being argued even by some Romanians. See I. E. Torouţiu, *Românii şi Clasa de mijloc din Bucovina* (Czernowitz, 1912), 11–13.

58. For a fuller discussion of these issues, see Irina Livezeanu, "The Politics of Culture in Greater Romania: Nation-Building and Student Nationalism, 1918–1927" (Ph. D. diss., University of Michigan, 1986), Chap. 6.

59. "Congresul profesorilor universitari la Cluj," *Transilvania*, Organul Societăţii Culturale "Astra" 60 (Sept. 1929): 717; and Constantin Kiriţescu, "Problema 'educaţiei dirijate' în legătură cu suprapopulaţia universitară şi şomajul intelectual," *Arhiva pentru ştiinţa şi reforma socială* 14 (1936): 848.

60. Dimitrie Gusti, "Cuvânt înainte," in *Un an de activitate la Ministerul instrucţiei cultelor şi artelor, 1932–1933* (Bucharest, 1934), ix.

62. Gusti, *Un an*, 316.

63. Ibid., ix.

64. See also Sabin Manuilă, "Suprapopularea universităţilor şi şomaj intelectual?" *Sociologie Românesca* 3, 4–6 (April–June 1938): 227–29 for an argument made by the director of the Romanian Central Statistical Institute in opposition to the intellectual unemployment thesis.

65. *Gând Românesc* 1, 1 (May 1933): 235–36.

66. *Abecedar* 1, 21–22 (5–12 Oct. 1933).

67. Arhivele Statului, Bucureşti. Fond Ministerul Instrucţiunii şi Cultelor (MIC) 1924/211/97; Ministerul Instrucţiunii, *Lege pentru învăţământul primar al statului şi învăţământul normal-primar* (Bucharest, 1925), 278; and Ministerul Instrucţiunii, *Proect de lege asupra învăţământului secundar teoretic* (Bucharest, 1928), 102.

68. See Marcela Felicia Iovanelli, *Industria românească, 1934–1938* (Bucharest, 1975), 27.

69. Ibid., 214.

70. Manuilă, "Suprapopularea," 228.

71. Ibid., 215.

9

Democracy and the Lower Middle Classes: Interwar Denmark

NIELS FINN CHRISTIANSEN
and
KARL CHRISTIAN LAMMERS

Introduction

As in most European countries in the interwar period, the urban lower middle classes in Denmark were a significant portion of the total population. In Denmark, as in other countries, they could scarcely be called a structural, social, and ideological unity, because they contained both traditional artisanal and commercial groups and new service employees, public and private. They felt and withstood constant economic, social, and political pressure from other classes and from the state. But there is much evidence that the threat of proletarianization, or "declassing," was considerably weaker in Denmark than, for example, in Germany. Market fluctuations were of course strong, but they were weaker than in the large capitalist states. Danish production and business structure left considerable room for small production units and trade. Several studies have indicated that before World War I the classic lower middle class—small, independent artisans and retailers—organized relatively early. Artisans especially were highly organized, whereas retailers were less so. The classic lower middle class represented its interests in the state and in local political institutions through vertical trade organizations partially inspired by the German *Mittelstandsbewegung*. The class was pluralistic in its party politics and ideology, dividing its loyalties between all the parties.[1]

Only a few studies of the Danish lower middle classes exist for the interwar period. An in-depth analysis of the growing number of public servants

---

This essay was translated by Barbara Dunn and revised by Rudy Koshar.

and salespeople and office workers employed in private enterprise is notably
lacking.[2] In this article we shall examine the interplay between urban lower-
middle-class political ideologies and trade organizations and the relationship of political parties to the urban lower middle classes. We shall discuss
the reasons why the lower middle classes, despite much wooing from right-
wing radicals and fascist or nazi groups, supported the general consensus
that upheld parliamentary democracy.

Politics and Classes to the End of World War I

The founding of the Conservative People's party in Denmark in 1915 completed the formation of a party system whose main outlines lasted until
the mid-1960s. The Conservative People's party was partly a reorganization
of the old Tory party *(Hojre)*, partly a new start. Its inaugural political
statement invoked a "sound conservatism" that should be mobilized "for
the protection and support of the middle class in town and country, first
and foremost because it is the social and cultural work of this class upon
which modern Denmark is built."[3] More than an opportune declaration
of devotion to potential voters, this was an expression of the recognition
that the middle class, especially in the towns, had for years been the mass
foundation of conservatism and the power base of the old Tory party.
At the same time, the statement referred to new sociostructural developments through which the old urban middle class (self-employed artisans
and retailers) was supplemented by a rapidly expanding group of public
servants, office workers, and salespeople. As early as the turn of the century,
the leading conservative theoretician, Arnold Fraenkel, had pointed out
the growing importance of office workers and the necessity of recruiting
them for the Conservative cause.

Following the introduction of representative democracy in 1848 and 1849
in the form of a constitutional monarchy[4], the urban middle classes were
politically conservative. But they were democratic, some even radically democratic in the 1840s, partly to oppose liberal capitalist developments that
threatened the social and economic bases of middle-class life. They found
partial support for their opposition to liberal capitalism in the Tory party,
which from the 1850s to the early 1870s crystallized in an alliance of
large landowners, high-ranking state officials, the military, and the remnants
of the National Liberal party, which was dominated by intellectuals. The
Conservatives ruled without interruption from 1866 to 1901 despite de-
creasing representation in the Rigsdag, the two-chamber national parliament that was later replaced by the present-day Folketing. Supported by
large landowners, local and state government officials, the military, the
urban middle classes (upper and lower), and parts of the working class,
the Conservative party was able to rule through provisional legislation.

In opposition to the Conservatives stood the Liberals *(Venstre)*, whose social base comprised freeholders, farmers, tenant farmers, and, later, parts of the radical urban intelligentsia. Freeholding farmers built a solid power base after the 1840s by forming an extensive network of cooperatives and political and cultural organizations. Compared to other countries, the farmer class achieved a very unusual degree of independence and identity. They gradually became the economically dominant class, and their political and cultural influence can be felt today, despite a rapid reduction of the rural population that began in the 1950s and 1960s. The Liberals had an absolute majority in the Rigsdag after 1872 and fought a long, hard battle to establish parliamentarism.

In the mid-1880s the Liberals and Social Democrats formed an alliance with the explicit purpose of breaking Conservative dominance in urban areas. The Social Democrats won a clear hegemony over the working class in the 1880s and 1890s. They simultaneously began to agitate for the support of the lower middle class, an effort that gained increasing votes and members for the party. Evidence from incomplete membership lists, lists of board members, and lists of delegates to party congresses indicate that small artisans and shopkeepers in the rapidly growing working-class districts of the towns joined the Social Democratic party.[5] Proprietors of small shops in these areas shared the same social conditions as the workers and participated fully in local social and cultural life. For most of them, it was also true that they could not have survived economically if it was known that they voted for right-wing parties. From the 1870s to the 1930s, artisans moved relatively frequently between the ranks of self-employed entrepreneurs and wage earners. The borderlines were, if not shifting, still comparatively easy to pass through in both directions. It must be emphasized that, at least until the 1930s, established and independent artisans as well as wealthier retailers were generally conservative. Nonetheless, their status mobility gave the Social Democrats a chance to win members in this social group.

In 1901 the Conservatives had to relinquish political power with the so-called Change of System, the recognition of parliamentarism. That meant that the Liberals—the farmers—took over government rule, and the alliance with the Social Democratic party was dissolved. The Liberal party was split in 1905 when radical Liberals, intellectuals, parts of the liberal professions, some capitalists, and cottagers formed the Radical party. This party formed an alliance with the Social Democrats shortly thereafter, an alliance that dominated Danish politics for better or worse until the 1960s. The constitution was revised in 1915; women won the suffrage; and a four-party system that characterized Danish political life in the following decades was formed. Reflecting the Danish class structure, the Liberal, Conservative,

Radical, and Social Democratic parties shaped a system of flexible cooperation and opposition that remained relatively stable from around 1900 to
the 1950s.

Danish Society in the Interwar Period

Denmark was neutral in World War I but friendly toward Germany. Neutrality was partially responsible for Denmark's ability to continue its vital
foreign trade. On the home front, broad political and class cooperation—a
kind of truce *(Burgfrieden)*—helped Denmark avoid serious social or economic friction as long as the war continued. Danish society therefore made
it through the war more or less in one piece, despite agricultural problems
and shortages of consumer goods. Meanwhile, Danish industry and crafts
reaped the advantages of gaining a larger portion of the domestic market.
When peace came, Denmark remained largely agricultural. Agriculture accounted for 25 percent of the gross national product (GNP) in 1920 and
employed one-third of the country's working population. Processing industries in agriculture represented a good 75 percent of Danish exports, and
a large part of industrial production was tied directly to agriculture. Industry and trade contributed 23 percent of GNP and employed 29 percent
of the population, but they were based on small enterprises that produced
for the domestic market and accounted for one-half of industrial production. A well-developed mercantile sector added a little over 25 percent
to GNP.

These basic economic conditions were the fundament of the class structure of Danish society. It was characteristic of Danish class structure between the two wars that the middle class (upper, middle, and lower) was
larger than the working class in 1921 and 1930, as illustrated in the table
on the Danish work force (see table). Numbering over 200,000 around
1930, freeholding farmers made up the largest share of the middle class
(upper, middle, and lower) throughout the period; their percentage of the
middle class was falling, though. Most of the remaining middle class lived
in towns, and the absolute number of urban middle-class groups, particularly civil servants and office workers or salespeople, was increasing. Overall, the class structure of Danish society underwent only small changes
from 1918 to 1939. The percentage of farmers fell, while those of the
working class and especially middle-class public servants, salespeople, and
office workers expanded.

Meanwhile, several economic crises hurt Denmark. The shift from a
war economy to peace "cleaned up" industry and trade, causing many
business failures. An agricultural crisis in the second half of the 1920s
depressed export prices, but the world economic crisis of the 1930s, milder
in Denmark than in other countries, damaged agriculture even more greatly.

CLASS STRUCTURE IN DENMARK 1921–1940

Class	1921		1930		1940	
Upper class	19,700	1.5%	20,900	1.3%	24,900	1.4%
Upper middle	37,400	2.8%	37,300	2.4%	51,200	2.8%
Middle class	444,500	33.4%	492,300	31.4%	480,500	26.0%
Lower middle	132,600	9.9%	172,000	11.0%	216,500	11.7%
Working class	521,700	39.2%	604,900	38.6%	879,500	47.7%
Domestic servants	175,500	13.2%	239,600	15.3%	192,100	10.4%
	1,331,400	100%	1,567,000	100%	1,844,700	100%

Still, these crises did not become serious enough to threaten the stability of Danish society. Relative political and social stability characterized the era, and the dramatic constitutional crisis of 1920, the Easter crisis, resulted in the strengthening of a parliamentary system that remained more or less undisputed throughout the period. Antiparliamentary groups from the Right and Left were marginal. This was a crucial political condition of the interwar years.

The Middle Classes and the Class Struggle, 1918–1924

A special characteristic of Danish political and social structure compared to that of other countries was the early, dense, and exhaustive organization of all classes and trades. In practice, the dense formation of business and employer organizations among self-employed master artisans continued earlier guild structures after obligatory guild membership was repealed by law in 1857 and made effective in 1862. In contrast, shopkeepers organized somewhat later, because they had to build their organizations from more modest beginnings. From the 1870s to about 1910, associations representing all trades and branches were formed at the national and regional levels and in the larger towns. The most important national organizations were the Danish Federation of Artisans and Industry (Faellesrepraesentationen for dansk Haandvaerk og Industri, 1878), Federation of Copenhagen Office Workers' Unions (De koebenhavnske Handelsforeningers Faellesrepraesentation, 1890), and the Danish Retailers' Federation (De samvirkende Detailhandlerforeninger i Danmark, 1907). New groups of office workers were also formed, including the Danish Trades and Office Workers' Union in 1900. These organizations formed in the same period that similar associations of independent farmers and workers appeared. Both as industrial organizations and as pressure groups, however, artisans', retailers', and office workers' associations never achieved the same economic or political influence that farmers' and workers' groups did. Thus, even when the Master Artisans' Association became a member of the Danish Master Artisans' and Employers' Association in 1896, the former never decisively shaped the policy of the latter organization.

Until World War I, organizations representing lower-middle-class groups concentrated on narrow economic interests and rarely tried to carve out an independent political or class position in the national polity. They acted as pressure groups vis-à-vis the Rigsdag, government, and political parties (except for the Social Democratic party, the enemy of many interest-group leaders from the lower middle classes). In the Rigsdag the lower middle classes had little direct representation, although they did have some electoral clout due to their numbers. Yet the size of lower-middle-class constituencies seems not to have been used very effectively as a basis for expanding their political influence. By the 1890s, group spokesmen of the lower middle classes called for independent Rigsdag representation either through the existing bourgeois parties or in a separate party. This last option gained no mentionable support from self-employed groups before World War I.

New possibilities appeared in the first years after the formation of the Conservative People's party. From 1915 to 1917 the party was almost divided over the question of how to interpret and implement its stated support for the middle class. The upper and lower middle class, large industry, and small proprietors opposed each other in the battle for power in the party. Large industry won, but only a few in the lower middle class drew the consequences and left the party. During the 1920s the wounds left over the struggle in the party were gradually healed. Simultaneously, the question of whether the lower middle classes should have their own political party was debated. Both developments signaled a growing desire in many quarters to politicize the lower middle classes, mobilize them to support their trade and class interests, and get small entrepreneurs and artisans in particular to look beyond their narrow concerns and consider broader class and national questions. As well, self-employed groups were disappointed about their lack of influence in the regulation of the war economy by the so-called Superior Commission (*Overordentlige Kommission*). There was a general feeling that small business and artisanal interests had been pushed aside by the politically more organized classes, especially the farmers and workers.

These conflicts resulted in the formation of the Trades and Industry party (*Erhvervspartiet*) in 1918,[7] which was to be the party of mainly urban large and small entrepreneurs in commerce, crafts, and industry. It was by and large a fiasco. Gaining no more than about 7,000 members, the party failed to mobilize significant parts of the lower middle class and gained no support at all in the upper middle class. Its electoral support peaked in 1920, when it had 30,000 votes and four parliamentary representatives. The party then went into decline, gaining no parliamentary deputies in 1924 elections and dissolving shortly thereafter. There are two obvious reasons for the failure. First, the party remained for the most part a Copenhagen affair, and despite energetic efforts, it never received official support from the business and interest organizations of the middle class. The most important of these, the Danish Federation of Trades and Industry, whose leadership was too closely associated with the Conservative People's party to offer substantial help to another party, never gave the *Erhvervspartiet* unambiguous backing. Only short-lived support came from local business organizations, especially the association of Copenhagen small retailers. Second, the party was weakened by potential conflicts between big capital and small business about such central problems as the protection of industry and import duties.

The Trades and Industry party never got wind in its sails, but it was nonetheless an important political and ideological symptom of developments in the lower middle classes. It was a signal that small businessmen wanted to create their own political profile vis-à-vis the state and in opposition to farmers, workers, and capitalists. Furthermore, ideologically the party contained most of the elements we find in movements of the lower middle classes in the 1920s and 1930s. The most coherent expression of party policy and ideology can be found in the 1922 party platform and in *The Trades and Industry Daily (Dagblad for Haandvaerk og Industri)*, which appeared from 1917 to 1922. The underlying aim of the party was, according to the rhetoric of its program,[8] "to rally people around an individualistic view of society, which acclaims personal freedom, which frees initiative in production and sales, and which demands that property rights be respected." With proper technical training of artisans and retailers as a prerequisite, as many independent businesses as possible were to be established, since "independent work sharpens the energies and feeds growth, which is the groundwork of economic progress." The party attacked both "economic conspiracy," that is, capitalist monopolies, and the "regulation of free competition by municipal socialism." Social security was to be based on the principle of "help to those who help themselves."

The core of this social ideology was the work ethic. "Hard work, skills, austerity, independence, and individual responsibility"—they read like an index from Weber's writings on the Protestant work ethic—were the key words. These were ideological elements that could unite the middle class across trade and political divisions. Time after time these themes were repeated, often in a direct frontal attack on the working class's alleged instrumental attitude toward labor. It was difficult for the small businessmen, artisans as well as retailers, to understand the priorities of the working class in putting issues such as wages or the length of the workday before the productive process itself, before "the joy of creation." The unemployed and welfare recipients received especially harsh criticism because they were thought to represent a general breakdown of the old, classic virtue of self-help. In *The Danish Merchants' News (Dansk Koebmandstidende)*, distributed widely among small artisans and retailers, it was argued in 1919 that the independent businessman should "reinstate the old morals" so that "the individual has responsibility for himself and his dependents, and cannot fall back on the state or the public sphere without first having done his best. We must depart from the whole system of support that does not differentiate between the honest and skilled worker and the idle poor. . . . We must on the whole depart from the present practice of appeasing poor and unwilling elements, a practice which means that all clear social boundaries are erased."[9] Undoubtedly this work ethic presupposed the small, independent shop, where each man worked for himself and perhaps his family. There was little room in this world view for capitalistic monopolies or for socialist attacks on private property and the market economy.

Unambiguously antisocialist, the *Erhvervspartiet* attacked "union tyranny" and constantly aimed part of its propaganda at Social Democratic supporters within the middle classes. Unions based on capitalist or socialist interests represented "egoistic class strife" and had to be eliminated. But liberalism was a dilemma for the movement. It supported free enterprise as "the groundwork of society and the driving force behind all progress,"[10] but admitted that an uncontrolled liberalistic market economy led to polarization between capital and the working class and threatened the existence of small business. Some reins had to be laid on liberalism.

Formed in response to the perceived inability and unwillingness of other parties to defend the interests of the middle classes, the Trades and Industry party initially criticized the old political system and its "cliches that drip from party leaders' mouths like heavy butter sauce."[11] Renewal was to come from legislation shaped in part by independent representatives of the middle classes, whose power in the Rigsdag would match their quantitative importance in the electorate. It is important to note that the party did not distance itself from democratic principles. Aside from sporadic criticism of favoritism in the other parties, no fundamental critique of parliamentary democracy emerged, and it seems that party leaders never considered using an antiparliamentary program to create mass support—a most realistic decision.

The party failed to get a mass following even though it gained support from the *Trades and Industry Daily,* aimed mainly at the middle classes. Published by the Danish Federation of Trades and Industry, the *Daily* was not a partisan paper, but its political and ideological stance was compatible with two features of the *Erhvervspartiet* program, namely a self-consciousness about the middle classes as "the bone and marrow of Danish society" and a realization that economic development constantly threatened the existence of the middle classes.[12] The *Daily* mounted a double attack on big capital and socialism. But during and immediately after World War I the paper attacked mainly the Social Democrats, the labor movement, and the syndicalists. It was the perceived need for cross-class national unity in the face of the working-class offensive of the postwar period—manifested in demands for control of capitalist business, in workers' councils, and in many long and exhausting labor conflicts—that caused this shift in emphasis. Nationalistic and even chauvinistic, the *Daily* refused to accept the necessity or suitability of social conflict, strikes, and lockouts.

The overall message was that "class politics" should be replaced by "practical reform politics" for the benefit of various social groups. "In a middle-class country like Denmark," the *Daily* wrote during the intense political strife of 1920, "theories fostered abroad in the big industrial proletariat of a vanished generation shall not determine the social structure of the future."[13] Using examples from the rest of Europe, the paper claimed that a decisive battle was being waged between a socialist and capitalist view of society. The middle class must form an effective bulwark against socialism, because "the road to a socialist state goes over the dead body of the middle class."[14] Social peace therefore became a primary demand, one that united small enterprise. It was class conflict and not the middle class that was to be eliminated. Labor conflicts, strikes, and lockouts were destructive of society. Strikes were evidence that workers used unions to exercise a "dictatorship of the minority" that threatened "all social order and all real freedom."[15]

Artisans and retailers received unambiguous support on these points from parts of the relatively new and rapidly increasing group of office workers employed in private business.[16] They were divided into two groups. The first of these, organized in the Danish Retail and Office Workers' Union (*Dansk Handels- og kontoristforbund*—HK), which was founded in 1900, supported the Social Democrats. The HK was accepted as a member of the National Trade Union Association in 1932. The other group consisted of various unions of office workers in private business that were united in 1922 in the Association of Office and Shop Workers in Private Business (*Privatfunktionaerernes Sammenslutning*—PS). The PS was decidedly anti-socialist and closely tied to the Conservative People's party despite its declaration of being nonpolitical. During the 1920s and 1930s, the HK organized far more office workers in private business than the PS did, and it gradually gained a near monopoly in organizing white-collar public employees. Differences between the two organizations reflected the general divisions in this social group between collectivism and individualism. The HK worked to achieve the right of collective bargaining and saw strikes as a necessary weapon. In contrast, working from the principal that harmony between office workers and employers should reign, the PS accepted only individual labor contracts and denied any justification for strikes. Conflicts between office workers and employers were to be settled through arbitration. Individual freedom was an irreplaceable good that would be lost in collective negotiations. They found little support on this point from the employers, who preferred collective negotiations regulated according to the September Agreement of 1899.[17]

The war against class struggle was waged through massive ideological campaigns in the press and trade magazines. On the practical level, it was demonstrated in active support for Save Society (*Samfundshjaelpen*, literally, Society Help). Founded in February of 1920 and modeled after the German emergency service *Technische Nothilfe,* this extremely antisocialist organization was dedicated to opposing strikes. It was founded by leading members of the Danish Employers' Association and had some links to existing paramilitary corps. Financing was organized partly through the Employers' Association, partly through private contributions from large banks, shipping firms, and big manufacturers. The aim of the organization was to provide labor where strikes threatened vital business and social interests, but only after the invitation of public authorities. Save Society organized roughly 7,000 active strikebreakers in 1920 and gave protection to workers willing to work during strikes. In its heyday in 1920 to 1922, Save Society received good police and military protection mainly in port and seamen's strikes. Its base was Copenhagen, but it had branches in many large provincial towns.[18]

Save Society's leadership lay securely in the hands of large capital and its representatives, but its membership was diverse. Splinter groups from the trade unions joined, but most members were minor office workers and representatives of small business, especially in retailing. Save Society also received full ideological and practical backing from the organizations and press of the lower middle classes,[19] who saw it was a defense against "union tyranny" and the Social Democrats. High unemployment in 1921 weakened the labor movement's ability to fight, however, and Save Society became redundant. It declined after 1923, and with the formation in 1924 to 1926 of the first Social Democratic government, it became more difficult to get official requests to mobilize strikebreakers.[20]

As in many other European countries, the extreme right wing tried to organize in Denmark in the wake of World War I. Using fear of Bolshevism as a justification, these groups found little support. In 1918–1919 sporadic anti-Semitic criticisms could be heard. They were touched off by the arrival of large numbers of East European Jewish emigrants, who were considered a threat to the livelihood of self-employed artisans and retailers in the towns.[21] In this period also, intellectuals, parts of the press, and even some Social Democrats became interested in race hygienics.[22] But neither anti-Semitism nor race hygiene became widely popular, and even Fascist and

Nazi organizations in Denmark would later keep their distance from such ideas.

In contrast, criticism of parliamentary democracy gained ground, and throughout the 1920s the question of the constitution was debated widely.[23] Not only within the lower middle classes but throughout society there was a diffuse discontent with a political system that suffered from inefficiency, endless discussions, half-finished solutions based on compromise, party and class egosim, and the hopeless ignorance and incompetence of government in dealing with the specific interests of the lower middle classes. This discontent combined with a desire for an effective government that replaced the ingrown tradition of minority rule with majority rule.

In this context, fascism was discussed as a possible solution. The *Aarhus Stiftstidende (Aarhus Times),* one of the most important mouthpieces of the lower middle class, agreed on a number of points with Young Denmark, which represented a nationalistic, critical line within the Conservative People's party. Young Denmark became the ideological center for criticism of parliamentarism and for fascist sympathies in the 1920s. In these circles fascism was considered a healthy popular reaction to a corrupt parliamentary system as well as a renewal of conservatism. It was said that belief in parliamentarism had become a dogma no one dared question. "It is therefore very refreshing," wrote the *Times,* "to see the unlearned Mussolini . . . do the unthinkable: within a couple of months being offered the dictatorship of a major modern state, while the parliament enthusiastically legislates its own redundancy and goes on vacation."[24] An even more concrete, positive reaction to the Fascist takeover appeared in the *Trade and Industry Daily* in the work of an obviously pro-fascist English correspondent, who characterized the Italian Fascist party as an "energetic middle-class party"[25] whose antisocialism was related to the Danish Save Society. But these attitudes were unique and were possibly rooted in a misunderstanding of fascism as a possible alternative to the Danish political system.

Despite many variations in political opinion, Denmark in general, and even the lower middle classes in particular, totally and unmistakably rejected fascism. Only "dreamers deluded themselves into believing that Denmark could be Italian and Fascist" wrote the *Danish Merchants' News* in 1925.[26] Along the same lines, we find artisans who criticized "the paralyzing lack of effectiveness of party strife" but who clearly rejected demands for a "strong man." "No, let us not expect too much of 'strong men'," wrote the newspaper *Danish Trades and Industry.* "Their miracles belong in other cultures. It is more likely true that only the people can solve the crisis."[27] Even among the majority of militant conservative circles, fascism was considered unsuitable for Danish conditions, even though a few young conservatives found its corporative ideas attractive because they theoretically eliminated class war. Some of the ingredients for a right-wing radicalization of Danish politics were present in these years, but there was no mass support for fascism.

The Campaign to Politicize the Lower Middle Classes, 1924–1930

There is no doubt that artisans, retailers, office workers, and sales personnel were hurt by the economic crisis of the 1920s; there is likewise no doubt that they were aware of their hardships. Bankruptcy, indebtedness, and unemployment threatened in the 1920s far more directly than during the breakthrough of the Depression in Denmark in 1929.[28] How could self-employed groups or minor office workers react, and what political choices were available when fascism was considered unfeasible?

Many seem to have chosen political resignation or passivity. Especially after the *de facto* collapse of the Trades and Industry party in 1924, many retailers and artisans viewed the possibility of establishing an independent political profile as exceedingly remote. The alternative was to fall back on narrow economic interests and trade identity, always a viable choice for these groups. Evidence from the trade journals indicates that artisans were particularly successful in establishing strong trade identities and in promoting the idea that craft skills would continue to be essential in spite of threats from big capital and state interference. This attitude can also be found among retailers. Individual responsibility for corporate interests was all-important for both groups.

These ideas sustained an ongoing battle to strengthen expertise in political life, to contribute something of the craft and trade mentality to political parties and the Rigsdag. Artisans and retailers were generally unrepresented in the Rigsdag after the collapse of the Trades and Industry party, and artisans' and retailers' associations worked tirelessly throughout the decade to politicize their members; that is, to engage them in national and local politics, to draw them out of their fruitless concentration on the trade or craft alone, and to exploit their expertise to enrich political life. The dominant theme was to get artisans and retailers to join the existing political parties and run as candidates in local and national elections. Leading the way were artisans, whose leaders called for a more precise view of craft interests. "Unfortunately, it has always been the 'what-use-is-it-all' spirit that has characterized the artisans' associations as soon as political questions were put on the agenda," *Danish Trades and Industry* wrote. "This spirit must be resolutely cast aside, artisans must go the polls. Artisans have exactly the same access to political influence as any other class. . . . What we want to encourage is not that you go and vote for a certain party. . . . We do not recommend that artisans form their own party either; that route has been tried and proved unnegotiable."[29] Artisans were to put pressure on the candidates of other parties to get them to promote the interests of the various crafts. Referring to the recently completed General Strike of 1926 in England, *Danish Trades and Industry* emphasized that it was "the English middle class who had repulsed the attack on society and reestablished law and order. . . . Everywhere, every time it has been the middle class who has been the real bearer of calm, healthy, and natural development, and therefore the price of damaging the natural conditions for the growth and future existence of the middle class is high."[30] Often referring admiringly to the results of effective working-class organization, artisans' associations campaigned unceasingly in 1926 and 1927 to activate their members politically.

In terms of membership and electoral support, independent artisans and retailers divided their loyalties among four parties, a point that the leaders of various organizations acknowledged. Minor office workers supported the Conservative People's party, the Social Democratic party, and to a lesser degree the Radical party, which gained office workers' support probably because it demanded mandatory arbitration in labor conflicts. In contrast, the Liberal party, favoring ultraliberalist policies and demanding a reduction of civil service wages, attracted office workers less successfully. But many retailers supported the Liberal party precisely for its championing of lower wages for public employees.

The Social Democratic party obviously presented a special problem for the lower middle classes. From the early 1920s the party enjoyed an indisputable hegemony in the working class. Syndicalism lay in ruins after the failed major strikes of 1920–1921 and never became an important factor again. The Danish Communist party provided a home for leftist opposition from 1920, but it was torn apart by internal conflicts in the next decade, its effect on the working class was extremely sporadic, and its electoral power was minimal. The absence of a serious left-wing revolutionary threat also made it impossible for the Right to use the Bolshevist specter in its propaganda. This gave the Social Democrats considerable room for maneuver, and the party exploited this opportunity to change policy in two areas. First, the Social Democrats formulated a plan for parliamentary "responsibility" in which they voiced their willingness to assume government power when the time was right, even without the certainty of realizing the party's principal ideas. Second, they tried to expand the social base of the party.

The class core of the party had until then been the urban working class. Appeals to the lower middle class had issued from working-class interests and from the argument that, at least in the long run, the lower middle and working classes had common interests. During the 1920s and the first half of the 1930s, the party defined itself as an alliance of workers, small entrepreneurs in town and country, and minor office workers. Social Democratic policies were now framed, not only in the interest of the working class, but also as a joint policy including other groups. In principle the party favored the working class, but in practical matters it gave considerable consideration to the lower middle class. The Social Democratic program now emphasized "social peace" rather than social conflict, a change that was evidenced in Social Democratic backing for state involvement in labor conflict and for industrial councils in large firms. The new program could also be seen in the formation of a Danish version of totalitarianism theory in which communism and fascism or nazism were described as equally serious threats to peaceful democratic, parliamentary government in Denmark.

This shift in Danish Social Democratic politics paralleled similar changes in the German Social Democratic movement in the 1920s. But these policies were implemented more consistently in Denmark, probably because the Danish party was not in competition with strong communist or left-wing reformist groups. The lower middle classes responded by voting more for the Social Democratic party and voicing support for its policies in some of their interest groups.[31] This allowed the Social Democrats the opportunity to adjust their social reform and business policies to satisfy the demands of at least part of the middle classes. That this adjustment occurred failed to make a deep impression on the leaders of artisans' and retailers' associations, who remained undividedly conservative or liberal. These association leaders waged an intense campaign in the 1920s against Social Democratic agitation in their constituencies. They were aware that many of their members had joined or were about to join the Social Democratic party, but they argued that these ordinary artisans and retailers were working against their own interests.[32]

This anti–Social Democratic propaganda criticized "municipal socialism," the Social Democrats' allegedly ambivalent attitude toward private property and private initiative, and especially the party's wish for state intervention on almost all levels of society. Undoubtedly the Social Democrats' understanding of economic development was somewhat ambiguous. On the one hand, the party appealed to the lower middle classes on the basis of the actual situation, but on the other hand, it often argued that big industry would dominate all production and be the foundation of all future wealth. The Social Democratic prime minister Theodor Stauning's belief in big industry was clear when he said in 1930 that "the world has changed greatly in the last fifteen years. Production forms are altered daily. Cottage industry has ceased to exist, small business disappears. Technological miracles produce as much in one hour as it takes artisans days to make. Production costs are reduced. Consumption grows and demand increases."[33] This pessimism about small business was promptly answered in a commentary in *Danish Trades and Industry* in which Stauning's arguments were reversed: "It is true that many branches have withered on the great tree of artisanry. But for every withered branch, new and fresh twigs have budded. . . . And thanks to technology, all these crafts—old as well as new—are today better equipped than ever before. . . . . It is technology that has given crafts wind in their sails as never before."[34] On the threshold of the international Depression, this was a daring, but as it turned out, not unjustifiable optimism on behalf of small business firms. Despite these disagreements, the Social Democrats' position as a potential government party became so strong that by the end of the 1920s the leaders of artisans' and retailers' associations stopped recommending that their members vote only for the Liberal or Conservative parties.

In the Depression: Consensus or Radicalization?

The full impact of the Depression was not felt in Denmark until 1931 and the most serious repercussions of the crisis came only in 1932.[35] Like the earlier crises in world market prices, the Depression affected Danish exports, especially in agriculture, where production was mainly export-oriented. The Depression brought about falling prices, decreased sales, and falling incomes for farmers, who initially tried to offset the crisis by increasing production, which only made things worse. The Depression spread from agriculture to urban industry, where production, sales, and income were tied in part to the agricultural sector. For urban industry, the Depression led to stagnation, cutbacks in production, and increasing unemployment, all culminating in 1932.

Aside from agriculture, however, the Depression turned out to be less serious in Denmark than in other countries. Industrial production in Denmark was reduced by 5 to 10 percent in 1932, the worst year of the crisis, even though unemployment was considerably higher. One of the reasons for Denmark's relatively milder experience was that, partially and whenever possible, state intervention kept the Depression from running its full economic course. Starting in late summer of 1931, an almost exemplary state policy effected agricultural assistance, currency devaluation, trade agreements, tax relief, Depression loans, limitations on production, and price increases. The state also protected the domestic market through exchange controls, protectionism, social programs, and a limited, growth-oriented economic policy that subsidized housing and started public works. Agriculture's dependency on world market conditions limited that sector's ability to benefit from state intervention; on the other hand, state intervention was important for domestic industry and commerce, which gained a larger portion of the home market for Danish goods. Thus Danish production was sheltered by the state in areas where Danish goods had had difficulty competing until then, a situation that pleased Danish artisans, who for years had disapproved of strong competition from imports. Based on broad political agreement and a balancing of group or class interests, state policy was socially conservative and static. It was not a policy aimed toward changing the structure of the Danish economy or its one-sided dependency on the world market. Oriented toward ensuring domestic buying power, Depression policy tried to improve farmers' living conditions, protect Danish production and the domestic market, alleviate unemployment, and provide for the unemployed. The crisis was not supposed to "clean up" the Danish economy, but stabilize it.

That the political system was able to master the Depression and avoid the kind of crisis Germany experienced was important to Danish democracy and the political climate of the 1930s. The great concern was to get through the Depression as painlessly as possible on the basis of political—and class—cooperation. This does not mean that serious political and ideological differences did not arise on specific issues. But because state policy tried to satisfy all interest groups—if not to the same degree—it was possible even in the Depression to maintain the political consensus underlying the four old parties and thereby to maintain the political system itself. The key point again was that Denmark was determined not to let the Depression develop into a legitimation crisis of the political system as it had in some other countries. This consensus extended to the Social Democratic party, which openly acknowledged that its support of Depression policies was intended to combat radicalization, antidemocratic tendencies, and even Nazi influences within the groups that were hardest hit in the crisis.

Depression policies were certainly part of the reason for Danish democracy's ability to maintain a basic consensus, even though various radical currents, hostile to the political system, appeared. Members of anti-democratic groups numbered 200,000 in the 1930s, and electoral support for the Nazi party (Danish National Socialist Workers' party, DNSAP) and other antidemocratic right-wing parties grew from 0.7 percent in 1932 to almost 7 percent in 1939, while the Communist party's share of the total vote grew from over 1 percent to 2.4 percent.[36] But these numbers indicated that the basic consensus of the system and support for state policies were unshaken. As well, however, they reflected a fear of radicalization and ideological rejection of nazism, which found expression in legislation limiting democratic rights of civil unrest in 1933, and in the Social Democrats' greatest electoral victory ever in 1935, when the party used the slogan "Stauning or chaos."

When there was open dissatisfaction with state policies, it was usually farmers who led the criticism, although workers and the unemployed, among whom the Communist party found increasing support, also added to the disharmony and unrest. Antiparliamentary groups benefited from such protests. Fear of nazism and fascism played a big role in Danish politics because of the sympathy expressed in some circles for fascist-inspired ideas and an alternative to parliamentary democracy in the form of corporative, estate-like organization of society and a strong state.[37] The influence of these ideas was clear in the so-called crisis movements that appeared in Denmark after 1930.[38] The most noticeable protest movement was the Farmers' Association *(Landbrugernes Sammenslutning*—LS), which at its zenith mobilized 100,000 farmers, or one-half of all Danish farmers, and criticized what it considered to be insufficient Depression programs and the all-too-tame policies of the agrarian organizations. Earth, Work and Capital *(Jord, Arbejde og Kapital)* was another protest movement; it mobilized farmers against so-called interest slavery. As a result of this dissatisfaction, the Liberals were split, and the Free Farmers' party, a new agrarian protest party, gained parliamentary representation.

Urban protest movements arose also, the most radicalized being the youth group of the Conservative People's party, Conservative Youth (*Konservativ Ungdom*—KU).[39] KU's political and ideological line imitated fascism in the 1930s. It enthusiastically informed the public of Fascist rule in Italy, advocated a strong government and corporativism, and imitated fascist and nazi styles by using fascist salutes and uniforms and by mounting demonstrations and riots. These activities found little enthusiastic support in the general population or in the Conservative People's party itself. At its height the KU could boast of 30,000 members, of which some were organized in storm trooper divisions. KU emphasized a youthful, activist style, winning support especially from salespeople, office workers, and students. KU courted the middle classes, telling them of events in Italy and Germany, where allegedly the middle classes had found their political identity. The lesson, according to the KU, was that the Danish middle classes should also become a powerful political factor.[40] Even more directly imitative of nazism was the DNSAP, which copied the German National Socialist party so slavishly that it adopted verbatim most of that party's twenty-five-point program. It was a "cross-class" party without clear class characteristics, even though small businessmen seem to have been overrepresented in the party at the end of the 1930s. Gaining representation in the Folketing in 1939, the DNSAP had 5,000 members in that year, most of them from Southern Jutland.[41]

Sympathy for dictatorship and antidemocratic sentiment were more widespread in the general public than was direct support for nazi groups.[42] The reasons for this become clearer if we focus on the development of various groups in the middle classes in the 1930s. Because the economic and social repercussions of the Depression were less severe for urban industry than for agriculture, times were not especially harsh for the urban middle classes. Of course, one cannot overlook problems in the construction industry, nor can one ignore artisans' complaints that state assistance was being given primarily to agriculture.[43] But the prophesies (and wishes) of some Social Democrats that artisans would be declassed and proletarianized remained unfulfilled. There were bankruptcies, and fears of being declassed spread in some circles in the urban middle classes. But such anxieties ultimately had little objective foundation, and therefore subjectively this fear did not seem to have been a determining factor in the Danish urban middle classes' reactions and political options. The contrast with the German middle classes is obvious.

Perhaps in one specific connection there was a fear of declassing. Artisans voiced great concern about the political influence of the crafts as such compared with farmers and workers, who had won political influence and who could be sure of having their interests satisfied. For craftsmen, this concern was translated into a feeling of being politically invisible in the process of determining subsidies for various groups during the Depression. "The crafts are badly hurt by the Depression, left to themselves," an article in *Danish Trades and Industry* read before the November 1932 parliamentary election, "while workers, farmers, and fishermen enjoy the state's provisions in the form of welfare and other kinds of protection. At the same time, in the Landsting (Upper Chamber) a law regulating apprentices is pending that, if passed, will ensure the demise of the crafts and shake the foundations of the tradition of apprenticeship."[44] But neither the Depression nor—for the artisans—insufficient state policies dealing with it were of great significance to the urban middle classes in political and ideological terms. Still, one must differentiate between the lower middle class and wage earners and, within independent business, between artisans, small industry, and retailers.

Let us start with the artisans, who are easiest to describe.[45] The 1930s did not bring great political and psychological change to the artisanal crafts. One-half of all artisanal businesses was to be found in the towns, and the other half in the country. As in the 1920s, over 80 percent of all artisans were organized; but whereas urban artisans were almost completely organized, the level of organization in the country was much lower. This led to a lack of discipline in bidding on contracts, with organized members often complaining that they were underbid by unorganized master artisans.

The Federation followed the line it had since the middle 1920s; namely, that the trades were neutral in party politics. This acknowledged that, with regard to membership and voting, artisans supported the four old parties. Artisans may have been more closely tied to the Conservative People's party—Pitzner, the Federation chair, was a Conservative deputy in the Folketing—but the Liberals, Social Democrats, and the radical Left also numbered artisans among their members. In 1932 two artisans were Rigsdag deputies for the Liberals. But as early as the 1920s and even more noticeably in the 1930s, there were clear indications that artisans felt they were in a political bind because they, unlike workers and farmers, who had their own parties, could not make their political influence felt as members of their particular crafts. Like other groups, the Federation worked to ensure that the parties put up candidates with whom artisans sympathized. There was even sympathy in the Federation for an industrial or class-organized political system in which artisans, ignoring party differences between crafts, gained political influence as artisans in a form of corporative organization.[46] It would be unreasonable to assume that this was an example of antiparliamentary or antidemocratic attitudes among artisans. Not only Prime Minister Stauning but also the Conservative People's party suggested that the Upper Chamber be turned into a kind of business chamber. Still, on the whole, artisans were fairly satisfied with the existing political system, which directly or indirectly gave them a chance for political influence. In the early 1930s the Federation did complain that it, unlike other business organizations, was not invited to meetings discussing exchange regulations,[47] but from the middle of the 1930s it was included in some of the bodies overseeing exchange policies.

Of course, artisans were not always pleased with the policies supported by the Rigsdag and government, especially the Social Democratic government. This applies particularly to business policies, such as those regarding apprentice laws, bidding, and so-called municipal socialism. In the case of municipal socialism, local branches of publicly employed artisans were accused of undermining the working conditions of artisans in general, a campaign that took place in particular during Social Democratic rule. We have already noted artisans' dissatisfactions with government Depression policies, particularly with what was alleged to be favoritism toward agriculture in such matters as the granting of subsidies. Yet even here, certain policies—state subsidies for housing, some public works programs, and especially protection of Danish production following the establishment of an exchange commission in 1932—were advantageous for artisans. Indeed, these policies suited them perfectly because they increased Danish producers' share of the domestic market.

The main exception to this general picture of artisans' satisfaction with the system was the protest movement centering around Skive and Himmerland in Jutland. Judging from the evidence, this movement was supported mainly by nonorganized rural artisans. Openly paralleling the agricultural protest movement, the artisans' movement called itself the Artisans' Association (*Haandvaerkernes Sammenslutning*—HS). In 1932 it presented a program of eleven points designed to combat the crisis in the crafts. The program reflected a mix of short-run solutions for the Depression and more anticapitalist and middle-class socialist ideas regarding big capital and the question of interest. Designed to ensure the continued existence of artisans, the demands were not particularly extreme. The most noteworthy were the attacks on monopolies, on exploitation of artisans by big capital, and on "interest slavery."[48]

It is worth underlining that although the Artisans' Association seems to have been limited primarily to rural artisans in north Jutland, the movement created unrest among organized artisans in the Federation, which warned against the division of artisans. The Federation also attacked the HS's criticism of big capital and interest oppression, saying that it was a short-sighted criticism that "hits the self-employed artisan himself right in the face." The Federation encouraged people to join together to institute "provisions that can also put troubled artisans on equal footing with agriculture with regard to subsidies and social assistance to compensate for the wounds of the Depression."[49] HS ideas won some sympathy in 1932 and 1933 but, unlike the LS, the movement ebbed relatively quickly and was silent by 1935. Most likely, the movement was partially responsible for sharpening the attitudes and demands of artisans in government and the Rigsdag.

But it would be a mistake to see the HS as an example of radicalization in the crafts. Danish nazism did not take root among artisans either, even though master artisans were slightly overrepresented in DNSAP membership in 1936 and 1939.[50] Fear of nazi influence was evidenced in the Federation's going out of its way to inform artisans about nazism and to combat the spread of nazism in Danish society and in the organization's ranks from the middle of the 1930s. This open disavowal of a particular ideology marked a clear shift from the Federation's policy in the early 1930s, when it commented approvingly on artisanal representation in the German Nazi party after Hitler's first significant electoral success in September of 1930. No drastic political and ideological changes occurred among the well-organized Danish crafts, therefore, and this absence of significant change was justified both objectively and subjectively. Craft groups, especially those in the building industry, were badly hurt by the Depression, and a crisis atmosphere prevailed. But the instinct to survive as a class played a part in hindering widespread anxiety about declassing. On top of this, the consequences of the Depression were rather quickly alleviated; Depression programs did provide extensive help for craft groups, even if these programs failed to fulfill all the artisans' demands; and artisans gained the opportunity to shape policy by being included in the administration of Depression relief programs. Politically, artisans behaved respectably, retaining their traditional party loyalties, or, possibly, allowing Social Democrats to gain a more solid footing among artisans during the 1930s.

More problematic is the other large group in the urban, self-employed lower middle class—the retailers. Numbering a little over 80,000, retailers constituted a group about as large as the artisans'. However, only one in four retailers belonged to professional associations, making this group far less organized than the artisans'. Furthermore, retailers' organizations were divided into a large number of branches and regional groupings, and it is difficult to locate a specific mouthpiece for this group. The Depression hit the small retailer hard, causing decreased economic activity, reducing incomes by 10 to 20 percent, and therefore reducing sales. Many retailers were forced to close their shops; but, just as for artisans, mass bankruptcy did not occur, and proletarianization and fear of declassing were not widespread. On the contrary, new businesses such as ice cream shops and beauty salons arose, and it is likely that many former wage-earners started their own businesses during the 1930s. These circumstances complicate the discussion of the politics of retail trade. We noted earlier that retailers had been active in forming the Trades and Industry party. But after the demise of the party, retail trade became much less active despite the participation of small businessmen in the bourgeois parties. Retail trade wanted a free market and was therefore most likely tied to the Liberals, although it is probably true that some groups such as wholesalers supported the Conservatives. Social Democrats probably did not find much backing in this group. Not much change occurred in this general pattern of allegiances during the 1930s despite the unpopularity among retailers of the state's Depression policies of regulation and control of sales and prices. This conflict of interest did not have serious political consequences. Aside from the fact that retailers seem to have been slightly overrepresented in the DNSAP in 1939—though to a lesser extent than other small, independent businessmen—there is no indication that this sector became more radical.

Wage-earning office workers and minor civil servants—the new middle class groups—composed a little over 10 percent of the labor market around 1930. Industrial development and the expansion of the public sector in particular made for the mild expansion of these groups, although they grew at a far slower pace than in the period before 1930. On the whole, office workers did not seem to have been hurt quite as badly as manual laborers by unemployment in the Depression. It must be added, however, that women dominated the new middle-class work force, and female unemployment was often difficult to measure. Already low, wages decreased during the Depression among this predominantly female work force. Still, just as for artisans and retailers, fear of being declassed or proletarianized was not widespread among service workers.

Office workers were relatively poorly organized even though the large HK had long functioned as a union for this group. But office workers were divided between a middle-class and a working-class point of view, and this division left its mark on the HK also. The HK did not join the working-class trade union movement, the DSF, until 1932, and the delay was surely caused by the fact that office workers, like the middle class as a whole, were politically and ideologically divided. For some, class and work attitudes were most important, and therefore they would not join a working-class union or be associated with the Social Democratic party;

they felt closer to the Conservatives or, to a lesser degree, the Radicals. For the majority of organized office workers, wage-earning status was decisive, and they felt they belonged with the Social Democratic labor movement and party. Even when the HK joined the DSF, not everyone in the office workers' union was convinced. In 1932 the KU encouraged office workers to quit the HK and thereby stop their support of the Social Democrats.[51] The KU claimed that it was the duty of the middle class to form a defense against socialism, and that the middle class had no class feeling and should therefore not be tied to the labor movement. KU spokesmen appealed mainly to office workers in private business, where some did quit the HK. But the KU could not stop the flood of people joining the HK, which throughout the 1930s campaigned energetically and successfully to increase membership. It is also likely that the KU's increased sympathy for fascism pushed some office workers toward the Social Democrats.

Civil servants were an extremely differentiated group, comprising postmen as well as directors of government departments. They had different work contracts and wage agreements from office workers in private business. They had job security, but their wages were often a matter of public discussion, and the Conservative People's party in particular saw to the working conditions of civil servants. Therefore, civil servants were probably sympathetic to the Conservatives and Radicals, while support among them for the Social Democrats was more limited. This situation did change somewhat, however, during the 1930s, when civil servants' work conditions improved. It can be claimed that specific job-related circumstances such as loyalty to the state and increased wages hindered civil servants from adopting extreme political viewpoints. Some young civil servants did join the KU, but on the whole, civil servants were slightly underrepresented in the DNSAP.

Salespeople and office workers employed in private business, especially the younger workers, did become more politically radical. They were disproportionately represented in the DNSAP in 1936 and 1939. The KU seems to have had great appeal to personnel in shops, banks, and offices, and the best basis for antiparliamentarism and radicalization was found in these groups. According to available sources, minor office workers and salespeople, and probably some civil servants as well, constituted a relatively large part of KU membership, almost equaling the students.[52] These groups were attracted to the KU's fascist-like politics and were inspired by fascist ideas. There were other tendencies among office and sales personnel. The HK almost doubled its membership during the 1930s, and this indicated that wage-earner consciousness was on the rise within these groups. This growing wage-earner consciousness is due partly to the fact that after 1932 the DSF worked hard to gain negotiation rights for office and sales workers and thereby raise their wages, and partly to the fact that the Social Democratic party was establishing a profile as a people's party and gaining votes from the middle classes. Support for the Social Democratic party among office workers, salespeople, and civil servants indicates that growing numbers of these groups supported the party's defense of democracy against Danish political extremism and antiparliamentarism.

The picture of the urban middle classes in the 1930s is therefore one of division and conflict. Political division was evidenced in a fragmentation of party loyalties, ideological division in a variety of attitudes toward the democratic system and toward various antidemocratic and antiparliamentary tendencies. If conflict and the potential for radicalization were present, the political and ideological climate of the 1930s nevertheless tended toward cooperation, solidarity, and defense of democracy; there was not much room for radical and antidemocratic groups to gain a foothold in the urban middle classes. Radical and antidemocratic groups did increase their support gradually during the 1930s, but at no time before the German occupation could they mobilize more than 10 percent of the Danish population. They were therefore unable to destablize the Danish political system, which successfully used various means to protect itself from the beginning of the 1930s.

Conclusion

The interwar period is justifiably characterized as the "age of fascism."[53] But this term is inappropriate from the Danish point of view. It would be more suitable to talk of the first "golden age" of class reconciliation and class cooperation. Class reconciliation became the dominant trait in the 1920s, even more so in the 1930s, and this meant that the urban middle classes remained or were detained within the framework of the democratic parliamentary system. Some urban middle-class groups changed parties while others worked to find a new political standpoint, but by and large, these classes retained their traditional ties and loyalties; all were part of the general consensus on the democratic parliamentary system.

This cannot be explained by reference to the absence of fascist and nazi alternatives. On the contrary, Denmark was the country in which there were more fascist and nazi organizations than anywhere else in Europe, but it was also the country in which these groups achieved the least support.[54] Although right-wing extremists courted the middle class energetically, they had as good as no effect in these classes. There are many possible explanations for this. First, the economic and business situation was apparently not quite as catastrophic in Denmark as it was in most other European countries. Denmark was dominated by petit-bourgeois production forms both in the country and in towns, and this was not changed by the crisis of the 1920s and the 1930s. Second, there was a long tradition in the lower middle class of political and ideological pluralism and relatively close ties with the existing political parties; initially with the Conservatives and Liberals, later with the Social Democrats. Not at the center of the political scene, the lower middle class was nonetheless considered decisive in winning political power. The class was not marginalized, and all parties demonstrated a willingness to incorporate its class demands. The four dominant parties were flexible, contributing to the integration of the political system through programs such as social security, which in principle applied to all classes rather than the working class alone.

Third, guidelines for a parliamentary system that produced results through party cooperation and compromise were developed early, and it was difficult for critics of the inefficiency of parliamentarism to make themselves heard. Fourth, after 1917, no revolutionary, Marxist, or Bolshevist parties were strong enough in the working class to provoke a right-wing reaction. Fifth, Danish fascist and nazi groups simply lacked the dynamism and ability to integrate the masses that German nazism had. Attempts to imitate the German party's politics in Denmark had little appeal in the lower middle class. Last, leading forces in Danish politics could take advantage of the success of fascism or nazism in other countries. At an early stage they were aware of the threat of right-wing radicalism and could mount their defense by mobilizing against nazism but also by making moderate adjustments to some fascist and nazi elements that might have had an appeal in Denmark. Thus Danish politics represented a completely different dimension of the interwar experience from German politics. Denmark's history in this era suggests that there was no necessary causality between the Depression and nazification of, or sense of crisis in, the lower middle classes.

Notes

1. Vagn Dybdahl, *Partier og erhverv: Studier i partiorganisation og byerhvervenes politiske aktivitet 1880–1913* 1–2 (Aarhus, 1969); idem, *Det nye samfund på vej 1871–1913*, in *Dansk Social Historie 5* (Copenhagen, 1982); Joergen Fink, "Middelklassen," in *Socialhistorie og samfundsforandring*, ed. S. Eriksen et al. (Aarhus, 1984), 210–24; Bjarne Hastrup, *Haandvaerkets oekonomiske historie 1879–1979* (Copenhagen, 1970).

2. This is treated in depth in Svend Aage Hansen and Ingrid Henriksen, *Sociale brydninger 1914–1939*, in *Dansk Social Historie 6* (Copenhagen, 1980).

3. Quoted from Alfred Bindslev, *Konservatismens historie i Danmark* (Copenhagen, 1938), 2:269.

4. With the Constitution of 1849 the Danish form of government was changed from

an absolutist monarchy to a constitutional monarchy. Parliament (Rigsdag) was divided into two chambers, the lower chamber (Folketing), where there was universal male suffrage, and the upper chamber (Landsting), which was elected indirectly with considerable conservative restrictions. A revision of the constitution in 1866 strengthened the conservative character of the Landsting.

5. Dybdahl, *Partier og erhverv*, 224–48.

6. Heine Andersen, "Klassestruktur i Danmark i mellemkrigstiden" (unpublished MS, 1976), 6.

7. Erik Nordholt, *Erhvervspartiets historie og dets samfundsopfattelse* (Erhvervshistorisk Årbog, 1972), 78–159.

8. Ibid., 147–49.

9. *Dansk Koebmandstidende*, 2 Sept. 1919.

10. Nordholt, *Erhvervspartiets historie*, 97.

11. Ibid., 98. The same theme is heard regularly in the following years. See *Dagblad for Haandvaerk og Industri* (hereafter DHI) 3 and 4, Sept. 1918, 22 April 1920.

12. DHI, 3 July 1917.

13. Ibid., 1 Jan. 1920.

14. Ibid., 31 March 1920.

15. Ibid., 22 Feb. 1920.

16. *Privatfunktionaeren: Tidsskrift for Privatfunktionaerstanden*, 1 Jan. 1921 and 15 March 1921.

17. The September Agreement was the main agreement made in 1899 between the Danish Employers' Association and the Danish Trades Union Association. Rules for announcing strikes and lockouts and for abiding by collective agreements were set down.

18. Anders Ture Lindstroem, *Samfundshjaelpen: Traek af en kontrarevolutionaer organisations historie* (Erhvervshistorisk Årbog, 1978), 7–48.

19. DHI, 22 Feb. 1920, 5 May 1920, 16 May 1920, and 22 March 1921.

20. Save Society was dissolved in 1942, but its importance between 1922 and 1942 was sporadic.

21. *Aarhus Stiftstidende*, 6 Nov. 1919.

22. See, for example, K. K. Steincke, *Fremtidens Forsoergelsesvaesen*, 2 vols. (Copenhagen, 1920). In the following years Steincke became in turn Minister of Justice and Minister of Health and Welfare in the Social Democratic governments.

23. For example, note C. Thalbitzer et al., *En dansk forfatningsaendring?* (Copenhagen, 1923), and *Gads danske Magasin*, 1928, esp. 11–26.

24. *Aarhus Stiftstidende*, 30 Nov. 1922.

25. DHI, 31 Oct. 1922.

26. *Dansk Koebmandstidende*, 5 May 1925.

27. *Dansk Haandvaerk og Industri* (hereafter, *Dansk Haandvaerk*), 18 Dec. 1926 and 25 Dec. 1926.

28. Hastrup, *Haandvaerkets oekonomiske*, 233 et seq.

29. *Dansk Haandvaerk*, 13. Nov. 1926.

30. Ibid.

31. Hastrup, *Haandvaerkets oekonomiske*, 292.

32. *Dansk Haandvaerk*, 1 Aug. 1928, 22 Aug. 1928, 6 Oct. 1928.

33. Hastrup, *Haandvaerkets oekonomiske*, 290.

34. *Dansk Haandvaerk*, 4 Jan. 1930.

35. Information on the Depression is based on Vagn Dybdahl et al., *Krise i Danmark* (Copenhagen, 1975); Karl Christian Lammers, "Verdenskrisen og krisen i Danmark," *Historievidenskab* 13/14 (1978): 15–69; Hansen and Henriksen, *Sociale brydninger*.

36. The figures are from Ulf Lindstroem, *Fascism in Scandinavia, 1920–1940* (Stock-

holm, 1985), 115.

37. Note in this connection Richard Andersen, *Danmark i 30'erne* (Copenhagen, 1968), 165 et seq.; Alex Quade and Ole Ravn, *Hoejre Om: Temaer og tendenser i den anti-parlamentariske debat, 1930–39* (Copenhagen, 1979); Karl Christian Lammers, "Magt og Masser: Om styreformer i mellemkrigstiden," in *Magt og Masser* (Copenhagen, 1985), 5–28, esp. 15 et seq.; Lindstroem, *Fascism in Scandinavia,* 6 et seq. Note further, with regard to the degree of antidemocratism, Jesper Vagn Hansen's, *Hoejreekstremister i Danmark, 1922–45* (Odense, 1982).

38. Note in general Quade and Ravn, *Hoejre Om.*

39. Note on the KU, Erik Jensen, *Mellem demokrati og fascisme* (Odense, 1983); Jim Skov Jensen, "KU og Fascismen" (unpublished MS, Copenhagen, 1984). Fascism's influence on the KU comes through clearly in Ole Bjoern Kraft, *Fascismen. Historie. Lære. Lov* (Copenhagen, 1933), as well as in two KU political statements of April and September 1934, printed in Skov Jensen, "KU og Fascismen," 117 et seq.

40. Aksel Moeller in 1935, quoted in Skov Jensen, "KU og fascismen," 15.

41. Note on this point, Malene Djursaa, *DNSAP: Danske nazister, 1930–1945* (Copenhagen, 1981), which is an exhaustive sociological study of the Danish Nazis. Her results were presented earlier in Henning Poulsen and Malene Djursaa, "Social Basis of Nazism in Denmark: the DNSAP," in *Who Were the Fascists: Social Roots of European Fascism,* ed. Stein Ugelvik Larsen, Bernt Hagtvet, Jan Petter Myklebust (Bergen 1980), 702–14; and in Lindstroem, *Fascism in Scandinavia.*

42. Andersen, *Danmark i 30'erne,* 18 et seq.; Quade and Ravn, *Hoejre Om.* In the Danish public sphere it was mainly the largest provincial newspaper, *Jyllands-Posten,* that led in criticizing democracy and calling for a dictator.

43. See, for example, the request of the Federation of Artisans and Industry to the Rigsdag, 20 Oct. 1932, in which artisans demanded the same support given to other sectors in the Depression. See *Dansk Haandvaerk,* 29 Oct. 1932.

44. Ibid., 11 Nov. 1932.

45. On this point, see in general Hastrup, *Haandvaerkets oekonomiske,* 281 et seq., and also Hans Mathiesen, "Faellesrepraesentationen for Haandvaerk og Industri" (unpublished MS, Copenhagen, 1983).

46. *Dansk Haandvaerk,* 28 Jan. 1933.

47. Ibid., 14 May 1932.

48. The Artisans' Association's eleven demands are printed in *Dansk Haandvaerk,* 24 Aug. 1932. See also Hastrup, *Haandvaerkets oekonomiske,* 293.

49. *Dansk Haandvaerk,* 24 Aug. 1932.

50. Compare with the tables in Djursaa, *DNSAP,* 2:116–17.

51. On the relation between the KU and office workers and salespeople, see Skov Jensen, "KU og Fascismen," 143 et seq.

52. Ibid., 11.

53. This characterization goes back to Ernst Nolte, *Der Faschismus in seiner Epoche* (Munich, 1963). See also Lammers, "Magt og Masser."

54. Djursaa, *DNSAP,* 17.

10

Corporatism and the Lower Middle Classes: Interwar Belgium

CARL STRIKWERDA

It has often been argued that fascism flourished in Europe because the lower middle class was particularly vulnerable to the economic crisis and structural changes of the interwar period. Frightened first by the growth of organized labor and big business and then by the Depression of 1929, shopkeepers and white-collar workers rejected parliamentary democracy and turned to authoritarian, right-wing movements. The strident nationalism of the Right, it is contended, appealed to the lower middle class because it felt peculiarly threatened by the class antagonisms fascist leaders purported to resolve. Because the long-run trend toward economic concentration, such as the growth of large department stores, threatened small retailers, some kind of "corporatism" in which each economic group—agriculture, commerce, industry, and labor—would be regulated in a state-controlled economy was also attractive. For these reasons, the lower middle class rejected ineffective or deleterious *laissez-faire* economics and parliamentary politics and turned to an authoritarian, nationalist, and coporatist vision that promised to rescue them from a very troubled world.[1]

Belgium, the oldest industrial country in continental Europe, provides an excellent area for testing this interpretation. After World War I, giant banks and holding companies increased their hold on Belgian industry, and the Socialist party and labor unions grew enormously. A large lower middle class, many observers feared, was losing its position to big business and the working class. A variety of antitax, antilabor, and "shopkeeper" movements sprang up in the 1920s and early 1930s. Then, in 1936, two movements with strong fascist tendencies, the Rexists and the Flemish nationalists, together captured almost 20 percent of the national vote.

Nonetheless, the case of Belgium challenges the view that the economic and political trends of the interwar period were delivering the lower middle class into the hands of authoritarianism or fascism. It is not clear that shopkeepers (that is, the commercial lower middle class) were doomed by long-term economic trends; nor did many of the "corporatist" demands of the lower middle class require recourse to authoritarianism or fascism. Although it has been overlooked by many historians, in the late 1930s the Belgian government took a whole range of actions designed to convince the commercial lower middle class that its economic grievances were being met. The solutions to these grievances, furthermore, were not simply hopeless attempts to stop economic progress; instead, they became, in many ways, the model for how the Belgian political and economic system has evolved for the last fifty years.

Although the place of white-collar workers in the rise of fascism has received much less attention than that of shopkeepers, here, too, the case of Belgium may be instructive. It has been argued that white-collar workers, the "new middle class," feared that they would fall into the proletariat or see their status and wages drop below that of unionized, blue-collar workers. White-collar workers in Germany, for example, were afraid that they would become "déclassé," and hoped that fascism would transcend the class politics that threatened their position.[2] In Belgium, however, there is little evidence that these workers turned disproportionately to the Right because of economic uncertainty. Instead, there is some indication that these workers were open to conventional labor-union organizing by Catholics and Socialists and that they did not provide a fertile recruiting ground for fascism.

That Belgian democracy eventually used state intervention to alleviate the problems of the commercial lower middle class represented a major change from the country's history, which had been dominated by heavy industry and by liberal, laissez-faire economic policies. In the 1920s, like Britain, Belgium still had a higher percentage of industrial workers in the labor force than did France or Germany.[3] The resemblance to Britain extended to economic policy; Belgium kept its tariffs very low from the pre–World War I period through the interwar years.[4] Liberal influence meant that Belgium had little of the statist tradition that Germany or France possessed. Internal government was largely directed by elected provincial councils, not by appointed officials such as prefects, and the government controlled very few economic enterprises.[5] Entrance into commercial trade or any other kind of business was virtually wide open.[6] Even when the state, in the late nineteenth century, gradually became involved in providing unemployment and health insurance, working-class housing, and other services, a statist tradition did not emerge. Much of the government involvement in these areas came through subsidies to labor unions, mutual insurance societies, and voluntary associations, a process known as "subsidized liberty."[7]

The liberal tradition arose because both of the nineteenth-century political parties, Liberal and Catholic, helped create it. Liberal and Catholic parties monopolized Belgian politics until universal male suffrage, based on a skewed system of plural voting, came in 1894, and, along with the Socialists, remained two of the three dominant parties in the interwar period. Both Liberals and Catholics accepted Belgium's constitutional monarchy, and they disagreed primarily over the issue of state funding of religious education. For almost the whole of the pre–World War I period, then, the lower middle class followed the economic liberalism of the established Catholic and Liberal parties.[8]

Although socialism, after its early years, did not challenge the parliamentary, monarchical form of government, its rise and the reactions to it by Liberals and Catholics left the lower middle class more and more isolated. Because of Belgium's large number of industrial workers and the failure of both traditional parties to mitigate their economic liberalism, Socialists quickly became the second largest party in 1894. The Belgian Socialists generally advocated a reformist brand of socialism, especially after they began participating in governing coalitions during World War I. By the 1920s, Socialists had built up an impressive chain of consumer cooperatives, mutual insurance societies, and labor union federations. As a crowning edifice on this network, Socialists created a Labor Bank, complete with shares traded on the Brussels stock exchange.[9] Although Belgian Socialist consumer cooperatives were commercially less important than the German and British cooperatives, they had an importance all out of proportion to their size. They regularly gave financial aid to the Socialist party, and, very often, they set the prevailing price for goods in many towns and neighborhoods.[10] The industrial upper middle class represented by the Liberals responded to the rise of socialism and to growing international competition by creating industrial federations and holding companies. Supported by very large banks, these federations and companies often succeeded in setting uniform prices, in lobbying the government for transportation improvements, and in controlling wages.[11]

Although the Catholic party also had the support of some bankers and industrialists, the most important development within its constituency was the rise of a huge federation of Catholic small farmers' leagues, the *Boerenbond,* and a Catholic labor union movement.[12] Much like the Socialists, the Catholic farmers created a huge investment fund that controlled its own bank.[13] While the Liberals clung, officially at least, to *laissez-faire,* Catholic social theory proved multifaceted enough for these new lower-class movements to call for more state action in the name of Christian moral teaching. The evolution of the Catholic party from an upper-class rival of the Liberals into a group of institutions representing different classes was enshrined in 1921 in a reorganization of the party's structure. The party reemerged as a loose alliance of four *standen*, estates or orders. The four *standen* were: first, the old, upper-class, conservative *Fédération des cercles*, which had been the only Catholic party before the rise of the unions and farmers' leagues; second, the Flemish farmers' *Boerenbond* and similar, though much smaller, French-speaking farmers' leagues; third, the Catholic labor movement; and fourth, the Catholic middle class. Of these, the middle class, which included the Catholic lower middle class, was by far the weakest and least institutionalized.[14]

The relative weakness of the middle class, particularly the lower middle class, was clear from the response of the government to the different groups after World War I. Workers received the eight-hour day, the first government-sponsored collective bargaining committees, and the expansion of unemployment and health insurance subsidies. Farmers received additional subsidies for their insurance societies. Industrialists and bankers received a government-sponsored industrial credit fund and enormous influence over government financial policy.[15] By the 1920s, then, the Belgian political system had begun edging away from *laissez-faire*, but the one group largely excluded remained the lower middle class. No white-collar workers were represented by the collective bargaining committees, and shopkeepers acquired little protective legislation.[16]

This political powerlessness did not mean that the Belgian commercial lower middle class was a group declining in size. Between 1910 and 1930, the number of shopkeepers and commercial employees increased by about one-third, while the country's population increased by less than 10 percent. This made commerce, along with public employment, the fastest-growing sector of the economy.[17] Growth in the number of people employed in the commercial sector is common in the second phase of industrialization, since the number of industrial workers reaches a plateau and rising productivity allows the economy to put more of its output into consumer goods. In Belgium, however, unlike some other countries, small retail merchants were the key to the distribution of consumer goods. Thus, the increasing number of people employed in the commercial sector came in Belgium from the growing number of small business establishments—not, as in some other countries, from a growing number of large businesses with many employees. Furthermore, the Depression accelerated rather than weakened this trend. As one observer noted, "a crisis tends to channel into retailing the workers laid off in other areas."[18] From approximately 200,000 small retailers in 1910, the number grew to 231,000 in 1930, or an increase of 15 percent in twenty years; by 1937, the number had grown to 291,000, an increase of 26 percent in only seven years. According to a study in the 1930s, Belgium, in proportion to its population, had the highest number of small commercial establishments in the industrialized world. (Small stores were those with four employees or fewer.) France, for example, had one small store for every 169 people, Germany had one for every 80 people, England one for every 70, and Austria one for every 61. Belgium had one for every 37 people.[19] Simply because Belgium supported so many commercial establishments, it had a huge number of workers employed in this sector. A 1947 study, whose figures correspond closely to those of the 1930s, showed Belgium had 54 workers in commerce for every 1,000 inhabitants, while the average for Western Europe was 34.[20] What is more, these figures do not include hotels, cafés, and restaurants, of which Belgium had extremely large numbers, perhaps as many as 190,000. In the 1930s, despite a series of restrictive drinking laws passed in 1920, the country still had one bar for every forty households, one of the highest rates in the world.[21]

Neither the economic upheavals of World War I and the Great Depression nor the expansion of the tertiary sector caused a decline in the viability of the small commercial establishment. Instead, the scarcity of goods during and immediately after the war raised the profits of many stores. In the prosperity of the 1920s, the influx of new goods, such as radios, record players, and automobiles, and the increased availability of household items, such as margarine, electric lamps, and synthetic clothing, caused another surge of new retailers. In fact, one economist believed that the persistence of small shopkeepers ensured that the policy of deflation pursued by the Belgian government in the early 1930s would fail. Shopkeepers refused to cut their prices as unemployment rose and demand fell. Between 1929 and 1933, wholesale prices in Belgium dropped 42 percent, but retail prices fell only 17 percent. The same tendency was at work in more normal times of economic growth when an increase in the number of retailers in Belgian towns did not lead to more competition and lower prices. Instead, retailers raised prices, so that with a smaller volume, all stores could stay in business.[22]

That this population of retailers was large and growing did not mean that it lacked grievances; but rather that its discontent was quite different from that commonly attributed to the German shopkeepers, who have been used as the prime evidence for the theory about the lower middle class. Both demographic factors and social attitudes kept the population of Belgian retailers large, and these forces, in turn, powerfully shaped this group's flirtation with fascism. Belgian shopkeepers, for example, lived disproportionately in small towns. Although Belgium was extremely industrialized and densely populated, it was not highly urbanized in the usual sense. Belgium, in 1947, ranked only fifth among West European nations in cities with populations of over 10,000, although only Britain had a larger percentage of its population outside agriculture and only the Netherlands had a more densely populated territory.[23] Rather than crowding into larger and larger cities, much of the industrial work force stayed in a myriad of small to medium-sized cities. Between 1890 and 1930, the percentage of the population in cities between 5,000 and 25,000 grew by more than one-third, while the proportion of the population in the countryside fell by almost a third, and the population in cities of over 100,000 was stationary. In 1930, 54 percent of the population lived in the countryside or in towns of fewer than 10,000 people. During the Depression, in fact, the number of people in places of under 10,000 rose 15 percent, as the population in towns of 10,000 and over fell.[24]

One reason why Belgium had so many retailers, in other words, is that the dispersion of the population in small towns preserved the viability of small shops. The population tended to be dispersed, in part, because the government encouraged workers to commute into the large cities to work, rather than to move to the large cities permanently. The national railroads offered inexpensive workmen's tickets, and the government under-wrote the building of a dense network of tramways, which linked hamlets and small towns to major rail lines.[25] The dispersion of the population meant, too, that large department stores and supermarkets had a difficult time expanding in Belgium. In 1936, the country, with a population of over eight million, had only 100 large department stores and 25 large discount stores. Even the chain-store outlets, of which there were 6,000, were often no larger than the individually owned family stores.[26]

Small commerce also continued because of the centralization of credit and the desire for social status. Very large banks, particularly the *Société Generale* and the *Banque de Bruxelles,* dominated finance. In part through holding companies, these banks kept financial resources away from retailing and confined to heavy industry, especially coal and metallurgy.[27] As one economic observer noted, "It was easier to borrow a million francs than 10,000."[28] Just because Belgium had deep class divisions between workers and other classes, owning one's own store carried a great deal of prestige. Over 96 percent of the commercial retail outlets were privately owned businesses, and over 40 percent had no employees other than family mem-bers.[29] As one international economist commented, "The desire to become or remain one's own master pushes people towards commerce, even when the income they are counting on will be inferior to the income they're making at the time. This consideration is very much at work in countries such as Belgium. . . ."[30] As a result, about one-third of the retailers had another full-time or nearly full-time job, and, as one might expect, wives and daughters of shop owners provided an important part of the commer-cial work force.[31]

Thus, the Belgian small retailers did not demand the control of consumer cooperatives and large department stores nearly as frequently as their counterparts in countries such as Germany. In 1936, cooperatives, company stores, and modern department stores and supermarkets accounted for only eight percent of all retail sales in Belgium.[32] Instead, the commercial lower middle class in Belgium worried about competition from newer, still smaller competitors, especially blue-collar workers moonlighting as store operators, the wives of white-collar workers running businesses on the side, and street peddlers. Members of the lower middle class felt threatened by *other*, more marginal members of the lower middle class as much as they did by other classes. They also resented the universal power of the handful of Brussels (that is, big-city) banks, which monopolized credit and influenced government policy. And the lower middle class felt aggrieved that the government and the rest of the public at large appeared unresponsive to their plight, preoccupied by the demands of more organized groups, or simply incapable of action.

The line of protest that drew some of this discontent towards fascism for a time focused on the "rule of parties," *particratie*. Belgian parliamentary democracy after World War I, many observers believed, seemed reduced to perpetual wrangling and incapable of producing any clear-cut decisions. From the time formal political parties began in the 1860s, until World War I, Belgium had not known coalition governments. From 1884 to 1914, only homogeneous Catholic cabinets had held power. From 1918 on, the institution of genuine universal male suffrage gave more votes to the Socialists' worker constituency and brought the Catholics below a majority. For the entire interwar period, coalitions, usually between Liberals and Catholics, were the only way to govern. The splits and alliances between and within parties were incredibly complicated. The Catholic party, which participated in all coalitions, was torn as its Christian Democatic wing, representing the unions and farmers, tried to push aside the old *Fédération des cercles,* representing the upper class. The conservative *Fédération* tended to ally with the much-reduced Liberal party on economic issues, while the Christian Democrats at times allied with the Socialists. Yet the anticlerical issue pulled all Catholics together against the Liberals and Socialists.[33]

The politics of the interwar period became truly complicated, however, as these essentially nineteenth-century issues of religion and class were overshadowed by the division between French-speakers and Flemings. Although Flemings—that is, Dutch-speaking Belgians—had always made up half or more of the population, French had served as the language of education, the church, government, and business, even in the Flemish-speaking areas. With universal male suffrage in 1894, and especially after the suppression of plural votes in 1919, and with the growing economic development of previously agricultural Flanders, lower-class Flemings demanded the right to use Dutch on an equal basis with French. Step by step, the Flemish tried, with much success, during the interwar period, to make Flanders a unilingual, Dutch-speaking area. Accommodating Flemish demands was a protracted and laborious process, however, because Flemish political spokesmen were themselves divided between hard-liners and moderates. A loose group of Flemish nationalists in Parliament made up the hard-liners, while the moderates were mostly Christian Democratic deputies representing Catholic farmers and workers, but increasingly including some Socialists and a few Liberals as well. When the Flemish groups could unite, they often won their demands, as they did in forcing the State University of Ghent to become a solely Flemish institution in 1930. On the other hand, the larger political agendas of the traditional parties kept moderates from working with the hard-liners on many occasions.[34] While the result was a slow success of the moderate Flemish program, for the average voter, Parliament often appeared consumed by unproductive infighting. Endless consultations behind the scenes between Catholics, Liberals, and Socialists, between Christian Democrats and conservatives, and between Flemish- and French-speakers produced only a series of compromises that were very difficult to understand from the outside. The "rule of parties" seemed to satisfy no one.

As the historian Hermann Balthazar has pointed out, in fact, the interwar parties were too weak, rather than too strong. The numerous conflicting demands of the parties faithfully represented the demands of the interest groups within and around the parties, demands the party leaders had difficulty turning down.[35] In 1933, in the midst of the Depression, the conservative Catholic-Liberal government acquired additional powers to deal with matters by executive order because it failed to reach a compromise in Parliament with Christian Democrats and Socialists. The multiple divisions meant that the thorniest issues, especially policies of deflation and devaluation of the currency, were acted on with extreme reluctance. At several points, nonelected experts from the financial community had to be called in as cabinet ministers to solve issues parliamentary leaders wished to avoid.[36]

This recourse to the banking sector only increased popular suspicion that shadowy behind-the-scenes wealth had undue power. This feeling mounted when, in 1934, the Socialist Labor Bank went bankrupt and the central fund of the *Boerenbond,* which had invested heavily in banking, nearly went bankrupt. Politicians' and businessmen's attempts to get the government to rescue the political banks fed the popular feeling, especially among the lower middle class. The association of artisans and merchants in Namur, for example, proclaimed, "We have as our enemies, on the one hand, high finance in all its forms . . . and on the other hand, the politicians who try to put us to sleep and who have given us poorly made legislation."[37]

The "rule of parties" may have been a particularly attractive rallying cry for the lower middle class because, of all the organized interest groups in Belgian politics, it was the least able to pressure the political parties and the government. Whereas farmers, blue-collar workers, and industrialists had begun organizing already before World War I, lower-middle-class organizations were largely a product of the 1920s. The new organizations, moreover, remained far too decentralized. By 1937, there were no fewer than 1,625 local associations in different occupations, and 1,059 associations linking different associations.[38] Only a handful of the national and regional federations uniting these local groups had any significance. The lower middle class was also pulled in different directions by its loyalties to the various political parties and factions. Even the large majority of the lower middle class that was Catholic could not unite: some aligned themselves with the Christian Democratic farmers and labor unions; others with the conservative, upper-class *Fédération des cercles;* while the most radical faction called for an autonomous middle-class movement that would ally with other political groups, including protofascist organizations.[39] By the mid-1930s, the frustration of the lower middle class was palpable; it was the most rapidly organizing group in Belgian politics, yet it lacked any leverage on the government and political parties.

Another strong current of protest that appealed to the lower middle class and on which right-wing groups capitalized was the moral laxity in society. Movies, radio shows, and modern literature appeared to be threatening a traditional Catholic, family-oriented society. These fears were especially strong among the Catholic shopkeepers for whom the work of family members was essential. A manifesto of the Catholic middle-class federation called, in its first article, for "the permeation of social and economic life with a constant and efficacious concern for the safeguarding of the family, especially the large family."[40] One of the strongest Belgian youth movements in the period, the *Association catholique de la jeunesse belge* (ACJB), took the struggle against pornography and the loss of moral standards as one of its chief goals. It was no coincidence that the ACJB increasingly represented the middle-class Catholic element and not other social groups, and that as a result it pushed the morality issue. Begun in 1921 as an umbrella organization for Catholic youth movements, the ACJB saw separate Catholic youth organizations split off for young workers, young farmers, and students during the 1920s, leaving it with the campaign for morality as one of its few claims to being a mass movement.[41]

All these elements of protest—the distrust of high finance, the disgust at a weak parliament and seemingly dominant parties, and the fear of immorality—came together in the success of the protofascist Rex movement. Rex exploded on the political scene in 1936, suddenly rivaling the Liberals as the country's third-largest party. Rex began in 1931 as a Catholic publishing house—hence the name, "Christ the King"—run by a young former law student, Leon Degrelle. Degrelle, like a great many Catholic students of the time, had been deeply influenced by the ideas of the French reaction-ary Charles Maurras of the *Action française*. Between 1931 and 1935, Degrelle, a personal friend of the chaplain of the ACJB, used his position as director of the publishing house to campaign for a reform of the Catholic party, and, by extension, of Belgian politics. Eventually, Degrelle's denunci-ation of corruption among Catholic party politicans forced the young firebrand—he was still in his twenties—to set up Rex as a separate organiza-tion from the Catholic community. Then, in late 1935, Degrelle chose to transform Rex into a new political party to contest the elections of May 1936.[42]

Rex, under Degrelle's brilliant if demagogic leadership, hit all the respon-sive chords among discontented Belgians. Degrelle's solution to the dilly-dallying and corruption in Parliament was "Sweep out the bastards!" Degrelle coined his own term for corrupt politicians and financiers: "bank-sters."[43] At the same time, one of the "Rexist Principles" was that, "Without a moral revolution, there can be no revolution at all."[44] The weekly newspa-per *Rex* ran a regular feature on the family, calling for more respect for mothers and daughters.[45] Although a few followers provided much of the written propaganda for Rexism, Degrelle was the soul of the movement and the movement's sole leader. He could reputedly deliver sixteen public speeches a day. Degrelle managed to combine vituperative, absurd attacks on his opponents with bizarre, pious claims of idealism. One wit described him as "P. T. Barnum as Jesus Christ."[46]

On a more serious level, Degrelle's Rexism tried to identify a common enemy of its constituents and to formulate a positive program. Jose Streel, as much of a theorist as Rexism had, tried to attack the big banks in a way that would appeal to workers, shopkeepers, and small businessmen: "Industrial capitalism, the capitalism of enterprise, is an economic form which, correctly regulated, can be socially defensible. It's a capitalism of work and saving, that is, of real value. Banking capitalism [however] sepa-rates work from power and wealth. It is false and can only lead to disas-ters."[47] In the same vein, Rexist propaganda urged "Workers of all classes, unite!"[48]

To make real this fundamental unity, parasitic banking capitalism would be rigorously controlled by the state, and each "healthy" economic sector—commerce, industry, agriculture, the liberal professions—would be allowed to organize its own affairs and be given control over government economic policy for its domain. Parliament would still exist, but with greatly reduced sessions and powers. Political parties would be suppressed. For the lower middle classes, associations of shopkeepers would acquire legal standing, utility rates would be lowered for small establishments, large wholesalers and department stores would be regulated, and the status of white-collar workers would become a legally controlled profession. For blue-collar workers, Rexism called for "self-management." All women were promised the right to vote, not merely those enfranchised in a 1919 electoral law.[49]

Although Degrelle tried to appeal to a variety of groups, his special attraction for the lower middle class was clear in his success in garnering support from the numerous, fragmented lower-middle-class organizations. In March of 1936, two months before the national elections, Rex formed an alliance with a loose coalition of organizations that had come together in an *Eenheidsfront van de Middenstand*. In many election districts, especially in Flanders, the Rexist slates of candidates were recruited from, or actually named by, the existing lower-middle-class organizations belonging to the *Eenheidsfront*.[50]

Given the traditional party loyalty of most Belgian voters, the success of Rexism in the May 1936 elections marked an enormous break in the country's political history. Only six months old as a party and led by the 29-year-old Degrelle, Rex won 11.5 percent of the nation's votes and captured 21 seats in a 202-seat parliament. Though unable to attract strong support in Flanders, Rex had won the votes of one out of every six French-speaking Belgians. Nationwide, this put Rex just behind the Liberals, the traditional third party. The threat of Rex was magnified because it was accompanied by other challenges to the stability of Belgian politics in the fateful year of 1936. The Flemish Nationalists, who had taken on a fascist-style program themselves in the mid-thirties, saw their total vote go from 5.9 percent to 7.1, which, because of the peculiarities of the election laws, doubled their seats in Parliament. The Communists at the same time went from 2.8 to 6.1 percent, their parliamentary seats from 3 to 9.[51] Thus, the extreme Right and extreme Left together had won almost a quarter of the country's votes. Meanwhile, both the international and internal Belgian situations immediately before and after the elections heightened the sense that the nation was at a crossroads. In March of 1936, two months before the elections, Hitler occupied the Rhineland, violating the Locarno treaties, which had been the bedrock of Belgian security for a decade. While the Belgian elections were taking place, a wave of strikes for the 40-hour week occurred in France, and were soon followed by similar strikes in Belgium in June and July.[52] Furthermore, both Rex and the Flemish Nationalists were known to be connected to international fascism: Mussolini's government certainly subsidized the Rexists in 1937 and probably did so as early as August 1936, while the Nazis aided the Flemish Nationalists. In January 1937, Degrelle broadcast to Belgium in French on an Italian government radio station.[53]

Whom did Rexism moblize? On a nationwide basis, Rex drew support from rural and urban areas in an approximately proportional fashion. But the support Rexism received in Flanders and francophone Wallonia differed radically. In Flanders, Rex received very little rural and small-town support, usually less than four percent. (The Flemish Nationalists, by contrast, were predominantly a rural and small-town party.) What electoral support Rex received in Flanders came from medium-sized to large cities, and predominantly the middle-to-upper class areas within them. In Wallonia, on the other hand, rural and very small towns provided the main source of Rex's support. In Bouillon, Degrelle's home town in rural Luxembourg, Rex was the largest party in 1936, with 35.6 percent of the vote. Bouillon, however, had only 2,203 voters. Rex's other greatest support came from the largest cities, especially the more administrative, less industrialized cities. Rex was the largest vote-getter with 24 percent of the vote in St. Josse-ten-Noode, a mixed commercial, white-collar, and working-class area of Brussels; while in Anderlecht, a more working-class area, it won only 13 percent. In small, industrial towns like Marchienne-au-Pont and Boussu in the coal and metallurgical province of Hainaut—towns where Communists were the second-largest party after the Socialists in 1936—Rex drew only 6 percent of the votes. Even in Liège, the industrialized province in which Rex did the best with almost 20 percent of the votes, there was the same split between rural, industrial, and commercial or administrative districts. In the agricultural commune of Dalhem, Rex received 30 percent of the vote and was only 4 votes short of being the largest single party. In the commercial and administrative city of Liège, Rex drew 23 percent, but in heavily industrialized Seraing, it received only 13 percent.[54]

In terms of its electoral support, then, Rex, in the French-speaking areas of Wallonia and Brussels, was disproportionately a rural and small-town party, and, nationwide, was an urban commercial party. That Rex attracted not only French-speaking farmers, but also small shopkeepers and white-collar workers, is also clear from its membership and candidates for elections. Of the rank-and-file Rex membership in St. Josse, the commune of Brussels where Rex did the best in 1936, 28 percent were small retail businessmen, the largest single occupational category, and 15 percent were white-collar workers. About 15 percent were lawyers, managers, and businessmen. In two samples of Rex candidates for elections, shopkeepers and other small retail businessmen (commerçants) made up the largest single group, 24.5 percent in the 1936 national and provincial elections, and 31 percent in local elections in Brussels during 1938. White-collar workers (employés) made up 12 and 16.6 percent, respectively. These percentages of shopkeepers and white-collar workers appear to be higher than on most Liberal and Catholic party slates, the slates that usually drew the votes of the lower middle class. Politically, Rex faithfully reflected its lower-middle-class, commercial constituency: Rexist deputies in Parliament, three of whom had been officers of the Eenheidsfront van de Middenstand, introduced bills to prevent the opening of department stores, to ban sales with prizes—sales small shopkeepers found it impossible to compete with—and to ban discount stores.[55]

Nonetheless, among its candidates for elections, Rex still had a large number of leaders from the liberal professions and big business, just as most other Belgian parties did. If one groups together the teachers, engineers, lawyers, managers (cadres supérieurs), and businessmen (industriels), they together made up 36.5 and 30.7 percent of the Rex candidates in the 1936 and 1938 elections. The Rex representatives in Parliament, too, show the same pattern: a large proportion of lawyers, teachers, journalists, and professional politicans—just as most parties had—but also a slightly higher percentage of shopkeepers than normal. Among the twenty-one Rexist parliamentary deputies, there were seven lawyers, four journalists, one businessman, one worker, one town mayor, and five shopkeepers, as well as two individuals whose occupations cannot clearly be categorized.[56]

By comparison with right-wing and fascist movements in other countries, Rexism may have been less able to mobilize workers. Whereas the German and Austrian Nazis, for example, regularly got anywhere from 15 to 35 percent of their support from workers, and even recruited those percentages of their candidates among workers; in Belgium, no more than 10 percent of the Rexist support may have come from workers.[57] In St. Josse, one of the urban areas with a relatively high percentage of industrial workers where Rex did well, only 10 percent of the members in 1937 were workers.[58] And among urban areas, typically the higher the percentage of workers, the lower the percentage of Rexist votes. The low level of worker support for Rex, furthermore, was a marked contrast to the Flemish Nationalists. Even though the Flemish Nationalists received most of their votes from small towns and the countryside, they succeeded in winning a fair degree of support from workers. Many workers in Flanders, in fact, lived in small towns and the countryside and commuted to cities. There they encountered discrimination from French-speakers and came to support Flemish nationalism.[59]

Yet the socioeconomic composition of Rexist support is not the only key to understanding it. Rather, what led groups to support Rexism, was, in part, the failure of the political system to give these groups access to power. Rex mobilized, in particular, French-speaking farmers in Wallonia, who (unlike the Catholic Flemish farmers in the highly organized Boerenbond) lacked a strong institutional voice in Belgian national politics. Similarly, the lower middle class was the interest group with greatest degree of fragmentation and the least clout on the national level. In the 1930s, even among the twenty-six largest professional associations in what could be considered the lower middle class, only one—the association of hotel, café, and restaurant owners, with 51,000 members in 1932—had any significant size. One attempt to unite the lower middle class came in November of 1932, with the formation of a non-partisan National Union of the Middle Classes. The Union soon claimed 100,000 members. The first point in its program called for support for "the legitimate claims of the associations making up the middle classes, associations presently isolated and, therefore, deliberately unrecognized by the public powers."[60] Similarly, the national Catholic middle-class federation called for the "end of the disdain of the public powers with regard to the middle class."[61] Unfortunately for these groups, however, the enormous political deadlock over devaluing the Belgian franc and ending the policy of deflation meant that the government in the mid-1930s barely started to address lower-middle-class grievances. Frustration with the government's lack of action led leaders of the National Union to participate in the *Eenheidsfront van de Middenstand*, which allied with the Rexists in the 1936 elections.[62]

The timing of the Rexist explosion, moreover, strengthens the argument that access to political power, and not simply economic distress, was a key element in lower-middle-class discontent. The Belgian economy revived significantly after devaluation in March 1935, and by the May 1936 elections, unemployment had dropped almost in half, profits and exports were up, and bankruptcies were down. Nonetheless, Rex tapped a current of discontent. By the same token, in the elections of 1939, after a new recession in 1938 had led to worsened economic conditions, support for Rexism dramatically declined.[63]

Rexism, in other words, mobilized significant discontented groups and proclaimed its intentions both to satisfy the lower middle class's grievances and to radically transform, if not destroy, the parliamentary system. The Belgian political system survived this challenge. In the process of trying to satisfy the lower-middle-class discontent, political leaders laid the foundation for the interest-group state that emerged in Belgium after the Second World War. To understand the failure of fascism in Belgium and the pivotal role of the lower middle class, it is helpful to examine, first, the political obstacles Rexism faced, and second, the positive steps taken by democratic parties to hold the loyalties of the lower middle class and thus to undercut the threat of fascism.

One key problem for Belgian right-wing leaders (and, in a sense, for all Belgian political leaders of the twentieth century) was how to ensure that nationalism would hold together rather than divide a multiclass movement. The Flemish issue, by complicating parliamentary government, made fascist appeals attractive, but it also presented a major obstacle to unifying all right-wing elements. As francophones, Degrelle and his chief lieutenants appealed most easily to other French-speaking Belgians. Whereas Rex won 15 percent of Walloon votes and 18.5 of the largely French-speaking Bruxellois, it received only seven percent of the votes in Flanders, which had a majority of the country's population. Rex could not hope to become a major political force without obtaining more support in Flanders. The Flemish Nationalists, meanwhile, had won 13.5 percent of the votes in Flanders, as well as 2.8 in Brussels—and almost none in Wallonia. There were, moreover, some similarities between the two movements: in 1933, the Flemish Nationalists had united in one party and turned toward the Right, adopting a program opposed to parliamentary democracy. Consequently, Degrelle led Rex to reach an alliance with the Flemish Nationalist party in October 1936, an alliance in which each party would organize its own section of the country.[64]

Yet some of the votes Rex had won in Flanders had come from middle- and upper-class Flemings who spoke French and who may have voted for Rex in protest against Flemish nationalism. These francophones were threatened by lower-class Flemings' demands that they stop using French. Others among his supporters in French-speaking Wallonia and Brussels resented Flemish nationalism as antipatriotic, even pro-German. Degrelle's idealistic goal of reconciling social divisions in a new corporate community had sounded to many francophones like a program to suppress both Flemish linguistic separatism and lower-class interests. In allying with the Flemish Nationalists, Degrelle could claim that he was simply trying to carry out his program of national reconciliation, but his anti-Flemish francophone followers saw the tactic as a betrayal. Although the exact terms of the Rex–Flemish Nationalist accord were kept secret, it was known that an agreement had been reached. During the winter of 1936–1937, dissatisfaction with Degrelle's leadership spread among his recently recruited followers.[65]

The biggest blows to Rexism came from several quarters. First, from the determined opposition of the Catholic church, which, though conservative, had never given up its support for a constitutional, parliamentary regime. Second, Rexism encountered the willingness of the democratic parties, especially the Socialists, to bury their differences with each other and unite against the threat of fascism. Degrelle's Rexism, like many other would-be revolutionary organizations, depended on continued activity. The movement could not simply organize and exercise some influence; it had to be gaining strength or be engaged in some dramatic combat, otherwise it would decline. In March of 1937, fearful that the movement was losing momentum, Degrelle provoked a by-election in Brussels, announced his own candidacy, and challenged the governing Liberal, Catholic, and Socialist coalition to oppose him. At the Socialists' suggestion, the coalition put forward only one candidate, the prime minister Paul Van Zeeland, a Catholic but not an official member of the Catholic party.[66] Even the Communists, following Popular Front tactics, supported Van Zeeland, a former official of the National Bank. The Flemish Nationalists, still formally allied with the Rexists, supported Degrelle's candidacy, although they had only won 2.8 percent of the vote in Brussels in 1936. Degrelle's opponents succeeded in forcing him to publicize the secret terms of the Rex–Flemish Nationalist accord, prompting some francophone and Belgian nationalist voters to desert Degrelle. Degrelle added to his own risks by implying in an election rally that the Catholic church, by not having condemned Rex, tacitly approved the movement. In response, two days before the election, the archbishop of Mechelen, head of the Belgian church, condemned Rexism as "a danger to the country and the Church," and forbade Catholics to vote for Rex—and forbade them even to abstain. The results of the election dealt Degrelle a crushing defeat: Van Zeeland received 75 percent of the vote, Degrelle 19 percent—less than the combined total of Rex and the Flemish Nationalists in the same district the previous year. A number of Rexist leaders soon left the movement, a trend that would continue over the next two years as Degrelle led the movement closer to complete fascism and closer to a complete identification with nazism. Already in June 1937, two months after Degrelle's defeat in Brussels, the Flemish Nationalists rejected their alliance with Rex, fearing that some of their supporters saw Rexism as too francophone to be trusted. In reaction, Degrelle tried to organize more of an authentic, Flemish-speaking version of Rexism. Neither he nor his Flemish followers ever solved the problem of how to defend a strong, authoritarian state while simultaneously defending Flemish demands for greater regional and linguistic rights.[67]

One other problem for Rex was that the two biggest lower-middle-class elements among its supporters, the small retailers and white-collar workers, did not form a coherent group. The fragile unity between the two sections of the lower middle class could come from a common feeling that they were both set apart from the blue-collar, unionized workers. Yet there was always the danger that white-collar workers would choose to ally with their blue-collar compatriots, who were also salaried and employed by large firms, rather than ally with retailers with whom they shared a sense of elevated status. In order to lessen tensions between white- and blue-collar workers, Belgian labor unions tried to assure white-collar workers that they would not lose their status in a labor movement dominated by less-skilled workers. The unions, in other words, usually decided that it was preferable to put up with a certain amount of elitism in white-collar workers in order to prevent them from being radicalized outside the labor movement by organizations such as Rex. Thus, in 1922, the public-service workers' union agreed to allow white- and blue-collar workers to organize and bargain as separate units within the union. Many national collective bargaining agreements in the interwar period began designating separate categories for white- and blue-collar workers.[68]

There were also tensions between small retailers and the white-collar workers that made an alliance between the two groups difficult. One of the major complaints of small retailers was that public employees, who made up at least a quarter of white-collar workers, engaged in commerce on the side. Without needing a full-time income from commerce, and often able to use their public position for special connections, public employees could gain an unfair advantage. In response to retailers' complaints, the government in 1930 even forbade wives of public employees from engaging in trade without the permission of the authorities.[69]

White-collar workers, too, appeared to have responded differently to the Depression and the political crisis of 1936. In part because unemployment insurance in Belgium was usually offered through labor unions, the massive unemployment of the Depression finally drove many white-collar workers to join unions. The number of white-collar workers who were labor union members more than tripled between 1929 and 1938. It is particularly important that the vast majority of these new union members, furthermore, went into the Catholic and Socialist labor union federations; attempts to enlarge or create new "autonomous" white-collar worker unions largely failed. The Catholic and Socialist unions both vehemently opposed Rex, the Flemish Nationalists, and other protofascist movements. The unions also worked to keep white-collar workers from allying with the right-wing lower-middle-class movements.[70] The result was a marked contrast to France and Germany, where unionized white-collar workers often opposed the dominant Socialist labor union federation.

In addition, although some white-collar workers voted for Rex in May 1936, many still actively participated in the strike wave during June of the same year. In fact, the participation of white-collar workers in the strike wave of 1936 led large numbers of them to become actively involved in labor unions for the first time. As a result of the 1936 strikes and the traditional unions' success in offering unemployment insurance, white-collar union membership had grown much faster by 1938 than union membership as a whole. While Socialist union membership overall stagnated in the 1930s, the Socialist white-collar workers' union went from 7,900 to 23,000. Catholic union membership as a whole grew an impressive 70 percent, but the white-collar workers' union went from 7,000 to 28,653, a growth of over 300 percent.[71]

The Catholic, Socialist, and Liberal coalition governments that ruled between 1936 and 1939 also tried to win over the discontented lower-middle-class individuals by a series of laws, executive orders, and administrative actions. In fact, some small businessmen deliberately threatened to support Rex in order to force the government to listen to them. Just before the local elections of 1938, the national association of café, hotel, and restaurant owners (as mentioned above, the largest lower-middle-class professional association) announced that it would support Rex if the government failed to change the laws on alcohol like the association wanted.[72] Much of the government intervention for the lower middle class came in this piecemeal fashion, in response to complaints. Yet the overall thinking behind the interventions was unmistakable: to abandon *laissez-faire* for the commercial sector and to use the state's economic power to tie a group politically to the regime. In other words, to use the state's power to regulate, to tax, and to control credit in order to pacify an interest group and give it a stake in maintaining the regime.

Some of the specific actions the state took on behalf of the lower middle class had begun before 1936, during the years when the government tried to deflate the economy in order to fight the Depression. An executive order in 1935, for example, increased the government's power to establish quality standards for goods, one of the complaints of small retailers being that discount and chain-stores often sold shoddy merchandise. But many of the government's most important and best-publicized actions came after the 1936 elections in which Rex did so well. In September of 1936, the government created the Retailing Commission to investigate the complaints of small commercial businessmen.[73] In October 1936, the government appointed Fernand Collin, a professor from the Catholic University of Louvain, to be Royal Commissioner for the Middle Classes. Collin held hearings in which small businessmen testified, did a survey on retailing, and published "Report on the Artisanal and Commercial Classes," which went through several editions and included most of the complaints of retailers.[74] In 1937, the regulations against moonlighting civil servants were tightened up, and civil servants were forbidden to participate in the management of consumer cooperatives. In 1938, the government also upgraded the Office of the Middle Classes to a separate Department within the Ministry of Economic Affairs. Some of the government's most important actions may have played a key role in the major elections in which Rex posed a challenge. On 13 January 1937, with what became known as the "padlock law," the government froze all diversified stores above a certain size (five employees in cities of over 100,000 inhabitants, three in smaller towns). The Ministry of Economic Affairs henceforth controlled whether or not these stores could be opened or enlarged, or add new lines. This law was strengthened in 1938 when large stores were also forbidden to manage another retailer's activity. In addition, the government in the late 1930s expanded professional education for the lower middle classes, gave middle-class professional associations more rights, and announced the creation of the "Institute for the Economic and Social Study of the Middle Classes."[75]

The other crucial aid given to the commercial lower middle class came in the area of credit, the sector that had provoked the popular ire against the big banks. In 1929, the government had created several credit organizations that could make loans to small businessmen, but these organizations were small and lacked visibility. The government also created temporary funds in 1934 to prevent bankruptcies among small businessmen. In 1937, however, all these credit institutions were grouped together under a new coordinating council for middle-class credit institutions, and the temporary funds created in 1934 became permanent. What is more, professional associations were given a stake in the system by being able to name representatives to oversee these credit institutions. This directly answered one of the demands of the lower-middle-class movement: as the Catholic federation had put it, "representation of the middle class in important public institutions."[76]

In other words, the state assured the loyalty of the lower middle class by the flow of money, and the formerly powerless professional associations now could use government patronage to keep their members organized and politically reliable. These credit institutions were a significant expansion of a particular genre of Belgian institutions, known as "para-statal" organizations. In the post–World War II era, the state has granted these organizations money and given them legal standing, like the middle-class credit institutions, but has allowed the sector they served to participate in administering them. In the post–World War II era, labor unions, education, agriculture, and industry have all benefited from these institutions, and the government and political parties have used them to keep the various interest groups tied to the state. In many ways, I would argue, credit institutions for the lower middle class in the 1930s provided the model for the postwar expansion of the para-statal system and for the political economy of Belgium.[77] In sum, the government intervention for the lower middle class marked an enormous change in economic policy. As J. Boddewyn, one of the authorities on Belgian commerce, later wrote:

> In 1912, the Belgian governmnent still could state that: "In Belgium, freedom of trade is a fundamental principle, formally embodied in the [patente] law of May 21, 1819, and deeply rooted in customs. Every citizen has the right to engage in business, but for the facts that he must obey fiscal regulations, and cannot injure others." Twenty-five years later, the voices of old-fashioned liberals who accepted the natural disappearance or streamlining of petty traders had been drowned largely by those favoring some tampering with competitive forces; and the government exhibited a willingness to intervene and regulate which would have been unthinkable or unacceptable before.[78]

After 1936, the government also acted to grant greater union rights to public employees, many of whom were white-collar workers. These actions, too, served to tie a section of the lower middle class to the regime and lessened the possibility that it would support radical movements such as Rex. Athough public employee unions had existed since 1921, they had lacked legal protections or guaranteed rights to consult with managers.

Two executive orders in 1937 granted legal recognition to public employee unions and allowed the creation of personnel committees that could bargain with managers.[79]

Much of the impetus for the government's actions in the late 1930s came from Catholic politicians for whom the lower middle class was an essential constituency they could not afford to lose. The first parliamentary caucus for the defense of the lower middle class—created in 1901—had been composed exclusively of Catholic deputies.[80] Since the 1890s, some elements of the lower middle class had been crucial allies for the Catholic farmers' leagues and labor unions, allies who had often given the Catholic unions, for example, a crucial edge over the Socialists.[81] Perhaps as much as 70 percent of the Rexist vote in 1936 had come from formerly Catholic voters.[82] In responding to the threat of Rexism, however, the Catholic leaders could also draw on the tradition of Catholic social theory. Beginning in the late nineteenth century, some Belgian Catholic leaders had begun looking for an alternative to *laissez-faire* economic and liberal individualism that also avoided what they saw as the dictatorial tendencies of socialism. At times, this search for a "third way" between liberalism and socialism could lead to flirtation with authoritarianism or fascism—as with Degrelle and his followers. At its best, however, it aimed at preserving what most Catholics saw as the best elements of liberalism (democracy and private property) and of socialism (the mitigation of economic oppression), while somehow avoiding either system's faults. These ideas had helped justify the reorganization of the Catholic party into the four *standen* in 1921. During the interwar period, some Catholic leaders tried to develop a Christian "democratic corporatism," in which parliamentary government would be maintained but the state would commit its resources to maintaining each economic group.[83] One could argue that by creating the para-statal credit institutions and regulating commerce, and by giving the lower middle class a stake in the political system that it had lacked, these leaders began forming a kind of "democratic corporatism."

This corporatist politics appears to have succeeded in winning back the loyalty of the lower middle class after its flirtation with Rexism. Whereas in the elections of 1936 Rex had won 11.5 percent of the vote, in 1939 Rex received only 4.4 percent. Already in local elections in October 1938, Rexism had suffered heavy defeats. In Brussels, it lost over a third of the votes it received in 1937. In the few towns where conservative Catholics ran joint slates with Rex in the local elections in 1938, many Catholic voters turned in masses of blank votes in protest.[84] It is true that in the national elections of 1939, other factors than the government's policy towards the lower middle class had an impact. The Flemish-French split and Rex's turning towards nazism hurt Degrelle's appeal, and the more dangerous international climate encouraged a return to the traditional democratic parties. Still, it is striking that of the three traditional parties, the Socialists, who had lost the least to Rex in 1936, lost votes in 1939 while the Catholic and Liberal parties' vote went up. The biggest single shift of votes between 1936 and 1939 was from the Rexists to the Catholics.

It was ironic that the Socialists gained so little from the coalition government's actions toward the lower middle class. The Socialists supported most of the actions to help small retailers. Indeed, the crucial legislation establishing the new credit institutions passed Parliament unanimously.[85] The Socialists' own programs in the mid- to late 1930s also helped create a climate in which the government could take the actions that it did. The most important Socialist theorist of the 1930s was Henri de Man, whose *Plan du travail* has often been described as a proto-Keynesian program to stimulate demand. What is striking about the *Plan* from the Belgian perspective is that de Man was deliberately appealing for lower-middle-class support: the only part of the economy to be completely nationalized under the *Plan* was the large banks, the common enemy of workers and small businessmen. De Man also called for a stronger executive, and by the late 1930s was close to supporting an outright authoritarian regime.[86] Yet Socialists may have also found it easier to vote for the protective legislation for small retailers because, apart from theory, their own commercial practices resembled that of the lower middle class. Many Socialist consumer cooperatives favored small, neighborhood branches—*magasins de quartier,* the corner cooperatives—rather than large establishments.[87]

The biggest reason why the Socialists appear to have to supported the new economic policies of the late 1930s, however, was their desire to prevent the further radicalization of the lower middle class by Rex. Although the Socialists, unlike the liberals and Catholics, won no votes back from the Rexists, they succeeded in helping depoliticize the discontent of the shopkeepers and other small businessmen. L. T. Léger, the Catholic president of one of the middle-class credit institutions, had already noted in 1938 that one of the keys to the Belgian policies had been their success in getting both the lower middle class and the political parties to substitute government financial aid for political conflict. One should modify, he suggested, the celebrated quip of Necker, the finance minister trying to balance the budget before the French Revolution, to fit the Belgian situation. Necker had told the French government, "Give me good policies, I'll give you good finances." The Belgian government had told the political parties and the lower middle class: "Don't make politics, and I'll give you good credits."[88]

In this sense, the case of Belgium may suggest that the key problem of the lower middle class during the interwar period was its role in the political system. The general theory about the lower middle class, however, has argued that socioeconomic causes pushed it towards right-wing extremism and that these causes were part of a general European or worldwide trend. The commercial lower middle class, in other words, was doomed in the face of increasing concentration and capitalist expansion. Yet in Belgium, with much different economic circumstances from Germany's, the lower middle class first turned to the Right, then rejected it when the democratic government responded with remedial measures. The experience of Belgium, in other words, may suggest that too much of the general theory about the lower middle class has been derived from Germany. Social and economic trends affecting the lower middle class varied widely across the industrial world, and could be radically different in a country right next door to Germany that had an equally industrialized economy. It is particularly striking, for example, that, in contrast with Germany, shopkeepers in Belgium were less threatened by department stores and cooperatives than by the *lower* lower middle class—peddlers, moonlighters, and part-time retailers. It appears the argument that increasing capitalist concentration was an inevitable trend should be seriously modified. Furthermore, the Belgian government in the late 1930s did severely curtail the more marginal traders, and thereby satisfied some of the demands of the commercial lower middle class. Perhaps the governments in countries such as Germany could have similarly addressed the grievances of the lower middle class. Thus, the radicalization of the lower middle class in Germany may have have been due more to the failure of the political system, a failure democratic regimes in countries such as Belgium succeeded (though not with difficulty) in avoiding.[89]

It is also striking that so much of the analysis of the interwar political systems has overlooked the role of the lower middle class in developing the interest-group or corporate welfare state. When historians and social scientists describe how western European states began to evolve the kind of politics in the interwar period that would eventually shape the post-1945 world, they almost always emphasize the relations between industry and labor, and, secondarily, banking, the government bureaucracy, and agriculture. Even Belgium's own Ernst Mandel, in his influential Marxist analysis *Late Capitalism,* describes how the corporate welfare state developed without mentioning the lower middle class—except to say that it was doomed.[90] Not only was the lower middle class more economically viable than has usually been believed, and its political loyalties more varied, but, in Belgium, it was critically important for the evolution of postwar politics. Recently, in an important reinterpretation of Scandinavian politics, Gøsta Esping-Andersen has argued that the lower middle class played an important role in bringing about a socialist system.[91] In Belgium, the lower middle class, perhaps with less initiative of its own but with no less importance, played a key role in ensuring that neither a fascist, nor a socialist, but a corporatist welfare state, under democratic Catholic influence, would emerge.

The author would like to thank Venita Jorgenson, Janet Moores, and Cynthia Tenpas of the University of California, Riverside Inter-Library Loan Office, without whose excellent professional assistance this essay could not have been written, and to thank Jean Beaufays, Gail Bossenga, Rudy Koshar, Vic Magagna, Wouter Steenhout, and Guy Vanthemsche for their helpful criticism and bibliographical suggestions.

Notes

1. For this argument, see Seymour Martin Lipset, *Political Man* (Garden City, 1967), 127–29; William Sheridan Allen, *The Nazi Seizure of Power*, 2nd ed. (New York, 1984); S. J. Woolf, "Introduction," 9, and H. R. Trevor-Roper, "The Phenomenon of Fascism," 27, in *Fascism in Europe*, 2nd ed. (New York, 1981); on Italy, Charles Maier, *Recasting Bourgeois Europe* (Princeton, 1975), 313; David Schoenbaum, *Hitler's Social Revolution* (Garden City, 1966), 5.
   As the result of new scholarship since the mid-1970s, a much broader view of the lower middle class has emerged, although most studies still agree that the fascist and extreme right-wing movements drew support disproportionately from the lower middle class. Some of the new scholarship does emphasize, however, that the lower middle class was not overwhelmingly attracted to fascism. See Thomas Childers, *The Nazi Voter: The Social Foundations of Fascism in Germany, 1919–1933* (Chapel Hill, 1983), especially 64–80, 142–59, 262–69; Richard F. Hamilton, *Who Voted For Hitler?* (Princeton, 1982) is perhaps too extreme in pushing the argument that the German lower middle class was not decisively pro-Nazi. On the other hand, this new literature does not challenge the argument that the lower middle class's motivations were primarily economic; that is, that competition from larger enterprises like cooperatives and department stores prompted a large segment of the lower middle class to move towards right-wing extremism or fascism. See Geoffrey Crossick and Heinz-Gerhard Haupt, eds., *Shopkeepers and Master Artisans in Nineteenth Century Europe* (London, 1984), especially the introduction by the editors, "Shopkeepers, Master Artisans, and the Historians: The Petite Bourgeoisie in Comparative Focus"; Frank Bechhofer and Brian Elliott, eds., *The Petite Bourgeoisie* (London, 1981); Denise Fauvael-Rouif et al., *Petite Entreprise et croissance industrielle dans le monde aux XIXᵉ et XXᵉ siècles* (Paris, 1981); Geoffrey Crossick, ed., *The Lower Middle Class in Britain, 1870–1914* (London, 1978); John Garrard et al., eds., *The Middle Class in Politics* (Farnborough, 1978). In encouraging a new wave of research, the following were also important: Heinrich August Winkler, *Mittelstand, Demokratie und Nationalsozialismus* (Köln, 1972); Arno Mayer, "The Lower Middle Class as a Historical Problem," *Journal of Modern History* 47 (1975): 409–36; and Heinrich August Winkler, "From Social Protectionism to National Socialism: the German Small-Business Movement in Comparative Perspective," *Journal of Modern History* 48 (1976): 1–18.
2. Schoenbaum, *Hitler's Social Revolution*, 8. Historians of Germany point out that the *DHV*, the largest union of white-collar workers in Weimar Germany, was the only labor union of any significant size to support an extreme nationalist foreign policy and to espouse anti-Semitic rhetoric. More recent historical work, however, has pointed

out that the *DHV*, as well as other nonsocialist unions and workers' organizations, had other political tendencies than simply right-wing authoritarianism. See William Patch, *Christian Labor and the Politics of Frustration in Weimar Germany: The Failure of Corporate Pluralism* (New Haven and London, 1985), 199–200.

3. Calculated from B. R. Mitchell, *European Historical Statistics, 1750–1970* (New York, 1978), 51–61.

4. Heinrich Liepmann, *Tariff Levels and the Economic Unity of Europe*, reprint ed. (Philadelphia, 1980), 413.

5. See Aristide Zolberg, "Belgium," in *Political Development in the United States and Europe*, ed. Raymond Grew (Princeton, 1979).

6. J. Boddewyn, *Belgian Public Policy Toward Retailing Since 1789: The Socio-Politics of Distribution* (East Lansing, 1978), 12–13, 20–21.

7. B. S. Chlepner, *Cent ans d'histoire sociale en Belgique* (Brussels, 1956), 109–234.

8. Val Lorwin, "Belgium: Religion, Class, and Language in National Politics," in *Political Oppositions in Western Democracies*, ed. Robert Dahl (New Haven and London, 1966).

9. On the Socialists before World War I, Marcel Liebman, *Les Socialistes belges, 1885–1914* (Brussels, 1979); Andre Mommen, *De Belgische Werkliedenpartij, 1880–1914* (Ghent, 1980); and Carl Strikwerda, "The Divided Class: Catholics *vs.* Socialists in Belgium," *Comparative Studies in Society and History* 30:2 (1988). On the interwar period: Mieke Claeys-Van Haegendoren, *25 Jaar Belgische Socialisme* (Antwerp, 1967); Emile VanderVelde, *Le Parti ouvrier belge, 1885–1925* (Brussels, 1925). On the Labor Bank, see Fernand Baudhuin, *Histoire économique de la Belgique, 1914–1939*, 2 vols. (Brussels, 1944) 2:174–83.

10. M. J. VanderGucht, "Les Tendances actuelles du commerce de détail" [Banque Nationale de Belgique], *Bulletin d'information et de documentation* [hereafter *Bulletin*] 11 (1936).

11. Georges De Leener, *L'Organisation syndicale des chefs d'industrie*, 2 vols. (Brussels and Liepzig, 1909); Baudhuin, *Histoire* 2:132–151; Eric Bussière, "La Sidérurgie belge durant l'entre deux-guerres: le cas d'Ougrée-Marihaye (1919–1939)," *Belgische Tijdschrift voor Nieuwste Geschiedenis/Revue belge d'histoire contemporaine* [*BTNG/RBHC*] xv, 3–4 (1984); Isi Delvigne, *Le Terrain au combat* (Liège, 1918), 184–275.

12. Emmanuel Gerard, *De Katholieke Partij in Crisis: Partijpolitiek Leven in Belgie (1918–40)* (Leuven, 1985), esp. 80–90, 157–63; Alois Simon, *Le Parti catholique belge, 1830–1945* (Brussels, 1958), 112–14; Jean Beaufays, *Les Partis catholiques en Belgique et aux Pays-Bas, 1918–1958* (Brussels, 1973), 53–67, 82–88. Despite its title, S. H. Scholl, ed., *150 Jaar Katholieke Arbeidersbeweging in België*, 3 vols. (Brussels, 1966) could serve as a general introduction to Catholic social movements in Belgium. On the farmers' leagues, see V. Varzim, *Le "Boerenbond" belge* (Paris, 1935).

13. Baudhuin, *Histoire*, 2:184–99; B. S. Chlepner, *Belgian Banking and Banking Theory* (Washington, D.C., 1943), 64–66.

14. Significantly, the Dutch/Flemish term *standen* was almost always used, even in French: Beaufays, *Les Partis catholiques*, 103, and Simon, *Le Parti catholique*, 115, for example. The Catholic party usually drew two-thirds of its votes in the interwar years from Flemish voters, even though the Flemish represented only a little over half of the population. On the weakness of the middle-class element, see Gerard, *De Katholieke*, 90–93, 161, 163, 340–43; Simon, *Le Parti catholique*, 114. Another example comes from Frans Van Kalken, *Entre deux-guerres: esquisse de la vie politique en Belgique de 1918 à 1940* (Brussels, 1944), 35, where, after describing all the other elements in the Catholic party, the author can find nothing to say about the middle-class federation

except that it existed. For more on the re-formation of the Catholic party after World War I, see Emmanuel Gerard, *Documenten over de Katholieke Partijorganisatie in België/ Documents relatifs à l'organisation du parti catholique belge (1920–1922, 1931–1933)* (Leuven and Paris, 1981), 17–34, 49–123.

15. Jean Neuville, *L'Évolution des relations industrielles*, vol. 2, *La Lutte ouvrier pour le maîtrise du temps* (Brussels, 1981); Helene Antonopoulo, "Les Commissions paritaires d'industrie en Belgique," *Revue de l'institut de Sociologie Solvay* (March 1924), 264–87; ibid. (May 1924), 451–85; ibid. (July 1924), 67–99; Chlepner, *Belgian Banking*, 144–47.

16. Pascale Delfosse, "La Petite bourgeoisie en crise et l'état: le cas belge (1890–1914)," *Le Mouvement social* (Jan.—March, 1981), 114; Robert Philippot, *Classes moyennes et question sociale* (Namur, 1938), 38–40.

17. Boddewyn, *Belgian Public Policy*, 35.

18. Jean-Marcel Jeanneney, *Le Commerce de détail en Europe occidentale* (Paris, 1954), 45.

19. "Le Commerce de détail," *Bulletin* 13 (1938): 511; Boddewyn, *Belgian Public Policy*, 35.

20. Jeanneney, *Le Commerce de détail*, 28.

21. Fernand Baudhuin, "Essai sur les classes moyennes," *Bulletin* 25 (Nov. 1933): 321; "Le Recensement de l'industrie et du commerce," *Revue du travail* (Nov. 1935).

22. VanderGucht, "Les Tendances actuelles du commerce de détail," 290.

23. Jeanneney, *Le Commerce de détail*, 62–68.

24. Ministère des affaires économiques, *Démographie de la Belgique de 1921 à 1939* (Brussels, 1945), 260.

25. Ernest Mahaim, *Les Abonnements d'ouvriers* (Brussels, 1910); H. Demain, *Les Migrations ouvrières à travers Belgique* (Louvain, 1919).

26. "Le Commerce de détail," 511.

27. L.-Th. Léger, "Les Institutions de crédit d'état pour les classes moyennes en Belgique," *Revue économique internationale* (Aug. 1938), 264–68; Baudhuin, *Histoire* 2:132–51; Chlepner, *Belgian Banking*, 62–69.

28. Léger, "Les Institutions de crédit," 266.

29. "Le Recensement," 1441; Boddewyn, *Belgian Public Policy*, 35–36.

30. Jeanneney, *Le Commerce de détail*, 39.

31. "Le Recensement," 1445, 1450–51.

32. Boddewyn, *Belgian Public Policy*, 35–36. In Germany in 1929, department and chain-stores alone acounted for 5.1 percent of sales; if one adds together these stores with company stores and cooperatives, establishments other than small shops probably made up a much larger amount of retail trade by 1936 in Germany than in Belgium. See Schoenbaum, *Hitler's Social Revolution*, 5.

33. The best guides to Belgian politics in this period are Theo Luykx, *Politieke Geschiedenis van België van 1789 tot heden* (Burssels and Amsterdam, 1964), 318–65; Carl-Hendrik Höjer, *Le Régime parlementaire belge de 1918 à 1940*, reprint ed. (Brussels, 1969), especially 31–53; E. H. Kossmann, *The Low Countries, 1780–1940* (Oxford, 1978), 567–660; and J. Willequet, "Le Politique intérieur de 1926 à 1965," in John Bartier et al., *Histoire contemporaine de la Belgique, 1914–1970* (Brussels, 1975), 114–33. Van Kalken, *Entre deux-guerres*; Willem Verkade, *Democratic Parties in Germany and the Low Countries* (Leiden, 1965); Ludovic Moyersoen, *Prosper Poullet en de Politieke van zijn Tijd* (Brussels, 1943), esp. 255–439; and Thomas H. Reed, *The Government and Politics of Belgium* (New York, 1924) are also useful.

34. On the Flemish question in this period, besides the other works cited in note 33,

see Gerard, *De Katholieke*, 93–102, 122–26, 204–8, 295–99; Höjer, *Le Régime parlementaire belge*, 3–30; A. W. Willemsen, *Het Vlaams-Nationalisme: De Geschiedenis van de jaren 1914–1940* (Utrecht, 1969); and J. Wullus-Rudiger, *En Marge de la politique belge, 1914–1956* (Brussels, 1957), 69–267. The roots of the Flemish question can be traced in Harry Van Velthoven, *De Vlaamse Kwestie, 1830–1914* (Kortrijk, 1982); H. J. Elias, *Geschiedenis van de Vlaamse Gedachte,* vol. 4 (Antwerp, 1955); Lode Wils, "De Vlaamse Beweging," in *Algemene Geschiedenis der Nederlanden,* vol. 11, ed. J. A. van Houtte et al. (Zeist and Antwerp, 1959); Shephard Clough, *A History of the Flemish Movement in Belgium* (New York, 1930); Aristide Zolberg, "The Making of Flemings and Walloons: Belgium, 1830–1914," *Journal of Interdisciplinary History* 5, 2 (1974).

35. Herman Balthazar, "De Ontwikkeling van de Particratie voor de Tweede Wereldoorlog," *Res Publica* 1, 23 (1981).

36. Luykx, *Politieke Geschiedenis*, 332–40; and Höjer, *Le Régime parlementaire belge*, 327. H. Speyer, *Corporatisme ou parlementarisme reformé?* (Brussels and Paris, 1935) lists the executive orders the government issued in order to take action without trying to work through a deadlocked parliament.

37. Chambre des metiers et negoces de la province, *Rapport de l'exercice 1933* (Namur, 1934), 5, cited in Philippot, *Classes moyennes*, 83. On the political banks' crises, Henriette Schoetens, "Les Interventions de crise et les collusions politico-financières en Belgique entre 1930–1940"; and Daniele Wallef, "Les Collusions devant l'opinion," both in *BTNG/RBHC* 7, 2 (1976): 426–70; Chlepner, *Belgian Banking*, 70–81; Baudhuin, *Histoire*, 2:285–99. *The Van Zeeland Experiment* (New York, 1943), 16–32, is also useful.

38. Philippot, *Classes Moyennes*, 87. The intense development of associational life among the lower middle class in Belgium during the interwar period may have some similarities to what happened in Germany. See Rudy Koshar, "Two 'Nazisms': The Social Context of Nazi Mobilization in Marburg and Tübingen," *Social History* 7 (1982): 27–42, and Koshar, "From *Stammtisch* to Party: Nazi Joiners and the Contradictions of Grass Roots Fascism in Weimar Germany" *Journal of Modern History* 59, 1 (March, 1987): 1–24.

39. Gerard, *De katholieke*, 339–60; Etienne Verhoeyen and Frank Uytterhaegen, *De Kreeft met de Zwarte Scharen: 50 Jaar Rechts en Uiterst Rechts in België* (Ghent, 1981), 135–41.

40. Federation Chrétienne des classes moyennes, "Decalogue des classes moyennes de Belgique," cited in Philippot, *Classes moyennes*, 97.

41. Pierre Dion, "L'A.C.J.B. et le lutte contre l'immoralité l'entre-deux-guerre: Phantasmes et realité," *BTNG/RBHC* 1–2, 15 (1984): 75–79.

42. On Rexism and Belgian fascism generally, Andre Buttgenbach, "Le Mouvement rexiste et la situation politique de la Belgique," *Revue des sciences politiques* (Oct.–Dec. 1936); Höjer, *Le Regime parlementaire belge*, 245–60; Jean-Michel Étienne, *Le Mouvement rexiste jusqu'en 1940* (Paris, 1968); Jean Stengers, "Belgium," in *The European Right,* ed. Hans Rogger and Eugen Weber (Berkeley and Los Angeles, 1966); Giovanni Carpenelli, "Belgium," in Woolf, *Fascism in Europe*; Verhoeyen and Uytterhaegen, *De Kreeft met de Zwarte Scharen, passim;* R. Grabiner-Kupperberg, "La Montée de rexisme: étude de la presse bruxelloise non rexiste, octobre 1935–mai 1936," *Res Publica* 4, 11 (1969); J. Willequet, "Les Fascismes belges et la seconde guerre mondiale," *Revue d'histoire de la deuxieme guerre mondiale* 66 (April 1967); Pierre-Henri Laurent, "Belgian Rexism and Leon Degrelle," in *International Fascism,* ed. George Mosse (London and Beverly Hills, 1979); Luc Schepens, "Fascists and Nationalists in Belgium,

1919–1940"; and Daniele Wallef, "The Composition of Christus Rex," both in *Who Were the Fascists? Social Roots of European Fascism*, ed. Stein Ugelvik Larsen, Bernt Hagtvet, and Jan Petter Myklebust (Bergen and Oslo, 1980); Harold Callender, "Fascism in Belgium," *Foreign Affairs* 15, 3 (April 1937); Viktor Leemans, "Soziale Ideen und soziale Bewegung in Belgien von 1933 bis 1940," *Zeitschrift für Politik* 12, 33 (Dec. 1943). On the influence of Maurras, Eric Defoort, "L'Action Francaise dans le nationalisme belge, 1914–1918," *BTNG/RBHC* 7, 1–2 (1976) and "Le Courant réactionnaire dans le catholicisme francophone belge, 1918–1926," *BTNG/RBHC* 8, 1–2 (1977).

I am concentrating on Rex, the largest Belgian fascist or protofascist movement. The next largest fascist or protofascist movement was the *VNV,* Vlaamsch Nationaal Verbond, or Flemish National Union. Two other groups, which did not participate in elections, must be mentioned: the francophone *Légion Nationale,* an authoritarian paramilitary nationalist group based in Liège, and the *Verdinaso,* a largely Flemish authoritarian movement that called for a greater Belgium or a revived Burgundian state. See Guy Delmotte, *La Légion nationale* (mimeographed *mémoire,* Université libre de Bruxelles, 1964); Willemsen, *Het Vlaams-Nationalisme,* 371–449; and Stengers, "Belgium," 150–56.

43. Buttgenbach, "Le Mouvement rexiste," 519; Willequet, "La Politique," 128.

44. Jean Denis, *Principes rexistes* (Brussels, 1936), 17, cited by George Mosse in his "Introduction," in *International Fascism,* 17, 39.

45. Buttgenbach, "Le Mouvement rexiste," 522.

46. Pierre Fontaine in *Le Rouge et le noir,* 1935, quoted by Étienne, *Le Mouvement rexiste,* 39.

47. Buttgenbach, "Le Mouvement rexiste," 525.

48. Étienne, *Le Mouvement rexiste,* 118.

49. Buttgenbach, "Le Mouvement rexiste," 524–25, 529–32.

50. Verhoeyen and Uytterhaegen, *De Kreeft met de Zwarte Scharen,* 140–41.

51. Roger De Smet et al., eds., *Atlas des élections belges, 1919–1954,* 2 vols. (Brussels, 1958).

52. Carl Strikwerda, "The Belgian Working Class and the Crisis of the 1930s," in *Chance und Illusion/Labor in Retreat,* eds. Helmut Gruber and Wolfgang Maderthaner (Vienna, 1988).

53. Étienne, *Le Mouvement rexiste,* 84–86; Stengers, "Belgium," 164; Callender, "Fascism in Belgium," 354. The Nazi aid to the Flemish Nationalists—the *VNV*—was probably much more important in 1938–1939 than earlier: Wullus-Rudiger, *En Marge de la politique belge,* 241–42.

54. Calculated from De Smet, *Atlas.* On Catholicism and Socialism in pre–World War I Liège: Carl Strikwerda, "Urban Structure, Religion, and Language: Belgian Workers, 1880–1914" (Ph.D. diss., Univ. of Michigan, 1983), 265–82, 463–66. On the interwar period, Delmotte, *Le Légion nationale,* 10, 46–48, 100; Joseph Bondas, *Histoire anecdotique de le mouvement ouvrier au pays de Liège* (Liège, 1956), 354–57; Jean Beaufays, "Aspects du nationalisme belge au lendemain de la grande guerre," *Annales de la Faculté de Droit de Liège* 16, 1–2 (1971): 105–74; Verhoeyen and Uytterhaegen, *De Kreeft met de Zwarte Scharen,* 109.

55. Étienne, *Le Mouvement rexiste,* 64–66, 125; Verhoeyen and Uytterhaegen, *De Kreeft met de Zwarte Scharen,* 141.

56. Étienne, *Le Mouvement rexiste,* 64–65; Wallef, "The Composition," 519–23.

57. Peter Merkl, "Comparing Fascist Movements," in Larsen, *Who Were the Fascists?,* 765–76.

58. Wallef, "The Composition," 519.

59. The importance of workers for Flemish nationalism in the 1930s has probably been underestimated by many historians. Compare Willemsen, *Het Vlaams-Nationalisme,* 167–69, 371–83, and Verhoeyen and Uytterhaegen, *De Kreeft met de Zwarte Scharen,* 57, with Confédération des Syndicats Chrétiens, *Manual de'action syndicale* (Brussels, 1936), 116; *La Démocratie* (16 Feb. 1935), 1; "L'Ordre du travail flamande," *Mouvement syndicale belge* (20 Dec. 1936), 241–45.

60. Arthur Wauters, "Les Classes moyennes devant la crise," *Revue du travail* 8, 34 (Aug. 1933): 944–45.

61. Fédération Chrétienne des Classes Moyennes, *Decaloque,* cited by Philippot, *Classes moyennes,* 97.

62. Verhoeyen and Uytterhaegen, *De Kreeft met de Zwarte Scharen,* 139–40.

63. On an annual basis, unemployment among insured workers in Belgium was at its worst in 1932 at 23.5 and in 1934 at 23.4. Between 1935 and 1936 it dropped from 22.9 to 16.8, when Rex experienced its greatest success. By 1939, unemployment rose again to 19.3 and Rex's vote total dropped almost 60 percent in the elections of that year. See Mitchell, *European Historical Statistics,* 67. Using monthly figures: unemployment went from 273,520 in March 1935, when the franc was devalued, to 170,759 in March 1936, a drop of 39 percent. By June 1936, unemployment had dropped to 139,771. (The elections were held at the end of May.) See also *The Van Zeeland Experiment,* 104. On the Belgian devaluation from the French perspective, Kenneth Mouré, "Devaluation in France, 1934–1936" (paper delivered at the American Historical Association convention, Dec. 1986), 20–21. My argument that Rex's appeal was only indirectly related to the condition of the economy differs from that of some other historians: see, for example, Verhoeyen and Uytterhaegen, *De Kreeft met de Zwarte Scharen,* 110.

64. Étienne, *Le Mouvement rexiste,* 96–100; Willemsen, *Het Vlaams-Nationalisme,* 371–96, 413–23. I am using "Flemish Nationalist" in the mid- and late 1930s to describe the VNV, the *Vlaamsch Nationaal Verbond,* or Flemish National Union or League. See note 42.

65. Étienne, *Le Mouvement rexiste,* 127–30, 133; Schepens, "Fascists and Nationalists," 513–14.

66. Stengers, "Belgium," 160–62; Étienne, *Le Mouvement rexiste,* 134–37.

67. Gerard, *De Katholieke,* 478–80; Étienne, *Le Mouvement rexiste,* 137–40, 158–59; Kossmann, *The Low Countries,* 642; Beaufays, *Les Partis,* 118–19, 360—65; Callender, "Fascism in Belgium," 562; Willemsen, *Het Vlaams-Nationalism,* 424–29; Höjer, *Le Régime parlementaire belge,* 26–27, 289–90.

68. On the public service workers: *Revue du travail* (Feb. 1922), 227; as well as V. Crabbe, "Syndicalisme et fonction publique en Belgique," *Revue internationale des sciences administratives* 21, 4 (1955): 825–90. On separate categories for white- and blue-collar workers, R. Blanpain et al., "Le Rapprochement des statuts de l'ouvrier et de l'employé—étude juridique comparative," *Revue de travail* 69, 9–10 (Sept.–Oct. 1968): 1257–1322. On social divisions between white- and blue-collar workers, see Guy Vanthemsche, "Aspekten van de Bediendenwerkloosheid in de Jaren 1930–1939" (unpublished paper, Vrije Universiteit Brussel, 1987), 6, 18. (I would like to express my gratitude to Guy Vanthemsche for making his unpublished paper available to me.) One reason for separate categories for white-collar and blue-collar may have been that white-collar workers tended more often to be Catholic. Socialist unions appear to have agreed to let white-collar workers keep their special status in order to lessen the chance of Catholic unions' using the issue as a recruiting device. In Labor Court elections

for blue-collar workers in 1930, the Socialists won 65.5 percent of the vote, to the Catholics' 34.5, while the Catholics edged out the Socialists among white-collar workers. *Revue du travail* (July 1930): 1165.

69. Boddewyn, *Belgian Public Policy*, 39, 247.

70. Vanthemsche, "Aspekten," 7–9, 20; and Constance A. Kiehel, *Unemployment Insurance in Belgium: A National Development of the Ghent and Liège Systems* (New York, 1932), esp. 292.

71. On the general strike, Monica DeVriendt and Yvan VanDen Berghe, *De Algemene Werkstaking van 1936* (Hasselt, 1967), 16, 24. On the growth in numbers, Vanthemsche, "Aspekten," 7–8; Scholl, *150 Jaar,* 334–38; Jan Dhondt et al., "L'Influence de la crise sur les mouvements ouvriers en Belgique," *Mouvements ouvriers et dépression économique de 1929 à 1939* (Assen, 1966), 81–82. The Catholic unions aggressively recruited workers in hotels: "Onze Christelijke Vakbeweging," *De Lichtstraal* (Nov. 1931), 5.

72. Étienne, *Le Mouvement rexiste*, 157.

73. Boddewyn, *Belgian Public Policy*, 46–50.

74. Fernand Collin, *Rapport sur les classes moyennes artisanales et commerçantes,* 2nd ed. (Brussels, 1937).

75. Boddewyn, *Belgian Public Policy*, 49–54. For the importance of the "padlock" law in comparative perspective, see Winkler, *Mittelstand,* 190.

76. Fédération Chrétiennes des Classes Moyennes, *Decalogue,* cited in Philippot, *Classes moyennes,* 97. On the credit institutions, Léger, "Les Institutions de crédit," 264–98; Raoul Miry, "Beschouwingen over Middenstandskrediet," *Bulletin* 13 (10 April 1938); Chlepner, *Belgian Banking,* 141–42, 150–54.

77. There are striking parallels between how the lower middle class and its leaders were given a place in the para–statal credit institutions in the late 1930s and how the labor unions and other groups were given places in state-sponsored institutions in the post–World War II era: Val Lorwin, "Labor Unions and Political Parties in Belgium," *Industrial and Labor Relations Review* 2, 28 (Jan. 1975); and Zolberg, "Belgium," 131–32. The para-statal organization as an institution has a long history in Belgium: the *Credit Communal* bank was already created in 1860. Nonetheless, the expansion of the para-statals in the late 1930s, I would argue, represented a new use for them as a means of tying groups to the regime. See Chlepner, *Belgian Banking,* 141–54.

78. Boddewyn, *Belgian Public Policy*, 54.

79. Crabbe, "Syndicalisme et fonction publique," 843–47, 864.

80. G. Kurgan-van Hentenryk, "A Forgotten Class: The Petite Bourgeoisie in Belgium, 1850–1914," in Crossick and Haupt, *Shopkeepers and Master Artisans,* 127.

81. S. H. Scholl, *De Geschiedenis van de arbeidersbeweging in West-Vlaanderen (1875–1914)* (Brussels, 1953), 106.

82. Calculated from De Smet, *Atlas.*

83. For the pre–World War I period, see Ginette Kurgan-van Hentenryk, "Belgique," in Fauvel-Rouif, *Petite Entreprise,* 211; Scholl, *De Geschiedenis,* 111–61; Rudolf Rezsohazy, *Origines et formation du catholicisme social en Belgique, 1842–1909* (Brussels, 1958). On the interwar period, Joseph Arendt, *La Nature, l'organisation, et la programme des syndicats ouvriers chrétiens* (Paris and Brussels, 1925), esp. 83–108; Paul Crockaert, "Preface," in Philippot, *Classes moyennes,* 115–22; "Socialisme, fascisme, et corporatisme," *La Démocratie* (Aug. 1934), 1; "Corporatisme et démocratie," *La Démocratie* (14 Oct. 1932), 1; Gerard, *De Katholieke,* 385–91, 477–78, 511–28; L. Brouwers, *Vijtig Jaar Christelijke Werkgeversbeweging in Belgie* (Brussels, 1974), 106–15. For informative, though at times unsympathetic, Socialist and Communist views, see: G. Koulischer, "Après les congrés catholiques de Dinant et de Gand," *Mouvement*

syndical belge (Dec. 1933), 323–28; Pierre Joye and Rosinne Lewin, *L'Église et le mouvement ouvrier en Belgique* (Brussels, 1966), 245–57; Verhoeyen and Uytterhaegen, *De Kreeft met de Zwarte Scharen,* 37–49, 135–42.

84. Robert Leurquin, "Après les élections communales belges," *L'Europe nouvelle* (29 Oct. 1938), 1186.

85. Léger, "Les Institutions de crédit," 292.

86. G. D. H. Cole, "Introduction," Henri De Man, *Planned Socialism: The* Plan du Travail *of the Belgian Labour Party* (London, 1935); Erik Hansen, "Depression Decade Crisis: Social Democracy and *Planisme* in Belgium and the Netherlands, 1929–1939," *Journal of Contemporary History* 16 (1981); Steven Philip Kramer, "Neo-Socialism: The Belgian Case," *Res Publica* 1, 18 (1976); Eric-John Nachtergaele, "Les Relations Leopold III–Henri De Man," *Res Publica* 1, 20, (1978); Peter Dodge, *Beyond Marxism: The Faith and Work of Hendrik De Man* (The Hague, 1966).

87. Guy Quaden and Roger Ramaekers, "Le Socialisme coopératif," in *1885/1985: Du Parti ouvrier au parti socialiste* (Brussels, 1985), 114.

88. Léger, "Les Institutions de crédit," 292.

89. Even a scholar doing detailed work on the Belgian lower middle class, Pascale Delfosse, has asserted (incorrectly, I believe) that cooperatives and large stores were the biggest threat to the small shopkeepers. Kurgan-van Hentenryk points out that Delfosse's article in *Le Mouvement social* (see note 16) is probably mistaken on this point: Kurgan-van Hentenryk, "Belgique," 128. Boddewyn, *Belgian Public Policy,* 56–57, is particularly helpful in pointing out the complexities of this issue.

90. Ernst Mandel, *Late Capitalism* (London, 1975), especially 377–407, 474–99. In the existing literature as a whole, the lower middle class has been neglected as a factor in the reorientation of Belgian political economy in the interwar period. Baudhuin, in his standard economic history, mentions the discontent of the lower middle class, but neglects the reactions of the government to it. Unfortunately, much of the more recent historical literature on Belgian interwar politics focuses on the events leading to the crisis of 1936 and then jumps to the political developments leading to the Second World War and the immediate postwar period. The late 1930s as a period of important change in domestic politics is consequently overlooked: both Gerard, *De Katholieke,* and Verhoeyen and Uytterhaegen, *De Kreeft met de Zwarte Scharen,* barely mention the late 1930s. Other, more recent Marxist scholars than Mandel, when trying to explain how the corporate welfare state grew out of the changes of the 1930s, also barely mention the lower middle class: I. Cassiers, "L'Entre-deux-guerres: quelques notes sur la régulation du capitalisme et le rôle de l'état," and D. Spaey, "Réflexions sur les politiques économiques de 1934 à 1938," both in "État, accumulation du capital, et lutte des classes dans l'histoire de Belgique (1830–1980)," *Contradictions* 23–24 (1980). Historians' emphasis on heavy industry, banking, and organized labor, and their neglect of the commercial lower middle class, is all the more striking when one realizes that most of the attempts of reformers and Socialists to alter large-scale enterprises failed. See Guy Vanthemsche, "De Belgische Overheid en de Kartels tijdens het interbellum," *Revue belge de philogie et d'histoire/Belgisch Tijdschrift voor Filologie en Geschiedenis* 61 (1983–84); and "De Mislukking van een Vernieuwde Economische Politiek in Belgie voor de Tweede Wereldoorlog: de OREC (Office de Redressement Économique)," *BTNG/ RBHC* 13 (1982).

91. Gøsta Esping-Andersen, *Politics Against Markets: The Social Democratic Road to Power* (Princeton, 1985).

Contributors

MABEL BEREZIN is assistant professor of sociology at the University of Pennsylvania. The author of articles on mass media and public discourse in comparative perspective, she is preparing a book-length study of the theater and politics under Italian Fascism.

NIELS FINN CHRISTIANSEN teaches contemporary history at the University of Copenhagen. He is the author or coauthor of several books and many journal articles on Danish and European social and labor history.

HEINZ-GERHARD HAUPT, professor of history at the University of Bremen, has written widely on modern French and European history. His most recent book is a social history of France since 1789.

TOM JEFFERY, a civil servant who works in education administration in London, was educated at Jesus College, Cambridge, and the University of Birmingham. He is the author of articles on British politics between the wars and is completing a study of the British lower middle classes from 1918 to 1939.

RUDY KOSHAR, associate professor of history at the University of Southern California, is the author of *Social Life, Local Politics, and Nazism: Marburg, 1880–1935* (1986). He is at work on a study of the discourse of urban conservation and allegories of national identity in Germany and West Germany from 1900 to the present.

KARL CHRISTIAN LAMMERS teaches history at the University of Copenhagen. He has written widely on European and Scandinavian political and labor history, political theory, and the history of fascism.

IRINA LIVEZEANU, assistant professor of history at Colby College, Waterville, Maine, is the author of several articles on modern Romania and of *The Politics of Culture in Greater Romania* (Ithaca, N.Y., forthcoming).

CHARLOTTE NIERMANN is a research associate at the University of Bremen. She has published articles in *Le Mouvement social* and other journals on the social history of pre-1914 German shopkeepers and is at work on a study of Bremen small enterprise in the Weimar Republic.

SUSAN PENNYBACKER received her Ph.D. from Cambridge University and is presently associate professor of history at Trinity College, Hartford, Connecticut. The author of several articles on modern British social history, she is completing a book entitled *A Vision for London: Labor, Everyday Life, and the LCC Experiment 1889–1914* (London, forthcoming).

CARL STRIKWERDA is assistant professor of history at the University of Kansas. The author of articles and reviews on modern Belgian and European political and urban history, he is working on two books, one a study of Catholic and socialist politics in pre–World War I Belgium, the other (with Camille Guerin-Gonzales) a reader on the politics of immigrant workers.

STEVEN ZDATNY teaches history at Rice University. He has published several articles on the history of French artisans and has recently completed *The Politics of Survival: Artisans in Twentieth-Century France* (New York, 1990).

Index

International Peace Campaign, 106
Italian Nationalist Association, 149
Italian Union of Labor, 149
Italy: composition of middle class, 146–47; corporativism and class collaboration, 151–54; and cultural democratization, 157–58; humanistic lower middle classes, 24; middle classes as contested terrain in, 147–49; middle class and fascism, 142–58; middle class as historical problem, 142–44; Milanese actors and, 149–51; nationalism in, 148–49; professional middle classes in corporativist state, 154–56; social class in, 156–58; socialism in, 147–48, 158; working-class intellectuals, 147–48

Jeffery, Tom: on British interwar politics, 98

Kater, Michael: on National Socialism, 7–8
Kershaw, Ian: on petite bourgeoisie and Nazism, 43
Kettenacker, Lothar: on Hitler's appeal, 8; image of Nazi national community of, 31
Kiriţescu, Constantin: on Romanian education, 178
Kleinbürgertum, 34–35
Kocka, Jürgen, 25n, 48–49n
Kornhauser, William, 6

Labini, Paolo Sylos: on strata of lower middle classes, 147
Labor: in interwar politics, 14
Labor Charter (Italy), 152–53
Labour party (England): middle-class support of, 77–78
Landesverband, 57–58
Langdon-Davies, John: on Franco's rebellion, 107; lecturing for LBC of, 110
Laski, Harold, 88
Late Capitalism (Mandel), 231

League for the Betterment of Dramatic Actors (Italy), 150
League of National Christian Defense (Romania), 177
League of the Archangel Michael (Romania), 177
Left Book Club, 71, 85; activism of, 106; beginning of, 107–8; Communist party influence on, 88; groups of, 87; London County Council group, 97, 98; on pacifism, 109; Popular Front and, 95n; role of, 86; support of Labour Party policies, 109–10
Léger, L. T., 230
Lewis, John, 110
Ley, Hubert, 130: on artisanal collective conventions, 133
Linz, Juan: on origin of fascism, 7
Little Man, What Now? (Fallada), 34
Localism, 18–19; in Weimar Republic, 37–38
London County Council, 75, 77, 99–112; clerical workers, 100–101; Staff Association, 101–2, 110, 112–13; women on staff of, 103
London Dock Strike, 99
London Progressives, 99
London Town, 100, 112–13; book reviews in, 107–8; coverage of Fabian conference, 108; theme of diminishing incomes in, 103–4
Lopez, Guido, 149
Lower middle classes (interwar Europe): categories of, 9–10; centrality of politics in formation of, 12–13; in century before World War I, 9; collective disillusionment of, 20–21; compensatory belligerence in, 1–2; definitions of, 3; demagogic language of, 19–20; in European Left, 16; as forces of conservatism and resistance to change, 15–16; impact of on European history, 23; intellectual discourse of, 6; obstacles to formation of, 11; old and new, 10; party political options of, 15–17; political